TREASURY OF

NORTH AMERICAN

BIRDLORE

. . . to come upon warblers in early May
Was to forget time and death:
How they filled the oriole's elm, a twittering restless
                    cloud, all one morning,
And I watched and watched till my eyes blurred from the
                    bird shapes,—
Cape May, Blackburnian, Cerulean,—
Moving, elusive as fish, fearless,
Hanging, bunched like young fruit, bending the end branches,
Still for a moment,
Then pitching away in half-flight,
Lighter than finches,
While the wrens bickered and sang in the half-green hedgerows,
And the flicker drummed from his dead tree in the chicken-
                    yard.

               from Theodore Roethke's "The Far Field"

TREASURY OF NORTH AMERICAN BIRDLORE

Edited by

Paul S. Eriksson

& Alan Pistorius

PAUL S. ERIKSSON

Publisher

Middlebury, Vermont

Library of Congress Cataloging-in-Publication Data

Treasury of North American birdlore.

1. Birds—North America.   I. Eriksson, Paul S.
II. Pistorius, Alan.

QL681.T68   1987   598.297   87-27287
ISBN 0-8397-8372-8
ISBN 0-8397-8373-6   PAPERBACK

The editors wish to acknowledge the generous help of those who made suggestions of pieces for inclusion in this anthology and those who contributed towards its completion. The following is an abbreviated list of some of these people, not least of whom is Harry B. Logan:

Dean Amadon, Elizabeth Ball, G. Clifford Carl, Reginald L. Cook, Allan D. Cruickshank, Margaret Woods Eriksson, Alfred G. Etter, Edith N. Halberg, George E. Hudson, Rimsa Michel, Kenneth Morrison, Harry C. Oberholser, Dorothy C. Pallas, A. L. Rand, John Terres, John Vosburgh, Farida A. Wiley, Robert Woodward.

Grateful acknowledgment is made to the following authors and publishers for permission to use and adopt copyright material:

AUDUBON MAGAZINE. "Little Calamities," by Frank Graham, Jr. from AUDUBON MAGAZINE, September, 1985. Reprinted by permission of *Audubon Magazine*. CROWN PUBLISHERS, INC. Excerpt from *Life of the Hummingbird* by Alexander F. Skutch. Copyright © 1973 by Vineyard Books, Inc. Used by permission of Crown Publishers, Inc. HAWK MOUNTAIN SANCTUARY. Excerpt from *The Mountain and the Migration* by James J. Brett. Copyright © 1986 by James J. Brett. Reprinted by permission of Hawk Mountain Sanctuary Association. HILL AND WANG. Excerpts from *The Birdwatcher's Companion* by Christopher Leahy. Copyright © 1982 by Christopher Leahy. Reprinted by permission of Hill and Wang, a division of Farrar, Straus and Giroux, Inc. HENRY HOLT AND COMPANY. Excerpt from *Secret Go the Wolves* by R.D. Lawrence. Copyright © 1980 by R.D. Lawrence. Reprinted by

(*Continued on page 387*)

INTRODUCTION

On a West Coast birding expedition of two decades ago, a woman commented in passing on the trip leader's "love of birds." The leader, a bank officer and a serious birder, would not let the comment pass. "We cannot love what cannot love in return," he declared. "I find birds abundantly interesting, but I do not love them."

What brought this pointed exchange back to mind was a rereading of the second piece in this anthology, John Burroughs' "The Return of the Birds." Burroughs, the upstate New York farm boy who became our first widely admired nature essayist, was not at all embarrassed to admit that he loved birds. "Love is the measure of life," he declared; "only so far as we love do we really live." Burroughs led with the heart, not the head. When an admirer allowed as how his knowledge of birds must have been the result of long and careful study, Burroughs replied: "Studied the birds? No, I have played with them, camped with them, gone berrying with them, summered and wintered with them, and my knowledge of them has filtered into my mind almost unconsciously."

The contemporary "serious" birder (not to mention the establishment ornithologist) is likely to be uncomfortable with this. He will object to Burroughs' use of personal pronouns to refer to birds (curiously, bluebird, robin, and flicker are "he's" while the eastern phoebe is a "she"), to his characterization of the "pert little winter wren" and the "lithe, merry-hearted" bobolink as mere sentimental twaddle, and to the distinction between the "democratic" robin and the aristocratic orchard oriole and rose-breasted grosbeak as blatant anthropomorphism. (Perhaps we should point out that, before the modern apotheosis of "objectivity," layman and scientist alike habitually humanized the lower orders of creation.)

Whatever one thinks of Burroughs' image making, it is important to note that, while leading with the heart, he by no means commits senses and mind to somnolence. His talent for close observation is evident in this excerpt. The brown-headed cowbird, he writes, "seems literally to vomit up his notes. Apparently with much labor and effort, they gurgle and blubber up out of him, falling on the ear with a peculiar subtle ring, as of turning water from a glass bottle." Readers familiar with the courtship display of the species will appreciate not only the description of the notes, but also the reference to the peculiar swelling and head-dipping—so like the retching mechanism—that precedes them.

In addition, Burroughs asks astute questions along the way. He notes that the common flicker is "not quite satisfied with being a woodpecker," and wonders what effects—in terms of morphology, plumage

coloration, even voice—its ground-foraging behavior may ultimately
have. And in calling it a "question worthy of Darwin," he puts it in the
appropriate context of evolution. Burroughs also asks fundamental
questions about the impact on birds of basic land-use changes: "Where
did the bobolink disport himself before there were meadows in the
North and ricefields in the South?"

Admirers of John Burroughs—and judging by the sets of complete
works languishing on top shelves in used bookstores they are not now
abundant—applaud his "whole-man" approach to the natural world.
How better to come to nature than with alert senses, an inquiring
mind, and, above all, the heart's affections?

This approach can be—has been—attacked from both sides. Walt
Whitman, in journal selections newly anthologized here, defends the
Romantic line that intellection is destructive, that too much knowledge
kills appreciation. Man's proper role in nature is not analysis but celebration.

Science, of course, attacks from the opposite front. Man's business is
to know, to penetrate, to understand, which requires that the senses
serve the interests of the mind. The heart is odd man out: emotions
confuse, obfuscate. Burroughs may ask good by-the-way questions, but
he does not—cannot—*answer* them. What good is an inquiring mind if
you are unable or unwilling to develop the means (read science) to
satisfy it?

Unlike bird appreciation, ornithology has changed radically over our
short history. Broadly speaking, early ornithology was concerned with
nomenclature (naming) and taxonomy (arranging species), while mid-
dle-period ornithology busied itself with life history matters. Leading
lights (both professional and amateur) of this second period—A.C. Bent,
Elliott Coues, Margaret Nice, Edward Howe Forbush, Frank Chapman
—are here represented by essays mostly exploring the private lives of
birds.

Contemporary ornithology—like the other disciplines combined under the old rubric "natural history"—has become hard academicized
science practiced by a small cadre of (mostly) men in university, museum, and government agency. The results of their focused, quantified,
often arcane problem-solving are published in a few professional journals, a random sample of which writing looks like this:

There were statistically significant correlations between growth
parameters and concentrations of elements in both back (Table 2)
and tail (Table 3) feathers. Multiple linear regression models were
used to see if the entire chemical profile of feathers could be used as
a predictor of growth. When back and tail feathers were analyzed
separately, fledging age of females could be predicted by the ele-

mental composition of tail feathers ($F = 8.39$, df $= 7,4$, $R^2 = 0.936$, $P < 0.05$, with significant sources of variation being Mg, Mn, and Ca concentrations), and the fledging age of males could be predicted by the elemental composition of back feathers ($F = 3.61$, df $= 5,19$, $R^2 = 0.487$, $P < 0.02$, with significant sources of variation being Mn concentrations). When the concentrations of back and tail feathers were used together, models predicting the $a(F = 82.60$, df $= 10,2$, $R^2 = 0.998$, $P < 0.02$, all variables contributing significantly) and $K(F = 21.76$, df $= 10,2$, $R^2 = 0.991$, $P < 0.05$, with significant sources of variation being Na, Al, Cl, and Ca concentrations in tail feathers) parameters of the weight growth equations of females were statistically significant.

If the work of contemporary scientific ornithology is underrepresented in this volume, it is because that literature is largely inaccessible to the intelligent non-scientist, and few practitioners attempt to translate their work for general consumption.

This does not mean that scientific ornithology is irrelevant to the contemporary bird literature. Some of that work is mediated through a new generation of natural history writers who, in forms as diverse as the magazine article and the encyclopedia, make bits and pieces of the accumulated knowledge available in palatable form. (This situation is not ideal; few of the writers publishing "popular" ornithology know enough biology—much less mathematics and statistics—to appreciate exactly what the scientists are up to.) Much of Parts 2 and 3 of this anthology, for example, piggy-backs on decades of painstaking lab and field work around the world.

Whatever their provenance and whatever their perspective, the selections in this book are first of all about North American birds—songbirds and waterfowl, divers and waders, raptors and pelagics, terns and turkeys and hummingbirds. (Scarce and dramatic species like the bald eagle and the trumpeter swan figure here; so do the exotic anhinga and the anomalous American dipper, the familiar eastern meadowlark and gray catbird, and the ubiquitous house sparrow.) Other sections address key questions about birds as living organisms (what does the world look like, smell like to a bird? how do birds accomplish those amazing long-distance migrations?), about the multifarious—and sometimes unexpected—relationships between birds and people, about conservation issues happy and sad.

This is a book about people as well as birds. There are tales of (or by) men and women who, in one way or another, care(d) about birds, from bird lovers and bird painters to bird shooters and competitive listers. There is the story of Audubon warden Guy Bradley, martyred by south

Florida plume hunters, and of Charles Broley, who retired from a financial career to climb to eagle eyries. There are the stories of two well-born presidents of the United States as well as that of Alexander Wilson, a Scottish slave-wage weaver, second-rate poet, and jailbird who became North America's first important birdman.

This is a book about American times, from the vanished worlds of Catesby and Audubon to our own, and of special American places and the men who defined them: from William Bartram's Florida swamps to John Muir's Yosemite; from Aldo Leopold's sand county Wisconsin to Henry Beston's Cape Cod; from Wendell Berry's Kentucky River country to Sigurd Olson's Quetico canoe country; from Maurice Broun's Hawk Mountain to Albert Hochbaum's south Manitoba waterfowl marshes; from R.D. Lawrence's Canadian subarctic to the southwestern deserts of Joseph Wood Krutch and Mary Austin.

We showcase here a rich variety of moods and voices. There are essays informative and celebratory, momentous and lighthearted, quiet and dramatic, hopeful and melancholy, contemplative and adventuresome (speaking of adventure, readers troubled by nightmares would do well to avoid George Sutton's tale of claustrophobic entrapment in a vulture's "den"). You will hear the puckish and irreverent Will Cuppy as well as the lyrical voice—rich in atmosphere, rich in emotion—of Sally Carrighar and the eloquent periods of Peter Matthiessen. By whomever and about whatever, these essays communicate, we think, something of man's continuing fascination with birds, those feathered vertebrates which, as Barry Lopez writes, "tug at the mind and heart with a strange intensity."

CONTENTS

PART SIX: BIRDS AND PEOPLE

Part

One

BIRDS THROUGH THE SEASONS

SPRING IN

A NEW LAND

John Muir

What a glorious night it was for eleven-year-old John Muir—and, in retrospect, for the American conservation movement—when his father interrupted him and his younger brother David, hard at their hated school lessons, with the news: "Bairns, . . . you needna learn your lessons the nicht, for we're gan to America the morn!" The boys were overjoyed at the immediate prospect of leaving dour, theocratic—and relatively wildlife-poor—Scotland for what the young Muir thought of as the "wonderful schoolless bookless American wilderness." (It is unrecorded whether thirteen-year-old Sarah, who accompanied them, was equally enthusiastic.)

By stages the Muir family (or rather half the Muir family; mother and three younger children were left behind for the time being) worked its way westward, and in this passage John Muir remembers his feelings upon coming at last in a new spring to a new home in the wild Wisconsin woods.

A land-agent at Kingston gave father a note to a farmer by the name of Alexander Gray, who lived on the border of the settled part of the country, knew the section-lines, and would probably help him to find a good place for a farm. So father went away to spy out the land, and in the mean time left us children in Kingston in a rented room. It took us less than an hour to get acquainted with some of the boys in the village; we challenged them to wrestle, run races, climb trees, etc., and in a day or two we felt at home, care-free and happy, notwithstanding our family was so widely divided. When father returned he told us that he had found fine land for a farm in sunny open woods on the side of a lake, and that a team of three yoke of oxen with a big wagon was coming to haul us to Mr. Gray's place.

We enjoyed the strange ten-mile ride through the woods very much, wondering how the great oxen could be so strong and wise and tame as to pull so heavy a load with no other harness than a chain and a crooked piece of wood on their necks, and how they could sway so obediently to right and left past roadside trees and stumps when the driver said *haw*

From *The Story of My Boyhood and Youth*. Boston: Atlantic Monthly Company, 1912.

and *gee*. At Mr. Gray's house, father again left us for a few days to build a shanty on the quarter-section he had selected four or five miles to the westward. In the mean while we enjoyed our freedom as usual, wandering in the fields and meadows, looking at the trees and flowers, snakes and birds and squirrels. With the help of the nearest neighbors the little shanty was built in less than a day after the rough bur-oak logs for the walls and the white-oak boards for the floor and roof were got together.

To this charming hut, in the sunny woods, overlooking a flowery glacier meadow and a lake rimmed with white water-lilies, we were hauled by an ox-team across trackless carex swamps and low rolling hills sparsely dotted with round-headed oaks. Just as we arrived at the shanty, before we had time to look at it or the scenery about it, David and I jumped down in a hurry off the load of household goods, for we had discovered a blue jay's nest, and in a minute or so we were up the tree beside it, feasting our eyes on the beautiful green eggs and beautiful birds,—our first memorable discovery. The handsome birds had not seen Scotch boys before and made a desperate screaming as if we were robbers like themselves, though we left the eggs untouched, feeling that we were already beginning to get rich, and wondering how many more nests we should find in the grand sunny woods. Then we ran along the brow of the hill that the shanty stood on, and down to the meadow, searching the trees and grass tufts and bushes, and soon discovered a bluebird's and a woodpecker's nest, and began an acquaintance with the frogs and snakes and turtles in the creeks and springs.

This sudden plash into pure wildness—baptism in Nature's warm heart—how utterly happy it made us! Nature streaming into us, wooingly teaching her wonderful glowing lessons, so unlike the dismal grammar ashes and cinders so long thrashed into us. Here without knowing it we still were at school; every wild lesson a love lesson, not whipped but charmed into us. Oh, that glorious Wisconsin wilderness! Everything new and pure in the very prime of the spring when Nature's pulses were beating highest and mysteriously keeping time with our own! Young hearts, young leaves, flowers, animals, the winds and the streams and the sparkling lake, all wildly, gladly rejoicing together!

THE RETURN

OF

THE BIRDS

John Burroughs

We cannot greet every new spring in a new land, but we can in every spring celebrate the miraculous return of the birds, whose disappearance in autumn is as sweetly sad as the falling of the leaves, and whose return is as cheering as the first flower to bloom in the woods.

John Burroughs was neither the first nor the greatest American nature writer, but he was observant and sound, and he won a wider audience than any previous writer who had invited his fellow countrymen to consider the richness of their continent's wildlife and the rewards to be reaped by those who saw it as something to be enjoyed rather than merely exploited.

SPRING in our northern climate may fairly be said to extend from the middle of March to the middle of June. At least, the vernal tide continues to rise until the later date, and it is not till after the summer solstice that the shoots and twigs begin to harden and turn to wood, or the grass to lose any of its freshness and succulency.

It is this period that marks the return of the birds—one or two of the more hardy or half-domesticated species, like the song sparrow and the bluebird, usually arriving in March, while the rarer and more brilliant wood-birds bring up the procession in June. But each stage of the advancing season gives prominence to certain species, as to certain flowers. The dandelion tells me when to look for the swallow, the dogtooth violet when to expect the wood-thrush, and when I have found the wakerobin in bloom I know the season is fairly inaugurated. With me this flower is associated, not merely with the awakening of Robin, for he has been awake some weeks, but with the universal awakening and rehabilitation of nature.

Yet the coming and going of the birds is more or less a mystery and a surprise. We go out in the morning, and no thrush or vireo is to be

From *Wake Robin*. Boston: Houghton Mifflin Company, 1895.

heard; we go out again, and every tree and grove is musical; yet again, and all is silent. Who saw them come? Who saw them depart?

This pert little winter wren, for instance, darting in and out the fence, diving under the rubbish here and coming up yards away—how does he manage with those little circular wings to compass degrees and zones, and arrive always in the nick of time? Last August I saw him in the remotest wilds of the Adirondacks, impatient and inquisitive as usual; a few weeks later, on the Potomac, I was greeted by the same hardy little busybody. Does he travel by easy stages from bush to bush and from wood to wood? Or has that compact little body force and courage to brave the night and the upper air, and so achieve leagues at one pull?

And yonder bluebird with the earth tinge on his breast and the sky tinge on his back—did he come down out of heaven on that bright March morning when he told us so softly and plaintively that, if we pleased, spring had come? Indeed, there is nothing in the return of the birds more curious and suggestive than in the first appearance, or rumors of the appearance, of this little blue-coat. The bird at first seems a mere wandering voice in the air: one hears its call or carol on some bright March morning, but is uncertain of its source or direction; it falls like a drop of rain when no cloud is visible; one looks and listens, but to no purpose. The weather changes, perhaps a cold snap with snow comes on, and it may be a week before I hear the note again, and this time or the next perchance see the bird sitting on a stake in the fence lifting his wing as he calls cheerily to his mate. Its notes now become daily more frequent; the birds multiply, and, flitting from point to point, call and warble more confidently and gleefully. Their boldness increases till one sees them hovering with a saucy, inquiring air about barns and outbuildings, peeping into dove-cotes and stable windows, inspecting knotholes and pump-trees, intent only on a place to nest. They wage war against robins and wrens, pick quarrels with swallows, and seem to deliberate for days over the policy of taking forcible possession of one of the mud-houses of the latter. But as the season advances they drift more into the background. Schemes of conquest which they at first seemed bent upon are abandoned, and they settle down very quietly in their old quarters in remote stumpy fields.

Not long after the bluebird comes the robin, sometimes in March, but in most of the Northern States April is the month of the robin. In large numbers they scour the fields and groves. You hear their piping in the meadow, in the pasture, on the hillside. Walk in the woods, and the dry leaves rustle with the whir of their wings, the air is vocal with their cheery call. In excess of joy and vivacity, they run, leap, scream, chase each other through the air, diving and sweeping among the trees with perilous rapidity.

In that free, fascinating, half-work and half-play pursuit—sugar-making—a pursuit which still lingers in many parts of New York, as in New England—the robin is one's constant companion. When the day is sunny and the ground bare, you meet him at all points and hear him at all hours. At sunset, on the tops of the tall maples, with look heavenward, and in a spirit of utter abandonment, he carols his simple strain. And sitting thus amid the stark, silent trees, above the wet, cold earth, with the chill of winter still in the air, there is no fitter or sweeter songster in the whole round year. It is in keeping with the scene and the occasion. How round and genuine the notes are, and how eagerly our ears drink them all in! The first utterance, and the spell of winter is thoroughly broken, and the remembrance of it afar off.

Robin is one of the most native and democratic of our birds; he is one of the family, and seems much nearer to us than those rare, exotic visitants, as the orchard starling or rose-breasted grosbeak, with their distant, high-bred ways. Hardy, noisy, frolicsome, neighborly, and domestic in his habits, strong of wing and bold in spirit, he is the pioneer of the thrush family, and well worthy of the finer artists whose coming he heralds and in a measure prepares us for. . . .

Another April bird, which makes her appearance sometimes earlier and sometimes later than Robin, and whose memory I fondly cherish, is the phoebe-bird, the pioneer of the flycatchers. In the inland farming districts, I used to notice her, on some bright morning about Easter Day, proclaiming her arrival, with much variety of motion and attitude, from the peak of the barn or hay-shed. As yet, you may have heard only the plaintive, homesick note of the bluebird, or the faint trill of the song sparrow; and Phoebe's clear, vivacious assurance of her veritable bodily presence among us again is welcomed by all ears. At agreeable intervals in her lay she describes a circle or an ellipse in the air, ostensibly prospecting for insects, but really, I suspect, as an artistic flourish, thrown in to make up in some way for the deficiency of her musical performance. If plainness of dress indicates powers of song, as it usually does, then Phoebe ought to be unrivaled in musical ability, for surely that ashen-gray suit is the superlative of plainness; and that form, likewise, would hardly pass for a "perfect figure" of a bird. The seasonableness of her coming, however, and her civil, neighborly ways, shall make up for all deficiencies in song and plumage. After a few weeks Phoebe is seldom seen, except as she darts from her moss-covered nest beneath some bridge or shelving cliff.

Another April comer, who arrives shortly after Robin redbreast, with whom he associates both at this season and in the autumn, is the gold-winged woodpecker, *alias* "high-ole," *alias* "flicker," *alias* "yarup." He is an old favorite of my boyhood, and his note to me means very much. He announces his arrival by a long, loud call, repeated from the dry branch of some tree, or a stake in the fence—a thoroughly melodious April sound. I think how Solomon finished that beautiful description of spring, "And the voice of the turtle is heard in the land," and see that a description of spring in this farming country, to be equally characteristic, should culminate in like manner—"And the call of the high-hole comes up from the wood."

It is a loud, strong, sonorous call, and does not seem to imply an answer, but rather to subserve some purpose of love or music. It is "Yarup's" proclamation of peace and goodwill to all. On looking at the matter closely, I perceive that most birds, not denominated songsters, have, in the spring, some note or sound or call that hints of a song, and answers imperfectly the end of beauty and art. As a "livelier iris changes on the burnished dove," and the fancy of the young man turns lightly to thoughts of his pretty cousin, so the same renewing spirit touches the "silent singers," and they are no longer dumb; faintly they lisp the first syllables of the marvelous tale. Witness the clear, sweet whistle of the gray-crested titmouse—the soft, nasal piping of the nut-hatch—the amorous, vivacious warble of the bluebird—the long, rich note of the meadowlark—the whistle of the quail—the drumming of partridge—the animation and loquacity of the swallows, and the like. Even the hen has a homely, contented carol; and I credit the owls with a desire to fill the night with music. All birds are incipient or would-be songsters in the spring. I find corroborative evidence of this even in the crowing of the cock. The flowering of the maple is not so obvious as that of the magnolia; nevertheless, there is actual inflorescence.

Few writers award any song to that familiar little sparrow, the *Socialis;* yet who that has observed him sitting by the wayside, and repeating, with devout attitude, that fine sliding chant, does not recognize neglect? Who has heard the snowbird sing? Yet he has a lisping warble very savory to the ear. I have heard him indulge in it even in February.

Even the cow bunting feels the musical tendency, and aspires to its expression, with the rest. Perched upon the topmost branch beside his mate or mates—for he is quite a polygamist, and usually has two or three demure little ladies in faded black beside him—generally in the early part of the day, he seems literally to vomit up his notes. Apparently with much labor and effort, they gurgle and blubber up out of him, falling on the ear with a peculiar subtle ring, as of turning water from a glass bottle, and not without a certain pleasing cadence.

Neither is the common woodpecker entirely insensible to the wooing of spring, and, like the partridge, testifies his appreciation of melody after quite a primitive fashion. Passing through the woods on some clear, still morning in March, while the metallic ring and tension of winter are still in the earth and air, the silence is suddenly broken by long, resonant hammering upon a dry limb or stub. It is Downy beating a reveille to spring. In the utter stillness and amid the rigid forms we listen with pleasure; and, as it comes to my ear oftener at this season than at any other, I freely exonerate the author from the imputation of any gastronomic motives, and credit him with a genuine musical performance.

It is to be expected, therefore, that "yellowhammer" will respond to the general tendency, and contribute his part to the spring chorus. His April call is his finest touch, his most musical expression. . . .

May is the month of the swallows and the orioles. There are many other distinguished arrivals, indeed nine tenths of the birds are here by the last week in May, yet the swallows and orioles are the most conspicuous. The bright plumage of the latter seems really like an arrival from the tropics. I see them dash through the blossoming trees, and all the forenoon hear their incessant warbling and wooing. The swallows dive and chatter about the barn, or squeak and build beneath the eaves; the partridge drums in the fresh sprouting woods; the long, tender note of the meadowlark comes up from the meadow; and at sunset, from every marsh and pond come the ten thousand voices of the hylas. May is the transition month, and exists to connect April and June, the root with the flower.

With June the cup is full, our hearts are satisfied, there is no more to be desired. The perfection of the season, among other things, has brought the perfection of the song and plumage of the birds. The master artists are all here; and the expectations excited by the robin and the song sparrow are fully justified. The thrushes have come; and I sit down upon the first rock, with hands full of the pink azalea, to listen. With me the cuckoo does not arrive till June; and often the goldfinch, the kingbird, the scarlet tanager delay their coming till then. In the meadows the bobolink is in all his glory; in the high pastures the field sparrow sings his breezy vesper-hymn; and the woods are unfolding to the music of the thrushes.

MARCH: THE

GEESE RETURN

Aldo Leopold

Aldo Leopold spent his life in forestry, game management, and conservation. His writing was for the most part scattered over various somewhat obscure technical journals, and it was not until after his death that the collection of essays called A Sand County Almanac *first revealed to any large public that he was one of our most original and perceptive twentieth-century nature writers.*

ONE swallow does not make a summer, but one skein of geese, cleaving the murk of a March thaw, is the spring.

A cardinal, whistling spring to a thaw but later finding himself mistaken, can retrieve his error by resuming his winter silence. A chipmunk, emerging for a sunbath but finding a blizzard, has only to go back to bed. But a migrating goose, staking two hundred miles of black night on the chance of finding a hole in the lake, has no easy chance for retreat. His arrival carries the conviction of a prophet who has burned his bridges.

A March morning is only as drab as he who walks in it without a glance skyward, ear cocked for geese. I once knew an educated lady, banded by Phi Beta Kappa, who told me that she had never heard or seen the geese that twice a year proclaim the revolving seasons to her well-insulated roof. Is education possibly a process of trading awareness for things of lesser worth? The goose who trades his is soon a pile of feathers.

The geese that proclaim the seasons to our farm are aware of many things, including the Wisconsin statutes. The south-bound November flocks pass over us high and haughty, with scarcely a honk of recognition for their favorite sandbars and sloughs. "As a crow flies" is crooked compared with their undeviating aim at the nearest big lake twenty miles to the south, where they loaf by day on broad waters and filch corn by night from the freshly cut stubbles. November geese are aware that every marsh and pond bristles from dawn till dark with hopeful guns.

March geese are a different story. Although they have been shot at most

From *A Sand County Almanac*. New York: Oxford University Press, 1949.

of the winter, as attested by their buckshot-battered pinions, they know that the spring truce is now in effect. They wind the oxbows of the river, cutting low over the now gunless points and islands, and gabbling to each sandbar as to a long-lost friend. They weave low over the marshes and meadows, greeting each newly melted puddle and pool. Finally, after a few *pro-forma* circlings of our marsh, they set wing and glide silently to the pond, black landing-gear lowered and rumps white against the far hill. Once touching water, our newly arrived guests set up a honking and splashing that shakes the last thought of winter out of the brittle cattails. Our geese are home again!

It is at this moment of each year that I wish I were a muskrat, eye-deep in the marsh.

Once the first geese are in, they honk a clamorous invitation to each migrating flock, and in a few days the marsh is full of them. On our farm we measure the amplitude of our spring by two yardsticks: the number of pines planted, and the number of geese that stop. Our record is 642 geese counted in on 11 April 1946.

As in fall, our spring geese make daily trips to corn, but these are no surreptitious sneakings-out by night; the flocks move noisily to and from corn stubbles through the day. Each departure is preceded by loud gustatory debate, and each return by an even louder one. The returning flocks, once thoroughly at home, omit their *pro-forma* circlings of the marsh. They tumble out of the sky like maple leaves, side-slipping right and left to lose altitude, feet spraddled toward the shouts of welcome below. I suppose the ensuing gabble deals with the merits of the day's dinner. They are now eating the waste corn that the snow blanket has protected over winter from corn-seeking crows, cottontails, meadow mice, and pheasants.

It is a conspicuous fact that the corn stubbles selected by geese for feeding are usually those occupying former prairies. No man knows whether this bias for prairie corn reflects some superior nutritional value, or some ancestral tradition transmitted from generation to generation since the prairie days. Perhaps it reflects the simpler fact that prairie cornfields tend to be large. If I could understand the thunderous debates that precede and follow these daily excursions to corn, I might soon learn the reason for the priarie-bias. But I cannot, and I am well content that it should remain a mystery. What a dull world if we knew all about geese!

In thus watching the daily routine of a spring goose convention, one notices the prevalence of singles—lone geese that do much flying about and much talking. One is apt to impute a disconsolate tone to their honkings, and to jump to the conclusion that they are broken-hearted widowers, or mothers hunting lost children. The seasoned ornithologist knows, however, that such subjective interpretation of bird behavior is risky. I long tried to keep an open mind on the question.

After my students and I had counted for half a dozen years the number of geese comprising a flock, some unexpected light was cast on the meaning of lone geese. It was found by mathematical analysis that flocks of six or multiples of six were far more frequent than chance alone would dictate. In other words, goose flocks are families, or aggregations of families, and lone geese in spring are probably just what our fond imaginings had first suggested. They are bereaved survivors of the winter's shooting, searching in vain for their kin. Now I am free to grieve with and for the lone honkers.

It is not often that cold-potato mathematics thus confirms the sentimental promptings of the bird-lover.

On April nights when it has become warm enough to sit outdoors, we love to listen to the proceedings of the convention in the marsh. There are long periods of silence when one hears only the winnowing of snipe, the hoot of a distant owl, or the nasal clucking of some amorous coot. Then, of a sudden, a strident honk resounds, and in an instant pandemonium echoes. There is a beating of pinions on water, a rushing of dark prows propelled by churning paddles, and a general shouting by the onlookers of a vehement controversy. Finally some deep honker has his last word, and the noise subsides to that half-audible small-talk that seldom ceases among geese. Once again, I would I were a muskrat!

By the time the pasques are in full bloom our goose convention dwindles, and before May our marsh is once again a mere grassy wetness, enlivened only by redwings and rails.

It is an irony of history that the great powers should have discovered the unity of nations at Cairo in 1943. The geese of the world have had that notion for a longer time, and each March they stake their lives on its essential truth.

In the beginning there was only the unity of the Ice Sheet. Then followed the unity of the March thaw, and the northward hegira of the international geese. Every March since the Pleistocene, the geese have honked unity from China Sea to Siberian Steppe, from Euphrates to Volga, from Nile to Murmansk, from Lincolnshire to Spitsbergen. Every March since the Pleistocene, the geese have honked unity from Currituck to Labrador, Matamuskeet to Ungava, Horseshoe Lake to Hudson's Bay, Avery Island to Baffin Land, Panhandle to Mackenzie, Sacramento to Yukon.

By this international commerce of geese, the waste corn of Illinois is carried through the clouds to the Arctic tundras, there to combine with the waste sunlight of a nightless June to grow goslings for all the lands between. And in this annual barter of food for light, and winter warmth for summer solitude, the whole continent receives as net profit a wild poem dropped from the murky skies upon the muds of March.

MORNING IN

MOUNT VERNON

Louis J. Halle, Jr.

Here Louis J. Halle, Jr., formerly a member of our State Department and by avocation a naturalist, pays tribute to the contribution made by bird song to a Sunday morning's walk.

(*On Sunday, March 26, 1786, George Washington made the following entry in his diary at Mount Vernon: "The warmth of yesterday and this day, forwarded vegetation much; the buds of some trees, particularly the Weeping Willow and Maple, had displayed their leaves and blossoms and all others were swelled and many ready to put forth."*)

EASTER Sunday, April 1, was a golden day. The stars and a waning moon were out when I left for my excursion by bicycle down the river. In the darkness by the Shoreham Hotel the robins were already caroling in chorus, anticipating daybreak. The sun rose in classic splendor as I passed the airport—as it had risen among the Aegean isles three thousand years ago (the golden-throned dawn) for a lonely wanderer striving to return to his home, as it had risen a thousand years ago over the misty valley of the Loire. Robins, titmice, wrens, sparrows, thrashers, cardinals, goldfinches, purple finches were all singing. At Dyke, in the sparkling haze and freshness of the new day, a pair of wood ducks flew clamoring from the big trees beside the road, circled, landed in the trees again, took off again. Other wood ducks, in pairs, flew through the trees or out over the marshes. Pine warblers, yellow-throated warblers, blue-gray gnatcatchers, and newly arrived black-and-white warblers contributed their notes to the dawn.

A week ago I had marked the first green bloom on the woods. Now, to my eager imagination, it seemed virtually summer, the trees in flower and foliage, though one could still see through them. Later in the season the leaves would hang in heavy masses, obscuring the view. Today they were still young and tender on the trees. The borders of the woods were

From *Spring in Washington*. New York: Harper & Brothers, 1947.

everywhere illuminated by the white dogwood, the pink dogwood, and the brilliant redbud, now in full flower. Near Mount Vernon I came upon Roger Peterson and a friend, out with cameras and tripods to make color photographs of the redbud. Peterson told me the flower and foliage was between two and three weeks ahead of last year's dates, basing his calculation on the blooming of the magnolias, now over. Who could remember such an early spring as this, with everything so far ahead of schedule? At Fort Belvoir young horned larks had left their nest two weeks ago.

(On April 21, 1785, Washington at Mount Vernon wrote in his diary: "The Sassafras not yet full out, nor the Redbud—Dogwood blossom still inclosed in the button." Two days later he wrote: "The Dogwood buttons were just beginning to open as the Redwood (or bud) blossom, for though they had appeared several days the blossoms had not expanded.")

On the morning of April 3, after a night of storm, the Bonaparte's gulls were moving north along the surface of the river as far as the eye could reach, flicking their wings, sparkling in the early sunlight. They acquire their summer plumage as the trees their foliage, and through my glasses I could see that some now had black heads while the heads of others were still white or mottled. Men, it occurred to me, are among the few creatures that undergo no seasonal changes. We don't even grow shaggy coats in winter.

That morning a Louisiana water-thrush sang loud, clear and repeatedly from a ravine in Rock Creek Park as I bicycled to work. Tzee, tzee, tzee, tzippy, tzippy-tzip he sang, with emphasis, so that I should think one could have heard him half a mile off. (Birds that haunt rushing streams have loud voices to rise above the uproar.) Brown thrashers were singing in the city now—really singing, for they are among the birds that do not merely emit signals but are musicians, consciously practicing their art, as if inspired to transcend their own mortality and achieve a heaven that lies, surely, just beyond mortal reach. One that sang constantly on Woodland Drive had a whole orchestra of bells and woodwinds in his throat. His song, every phrase with its echo, bubbled like a natural spring breaking from the ground in flood season. Yet there was a method in it, a repetition and return to the same themes. Before the week was out, barn swallows, spotted sandpipers, and ruddy ducks in Washington Channel had been added to the list of new birds.

This week, however, was bountiful chiefly in its flowers. The City of Washington might have been deliberately decked for a flower festival, as when the citizens hang out their flags because it is Flag Day. The lilac clusters came out in profusion overnight, among the young leaves, freshening the air. So did the azaleas, in all their variety, transforming the woodland parks and dooryards. A man from Mars might have stopped passers-by to inquire in what god's celebration the city was so garlanded.

SPRING

IN THE

KINGDOM

Ada Clapham Govan

Birds that come and go are—such is human perversity—usually more wel-come than those which stay with us. Here is an account of one woman's experience with hordes of visitors, the result of bad-weather migratory "dropout."

A SIDE from the visits of the field sparrow and the finches, our visitors up to that time consisted of a regular assortment of juncos, downy woodpeckers, brown creepers, tree sparrows, red-breasted nuthatches, white-breasted nuthatches, five darling chickadees, and, as a finishing touch, two golden-crowned kinglets. With these I was content and the days slipped by, pleasantly enough, till just two days before Easter. On Good Friday morning, I looked out of my window and discovered one lone fox sparrow feeding in the yard; eleven more were keeping him company by afternoon. The flock numbered fifty-three by Saturday noon, and more were arriving constantly. Apparently a migration of fox sparrows was keeping pace with spring. To have as guests fifty-three of these superb singers was something long to be remembered.

Meanwhile, five robins, a flicker, a gorgeous cock pheasant, and one unwelcome grackle had arrived in time for dinner; but it wasn't until Easter Monday that things really began to happen.

Easter Sunday was a mellow, sunny day, but a blizzard broke that night, catching the migrating hosts in their northward flight and slaying them by thousands and tens of thousands. The noise of that wild storm and a mixed chorus of bird calls outside awakened me at daybreak. Every feeding box was inches deep in snow; yet birds were everywhere, and in spite of the storm, they were singing lustily, joyously, as I had never heard birds sing before. By six o'clock I had scattered two large pans of food all over the yard. The manner in which it disappeared left no doubt of its being sadly needed.

From *Wings at My Window*. New York: The Macmillan Company, 1940.

Some gay little song sparrows joined the fast-growing assembly, and fox sparrows arrived in an ever-increasing stream. A few purple finches joined the throng, and strangers whom I could not identify, for their coloring was changed and dulled, so sodden were they all from the gale's buffeting. Why did so many come to us? What had told them that here they would find sanctuary?

There they stood within a few feet of the house, body-deep in slush and snow, blown and battered by the gale—between three and four hundred birds (nearly three hundred of them fox sparrows), and all singing gloriously. Any migration under such conditions would be unusual, but a gathering of almost three hundred fox sparrows, plus many other birds, in one back yard, is an event of a lifetime. To see a flock of even one hundred Foxies in our locality is something to boast about. No wonder people came from all over town, and farther, to hear them sing. Their song carried for blocks! The promise of springtime had betrayed them, yet it seemed that no sleet or snow or fiercely beating hail could quench the joy of homecoming in those valiant hearts.

Then I heard the squeaking of a wheelbarrow chorus far in the distance, and saw a cloud of midnight blackness coming towards me. Settling in the woods across the road, it quickly disintegrated into hundreds of rusty blackbirds still groaning their crazy song.

The peak of the invasion reached us on Tuesday morning. In one group there were more than eighty fox sparrows; two other groups were nearly as large, and there were several smaller bands. For several days we fed about four hundred birds, who consumed twenty pounds of wild bird seed and many pounds of sunflower seed, suet, and scraps, in less than three days.

Soon warm weather and a few sunny hours thinned the ranks of those who had come to us in their time of stress; but across the years I can still hear the wonderful singing that was wafted on high from dawn to dark in a never-creasing chorus of thanksgiving.

SUMMER ON

CHESTNUT RIDGE

David Rains Wallace

Many casual birders give over their avian pursuits in summer, when the excitement of spring migration and the grand choral effects have waned. But of course life goes on in the woods and meadows, as well as on Chestnut Ridge, a sandstone ridge off the western escarpment of the Appalachian Plateau, the fortunes of whose flora and fauna were followed over the course of a year by the contemporary nature writer David Rains Wallace.

O N a mildly windy day a seventy-year-old red oak beside the hay meadow toppled and broke in half. It was so eaten away by red oak borer beetle larvae that a few inches of healthy wood around the outside of its trunk had been all that sustained and supported it. The rest was rotten, full of beetle wings and woody tubes where the brown, shiny-headed grubs had eaten their way through the trunk, packing the tunnels behind them with digested cellulose as they burrowed. The ripening apples in the old orchards were coated with black-spot fungus and riddled with pink coddling moth larvae. Another parasite—probably a species of mite—had caused scarlet warts to sprout all over the leaves of small hawthorn trees that had grown up among the apples. On the ground, leaves of snakeroot or crowfoot, which had not been chewed up by larger insects, were usually marked with wavering yellow tracks of leaf miner caterpillars—moth larvae that are so tiny they can live inside the thinness of a leaf.

The young yellow-billed cuckoo found these conditions quite satisfactory. Its parents had fledged it and then left the ridge, so it had to find its own food now. It had little difficulty in doing so: caterpillars, beetles, tree crickets, and other cuckoo staples literally dripped from every branch. Particularly abundant at this time of year were the larvae of the pale tiger moth—white, hairy, black-headed caterpillars with a fanciful resemblance to the white-ruffed, black-capped Pierrot of French pantomime.

From *Idle Weeds: The Life of a Sandstone Ridge.* San Francisco: Sierra Club Books, 1980.

The fledgling found one of these Pierrot caterpillars dangling by a silken thread from a pawpaw leaf on a muggy afternoon and reached up to grab it. Suddenly a sound like a wave breaking on a beach came from the tree canopy overhead.

"Shoom!" The cuckoo pulled its head back in surprise and looked up. A flock of grackles had taken off from the treetops, and the concerted impact of their first wingbeats on the still air had made the sound. Smaller groups taking off after the main flock sounded as though a fitful breeze were shaking the branches. There was a moment of silence, then a pattering as of raindrops began further up the slope where the flock had realighted. The grackles were hopping from branch to branch, knocking dead twigs to the forest floor.

The cuckoo again reached toward the dangling caterpillar and plucked it from its thread. Flicking the larva up and down, it looked around nervously for a moment and abruptly swallowed it. Then it began to preen and pick rather uncomfortably at its breast and underwings; the young bird harbored a fair collection of parasites from the untidy nest it had recently left. The grooming session seemed to make it feel better, and it fluttered a few feet to another perch, made a few gurgling-drain sounds, and flew into the treetops.

The ridge looked very different from above the forest canopy than from below it. The cuckoo saw a billowing sea of leaves, which seemed about to flow down and inundate the lowland cornfields and houses. Birds and flying insects occasionally broke from the green billows as jumping fish break from the ocean, and once in a while a squirrel would leap porpoiselike along the treetops. At night raccoons and opossums prowled the canopy, and to the birds and butterflies they must have seemed monsters of the deep.

The cuckoo fledgling looked pale in the full sunlight: its plumage was lighter than its parents' and it wouldn't acquire their black and white tail markings until after its autumn molt. It opened its beak and spread its wings for relief from the heat and parasites, but then it saw one of the red-tailed hawks drifting toward it and ducked back under the canopy. The hawk soared along, so close to the treetops that its wingtips sometimes touched leaves, and suddenly found itself in the midst of the grackle flock. The grackles immediately began to make their harsh alarm calls and to fly at the hawk. The whole flock rose from the woods and took off in pursuit of the red-tail, which flapped its wings a few times as if in mild annoyance and dropped away down the eastern slope.

With the grackles gone, the only sounds in the woods for the rest of the afternoon were the whining of mosquitoes and the peevish calls of red-eyed vireos and wood pewees. A few ground crickets stridulated feebly, as though enervated by the heat. Even the cicadas stopped calling as the heat peaked in late afternoon, starting up again only after sunset. A rufous-sided towhee on the ridgetop sang "Drink you . . . Drink your te . . . uh . . . uh. Drink your t . . ." Skulking in a blackberry thicket, he seemed unable to summon the conviction to voice the normally accented "tea" syllable.

As the daylight faded, tree crickets and cone-headed grasshoppers began to sing with considerably more enthusiasm, although their noise was masked until after dark by the cicadas' whirring.

BIRD VOICES

OF

AUTUMN

Robert Cunningham Miller

With family duties concluded, many birds find voice once again in the fall. But it is a special sort of music they make at this time of year, a "chamber music" here described by Robert Cunningham Miller, former director of the California Academy of Sciences.

In the Pacific states Indian summer brings us some of our finest weather, and in coastal regions where there is considerable summer fog it constitutes quite a definite, well-marked season—the long, warm, golden interlude between summer fog and winter rain. It is almost a second springtime, only more subdued and mellow, with more subtle nuances of light and color and sound.

Nature has to be learned by ear as well as by eye. Every experience of the out-of-doors has a sound accompaniment—the crash of a water-fall, the roll of thunder, the sighing of wind in the trees, the crackling of twigs or the swish of grasses as little animals move about their business, the voices of insects and birds. Indian summer has it own complement of musicians, and its own musical score which, lacking the wild rapture of spring, requires more careful listening. If spring provides the crescendo of the symphony, autumn gives us nature's chamber music.

There is the industrious hum of bees, the rhythmic stridulation of grasshoppers, and the cheerful chirp of crickets which—as the weather grows cooler—will find their way indoors to sing their autumn song around the fireplace. And there are the voices of the birds, almost un-noticed till we try to contemplate what an Indian-summer day would be without them.

On a sunny morning in September the juncos pursue one another with cheerful trills and twitters, their song more playful and varied than the somewhat monotonous "territorial" chant of spring—a serious

From *Pacific Discovery*, September–October, 1951.

business then, when the males take up their posts and by persistent song announce their possession of the nesting area and their intention to defend it against all comers. Now the responsibilities of the nesting season are over, food in the form of ripened seeds of weeds and grasses is abundant, the sun is warm, and life is good. Flashing the white inverted V of their outer tail feathers, the juncos dart about with all the happy abandon of children on a picnic.

One hears the nasal *yank, yank, yank* of a wandering nuthatch, the shrill cry of a sparrow hawk, the loud shouts of jays—hardly musical sounds, yet each contributing in its own manner to the character of an Indian-summer day. From the distance comes the lilting trill of a white-crowned sparrow, while close at hand a Bewick wren tries a few exploratory notes, like someone practicing scales and runs on the piano. A pair of wren-tits, mated throughout the year, slip unobtrusively about among the shrubbery, conversing with one another in lovely, liquid syllables, occasionally interspersing gently scolding notes that provide just the right accent to this otherwise too perfect example of conjugal felicity.

The robins begin to gather into flocks. One notices half-a-dozen robins in the yard, and thinks perhaps it is a robin family. Then he sees a score or more of robins on a neighboring lawn, and presently they are going about in flocks of two or three hundred. Robins at this season are comparatively silent, especially considering the size of their flocks; however, they frequently give familiar robin calls, and occasionally, on any sunny day, a short phrase of song.

Many of the bird voices of autumn seem vaguely plaintive and at least one, the *tiu, tiu, tiu* of the rufous-crowned sparrow, sounds downright querulous. Happily it is unlikely that the little feathered complainants feel as dejected as they sound.

Most familiar of the plaintive voices of the autumn is that of the goldfinch, which in its several local races is found throughout most of North America. As goldfinches move about in little flocks in September and October, feeding on weed seeds or flicking out thistledown, their purling calls, marvelously sweet yet tinged with melancholy, bring to Indian summer the gentle sadness of remembered yesterdays.

There is another autumn voice that is still more poignant. As the days grow shorter and the noonday shadows lengthen to the northward, there comes one day a call so indescribably sad and sweet that it might almost be the voice of a disembodied avian spirit. Three notes there are in a descending cadence, not in the diatonic but in a chromatic scale. They have been compared to the opening bars of "Three Blind Mice," but this is only a loose approximation. "Oh, dear me," says the bird, recounting its woes, and then in a different key and with altered emphasis, it repeats, "*Oh, dear* me," as if its heart were bursting with all the sorrows of the avian world. This is the song of the golden-crowned sparrow, newly arrived on its winter feeding grounds; and when one hears it, he inevitably thinks of the lines of William Cullen Bryant:

"The melancholy days are come, the saddest of the year,
  Of wailing winds and naked woods and meadows brown and sear."

But nature never leaves us to despair. Even the melancholy days hold promise of happier ones to come. Just as the tide of out-door life seems at its lowest ebb, in the late, dark mornings of December, the Anna hummingbird begins its courtship, and in coastal California the song sparrow bursts forth with its nuptial song. Nature seems ever to be looking forward. Even as the dying year approaches its end, there are bird voices to remind us that we have passed the winter solstice, and that already the days are lengthening toward spring.

AUTUMN ON

THE PRAIRIE MARSHES

H. Albert Hochbaum

Is much of fall birdsong really in a minor key, or do we only hear it that way because it presages the exodus of many of our summer birds? A dramatic part of that exodus are the waterfowl flights, the majority of which originate in the "duck-hatchery" potholes and marshes of the prairie states and provinces. Among the most famous of these is the vast Delta Marsh at the southern end of Lake Manitoba. For many years the director of the Delta Waterfowl Research Station, the talented writer (and artist) H. Albert Hochbaum here describes the stage-by-stage autumn emptying of that raucous waterfowl nursery.

THERE come unforgettable evenings in late August when a soft calm settles over the marsh. The breeze is spent and the reeds duplicate themselves in perfect reflection. The sky is clear, yet with sundown comes a refreshing chill. The tinkle of water from the canoe paddle and the rustle of a wren in the tules are the only sounds. Here is the world as God made it. Deep in the heart of the wheatland is a pristine wilderness that can differ little from that so loved by the native Cree. This might be the marsh as seen two centuries ago by La Vérendrye. The dark bulrush, the green cattail, and the tall reed have not changed; sky and water are the same; the wren must be a direct descendant of one that chattered here when the explorer's canoe slipped past this very place. Surely all is the same except for the tall grain elevator that rises above the oak bluff six miles to the south.

The peace is broken suddenly by the chuckle of a teal. Who is there so solemn that he listens to the fall note of the Blue-winged Teal without a smile? Here is a challenge offered severely, the youngster's exclamation of its place in this ancient world of bulrush. Hardly before summer becomes routine, autumn is upon us. These Blue-winged Teal, whose voices break the tranquillity of the August evening, are birds-of-the-year. Bred in May, born in June, reared before the wheat is ripe,

From *Travels and Traditions of Waterfowl*. Minneapolis: University of Minnesota Press, 1955.

they are on their way to the wintering grounds before summer is gone. One evening after supper I flush a hundred from the cove; the next morning only a dozen are frightened from the same place. By the equinox the main flight has passed to the south; the end of the first week in October finds only a few stragglers remaining, although there is promise of more fair weather before the shallows close with ice. Whatever the urge, it surely is not the pressure of frost that sends the bluewings to their southland. . . .

What greater place in life can a man attain than a seat by the fire on an October evening? What finer thoughts than of bird, of dog, and of gun? What better companionship than of elder hunters who read aloud from their life stories as they gaze into the hearth? However artificial their environments become, however far from nature they must stray in search of fortune, all wise young men seek a place by the October hearthstone.

I have read many books, have spent many days on the marsh, but there is much I have learned from the words of older hunters. The north wind was their friend before I could hold my father's gun. In calm and storm they lived many years on marshland I am just beginning to know. As the birch logs crackled, I have learned that the Canvasback never wait for the heavy frost. Come mid-October and the cannies are done with Manitoba. In late September their numbers crowd the big marshes so that windrows of pondweed litter the shore downwind of the feeding places. In early October they parade daily, passing from their loafing grounds on open water to the sago beds where they feed. Then, when October is half gone, there comes upon the birds a wild restlessness. In a flock loafing on the water, one bird after another raises its body to flex its wings, so that there is a constant fluttering. Over the marsh, small bands join to form larger flocks. Then the Canvasback are gone, all but a few strays lingering on with the scaup. . . .

Casual as the teal flights may be, early as the Canvasback slip away, the freeze-up flight of Mallard and Lesser Scaup is quite another thing. They cling to the northland through October and on into November. Some travel southward, to be sure, like teal and Canvasback, but vast numbers hold to the north as long as open water remains. Then comes the time for passage. The temperature drops and remains below freezing all day; it may touch zero or fall below that mark. The barometer rises, a stiff wind strikes out of the northwest, and before noon the skies are clear. On such a day in November it is the wildfowler's duty to abandon all home ties and go at once to the marsh. It is usual for little flurries of southbound ducks to appear early that afternoon. First one, then another, then more and more, until one glance catches many flocks. They come out of the northwest, often so high that they would not be noticed but for the volume of the flock. They scurry past without stopping. By four o'clock there is not an instant without ducks in every corner of the sky. During the heaviest waves, fifty or sixty flocks a minute may pass over a section of marsh a mile wide; and as far east and west as one can see, waterfowl cross over in steady numbers, small bands and large. The stream of their passage seems endless; then after sundown the rosy twilight changes to cold blue, and the last ducks have passed. Another autumn is gone.

ON THE

WINTERING GROUNDS

OF THE SNOW GEESE

Barry Lopez

Along the coast and on the interior lakes of California, autumn means the beginning rather than the end of waterfowl activity, for these waters concentrate impressive numbers of wintering ducks and geese. In the following passage, the young writer Barry Lopez treats us to images of one such concentration on Tule Lake, situated near the Oregon border.

IT was still dark, and I thought it might be raining lightly. I pushed back the tent flap. A storm-driven sky moving swiftly across the face of a gibbous moon. Perhaps it would clear by dawn. The ticking sound was not rain, only the wind. A storm, bound for somewhere else.

Half awake, I was again aware of the voices. A high-pitched cacophonous barking, like terriers, or the complaint of shoats. The single outcries became a rising cheer, as if in a far-off stadium, that rose and fell away.

Snow geese, their night voices. I saw them flying down the north coast of Alaska once in September, at the end of a working day. The steady intent of their westward passage, that unwavering line, was uplifting. The following year I saw them over Banks Island, migrating north in small flocks of twenty and thirty. And that fall I went to northern California to spend a few days with them on their early wintering ground at Tule Lake in Klamath Basin.

Tule Lake is not widely known in America, but the ducks and geese gather in huge aggregations on this refuge every fall, creating an impression of land in a state of health, of boundless life. On any given day a visitor might look upon a million birds here—pintail, lesser scaup, Barrow's goldeneye, cinnamon teal, mallard, northern shoveler, redhead, and canvasback ducks; Great Basin and cackling varieties of Can-

From *Arctic Dreams: Imagination and Desire in a Northern Landscape.* New York: Charles Scribner's Sons, 1986.

ada geese, white-fronted geese, Ross's geese, lesser snow geese; and tundra swans. In open fields between the lakes and marshes where these waterfowl feed and rest are red-winged blackbirds and Savannah sparrows, Brewer's sparrows, tree swallows, and meadowlarks. And lone avian hunters—marsh hawks, red-tailed hawks, bald eagles, the diminutive kestrel.

The Klamath Basin, containing four other national wildlife refuges in addition to Tule Lake, is one of the richest habitats for migratory waterfowl in North America. To the west of Tule Lake is another large, shallow lake called Lower Klamath Lake. To the east, out past the tule marshes, is a low escarpment where barn owls nest and the counting marks of a long-gone aboriginal people are still visible, incised in the rock. To the southwest, the incongruous remains of a Japanese internment camp from World War II. In agricultural fields to the north, east, and south, farmers grow malt barley and winter potatoes in dark volcanic soils.

The night I thought I heard rain and fell asleep again to the cries of snow geese, I also heard the sound of their night flying, a great hammering of the air overhead, a wild creaking of wings. These primitive sounds made the Klamath Basin seem oddly untenanted, the ancestral ground of animals, reclaimed by them each year. In a few days at the periphery of the flocks of geese, however, I did not feel like an interloper. I felt a calmness birds can bring to people; and, quieted, I sensed here the outlines of the oldest mysteries: the nature and extent of space, the fall of light from the heavens, the pooling of time in the present, as if it were water.

There were 250,000 lesser snow geese at Tule Lake. At dawn I would find them floating on the water, close together in a raft three-quarters of a mile long and perhaps 500 yards wide. When a flock begins to rise from the surface of the water, the sound is like a storm squall arriving, a great racket of shaken sheets of corrugated tin. (If you try to separate the individual sounds in your head, they are like dry cotton towels snapping on a wind-blown clothesline.) Once airborne, they are dazzling on the wing. Flying against broken sunlight, the opaque whiteness of their bodies, a whiteness of water-polished shells, contrasts with grayer whites in their translucent wings and tail feathers. Up close they show the dense, impeccable whites of arctic fox. Against the bluish grays of a storm-laden sky, their whiteness has a surreal glow, a brilliance without shadow.

When they are feeding in the grain fields around Tule Lake, the geese come and go in flocks of five or ten thousand. Sometimes there are forty or fifty thousand in the air at once. They rise from the fields like smoke in great, swirling currents, rising higher and spreading wider in the sky than one's field of vision can encompass. One fluid, recurved sweep of ten thousand of them passes through the spaces within another, counterflying flock; while beyond them lattice after lattice passes, like sliding Japanese walls, until in the whole sky you lose your depth of field and feel as though you are looking up from the floor of the ocean through shoals of fish.

WINTER COMES

TO CHESTNUT RIDGE

David Rains Wallace

Winter on the Gulf Coast or on the waterfowl lakes of California is a time of bustling avian activity, but for most of North America—including Chestnut Ridge—the short days signal retrenchment in the face of the spare economies of a cold and food-short season.

T HE creeks ran open for a few days more, then the cold returned—a still, metallic frost that hung over the ridge day after day until the ground was brittle from the ice crystals growing in it. Earthworms and salamanders moved deeper. Mites, springtails, nematodes, protozoans, and fungi froze to death in multitudes—and survived in even greater multitudes by finding sympathetic microclimates or taking refuge in cysts and spores. The chipmunks joined the groundhogs in winter sleep, and the woods were quiet, almost prim. They seemed a little tidier now that the leaf litter was frozen hard and the branches were not disarrayed by warm air currents. Red-bellied woodpeckers and white-breasted nuthatches hitched themselves around the trees making nasal, peevish sounds—spinsters and bachelors in their wintry parlors. . . .

The first snow that would lie on the ground through the winter fell at midnight two days before the solstice. It was not a heavy snow, and stopped after a few hours. The sky cleared, and the white landscape glittered in the bright dawn. The air was very cold, and the snow did not melt even though there was little more than an inch on the ground. It remained powdery and undiminished through the afternoon, and the glare of sunlight reflected off snow made the ridge seem insubstantial—only the bright blue tree shadows indicated the contours of slopes and gullies. Against the whiteness the quarry cliffs and spring pool resembled black holes more than surfaces of rock or water.

A wind from the southwest blustered through most of the day, raising little cyclones of snow crystals along the ridgetop, baring some

From *Idle Weeds: The Life of a Sandstone Ridge*. San Francisco: Sierra Club Books, 1980.

spots and burying others in drifts. It filled the tracks left by early morning squirrels and rabbits and kept the songbirds sheltering in thickets. Often the wind was the only thing moving, but some birds seemed to enjoy playing in it. Goldfinches made swift, arching flights above the old fields. Occasionally the wind blew them off course and nearly upended them as surf lifts and rolls swimmers. Mourning doves flew in and out of pine plantations with a headlong clapping of wings, seeming almost able to outrace the wind. The red-tailed hawk pair stilled above the ridge for long moments, facing into the wind so it buoyed up their broad wings, until a strong gust knocked them backward and they had to turn and glide a little before facing it again. It was an easy way to look for meadow mice, although there were few mice to be seen.

The wind died down after an early, almost colorless sunset. The horned owls' calls were very clear in the stillness that followed—the deep "Hoo *hoo* hoo hoo" answered by the higher, excited "Hoo hoo *hoo* hoo hoo." The deep call came from a vine-tangled hickory on the ridgetop, and the last of the short-tailed shrew's autumn litter heard it.

The shrew's heart raced for a moment, but it was safe underground. It had used the warm weather after its mother's death to make new tunnels in the leaf litter and had broken into a carpenter ant's nest in a stump. The sluggish ants, woodlice, beetles, and other inhabitants of the nest had filled its stomach many times, and its condition was much improved. It had the strength to forage and seek new food sources now that the cold weather had returned. It remained timid, reluctant to leave its tunnels, so it didn't emerge to explore the new snow as had its mother a year before.

The owl saw nothing of interest on the ridgetop and flew away to look for mice along the marsh edges. Although the sun had just set, the air was so clear and dry that the winter constellations were out already, Orion in the southeast, Aquarius on the western horizon, the Great Bear low in the north—a polar bear. It was getting very cold indeed.

Part

Two

FLIGHT AND MIGRATION

THE PERFECT

FLYING

MACHINE

Guy Murchie, Jr.

Birds move through the seasons by "winging it." We are fascinated by flightless birds precisely because we consider flight the preeminent avian characteristic. From the birds themselves man learned some of the indispensable secrets of successful flying, but he could never have put them into practice had he not been able to summon to his aid his own unique invention—the art of using for his own purposes an external source of power. Aviation first became possible when engineers had developed the internal combustion engine to the point where the ratio of weight to power was as low as that achieved millions of years ago by the birds! And birds, as the author of the following article convincingly argues, are still the most perfect of all flying machines.

1

THE birds that we see flying successfully around us every day are only the surviving ten per cent or so of much larger numbers that hatch from eggs, who in turn represent far less than one per cent of all that would be hatched if the extinct birds survived in their former numbers. In other words, our present birds are a very select bunch, being actually only the topflight athletes, the champions who have won the flying tournament of evolution by their prodigious feats of soaring, of diving at terrific speed, plunging deep into the sea, or fighting in the air.

Can you imagine any better example of divine creative accomplishment than the consummate flying machine that is a bird? The skeleton, very flexible and strong, is also largely pneumatic—especially in the bigger birds. The beak, skull, feet, and all other bones of a 25-pound pelican have been found to weigh but 23 ounces. Yet the flesh too is pneumatic, and in some species there are air sacs around viscera, muscles, and, where balance and streamlining permit, immediately under the skin. The lungs are not just single cavities as with mammals but whole series of chambers

From *Song of the Sky*. Boston: Houghton Mifflin, 1954.

around the main breathing tubes, connected also with all the air sacs of the body, including the hollow bones. Thus the air of the sky literally permeates the bird, flesh and bone alike, and aerates it entire. And the circulation of sky through the whole bird acts as a radiator or cooling system of the flying machine, expelling excess humidity and heat as well as exchanging carbon dioxide for oxygen at a feverish rate.

This air-conditioning system is no mere luxury to a bird but vitally necessary to its souped-up vitality. Flight demands greater intensity of effort than does any other means of animal locomotion, and so a bird's heart beats many times per second, its breathing is correspondingly rapid, and its blood has more red corpuscles per ounce than any other creature. As would be expected of a high-speed engine, the bird's temperature is high: a heron's 105.8°, a duck's 109.1°, and a swift's 111.2°.

Fuel consumption is so great that most birds have a kind of carburetor called a crop for straining and preparing their food before it is injected into the combustion cylinders of the stomach and intestines, and the speed of peristaltic motion is prodigious. You may have heard of the young robin who ate fourteen feet of earthworm the first day after leaving the nest, or the house wren who was recorded feeding its young 1217 times between dawn and dusk. Young crows have been known to eat more than their own weight in food per day, and an adolescent chickadee was checked eating over 5500 cankerworm eggs daily for a week.

The main flying motors fed by this bird fuel are the pectoral muscles, the greater of which pulls down the wing against the air to drive the bird upward and onward, while the lesser hoists the wing back up again, pulling from below by means of an ingenious block and tackle tendon. This extraordinary halyard which passes through a lubricated pulley hole at the shoulder is necessary because the heaviest muscles must be kept at the bottom of the bird so that it will not fly top-heavy. Just as the motor may weigh half of a small airplane, the powerful wing muscles of a pigeon have been found to weigh half the whole bird. These pectorals, by the way, are the solid white meat attached to the breastbone or keel, a location insuring the lowest possible center of gravity—just forward of such other low-slung ballast as gizzard and liver, and well below the very light lungs and air sacs.

If you want to see the ultimate in vertebrate flexibility, you must examine a bird's neck. More pliant than a snake, it enables the beak to reach any part of the body with ease and balances the whole bird in flight. Even the stocky little sparrow has twice as many vertebrae in its neck as the tallest giraffe: fourteen for the sparrow, seven for the giraffe.

The most distinctive feature of all in a bird, of course, is its feathers, the lightest things in the world for their size and toughness. The tensile strength of cobwebs is great but feathers are stronger in proportion in many more ways, not to mention being springy and flexible.

The growth of a feather is like the unfoldment of some kinds of flowers and ferns. Tiny moist blades of cells appear on the young bird, splitting lengthwise into hairlike strands which dry apart into silky filaments which in the mass are known as down. At the roots of the down lie other sets of cells which, as the bird grows older, push the down from its sockets. These are the real feathers, and when the down rubs off they appear as little blue-gray sheaths which may be likened to rolled-up umbrellas or furled sails.

Each of these sheaths is actually an instrument of almost unimaginable potentiality and at the right moment it suddenly pops open—revealing in a few hours feathers that unfold into smaller feathers that unfold again and again. Each main shaft or quill sprouts forth some 600 dowls or barbs on either side to form the familiar vane of the feather. But each of the 1200 barbs in turn puts out about 800 smaller barbs called barbules, each of which again produces a score or two of tiny hooks known as barbicels. The complete interwoven mesh of one feather thus contains some thirty million barbicels, and a whole bird normally is encased in several hundred billion tiny clinging barbicels.

It is hard for the human mind to take in the intricacy of this microscopic weaving that is a feather. There is nothing chemical about it. It is entirely mechanical. If you pull the feather vane apart in your fingers it offers outraged resistance: you can imagine the hundreds of barbules and thousands of barbicels at that particular spot struggling to remain hooked together. And even after being torn the feather has amazing recuperative power. Just placing the split barbs together again and stroking them lengthwise a few times is sufficient to rehook enough barbicels to restore the feather to working efficiency—by nature's own zipper action.

The feather webbing is so fine that few air molecules can get through it and it is ideal material for gripping the sky. In a sense the feather is as much kith to sky as kin to bird, for by a paradox the bird does not really live until its feathers are dead. No sooner is a feather full grown than the opening at the base of the quill closes, blood ceases to flow, and it becomes sealed off from life. The bird's body does not lose track of it, however, for as often as a feather comes loose from a living bird, a new one grows in its place.

Did you ever notice how similar are a feather and a sail? The quill, though it can be bent double without breaking, is stiff enough for a mast. The forward or cutting vane is narrow as a trimmed jib, the aft or lee vane wide like a mainsail. The barbs correspond to the bamboo lugs of a Chinese junk, strengthening the sail, enabling it to withstand the full typhoon of flight. The primary feathers of some sea ducks, however, can be as jibless as catboats, having virtually no vane forward of the quill, which thus itself becomes the leading edge. The cross-section of such a feather is rather like an airplane wing and highly efficient in lift.

Besides its individual qualities a feather is a perfect part of a whole, its shaft curved to blend exactly into the pattern of the wing, its shape to fit the slipstream of the sky. Like roof tiles, feathers are arranged in overlapping rows, the forward part of the bird corresponding to the top of the roof. Which explains why birds do not feel right unless they are facing the weather, why when they turn to leeward the wind blows against their grain letting the rain soak through to the skin just as shingles reversed will funnel the wet into the house instead of shedding it away.

Different feathers naturally have different functions and shapes. The wing-tip feathers are called the primaries, usually ten in number, and serve to propel the bird. These grow out of what corresponds to the bird's hand. The forearm feathers nearer the body are the secondaries, twelve to fourteen of them—they mainly support the bird—while the upper arm tertiaries or tertial feathers fair in the secondaries with the body and stabilize the bird in the air. The tail feathers average about fourteen, overlapping from the center outwards, but they vary so much in different birds that hardly any generalization can be made about them. They are rooted in a pincushionlike muscle mound, the pope's nose, which in some species has been found to house more than a thousand individual feather muscles, each capable of moving one feather in one direction.

One might think that as a bird moults, shedding feathers from once to three times a year, the uneven loss would sometimes set the bird off balance in flight. But nature provides that at least the important primary feathers drop off exactly in pairs, one from the right wing with the corresponding feather from the left wing, waiting then for two new feathers to replace them before moulting the next pair.

2

When Leonardo da Vinci and later Otto Lilienthal and the French glider pioneers studied birds in order to learn the principles of flight, their concentration naturally was focused on the motions of wings and tail. But these movements turned out to be so fast, complex, and subtle that their analysis was extremely difficult. Even today much remains to be learned of them.

One of the first facts revealed by close observation and the high-speed camera was that wings do not simply flap up and down. Nor do they row the bird ahead like oars. The actual motion is more that of sculling a boat or screwing it ahead by propeller action, a kind of figure-eight movement.

A bird's "hand" (outer wing) is longer than the rest of its "arm" (wing) but it has almost as complete control over it as a man has. It is true that two of the original "fingers" have fused into one and the others have disappeared, but the big primary feathers have replaced them so completely that it has gained many more digits and muscles than it has lost. It can twist its "hand" to any position, spread its ten primaries, waggle or twiddle them, shrug its shoulders, even clap its "hands" together behind its head and in front of its breast. That is why wing motion is so complex, variable, and hard to comprehend.

The powerful downstroke that obviously lifts and propels the bird also is a forward stroke, so much so that the wings often touch each other in front of the breast and almost always come close at take-off and climb. Many people have trouble understanding this fact proven by the camera until they reflect that it is likewise forward motion of the airplane wing that generates lift. Just as a sculling oar or a propeller drives a boat ahead by moving at right angles to the boat's motion, so does the force of the bird's wing resolve itself into a nearly perpendicular component.

Even the wing's upstroke plays its part in driving the bird upward and onward—for the same reason. This quick flip of recovery takes half the time of the downstroke and has much less power, but is still part of the sculling motion that is almost peristaltic—like a fish in the sea or a snake in the grass—probably closest of all to the rotor screw action of a moving helicopter: forward and down, backward and up and around.

A fuller understanding of this marvel can be gained by careful study of photographs taken at very high speed, flashed in slow motion on a screen or strangely frozen in stills. The pliable feathers at the wing's tip and trailing edge are then seen to bend according to the changing pressures, revealing how the air is moving.

The downstroke plainly compresses them tightly upon each other the whole length of the outstretched wing, each feather grabbing its full hold of air, while the upstroke, lifting first the "wrist," then the half-folded wing, swivels the feathers apart like slats in a Venetian blind to let the air slip by. It is an automatic, selective process, probably nature's most graceful and intricate valve action, the different movements overlapping and blending smoothly, the "wrists" half up before the wing tips stop descending, the "forearms" pressing down while the tips are yet rising. The convexity of the wing's upper surface and the concavity of its lower aid this alternate gripping and slipping of the air—this compression of sky into a buoyant cushion below the wing while an intermittent vacuum sucks from above—this consummate reciprocal flapping that pelicans accomplish twice a second, quail twenty times, and hummingbirds two hundred times!

Birds are clearly way ahead of the airplane in aileron or roll control; and some, like ravens and roller pigeons, close their wings to make snap rolls just for fun or courting. And the same bird superiority holds in the case of flaps which brake the air to reduce speed in landing, the birds fanning out their tails for this purpose as well as their wings. Web-footed birds such as geese usually steer and brake with their feet also, and inflect their long necks like the bow paddle of a canoe to aid in steering and balancing.

The tail is of course intended primarily for steering—steering up and down as well as to right and left. Some birds with efficient tails can loop the loop, fly upside down, or do backward somersaults like the tumbler pigeon. Small-tailed birds such as ducks are handicapped by not being able to make any kind of sharp turns in the air, though their tails steer well enough in water and in slapping the waves on take-off from water. The male whidah bird has such a long tail that on a dewy morning he actually cannot get off the ground until the sun has evaporated the extra weight from his trailer. The variety of bird tails never ends, nor does the multiplicity of functions. Furled to a mere stick or fanned out 180° and skewed to any angle, tails serve for everything from a stabilizing fin to a parachute, from a flag to a crutch.

3

Man cannot hope to match the bird in sensitivity of flying control, mainly because he usually has to think air or read it off instruments, while the bird just feels air everywhere on his feathers and skin. This is not to say, however, that the bird is a faultless flyer. Birds make plenty of mistakes—even forced landings! Not a few are killed in crashes. Usually bird slip-ups happen so fast they go unnoticed. But when you get a chance to watch a flight of birds coming in to land in slow-motion movies you can see them correcting their errors by last-moment flips of tail or by dragging a foot like a boy on a sled. If a landing bird discovers he lowered his "flaps" too soon he still can ease off these air brakes by raising his wings so that his secondaries spill wind, his primary feathers remaining in position for lateral or aileron control. Buzzards do something almost similar called a "double dip" to correct a stall. But lots of times excited birds do not notice their mistakes soon enough and lose flying speed while trying to climb too steeply, or fall into a spin from tight turns or from simply misjudging the wind. Once they have ceased making headway they tumble downward just as surely as a stalled airplane.

I saw a heron one day muff a landing in a tree, stall, and fall to the ground, breaking his leg. This is particularly apt to happen to heavy birds like ducks when they are tired. Sometimes ducks lose half a pound on a long migratory flight and are so exhausted on letting down that they splash into the water and cannot take off again for hours.

The energy required of a heavy bird at take-off of course is very great. It has been estimated at five times normal cruising energy. Many birds, like the swan, need a runway in addition to the most furious beating of wings to get up enough speed to leave the ground. Others like the coot are lighter but low-powered and take off like a 1915 scout plane missing on three cylinders. All birds naturally take off against the wind for the same reason that an airplane does: to gain air speed, which is obviously more significant than ground speed at take-off. You have surely noticed that birds feeding by the lee roadside will often take off across the path of an approaching car, actually tempting death to gain the wind's help.

Heavy birds that dwell on cliffs of course have the advantage of being able to make a catapult take-off, dropping into a steep glide until they build up flying speed—but again they must beware of landing at a place where this needed gravitational asset is not available. The penalty for lack of such foresight can well be death.

I heard of a loon that made the mistake of alighting on a small pond set amid a forest of tall pines. When he wanted to take off an hour later he found himself stymied. He could not climb steeply enough to clear the trees or turn sharply enough to spiral out. He was seen thrashing along over the water, whipping the waves with his wings to get under way, even pedaling at the water desperately with his webbed feet before getting into the air. He almost made it a couple of times but also nearly got killed crashing into the big trees, then plowing back through the under-brush on his sprained wishbone. Finally he had to give up. But this particular loon was lucky. After four frustrated days in his pond jail a very strong wind came up and enabled him to take off and climb so steeply against it that he just brushed between the treetops and was free!

A very different and special capacity is required in bird formation flight or mass maneuvering. Did you ever see a puff of smoke blowing against the wind? I did—but it turned out to be a tight flock of thousands of small birds. When you get close enough to watch a large flight of star-lings feeding on a field you wonder how each bird can so completely lose its individuality as to become part of that smooth, flowing mass. Sometimes the flock moves like a great wheel, individual birds alighting and rising progressively as parts of the rhythm of the rim. Now it rolls as a coach on the highroad, now with uneven grace like a tongue of sea fog folding over and over.

Sandpipers, plover, turnstones, sanderlings, and other small shore birds are all expert in this sort of flying, which seems to depend on extreme quickness of eye and a speed of selfless response not equaled elsewhere in nature—not among its counterparts in the hoofed animals of the plains, not even among the mysterious schools of the deep sea where whales and the lesser fish have been seen to dive in wonderful co-ordination miles apart. No one knows exactly how this amazing unity of action is accom-plished or why. It may depend on much more than visual contact. It may be a part of one of the seams of life where the individual is granted a pretaste of absorption into a greater order of consciousness, far above and beyond his own little being.

When birds migrate they often fly in V formation and for the same reason that the Air Force does. It is the simplest way to follow a leader in the sky while keeping out of his wash and retaining good vision. Birds instinctively do it, peeling off from one heading to another and sometimes chasing after man-made gliders. They even have been seen pursuing power planes until they were unable to keep up with them. I know of a glider pilot who was followed for half an hour by a young sea gull who copied his every maneuver: figure-eights, vertical turns, spins, loops. It was only after the glider led the gull into a vertical dive for three thousand feet which blew most of the bird's feathers off that it realized it had been a little too gullible and left off the chase.

Lots of birds, far from feeling jealous of human trespassing in their ancient territory, seem to get such a kick out of airplanes that they hang around airports just like human kids watching the big ones take off and land. Many a time I've seen sea gulls at the big Travis Air Base near San Francisco flapping nonchalantly among the huge ten-engined B-36 bombers while their motors were being run up. The smoke whipping from the jets in four straight lines past the tail accompanied by that soul-shaking roar would have been enough to stampede a herd of elephants but the sea gulls often flew right into the tornado just for fun. When the full blast struck them they would simply disappear, only to turn up a few seconds later a quarter mile downwind, apparently having enjoyed the experience as much as a boy running through a hose—even coming around eager-eyed for more.

4

Of all birds the hawks have probably contributed most toward teaching man to fly—through their example of soaring over the zones of the earth where most men live. But how they accomplish their miracle has been discovered only a little at a time over long periods.

Sir George Cayley around 1810 concluded that a rook, whose weight is about a pound for each square foot of its wing area, would be able to glide horizontally as long as it could maintain a speed of at least twenty-five miles an hour. What could enable it to keep up that speed, however, he did not pretend to know.

A partial answer was revealed long afterward by a study of gulls circling close to the sea in autumn and winter, times of year when the relative warmth of the water often produces updrafts in which birds can soar indefinitely. Even in a fresh breeze when these warm columns of air are blown over to leeward until they lie almost flat upon the waves, the gulls have been observed soaring buoyantly along the invisible wind seams—gliding magically upwind upon a continuous fountain of air where two counterrotating columns adjoin.

But when they cannot thus coast "downhill" in air flowing "uphill," neither on thermal nor deflected updrafts, soaring birds somehow still manage to stay aloft on almost motionless wings—traveling at high speed as often against the wind as with it. A mission of the French scientist, Idrac, to the South Seas during the last century to solve the mystery of the albatross determined that this largest of soaring birds flies at the high average speed of forty-nine miles an hour. When soaring close to the waves and losing altitude, reported Idrac, the albatross uses his remaining speed to gain height. If he can rise only four or five times his wingspread of about eleven feet he usually gets into an air stratum fifty feet up where the wind is blowing three times as strongly as at the surface, thus giving him an extra boost just as a kite will be sent upward by a gust of wind.

The theory of this eventually expanded into one of the first real explanations of why birds soar in circles: since surface friction reduces wind speed at lower altitudes, the bird soars against the wind aiming slightly uphill to take advantage of higher wind velocity as he goes up, giving him the kite boost by *horizontal* shearing (by differences of wind speed at different horizontal levels). But as forward speed eventually falls off because of the climb, he turns away from the wind and coasts slightly downhill to leeward, again getting a boost from his increase in air speed as the tail wind decreases—then into the wind once more, and so on round and round.

The principles of "static soaring"—soaring on rising air currents—have been worked out in detail mainly during the last twenty-five years as sailplane pilots have experimented with thermal currents over sun-baked fields or up the windward slopes of hills or cold fronts. But only more recently has "dynamic soaring" come into use by man: this more difficult since it depends on the sudden variations of wind speed in gusty air to impart the kite boost by *vertical* shearing (by differences of wind speed in different vertical planes), relying of course on the pilot to be heading to windward at each increase of wind and to leeward at each decrease, a rhythm that can be irregular to the point of inscrutability.

All of these discoveries have helped explain how birds can glide on motionless wings against the wind, for it became clear that gravity is to the bird as the keel is to the sailboat or the kite string to the kite. All three hold the moving object firm against being blown to leeward, each in its own way.

The form of the wing is obviously another basic factor in flying effectiveness, and birds have adopted a great variety of special shapes just as have the airplane designers after them. There are the narrow, pointed wings of the fast and strong flyers: the falcons and swallows, the swifts and hummingbirds. There are the bent-wrist wings of the fast gliders like the nighthawk; the broad, fingered wings of the slow soarers, the red-shouldered and red-tailed hawks; the short, rounded wings of the woodland darters: grouse, quail, the small sparrows and finches.

Gulls and albatrosses also have narrow, pointed wings, theirs however adapted specially to long-range gliding and soaring over the open ocean. The albatross, in fact, so perfectly geared to the air that he cannot fold his lengthy wing restfully inside his flank feathers when on ground or sea, is thought to stretch out in sleep while actually on the wing—dozing aloft, even as some of us, but literally in his own feather bed upon the sky.

Little by little the factors of wing efficiency have resolved themselves into the separate relationships or dimensions of the wing: specifically, its aspect ratio or the proportion between its length and breadth, its degree of bluntness or pointedness, its camber or curvature fore and aft, its horizontalness or dihedral angle in relation to the other wing, its slotting or spacing of primaries (if any), its degree of sweepback, its fairing or smoothness of surface, its thickness, its flexibility, and innumerable minor points.

Aspect ratio in birds averages around 3:1. That is, their wings are generally about three times as long as they are wide. The albatross exceeds 5:1. Airplanes sometimes reach 7:1, and sailplanes as high as 18:1. Theoretically, the higher the ratio the greater the lift, but practically a limit comes when the wing gets so long and narrow that it may break in gusty air. And of course soaring birds have many considerations besides flying that affect their shape: things like catching food, preening their feathers, folding their wings, laying eggs, raising a family. Thus sailplanes, built solely for soaring, have a distinct advantage over the bird who must also be somebody's uncle or grandmother.

HUMMINGBIRD FLIGHT

Alexander F. Skutch

If Alexander F. Skutch knows a great deal about hummingbirds, it is partly because he has spent the bulk of his adult life in the American tropics, where most of the world's 340-plus species live. Here Skutch describes the remarkable flying abilities of these diminutive packages of feisty energy.

THE flight of hummingbirds is no less wonderful than their refulgent plumage. Watch a hummingbird as it sucks nectar from a spike or panicle of long, tubular flowers pointing in all directions. Now it hovers motionless on wings vibrated into unsubstantial blurs, while its long bill probes the depths of a corolla. Its drink finished, it flies backward to withdraw its bill from the tube, hovers briefly, then perhaps shifts sideways in the air, to place itself squarely in front of another blossom. With equal facility it adjusts its level up or down to reach higher or lower flowers. If the flower points sideward, the bird hovers with its body only slightly inclined; if it points downward, the hummingbird with equal ease drinks with its hovering body nearly vertical and its bill directed straight up. When it has satisfied its thirst, it may pivot around on a fixed point in the air before it darts swiftly away.

Although heavier than air, the hummingbird appears to be in perfect equilibrium with it, like a fish in water; with equal ease it moves in any direction, forward or backward, up or down, to the right or to the left, as well as pivoting on a stationary axis. No other bird can do all these things. The only limitation to the hummingbird's competence in the air is its inability to soar on motionless wings; this is a capacity reserved for larger birds with broader wings.

Among the hummingbird's other accomplishments is its ability to achieve practically full speed at the instant it takes wing. Indeed, it has been said to start flying before it leaves its perch; far from using the perch as a resistance against which to push with its feet and spring forward, it may lift a slender twig slightly at the moment of leaving it. Similarly, it has no need to reduce velocity as it approaches a perch; it

From *The Life of the Hummingbird*. New York: Crown Publishers, 1973.

may reach the perch at full speed and stop abruptly, in a way that would be disastrous to an airplane or a heavier bird.

Some of the hummingbird's flying abilities are useful not only when visiting flowers but also while nesting. Certain hummingbirds, notably the hermits, fasten their nest beneath the arching tip of a palm leaf, which they always face while incubating eggs or brooding nestlings. To leave, they start beating their wings while still sitting, fly upward and backward until clear of nest and leaf, then reverse and dart away. To return to the nest, hummingbirds of all kinds fly right into it instead of alighting on the rim or nearby and hopping in, as other birds do. By the time the newly arrived hummingbird's wings are folded, it is already incubating. When a white-eared hummingbird wishes to change her orientation in the nest, she sets her wings in motion, rises up slightly, and pivots around. When she wishes to turn her eggs, she flies upward and backward about one inch, to alight on the rim facing inward.

Another remarkable feat of the hummingbird is flying upside-down. If suddenly assailed from the front, as while visiting a flower, it may turn a backward somersault by flipping its spread tail forward, dart a short distance with its wings in reverse and feet upward, then roll over and continue in normal flight. . . .

When the hummingbird hovers motionless, its rapidly beating wings move forward and backward rather than up and down, their tips tracing a flat figure of eight in the air. With each reversal of the beat, the wings are pivoted through about 180 degrees, so that the front edge always leads and on the backstroke the undersides of the flight feathers are uppermost. Accordingly, while both forward and back strokes give lift, they cancel whatever tendency to horizontal displacement each may have and hold the bird in a single spot with no evident oscillation.

The great majority of hummingbirds appear unable to walk or hop. They scarcely ever alight on the ground, and to move a few inches on a branch, they fly. They depend wholly upon their wings for locomotion.

The rate of the wingbeats that in many species make a humming sound is difficult to determine, as it is far too rapid to be followed by the human eye. The most accurate counts have been made while the hummingbird was hovering rather than flying forward, by using a stroboscope in a darkened room. This apparatus emits extremely brief, bright flashes of light at exceedingly short intervals. If it is exactly synchronized with the wingbeats, they will always be illuminated in the same position, so that the bird will appear to float on motionless wings. The rate of the flashes can then be read on the instrument's dial. Using this method on a variety of hummingbirds, Scheithauer obtained frequencies of from twenty-two to seventy-nine wingbeats per second, the complete cycle of a down and up stroke being counted as one beat. The slowest rates were by the long-billed starthroat and the black-throated mango, large hummingbirds weighing respectively six and six and a half grams; the most rapid by the little white-bellied woodstar, which weighs only two and a half grams.

These results are in substantial agreement with those obtained earlier by C. H. Blake working with Harold Edgerton, by Crawford Greenewalt, and by other investigators. Just as a long pendulum swings more slowly than a short one, so a long wing beats more slowly than a short one. A mute swan's wing, twenty-eight inches long, flaps only one and a half times per second; a gnat's wing, a quarter of an inch in length, vibrates 500 times per second. Contrary to a prevalent impression, for their weight or wing length hummingbirds beat their wings less rather than more rapidly than other birds do. The giant hummingbird flaps only eight or ten times per second, whereas the much larger mockingbird does so about fourteen times. Many hummingbirds that weigh from five to seven grams flap at a rate of twenty to twenty-five times per second; but a chickadee, almost twice as heavy, beats its wings about twenty-seven times per second. Since only the chickadee's downstroke generates power, while both strokes of the hummingbird help to propel it, twenty-five beats of a hummingbird evidently count for fifty of the chickadee or some other "ordinary" bird. The hummingbird can afford to flap its wings more slowly because there is no waste motion.

In courtship flights ruby-throated and rufous hummingbirds have been reported to beat their wings at the rate of 200 times per second.

At a given velocity, a small body appears to move faster than a large one—an optical illusion that is responsible for exaggerated claims of the speed of hummingbirds. A carefully controlled measurement of a hummingbird's velocity, made in a wind tunnel by Greenewalt, demonstrated that the top speed of a female rubythroat was 27 miles per hour. When the velocity of the air current passing through the tunnel was increased to 30 miles per hour, the bird tried vainly to reach the coveted syrup by flying against the current. Bees and wasps trying to reach the feeder in the same tunnel flew at a rate of scarcely more than 10 miles per hour. Augusto Ruschi observed flying speeds ranging from 14 to 25 miles per hour for several species of Brazilian hummingbirds on outdoor courses; he believed that none could exceed 30 miles per hour.

It appears, however, that under special conditions or with stronger motivation some kinds of hummingbirds can go faster. By taking motion pictures of an Allen's hummingbird diving earthward under wing power in courtship display, Oliver Pearson calculated its maximum velocity to be about 60 miles per hour. Using a stopwatch to time a male violet-ear's flight from one isolated tree to another, Helmuth Wagner found an average speed of over 56 miles per hour. In Scheithauer's indoor aviary, two long-tailed, or blue-throated, sylphs were in the habit of chasing each other, sometimes eight to twelve times without stopping, over a standard course, roughly a figure of eight, that led them through tropical vegetation and avoided enclosing walls. This course was about seventy-four yards long. By timing the birds repeatedly with a stopwatch, the aviculturist obtained velocities ranging from 30 to 47 miles per hour, with a mean of 38.4 miles per hour.

Although this speed may not impress people accustomed to jet travel, that a bird could hurtle so fast through obstructing vegetation in a small enclosed space, without dashing itself to death, reveals marvelously precise control of flight. And when we recall that songbirds, including those as large as thrushes, mostly fly at velocities between 20 and 35 miles per hour, and pigeons hardly go faster, the tiny hummingbird's performance commands admiration.

HAWKS OVER

THE RIDGES

James J. Brett

Thanks to his position as curator of Hawk Mountain Sanctuary, James J. Brett has been privileged to witness autumn after autumn the great hawk flights down Kittatinny Ridge in Pennsylvania's Appalachian country. The several families of raptors employ radically different approaches to long-distance flight. A number of species make key use of "thermals" and "deflection currents," as Brett explains below.

Birds of prey are masters of flight. Buteos, the wide-winged soaring hawks, rely on air currents to help keep their relatively heavy bodies aloft. By contrast, the bodies of accipiters are streamlined, enabling them to maneuver with speed in their woodland habitats. Migrating accipiters take advantage of ridge currents for both uplift and propulsion. Falcons, our fastest raptors, make little use of air currents, relying instead on flapping. Peregrine falcons, kestrels, and merlins are more likely to follow coastal rather than ridge diversion lines. . . .

Two types of air currents are important to hawks migrating along the Appalachians or other ridge systems: thermal currents and deflection currents.

Thermals are produced by differential heating, as when warm air rising from the south side of a mountain ridge, plowed field, or rock outcrop is fed cooler air from a nearby north-facing ridge. Heated air expands but is held to the ground by cooler, heavier air, much like the bubbles on the bottom of a kettle whose water approaches the boiling point. After being sufficiently heated, the expanding air pocket rises from the ground, to be replaced by cooler air. The process continues with hot air "bubbles" being formed and released, sometimes combining as they sail aloft.

A bubble continues to expand as it rises, carrying moisture with it. Gradually it loses heat to the surrounding cooler air. As the temperatures equalize, water vapor within a bubble reaches its saturation point

From *The Mountain & the Migration: A Guide to Hawk Mountain.* Kempton, PA: Hawk Mountain Sanctuary Association, 1986.

and a cloud forms. Cumulus clouds mark the top of these thermals, whose lift will continue as long as they are supplied with energy and moisture from below. Hence, the beautiful billowing clouds rise higher and higher before disintegrating and vanishing.

Thermal production is most active in the spring, when the sun's rays strike the earth's surface at the most advantageous angle. Early autumn thermal production is also strong, but by late fall thermal activity slows dramatically as the earth's angle to the sun becomes more oblique.

Our wide-winged buteos are able to use thermals to good advantage; the broad-winged hawk, a master soarer, is king of the thermal. During the peak of the broadwing flight in mid-September, great movements of these hawks are seen along the ridges. Hawk watchers refer to a flock of thermaling broadwings as a "kettle"—from the boiling churning of birds in the heated bubble. Broadwings use thermal air currents as their main aid to travel all the way from the woodlands of eastern North America to northwestern South America.

A thermal typically begins to develop in mid-morning. Dust, leaves, insects—anything light enough to be drawn into the rising air mass—may be carried aloft with the cool, moist air. Broadwings detect the development of thermals by sighting the upward movement of materials within an invisible bubble and move towards it. As the sun rises and thermal activity quickens, broadwing after broadwing will begin to kettle in the rising air. It is not uncommon to see upwards of a hundred birds in a single kettle, and thousands are occasionally recorded. Thermal development is best on clear, calm days. Wind disrupts thermal production, and not only retards the heating of the ground, but also blocks the rise of heated air as well.

Hawks are lofted higher and higher, until they reach the point where the thermal begins to lose energy and dissipate. By then another thermal—or the kettle within it—has been sighted, and the birds stream out of the top of the present thermal and glide toward the bottom of the next. This hopscotching from one thermal to another allows the birds to travel great distances with minimal energy expenditure.

Although red-shouldered hawks and red-tailed hawks are also buteos, they utilize thermal air currents far less than do broadwings, in part because thermal activity begins to wane before most redtails and red-shoulders push southward.

Thermal air currents, while important, are used by only a few species, while deflected air currents are used by many species of northeastern ridge-flying raptors. Deflected air currents—called updrafts or deflection currents—occur when northerly or northwesterly wind strikes the vertical ridge and is forced up and over the top. Updrafts occur throughout the fall season as long as the wind blows. East and south winds are also deflected, but deflected northwesterlies are used to great-est advantage. . . .

The strength of deflected air currents is correlated with the passage of weather systems. . . . Southbound hawks use updrafts to sustain cruising speeds up to 60 mph. Birds glide mile after mile on out-stretched wings and can cut their sail-surface enough to maintain a steady balance relative to the lifting power of the rising air. Much as a surfer will ride the crest of a wave of water, birds ride the crest of a wave of air, receiving not only lift but also propulsion. On an ideal day, a raptor flying at an average speed of 40 mph may travel 250 miles.

THE

MIGRANT

BIRDS

Gonzalo de Oviedo

Just twenty-two years after Columbus first set sail for the Indies, one Gonzalo Fernandes Oviedo y Valdes was appointed Supervisor of the Gold Smeltings at San Domingo, and later, Historiographer of the Indies. In all, he paid six visits to the New World, and his Natural History of the Indies *contains a mass of curious information, much of it based on original observation. He was probably the first to comment on the migration of birds in the Western Hemisphere.*

EVERY yeere there passe from the end of Cuba infinite numbers of divers sorts of Birds, which come from the north of the firme Land, and crosse over the Alacrain Islands and Cuba, and flye over the Gulfe Southwards. I have seene them passe over Darien and Nombre de dios and Panama in divers yeeres, in the Firme Land; so many that they cover the skie: and this passage or march continueth a moneth or more about the moneth of March. I thinke they flie round about the World, for they never are seene to returne toward the West or North: and we see them not every yeere one after another; from morning to night the aire is covered, and some flie so high that they cannot bee seene, others lower yet higher then the mountaines tops. They come from the Northwest and North to the Southwards, and then turne South-west, occupying in length more than the eye can discerne, and a great space in breadth. The lowest are Eaglets and Eagles, and all seeme Birds of prey of many kinds and plumes: the higher cannot bee discerned in their plumes, but in manner of flying and quantitie appeare of divers sorts.

From *Summarie and Generall Historie of the Indies*, 1525, translated by Samuel Purchas.

BIRDS

OF PASSAGE

William Bartram

A vulture sailing high and effortlessly in the sky or a hummingbird poised before a flower are astonishing sights, but the most wonderful of all the birds' feats is one of which the incredible story has only recently become known. Even the ancient Greeks knew that some of them flew away to warmer climates when winter approached. But it is only within our own century that we have come to know about such feats as that of the Arctic tern, which migrates annually from the Arctic to the Antarctic and back again, or of the hummingbirds who fly non-stop across the Gulf of Mexico to their winter homes in Central or South America.

William Bartram, son of America's first botanist, was among the earliest of our naturalists to interest himself in the subject. The following passage is taken from the Travels, *in which he describes a naturalist's journey deep into Florida. It was one of the first American books to be widely read in England and it supplied hints to both Wordsworth and Coleridge.*

THERE are but few [birds] that have fallen under my observation, but have been mentioned by the zoologists, and most of them very well figured in Catesby's, or Edwards's works.

But these authors have done very little towards elucidating the subject of the migration of birds, or accounting for the annual appearance and disappearance, and vanishing of these beautiful and entertaining beings, who visit us at certain stated seasons. Catesby has said very little on this curious subject; but Edwards more, and perhaps all, or as much as could be said in truth, by the most able and ingenious, who had not the advantage and opportunity of ocular observation; which can only be acquired by traveling, and residing a whole year at least in the various climates from north to south, to the full extent of their peregrinations; or minutely examining the tracts and observations of curious and industrious travelers who have published their memoirs on this subject. There may perhaps be some persons who consider this enquiry not to be productive of any

From *The Travels of William Bartram,* edited by Mark Van Doren. New York: Dover, 1928.

real benefit to mankind, and pronounce such attention to natural history merely speculative, and only fit to amuse and entertain the idle virtuoso; however the ancients thought otherwise: for, with them, the knowledge of the passage of birds was the study of their priests and philosophers, and was considered a matter of real and indispensable use to the state, next to astronomy; as we find their system and practice of agriculture was in a great degree regulated by the arrival and disappearance of birds of passage; and perhaps a calendar under such a regulation at this time, might be useful to the husbandman and gardener.

But however attentive and observant the ancients were on this branch of science, they seem to have been very ignorant or erroneous in their conjectures concerning what became of birds, after their disappearance, until their return again. In the southern and temperate climates some imagined they went to the moon: in the northern regions they supposed that they retired to caves and hollow trees, for shelter and security, where they remained in a dormant state during the cold seasons: and even at this day, very celebrated men have asserted that swallows (*hirundo*) at the approach of winter, voluntarily plunge into lakes and rivers, descend to the bottom, and there creep into the mud and slime, where they continue overwhelmed by ice in a torpid state, until the returning summer warms them again into life; when they rise, return to the surface of the water, immediately take wing, and again people the air. This notion, though the latest, seems the most difficult to reconcile to reason and common sense, respecting a bird so swift of flight that it can with ease and pleasure move through the air even swifter than the winds, and in a few hours time shift twenty degrees from north to south, even from frozen regions to climes where frost is never seen, and where the air and plains are replenished with flying insects of infinite variety, its favourite only food.

Pennsylvania and Virginia appear to me to be the climates in North America, where the greatest variety and abundance of these winged emigrants choose to celebrate their nuptials, and rear their offspring, which they annually return with, to their winter habitations, in the southern regions of N. America; and most of these beautiful creatures, which annually people and harmonise our forests and groves, in the spring and summer seasons, are birds of passage from the southward. The eagle (i.e. *falco leucocephalus*), or bald eagle (*falco maximus*), or great grey eagle (*falco major cauda ferruginea*), (*falco pullarius*), (*falco columbarius*), (*strix pythaulis*), (*strix acclamatus*), (*strix assio*), (*tetrao tympanus*), or pheasant of Pennsylvania (*tetrao urogallus*), or mountain cock or grouse of Pennsylvania (*tetrao minor sive coturnix*), or partridge of Pennsylvania (*picus*), or woodpeckers of several species (*corvus carnivorous*), or raven (*corvus frugivora*), or crow (*corvus glandarius s. corvus crisatus*), or blue jay (*alauda maxima*), (*regulus atrofuscus minor*), or marsh wren (*sitta*), or nuthatch (*meleagris*), are perhaps nearly all the

land birds which continue the year round in Pennsylvania. I might add to
these the blue bird (*motacilla sialis*), mock bird (*turdus polyglottos*), and
sometimes the robin red breast (*turdus migratorius*), in extraordinary
warm winters; and although I do not pretend to assert as a known truth,
yet it may be found on future observation that most of these above mentioned are strangers; or not really bred where they wintered; but are
more northern families, or sojourners, bound southerly to more temperate
habitations; thus pushing each other southerly, and possessing their va-
cated places, and then back again at the return of spring.

Very few tribes of birds build, or rear their young, in the south or
maritime parts of Virginia and Carolina, Georgia and Florida; yet all these
numerous tribes, particularly the soft-billed kinds which breed in Pennsylvania, pass in the spring season through these regions in a few weeks
time, making but very short stages by the way: and again, but few of
them winter there, on their return southerly; and as I have never travelled
the continent south of New Orleans, or the point of Florida, where few or
none of them are seen in the winter, I am entirely ignorant how far southward they continue their route, during their absence from Pennsylvania;
but perhaps none of them pass the tropic.

When in my residence in Carolina and Florida, I have seen vast flights
of the house swallow (*hirundo pelasgia*) and bank martin (*hirundo ri-
paria*) passing onward north toward Pennsylvania, where they breed in
the spring, about the middle of March, and likewise in the autumn in
September or October, and large flights on their return southward. And
it is observable that they always avail themselves of the advantage of
high and favorable winds, which likewise do all birds of passage. The
pewit, or black cap flycatcher, of Catesby, is the first bird of passage
which appears in the spring in Pennsylvania, which is generally about
the first, or middle of March; and then wherever they appear, we may
plant peas and beans in the open grounds, (*vicia sativa*) French beans,
(*phaseolus*) sow radishes, (*raphanus*) lettuce, (*latuca*) onions, (*cepa*) pas-
tinaca, daucus, and almost every kind of esculent garden seeds, without
fear or danger from frosts; for although we have sometimes frosts after
their first appearance for a night or two, yet not so severe as to injure the
young plants.

In the spring of the year the small birds of passage appear very suddenly in Pennsylvania, which is not a little surprising, and no less pleasing:
at once the woods, the groves, and meads, are filled with their melody, as
if they dropped down from the skies. The reason or probable cause is
their setting off with high and fair winds from the southward; for a strong
south and southwest wind about the beginning of April never fails bringing millions of these welcome visitors. . . .

WINGS

ACROSS

THE MOON

Robert J. Newman

The fact that migrating birds tend to travel at night makes observation more difficult, but moonlight is a help—not so much because of the dim light that it affords as because a full moon silhouettes the individuals who cross it.

BIRD!"
The voice coming out of the semi-darkness had a lilt in it. It was as though a bird, *any* bird—not the first purple martin of spring necessarily, nor the last surviving ivory-billed woodpecker, nor a newly discovered subspecies, but just any bird at all—was a momentous matter. The voice continued:

"Eleven-thirty to five! Definition beautiful! About Two T."

A flashlight winked on. Another voice inquired, "Remarks?"

"Well, pretty fast, I'd say, but straight as an arrow."

Since 1946, this bewildering bit of dialogue, with minor variations, has been repeated more than 10,000 times. It has been heard on half-a-dozen college campuses; aboard a destroyer cruising the Gulf of Mexico; beneath the domes of astronomical observatories; at the fringe of tropical jungles; on the remote sandpits of the Dry Tortugas, and in plain backyards in the heart of great cities. But, varied as these settings have been, they have all had one thing in common. They have all been bathed in the pale light of the moon.

To understand what all this is about, we must go back to [1946] when George H. Lowery, Jr., curator of the Louisiana State University Museum of Zoology, was trying to find out whether any of the birds returning from Central America fly directly across the Gulf of Mexico or whether they all detour around it. What was needed was a means of measuring the amount of migration taking place at different times and

From *Audubon Magazine*, July–August, 1952.

places and in different directions. What is more, it had to be a method that would work at night, when most trans-Gulf flights were supposed to take place. Immediately, when you hear of this problem, you probably think of radar. So did Lowery. Radar had already on occasion detected the passage of large birds like geese. Unfortunately, so the electronics experts said, a device sensitive enough to do the same thing with small land birds would take hundreds of thousands of dollars, and a long time, to develop.

Then Lowery remembered several papers published around the turn of the century, describing the flight of migrating birds before the disc of the moon as seen through a telescope. Could these silhouettes be used somehow to obtain the information he was seeking? Lowery took the question to his friend, Professor W. A. Rense of the Department of Physics and Astronomy at Louisiana State. Rense's answer was yes, but not a simple, unqualified yes; it was an answer complicated with sines, cosines, and spherical triangles, with zeniths and azimuths, and with Greek letters like theta, eta and alpha.

Leaving these matters to the mathematicians, let us merely note what Rense eventually accomplished. The space in which one sees birds through a telescope pointed at the moon is constantly changing in size because of the movement of the moon. Rense devised equations that make adjustments for these changes. The equations permit one to use counts made with the telescope as samples to determine the probable number of birds per hour crossing over a one-mile line on the earth's surface. In order to carry out the computations, however, and to find out what the directional trend of the flight is, it is necessary to know the slant of each observed bird's pathway across the face of the moon. This information can be recorded by imagining that the moon is an upright clock with the rim marked off according to the 12 hours and with the midpoints between the hour marks considered as half-hours. Then the point on the rim where the bird appears and the point where it disappears can each be identified in terms of these hours, establishing its flight line.

This is the key to the strange snatches of conversation that are now being heard on moonlit nights all over the North American continent. "Bird!" is the call that the observer at a telescope uses to alert the recorder sitting beside him, and "eleven-thirty to five" is the description of the bird's path as it glides across the bright white background of the moon and over the silvery seas called lunar seas. Along with this "clock reading" goes other terse information regarding the speed of the bird, the curvature of its path, and the clarity of its focus.

And what about the two T? Well, that is a device to indicate the size of the bird's silhouette. Long ago the features of the moon received fanciful names, and some not so fanciful—names like the Lake of

Death, the Hurricane Ocean, the Sea of Showers, the Alps and the Appenines—and these names have stuck. One of the most prominent of these features is the crater Tycho, which stands out on the moon's surface like the navel on an immense floodlit plaster model of an orange. Moon-watchers refer to its diameter as T and use it to measure the bird's apparent length. Two T, for example, indicates a bird whose image is twice as long as the diameter of Tycho.

Lowery eventually had the satisfaction of sitting out on the Gulf of Mexico, at the end of a wharf, a mile beyond the surf, and watching 86 birds flash across the moon in a single hour as they left the coast of Yucatan and headed out over 600 miles of open sea toward the northern Texas coast and the heel of Louisiana. The moon was high over the water so that he was looking through a mere sliver of the night sky; and the birds that he counted through his telescope were the equivalent of 11,900 birds crossing over the one mile shoreline. That was on the night of April 23, 1948. By that time it had become apparent that flight studies by means of the moon were much more than a way of finding out whether any migrants cross the Gulf. They would permit us to peer into the very heart of age-old basic mysteries of mass migration.

It is necessary to pause a moment to grasp how revolutionary this development really is. Never before have we been able definitely to measure the volume of migration, even in daylight. When we go out on a May morning bird trip to look for migrant species, we can seldom tell for sure which is the process of migration itself and which are merely effects of migration. Five thousand birds interrupting their migration to flit about for an hour in search of food *within* a square mile of fields and woodland look to the observer much the same as 5000 individuals moving *through* the same area and being replaced every 10 minutes by another 5000. Yet the one case represents no migration, while the other means migration at the rate of 30,000 birds per mile per hour! This is only one of several reasons why the impressions gotten on a bird walk may be very misleading. All of the notions we have based in the past on such impressions may be correct, but there is a good chance that some of them are quite wrong. The moon and the telescope offer an opportunity to find out.

So, before he set out for Yucatan, Lowery had suggested that some observations be made in other places at the same time. It has been said that the bird enthusiasts of America tend to shy away from the scientific aspects of their subject, being in this respect unlike Europeans. However that may be, the response to Lowery's suggestion was gratifying. Telescopes were lifted toward the moon at 30 localities scattered over the continent. Before the season ended, more than 200 people had pooled their efforts to pile up more than 1000 hours of observation.

From the resulting accumulation of data many surprising things were discovered. Some of them had to do with night migrational routes. It has been pretty generally supposed, for instance, that the peninsula of Florida is a major avenue of flight. Nevertheless, at Tampico, on the east Coast of Mexico, almost as many birds were seen in a single *hour* as were seen over the Florida station, at Winter Park, on 11 *nights* of observation. Lunar studies have also indicated that, unlike birds in the daytime, nocturnal migrants rarely fly in definite flocks; that sometimes they fly *southward* in spring, and that they tend to ride the prevailing air currents toward their destination.

But more unexpected than any of these things, perhaps, has been the discovery relating to the basic hour-to-hour pattern of their nightly activity. Ornithologists used to suppose that nocturnal migrants either traveled all night long or that they usually confined their activity to the period directly after sunset or shortly before dawn. The moon has revealed that most of them follow none of these seemingly sensible courses. After sunset the majority of the migrants seem to rest a while. Then, hour by hour, they mount in increasing numbers into the dark sky. This process typically reaches a peak between 11 P.M. and midnight. Thereafter the birds begin to drop to earth again until by the hour before dawn almost none are left a-wing.

Whatever way you look at it, it appears that many birds must get up in the middle of the night just for the sake of making three or four hours' progress toward their destinations. Why they do so we cannot guess as yet. However, it is interesting to note that the pattern of their activity corresponds closely to the pattern of migratory restlessness displayed in spring by wild European birds confined in cages with electrically wired perches that register their movements from one part of the cage to the other.

All of these results have been based on observations in spring, made mostly in the central and southern parts of the United States. We still need to know how they apply in the northern tier of states and in all the region west of the Great Plains. We still need to know whether they hold good *anywhere* in autumn. And we still need answers to a whole host of other questions. Does the moonlight itself affect the volume of migration? Do the "chip" notes of small land birds give any indication of the number passing overhead in the darkness? Do migrants funneled onto peninsulas double back? Do they advance in a wide movement, with a nearly even distribution of numbers along a broad front? Or do they travel in narrow streams? Are such streams channeled along rivers, valleys, mountain ranges and coastlines?

THE

MIGRATION IMPULSE

Charles William Beebe

There is a Power whose care
Teaches thy way across the pathless coast—
The desert and illimitable air—
Lone wandering, but not lost.

So wrote William Cullen Bryant in To a Water Fowl, *once among the best known of American poems. Present-day ornithologists are little inclined to look with favor upon such notions and they are more likely to echo the words quoted in the selection which follows: "Annual migration cannot be looked upon as an act of volition, but as the automatic response to a state probably induced by a gonadial hormone"—which is after all an explanation only calling for another. It describes a mechanism which certainly exists but it does not account for the existence of that mechanism.*

To write honestly and with conviction anything about the migration of birds, one should oneself have migrated.

But not every millionaire who in the autumn goes in his private car to Palm Beach and returns in the spring can claim fellow feeling with the migrant birds, although there is a firm basis of communion. A single night in a lighthouse or in the torch of the Statue of Liberty might conceivably be a better preparation. But somehow or other we must dehumanize ourselves, feel the feel of feathers on our body, and the wind in our wings, and finally know what it is to leave luxury and safety, and yield to the compelling instinct, age-old, at the moment seemingly quite devoid of reason and object. . . .

One fortunate night . . . I squatted on the swaying floor of the torch of the Statue of Liberty when the fog drifted in from the sea and closed down grey and silent. With it came birds which before had been only disembodied voices, and the fog, which obliterated the heavens and the earth, made the migrating flocks visible to my eyes. More and more they came, until a swarm of golden bees was the only simile I could

From *Nonsuch*. New York: Brewer, Warren & Putnam, 1932.

think of. I dared not face them full, for now and then one struck the light with terrific impact. So I peered from behind the railing and watched the living atoms dash into view, shine for an instant, and vanish, so rapidly that when I looked through half-closed lids the driving sparks consolidated and lengthened into luminous lines. I think that I enjoyed it as a spectacle more in retrospect than at the time, for my emotion was distracted by the occasional thud at my feet of black polls and other warblers. It seemed such a cruel thing that even one of these lives which had been hatched and fed with such care in Hudson Bay or Labrador should be needlessly snuffed out because of the glare through a bit of glass.

Tens of thousands of facts have been gathered and collated concerning the migration of birds, but as to origins and causes we can only surmise and imagine.

To clarify the subject of migration I need to divorce it from the mere organism which manifests it—to emphasize the obsession, the absolute obligation to go and go, apart from the specific swallow or duck, lemming or butterfly which temporarily houses this mysterious daemon. I shall try to do this by continuing the simile of the swarm of golden bees about the lighthouse, and let the golden glow typify the migration instinct.

Even human history sheds a little light on our subject. Hannibal forged a tiny flicker of migratory flame over the Alps, the glow of which slowly died down in the plains of farther Italy. Attila and his following hordes were agleam with it when wave after wave of them broke against the Roman legions, finally to be smothered by the Eternal City itself. It is disturbing to think what our blood and mental equipment would be today had not our piratical ancestors—the winged hats —executed the most lasting migrations known to humans. A very cool, white flame burned in the Mayflower, and even today, our aforementioned Goddess of Liberty watches, perhaps a little humorously, faint sparks within the shawl-wrapped forms of the steerage, floating past, upstream, toward migration's melting-pot.

But these are all trifling migrations, whims of empire, tribe or family, variously originated and of brief duration. We must go to the lower animals to find migration in all the majesty of age-old tradition, its beginnings buried in past geological epochs, with routes fashioned by long forgotten configurations of continents, ancient before mankind had risen up on his hind legs or climbed into the trees—migrations whose times and seasons have been evolved and governed by countless centuries of revolutions of the planet earth.

From a lofty vantage point let us watch the coast lines of Labrador and Greenland and as far north as any frozen bit of earth distinguishes itself from sheer ice. It is July and the breathlessly short Arctic summer is at its height. As an icicle loses a few drops between clouds, so this northland relaxes its grip for a brief season, countable in days, and permits a few inches of thaw and of dwarfed and hasty growth of moss and flowers to slip through its icy fingers. All is grey and white—sea, old snowdrifts and birds. The birds have come, like the intermittent drops from the icicle, settling to earth from nowhere at the first hint of thaw, scratching a shallow hollow, and brooding four huddled eggs. The breast of the mother tern is a tiny oasis of warmth amid the Arctic waste; her food is inchling fish snatched at brief intervals from the edge of the ice. She stakes the hatching and the feeding of the young against the swift passing of the midnight sun, and scarcely is the brood awing before the meagre foliage blackens, the soil turns to iron, and the last ripple freezes over. She has won, but only by a margin of hours.

All along the Arctic shores from Labrador to within a few hundred miles of the pole, we from aloft now discern a faint glow—our imagined glow of the birth of the instinct of migration. It increases, and soon the restlessness of the birds is changed to impatience, and impatience to complete surrender and these bits of northernmost life beat southward across the face of the planet. There are thousands upon thousands of them. They have ceased to be every-Arctic-Tern-in-the-world, they are not *Sterna paradisaea*, they are no longer parents or young or this or that individual, but a unified cohort of organisms set apart, obsessed, glowing at fever heat with the thralldom of migration.

In the face of unknowable mystery I often imagine myself the Creator, or, as in this case, the Instigator of Instinct, and plan out what seems wisest and best. This exercise frequently shows me why the obvious is seldom probable. In regard to these migrants I should without hesitation lead them to Bermuda. Here . . . is a compact swarm of islands with an infinity of rocky crags and caves and beaches fit for safe perching and sleeping; here are multitudes of delectable fry of just the right size; here are man-made laws ensuring safety from molestation. Here also (although the least important of all natural reasons) are thousands of human eyes ready to see and admire, perhaps many human beings who would be better for having their thoughts diverted, by the sight of beauty, from the humor engendered by an ill lead at bridge or an irritating drive on the golf course.

Yet not a single migrant of this species veers eastward to these desirable isles. They hold steadfast to the south. They must sleep and eat, but, steady as the feather-end of the compass arrow, they swing on and on, covering only a little less than two hundred miles each day. If storms hold them back, they make up time, with ever warmer and warmer air whistling through their wings. Around Cape Cod, past Cape Hatteras, along Florida beaches—the hot sun of the tropics replacing the cold, blue shine of the Greenland midnight; threading the West

Indies, skirting Brazilian jungles, and diving for strange fish off the shores of the Argentine. The sun swings lower, the last breath of warmth is strained from the air, as Patagonia and Magellen's Straits vanish below the horizon. After eleven thousand miles have passed behind, the birds sight the gigantic ice barrier of the Antarctic, and here the migration glow dies down and expires. Here they sleep and preen their plumage, catching fish in company with penguins instead of polar bears, their grey and white feathers illumined by the sun for all the duration of their stay.

Four months pass. The ice is just as cold, the air as bitter, there is no change in the character or abundance of food, yet again comes the restlessness, and northward goes every bird, reflying the eleven thousand miles of whirling globe, and redistributing themselves. If the gods of little birds have been kind to any single pair, the chances are they will meet and mate again, and deposit their eggs in the selfsame hollow.

These are the facts. But what about the Why? One recent answer is that "annual migration cannot be looked upon as an act of volition, but as the automatic response to a certain physiological state probably induced by a gonadial hormone." And this, in spite of itself, is very probably true, and contains a core of dramatic interest equal only to the more perspicuous phase of the subject with which we are at present concerned. It is clear that our Arctic terns must move south from their breeding grounds or be starved and frozen to death. But now that we know that they crave ice and stress of storm and small fish in frigid seas, why should they go farther south than Labrador? It would seem that this obsession of migration sometimes acquires such an impetus that only the whole long length of the planet can dissipate it.

If we find mystery in the migration of the Arctic tern we are still less able to explain the annual movements of many other birds. Of those which are not forced to move by oncoming frost, some are content to shift a few miles southward, others to cross mountain ranges and wide stretches of open ocean, to winter in unfamiliar torrid jungles. If our fancied glow of the instinct was a reality, our spring and autumn nights would show an unending blaze of avian meteors which would dim the moon and stars. After exhausting our explanations of the means of guidance, such as landmarks, sea currents, winds, stars and a magnetic sense, we must, in some instances at least, fall back on an inexplicable sense of direction. And when we have taken refuge in this pleasantly all-comprehensive phrase, we remember those species in which the young migrate before their parents—and rather willingly change the subject.

NEW LIGHT ON

MIGRATION MYSTERIES

Alan Pistorius

During the half century since the publication of Beebe's book, the mysteries of bird migration have received more attention from field and laboratory ornithologists than had been expended upon them in the whole previous history of mankind, and we need not now be quite so eager to "change the subject."

Two complex problems, though recent work has clarified the issues, continue to elude solution. What triggers and controls migration, and how do birds navigate, or do they?

I F birds moved north and south in random fashion, breeding and wintering wherever the season happened to find them, we wouldn't need to ask the navigation question. But they do not. Banding and other sorts of marking have demonstrated that adults typically show a remarkable fidelity to the first breeding location. Northern shoveler hen No. 47-604004 returned four consecutive years (a long life for a game duck) to Lyle K. Sowls's Delta marsh study area in south-central Manitoba. Her four nests were all within a few hundred yards of one another. Nest placement among colonial-nesting seabirds may vary by only a foot or so from year to year.

Of course, waterfowl and pelagic birds are restricted in terms of breeding habitat, but the same fidelity to previous breeding territory obtains for the songbirds in your garden. Four out of five mourning doves and house wrens will return to nest in the same immediate neighborhood as long as they live. . . . Interestingly, young birds do not characteristically return to the immediate area of their hatching. The young of most songbirds apparently imprint on the last area visited during their first autumn's premigratory wanderings, a habit which assures healthy dispersion over the breeding range.

The return of adult birds to the same nesting area is well documented; evidence grows that they are similarly faithful to a particular

From *The Country Journal Book of Birding and Bird Attraction*. New York: W. W. Norton, 1981.

wintering area. How do these birds find their way from the one to the other? Students of migration differentiate among three possible strategies for getting from Point A to Point B. *Pilotage* means proceeding from known landmark to known landmark, the way your child learns to get from home to school and back. *Orientation* is the ability to determine and maintain directional flight, regardless of landmarks. *Navigation* is more demanding yet; it means the ability to get to a specific goal from unfamiliar areas.

Simple pilotage could account for much migratory homing. A flock of blue jays might well work its way south from somewhere in Ontario, say, to somewhere in Kentucky on the basis of landmarks known to older, experienced members of the flock; younger birds could learn the route while accompanying adults. The early German researcher Ernst Schüz's experiments with white storks show that there is, in fact, a large learning component involved in migration. European-nesting white storks are divided into two populations. Those nesting east of central Germany migrate southeast around the eastern end of the Mediterranean, while the storks nesting west of central Germany head southwest around the western end of the Mediterranean, both heading for Africa. Young storks from the eastern population were raised in western Europe, and were released at the normal migratory period. The young birds migrated southwest with the local birds. Young mallards taken from a nonmigratory English population were released in Finland, whose mallards do migrate. The English birds migrated with the latter.

But pilotage obviously cannot explain all migration. What about the young of those shorebird species whose adults depart the breeding grounds before the young can fly, leaving them to migrate independently later on? And how about nocturnal migration, which often proceeds when most terrestrial landmarks are invisible at flight altitudes? Schüz did a clever thing. He took more young eastern storks, raised them in the west, and released them as before, except that they were detained until all local storks had migrated. The color-marked young were subsequently plotted on a southeast track for the Adriatic, a track which, from their original home territory, would have taken them on their population's traditional route through the Bosporus and around the eastern end of the Mediterranean for Africa.

Other displacement experiments, with European hooded crows and starlings and with American herring gulls and blue-winged teal, confirmed what the storks had suggested: that the young of migratory species have an inherited directional tendency. That is, they migrate in a predetermined compass direction which they maintain when displaced from the breeding grounds or along the migratory route, even if this takes them to an inappropriate wintering area. That this ability is in fact innate has been proved by hand-raising birds from the egg, completely shielded from ordinary environmental information. These birds readily orient in the direction appropriate to their particular population.

How is this compass orientation managed? G. V. T. Matthews, working in England in the early 1950s, noticed that homing pigeons' initial homeward orientation after release was better under sun than under clouds. Then came the German researcher Gustav Kramer's classic experiments utilizing orientation cages. Birds in a migratory state show a characteristic restlessness, usually known by its German name, *Zugunruhe*. Placed in an orientation cage, the bird jumps and flutters in the direction of its intended migration. These movements are recorded, using sophisticated electronic equipment. (Originally the recorder was the researcher, who lay on the floor underneath the cage, watching the bird through a transparent floor!) Kramer's tame starling oriented northwest, and continued to do so when everything but the sun was blocked from view. Jumps were random under cloud cover. When mirrors were installed outside the cage's windows, deflecting the sunlight 90 degrees from its actual direction, the starling changed its orientation accordingly, heading for an apparent northwest but an actual southwest.

Kramer thus demonstrated what biologists now call sun-compass orientation: the ability to determine a compass direction on the basis of sun position. This ability has since been experimentally demonstrated for many other bird species, and appears to account for most short-range diurnal migration. The sun, however, because of its apparent movement during the course of the day, is useless as a compass without a clock. Birds' "biological clock," presumably either neural or hormonal in nature, operates automatically in roughly twenty-four-hour cycles (biologists call this cycle the "circadian rhythm," "circadian" meaning "approximately daily"). It is apparently fine-tuned by environmental pacemakers, of which photoperiod—the seasonally variable relative duration of daily light and darkness—seems to be most important. Indeed, the clock can be reset by exposing the bird to artificial light schedules; this clock skewing (like Kramer's mirrors) results in predictable orientation errors in orientation cages or in actual releases.

The combination of orientation cages and planetaria soon brought a breakthrough in the area of nocturnal migratory orientation. The German team of Franz and Eleonore Sauer showed that certain Old World warblers oriented properly when shown replicas of real skies, but could not orient when the simulated stars were obscured. German researcher Hans G. Wallraff discovered that ducks could orient when only parts of the sky were visible, and that they had the ability to memorize incredibly complex star patterns. Cornell's Stephen T. Emlen, testing hand-raised indigo buntings, found that young birds failed to orient well if denied visual experience of the sky until fall. Apparently, young buntings "learn" the sky during their first summer, and particularly the part of the sky which shows least rotational movement—i.e., the circumpolar sky. Clock-shifted birds of other species, which misorient predictably during the day, orient properly at night, suggesting that they, too, are cuing on the North Star (or nearby stars), whose apparent lack of movement renders their clocks superfluous. Emlen got some young buntings to treat Betelgeuse as if it were Polaris, simply by rotating the planetarium sky around that star.

Sun-compass and star-compass orientation can be made to explain most migration. A bird starting with an inborn directional tendency and the ability to choose and maintain a compass direction might well make its way back and forth from summer to winter territory, perhaps using landmark recognition near both ends of the trip. But neither sun compass nor star compass can explain homing, or true navigation—that ability to locate a goal from an unknown location.

Navigation has been demonstrated unequivocally for a relatively few species. Homing pigeons are famous for the ability, but then they are bred and trained for it. Among wild birds pelagic species seem most adept. One dramatic experiment involved eighteen adult Laysan albatrosses, removed from their nests on the Midway Islands in mid-Pacific and flown all over the Pacific. Released, among other places, on Oahu and Guam, from Honshu (Japan) and Luzon (Philippines), and on the coast of Washington State—places none had ever been—fourteen birds returned to their nests. A Washington coast bird covered the 3,200 miles back to Midway in ten days. A Philippines albatross negotiated 4,100 miles in a month.

Petrels, shearwaters, gulls, terns, swifts, and swallows have all proved capable of homing. Displaced Adelie penguins have navigated distances of over 1,000 miles, walking, of course, every step of the way. Dutch biologist A. C. Perdeck's classic displacement experiments showed something very interesting about European starlings. Thousands of the birds were trapped and banded as they passed through the Netherlands on their fall migration west to wintering quarters in northern France and England. The starlings were released nearly 400 miles south-south-east in Switzerland. When recoveries from later in the fall were plotted, Perdeck discovered that young birds, on their first migration, continued west, as they would have done from the Netherlands, and set up new wintering grounds in southern France and northern Spain. Adult starlings, however, were mostly heading northwest, in a line pointing toward the traditional wintering grounds. The immature birds, which either did not recognize the displacement or could not compensate for it, were orienting. The adults (like the Midway albatrosses, though in less impressive fashion) were navigating.

To navigate, to get "home" from an unfamiliar place, a bird (or person) needs either an inertial system or a bicoordinate mapping system for guidance. An inertial system assumes some sort of motion-sensitive organ to "record" the displacement trip, whether initiated by adverse winds or an experimenting biologist. Movie kidnappers are notorious believers in inertial systems: the victim is always blindfolded, driven a labyrinthine course, even spun around like a pin-the-tail-on-the-donkey candidate, all in order to make it difficult for him to locate the hideout after his release. The exact same things have been done to homing pigeons, and for the same reason. The birds are taken to release points in sealed boxes and driven complicated routes. They have been tumbled in drums and rotated on turntables during the trip out, all in hopes of confusing a presumed recording instrument; they have been transported heavily anesthetized, in hopes of deadening it. Various inner-ear organs, thought to be possible sites of directional recording, have been snipped, punctured, and cauterized. The birds homed anyway. (Why, in the latter case, they would *want* to is a question science isn't prepared to ask. Homing pigeons have many abilities; the ability to choose a reasonable course of action, which we sometimes define as intelligence, isn't one of them.)

A contemporary Italian school, under the leadership of Floriano Papi, believes olfaction is the key. (Salmon fry imprint on the odor of their hatching stream, to which they return, through the agency of olfaction, years later as breeding adults returning from the sea. Why not birds?) They argue that young pigeons map their loft area in terms of characteristic odors borne on winds from various directions. Detour experiments (in which the bird is expected to leave the release area in a direction opposite to the initial leg of a circuitous journey to the site) and nasal-pouch experiments (in which a pouch containing a strong-smelling substance is applied to the bill just prior to release) have proved ambiguous. Detoured pigeons expected to deflect clockwise often did so; those which ought to have deflected counterclockwise did not! Some birds flew off in a direction intermediate between expected and home directions. Nasal pouches result in more initial scatter at release, but homing success is not impaired. A German team completely deadened birds' olfactory nerves with xylocain. Results were ambiguous, but largely negative.

Most current research seeks the key to homing in terms of bicoordinate navigation. This would require, in addition to the compass and clock needed for orientation, a map. With these aids, a bird could determine the direction of its displacement in terms of both latitude and longitude, and then navigate home. But how is this system supposed to operate? The British ornithologist Matthews has vigorously defended the sun-arc theory which he propounded in the early 1950s. Matthews argues that the sun alone can provide the necessary bicoordinate information. It would work this way. Upon finding itself in a strange location, the bird observes the sun, measuring a short part of its movement along its arc. It then extrapolates from that segment to determine the sun's highest position. (At noon, of course, extrapolation would be unnecessary; simple observation would do.) Then, using its internal clock, the bird determines the sun's progress along its arc. Now the bird need only compare those two values (noon altitude and progress position) with remembered home values to determine its present location. If the sun's noon altitude is too high, the bird is south of home; if the sun is too far along on its arc, it is also east of home. It is now a simple matter to fly northwest. When sun values are correct, the bird is home.

Birds could, by the same token, navigate at night by the stars. They would determine the coordinates of an unfamiliar location by gauging the altitude of Polaris above the horizon, and the degree of westward rotation of the star field. These values would be compared with remembered home values, and a homeward direction could be deduced.

There is no question that sun-arc (or star-arc) theory *could* account for homing, but few students of migration have been convinced. Skeptics doubt that birds are capable of the fine measurements of sun movement and time required, or of the process of extrapolation. Among these critics are State University of New York (Stony Brook) biologist Charles Walcott and members of the Frankfurt school, whose work with pigeons and Old World robins and warblers, respectively, suggests that birds can orient by exploiting a sensitivity to earth's magnetic field; might they not navigate by it as well? The magnetic field theory, a century old now, holds that birds can detect varying inclination and/or declination intensities forming a grid over the earth. Until recently, most biologists believed this theory absurd, for there was no evidence that birds were sensitive to the low order of force involved. Experiments carried out in the 1970s, however, have given the notion new life.

Pigeons have now been taught, for example, to detect earth-strength magnetic fields in the laboratory, and pigeons released at locations known to represent magnetic-field anomalies have shown reduced orientation ability. Birds transported to release sites in altered magnetic fields have sometimes been affected, sometimes not. Wolfgang and Roswitha Wiltschko, prominent members of the Frankfurt school, spent a year with the Cornell group working with indigo buntings. Tests seemed to show the birds were sensitive to the horizontal component of the magnetic field, but some kinds of orientation cages showed better results than others.

Cornell's William T. Keeton attached magnets to pigeons' heads to see how the birds would perform when ordinary magnetic information was interrupted. The results are very interesting. Released under clear skies, experienced adult homers—both controls and experimentals—oriented well. Under overcast skies, controls oriented homeward, while experimental birds mostly scattered. Young, inexperienced homers, furthermore, scattered under sunny *or* overcast skies with magnets attached. Do young pigeons, then, as well as adults under overcast, utilize magnetic information? Or did the magnets somehow block the reception of other information? In either case, all the experimental birds eventually homed; somehow they solved whatever problem the magnets presented.

In 1926 Aberdeen professor J. Arthur Thomson published a three-volume work called *The New Natural History,* which fairly represents our knowledge in that area from the post-World War I period. With regard to the question of how birds navigate, Thomson fell back on "the interesting old view that birds have in a high degree . . . *a sense of direction."* That is, of course, a non-answer, and it would be worth the job of any academic researcher who uttered it today. But the question itself remains unanswered. Thomson pointed out that experiments with pelagics prove they do home, but the tests "do not throw any light on the problem of where the sense of direction has its seat." A great deal of time and money spent in modern laboratories hasn't pinned down that "seat" either. Possibilities we have. There's the pecten, for example, a curious structure in the avian eye, which presumably casts a straightedge shadow on the retina, such that horizon and sun image could be viewed simultaneously. The pecten could function as a compass, a sundial, even a sextant; so that it could, conceivably, make sun-arc navigation work. Then there are the rhodopsin molecules in the retina, and, just discovered between brain and skull, specialized cells rich in magnetite crystals, both of which have been proposed as possible centers of perception of magnetic-field forces.

But we simply don't know. Part of the problem is that birds obviously have access to redundant cues.* When you block one sort of input, and the bird performs successfully, you have not proved that it cannot or does not use that information, but only that, under the particular set of circumstances, it did not *require* that input. And it is very difficult to design experiments that control several sources of potential information simultaneously. Then, too, different species test differ-

---

* And new potential cues are complicating the situation. Pigeons have recently been shown to be sensitive to both ultraviolet and polarized light, and to be able to make fine discriminations of barometric pressure differences. There is also experimental proof that pigeons can hear low-frequency sounds over great distances, leading to speculation that a flock of migrating geese cruising high over the Midwest may be able to hear storms over the Rockies and the crashing Atlantic surf simultaneously. Any or all of these talents *might* help a bird navigate.

ently, making it difficult to generalize from necessarily limited experiments. Even within a given species, individuals show a frustrating variability of performance. (Charles Walcott's wonderful homing pigeon B38 was a fine navigator but a lousy pilot. She would fly unerringly for home, then shoot right past, failing to utilize landmarks near the loft. Five or ten miles down the road she seemed to realize her mistake, and a surprised homeowner would subsequently discover on his front porch an odd-looking pigeon, harnessed into a radio transmitter, patiently awaiting assistance. He would find the loft's telephone number on the transmitter, and B38 would soon arrive home in a taxi.) And a final, nagging doubt remains. Most navigation research utilizes pigeons, which are readily available from established lofts and are accustomed to human handling. But how much have homing pigeons, generations of directed inbreeding removed from wild stock, to tell us about the migratory behavior of wild birds? It is possible that we may figure out pigeon homing and still not know much more than we do now about warblers and shearwaters.

This is not to suggest that recent work has been in vain. Much has been learned by the way—about the hierarchy of cues used for orientation by night-migrating songbirds, for example. Stephen Emlen and Natalie J. Demong released white-throated sparrows at migrating altitude through the agency of a trap-doored box carried aloft by helium-filled balloons under different weather conditions. State University of New York (Albany) ornithologist Kenneth P. Able tracked migrants under similar circumstances with radar and portable ceilometers. Both studies, carried on in the northeastern U.S., found visual cues to be most important. Birds oriented best with a view of the stars, whatever the wind conditions. They also oriented successfully under overcast skies if post-sunset glow was visible before overcast set in. If neither stars nor sunset were available, Able found birds simply flew downwind. The white-throats, however, hovered or circled, apparently attempting to get a fix; they then oriented fairly accurately, but flew at subnormal speed, and often in a zigzag pattern.

These observations suggest that stellar cues are more important than wind, and wind—at least in Able's study—seems more important than landmarks or, in the short run at least, magnetic information. (Results of some research by the Wiltschkos suggest birds may consult a magnetic compass only occasionally, on the order of once a day or every other day.) Visual cues, then, seem most important under ordinary circumstances, at least for nocturnal songbird migrants. But it has been proved that visual information can be dispensed with entirely in some cases. Homing pigeons blinded by the attachment of opaque glasses have homed successfully. And the European robin has been shown to be capable of orientation in a totally dark room. The mystery remains.

It may be less immediately evident that migratory birds face a temporal as well as a spatial problem. In addition to the problems involved in getting from Point A to Point B is the problem of when to leave A, and how to know when B has been reached. For fall migration the plausible answer to the first would be that the bird leaves the North when cold weather and dwindling food supplies begin to make life uncomfortable. So-called "weather" migrants generally do operate this way. But not "calendar" migrants, many of which abandon even temperate zones long before weather or food shortage becomes a factor. Birds vacate the far North wholesale in August, just when the seed, berry, and insect crops are reaching a peak. (This works out very neatly on the tundra, where much of this food is preserved flash-frozen over the winter; the spring melt then makes it available to the returning birds, which otherwise would face a food shortage.)

The author of Jeremiah . . . seems to have sensed that typical long-distance migrants migrate on schedule rather than in response to environmental exigencies: "Yea, the stork in the heaven knoweth her appointed times; and the turtle and the crane and the swallow observe the time of their coming." The turtle dove and the swallow "know" their appointed times not in the brain, but in the blood. They initiate the repetitive events of their lives in response to an inborn annual (circannual) rhythm analogous to the daily (circadian) rhythm mentioned earlier.

Birds are programmed, through changing blood chemistry, to take life one thing at a time. The sequence, one biologist has written, is "rigid and inexorable." When baby house sparrows were introduced to adult house sparrows at the nest-building stage of breeding, the adults either tossed them out or used them for nesting material. A couple of weeks later, when they were physiologically prepared for attachment to young, the same house sparrows accepted and raised introduced young. This is not, obviously, an "intelligent" way to order life; indeed, it is a system which *substitutes* order for intelligence. The system works well enough, but it tolerates no deviation. This is especially evident in the far North, where the breeding season is short and timing is critical. Well-grown young redpolls have been found frozen in their nests by fall wanderers on the Alaska tundra. Probably the adults had, for one reason or another, laid the clutch of eggs late. Birds are famous for selfless dedication to their young. But only in season. The redpoll young matured on schedule, but high summer passes quickly on the tundra, and blood chemistry changes with the seasons. Area redpolls began to flock up, to experience migratory restlessness. Then, one day, the birds were up and away, and our pair with them, leaving a nest of hopeful young perhaps only days away from fledging.

The circannual rhythm, which controls and times these events, is automatic, at least to a point. Birds—including hand-raised young—will exhibit molt, *Zugunruhe*, and so on in the proper sequence even if denied normal environmental stimuli. Apparently those glands (especially the pituitary and hypothalamus) whose secretions stimulate migration-related processes such as fat deposition and gonad development will operate in response to the inborn annual rhythm alone. When Emlen kept indigo buntings under an unchanging light-and-dark schedule prior to fall migration, the birds molted, put on fat, exhibited *Zugunruhe*, changed bill color, and sang the following spring; but they did not molt into winter plumage the second autumn. He concluded that the circannual rhythm requires a late-summer environmental stimulus (the German term is *Zeitgeber*: "time-giver") to keep the cycle going.

More than one *Zeitgeber* may be at work here, but photoperiod is thought to be most important. Light-and-dark schedules are easy to manipulate in the laboratory, and the effect of photoperiod on the controlling glands is clear. It has been a half century now since Canadian biologist William Rowan amazed the scientific world by bringing juncos into breeding condition in midwinter Alberta simply by exposing them to artificially increasing day length. The birds' sexual organs became enlarged; the males sang. It seems clear that, under normal circumstances, photoperiod (and perhaps other external stimuli) synchronizes and fine-tunes innate rhythms.

The seasons turn, and once again the birds' circannual clocks read migration. But a physiologically prepared bird cannot fly on automatic; it must be able to suppress the urge to initiate migration until circumstances are right. Different species apparently respond to different immediate stimuli. Weather birds leave the North when temperatures fall, when food becomes scarce. Flocking migrants seem to require social stimuli of some sort; hand-raised social migrants have refused to migrate on their own. Presumably those great chattering flocks of redwings and tree swallows are synchronizing—or even stimulating—individual migratory drives ("awaiting the 'signal' to depart" is the popular expression). Typical long-range migrants wait on adequate fat deposition and favorable flying weather.

What ornithologists call the premigratory state is identified by *Zugunruhe*, migratory restlessness. The bird wakes at night, flutters from perch to perch. It has been noticed in the laboratory that *Zugunruhe*, at least for long-distance migrants, seems to persist throughout the migratory period. Migrants trapped halfway along their fall migratory route, then transported to the normal wintering grounds and released, have proceeded to fly the second half of their normal migratory flight to winter in new, sometimes inappropriate, areas. These observations suggest that the migratory drive may be quantitative, may burn itself out over the period of time required to complete a migration appropriate to the species. This would neatly solve the problem of how a bird—especially a solitary, inexperienced bird—knows when to quit migrating: "I don't feel like migrating any more; this must be Nicaragua."

If we do not perfectly understand what triggers and controls migration, how autonomous rhythms interrelate with environmental stimuli, it is not for lack of trying. Birds have been castrated. Pineal glands have been excised. Birds have been injected with hormones, thyroid extract, adrenaline. But the problems, like those concerning navigation, remain obdurate. Progress is made—but the frontiers recede. We earlier condescended to J. A. Thomson on the matter of navigation, but the good Scottish don's analysis of migration control was right on. He wrote that "the constitution of the creature has been, as it were, wound up to become restless at particular times of the year, but this is linked on to the regular changes of the seasons." Of course, no biologist would be caught dead saying that in the 1980s. He would say that "events in the endogenous circannual cycle are entrained by exogenous stimuli." The latter sounds more impressive, but the two statements mean exactly the same thing.

RUNNING

THE GAUNTLET:

MIGRATION HAZARDS

Frank Graham, Jr.

Whatever else migration may be, it is seldom a picnic. Veteran nature writer Frank Graham, Jr. details the sorts of problems birds too often encounter during migratory flights.

In fall a birder's thoughts turn to migration and the age-old questions: Where is *that* bird headed? How on earth does it find its way? (Scientists are still trying to piece together the facts of avian migration.) And there is always the sentimental query: Will it survive the trip?

For us confirmed sentimentalists, the last is the most pressing question and is the source of much of the sympathy we feel with birds. We fly in imagination with those indomitable bits of fluff as they travel thousands of miles over forests and oceans on the way to their exotic winter quarters. Their losses en route are incalculable, but most of them endure and in spring make the trip all over again. What are the hazards that birds in transit are likely to face?

In its dry, factual way, a paper in last April's issue of *The Auk*, the journal of the American Ornithologists' Union, painted a haunting picture of a doomed flock of chimney swifts. The paper's author, Peter Spendelow of the University of Washington, worked on his doctoral thesis in 1979 on Islas del Cisne, two tiny Caribbean islands about a hundred miles north of Honduras. These "Swan Islands" were then the site of a U.S. Weather Service station.

In October of that year a flock of two to three hundred chimney swifts landed on Islas del Cisne. The arrival was unusual in itself, for the tiny, remote islands (one and a half square miles) are incapable of supporting large numbers of birds, especially aerial feeders such as swifts and swallows. Weather records for several weeks past did not reveal any storms or heavy rains which might have forced the birds to

From *Audubon*, September 1985.

land, and the sun shone during most of the days the flock was on the islands.

"The swifts spent the daytime foraging over the islands and roosted at night on the trunks of two palm trees," Spendelow wrote. "On 19 October, a few days after the arrival of the flock, eleven swifts were found dead under the roosting trees, and many swifts were noticed to be roosting during the daytime. The bulk of the swift population died over the next two days, and not a single swift was seen alive after 24 October. It is not known if any swifts left the island during this period."

But comparing the number of bodies he and the Weather Service custodians collected with the estimated number of arriving birds, Spendelow concluded that most or all of the birds had died. He could find "no other record of an entire flock of any species arriving on an island and remaining until the last one perishes." Their bodies, on analysis, proved to be emaciated, with "severely atrophied pectoral muscles and no visible fat." Many were adult birds, already experienced migrants. Spendelow discovered the emaciated bodies of a few other migrant birds, mostly swallows and warblers, on the islands, though the three resident species (white-crowned pigeon, smooth-billed ani, and vitelline warbler) remained active.

If the swifts had flown on for another five or six hours, they would have reached an abundant source of flying insects in Honduras. But the weary birds detected a welcome speck of sand and palms in the sea and set down. The haven was a mirage. By the time they discovered the bleak reality, they were too weak to go on.

Everyone who spends much time at sea has witnessed these migratory calamities, on a smaller scale perhaps but no less affecting, as exhausted birds home in on ships as the only semblance of "terra firma" in all that watery world. Often their journey to the tropics ends far short of the latitude of Islas del Cisne. A man who operates a dragger off the Maine coast tells of dozens of small migrants, which probably set off over the Bay of Fundy from New Brunswick or Nova Scotia, descending on his boat's deck during bad weather.

"Some days there'll be mostly warblers—redstarts and things like that—all over the boat," he says. "I've seen birds that crouch there, not moving, and finally when you go over and pick them up they'll just die in your hand. Others will hop around the deck, pecking at fish scales stuck to the deck or bits of seaweed on a coiled rope. Gulls follow the boat, and when the little birds get their second wind and take off, the gulls pick them right out of the air."

Confusion, as well as exhaustion, often brings birds down at unlikely places. For nearly a century now, three islands off Nova Scotia—Brier, Sable, and Seal—have been familiar to ornithologists as outstanding places to view a variety of fall migrants, especially rarities. Birders compile impressive lists of "vagrants"—species that are clearly way outside their usual ranges or migration routes.

"The Nova Scotian islands are visited by an unusually large number and great diversity of vagrants, possibly more so than any other areas of comparable size in eastern North America," writes Ian McLaren of Dalhousie University in *The Auk,* April 1981.

Many of these birds belong to typically western species. Among those listed for the islands by McLaren are Swainson's hawk, black-billed magpie, yellow-headed blackbird, black-throated gray warbler, Townsend's warbler, hermit warbler, Cassin's sparrow, Harris' sparrow, and clay-colored sparrow. Contrary to older beliefs, their appearance is not linked to intense storms.

"There is an extraordinary convergence of air masses and wind streamlines in the vicinity of Nova Scotia during seasons of migration," McLaren writes. "During early autumn, streamlines from the midwestern to southeastern United States converge on Nova Scotia and carry out to the seas beyond." Apparently, navigational errors put some fall migrants off course, and even comparatively weak winds may push them eastward into the Atlantic, where they find temporary havens on islands off Nova Scotia. No one ever said migration was easy.

Those hazards and uncertainties are built into the phenomenon of migration, whereas human enterprise has thrown up new obstacles to a successful passage. In a sense, human predation has been part of the picture for a long time too, wildfowlers taking their share of the passing flocks along the way just as merlins and sharp-shinned hawks replenish their energy reserves en route by preying on their smaller traveling companions.

We sometimes tend to minimize those losses in the belief that most migrant species are protected by law, except for certain ducks, geese, and doves whose harvest is regulated by government agencies. But other species fall outside that category. The toll among small European migrants, such as buntings and thrushes, as they run the gauntlet of local gunners in France and Italy is legendary. In some years, native people in Greenland have shot as many as three-quarters of a million thick-billed murres (a declining species) during their post-breeding dispersal in the fall.

The roseate tern, a threatened species on our own coastlines, is a dramatic example of a bird whose main problems lie on its migratory route. Unlike most terns that nest in the northern United States, it seems to be doing reasonably well in finding sufficient food and breeding space while evading its natural predators. But Ian Nisbet, reporting last year in the *Journal of Field Ornithology,* wrote that an unusual proportion of the birds died on, or on the way to, their winter homes, especially in eastern Guyana, where terns are killed for sale in local markets. (Across the Atlantic, a large proportion of Europe's dwindling population of roseate terns is taken every fall and winter by small boys using snares on beaches in Ghana.)

Ironically, a strategy that enabled many migratory species to escape predation on the way to their winter homes has led them into different kinds of traps. Many migrants fly by night, often landing during the day to feed and rest. But birds, like insects (or you and me, for that matter), are often attracted to, or confused by, bright lights. During the nineteenth century and continuing into our own time, lighthouses have lured birds to their destruction. Confused by the glare, hundreds of migrants swirl in the vicinity, apparently unable to free themselves from the beam, and eventually they collide with the lighthouse and fall to their deaths among the grass and rocks below.

Later, tall buildings such as the Washington Monument and the Empire State Building, ceilometers at airports, and television towers added to the toll. One September morning some years ago, 2,117 individuals of thirty-seven species were picked up at the foot of a television tower in Eau Claire, Wisconsin. Modifications of some of these buildings or devices have helped to lower the toll.

Ceilometers, for instance, directed a steady, brilliant beam upwards to determine the cloud ceiling. Thousands of birds, attracted to the light, milled at the spot for hours, crashing into each other, the ground, or perhaps into nearby structures. Eventually the fixed-beam design was replaced by rotating beams that reduce the fatal attraction.

Often the total kill at man-made structures is never determined. Entire complexes of predators and scavengers form at the site, and owls, raccoons, coyotes, and other creatures feed on the victims before daylight. A sufficient number of birds is salvaged, however, to fuel an ingenious new cottage industry for scientists, who analyze the numbers and species of the victims to provide fresh insights into the mechanics of migration. In many cases scientists find that ovenbirds make up a prominent percentage of the kill, while blackpolls (which migrate far out at sea) are seldom present in the body counts. Thus opportunists frisk every ill wind for its dollop of good fortune.

Scientists in Hawaii have now gone full circle, altering modern technology to protect rare birds and at the same time extracting new benefits for humans. The birds in question are not true migrants but young seabirds leaving the nesting burrow on their first flight to the ocean.

For many years the Newell's shearwater, a race of Townsend's shearwater, was believed to have been wiped out by introduced mammals in the Hawaiian Islands. Then, in 1954, one flew into a lighted window on Oahu and the subspecies returned to the checklist. The shearwaters were finally traced to the mountains of Kauai, where a small but flourishing nesting colony had developed in the absence of major predators. The trouble is that each year more than a thousand young Newell's shearwaters (as well as fledglings of several other seabird species) fall victim to the bright lights around Kauai's resorts.

Three ornithologists (Jonathan Reed, John Sincock, and Jack Hailman) tell the story in the April *Auk*. Working at a large beach resort, they placed hoods over the lights on alternate nights, re-directing the radiation to the grounds and buildings below. The toll of birds dropped significantly on those "experimental" nights. Meanwhile, the hoods increased the efficiency of the lighting for human purposes.

"The attraction of birds to bright point sources may mean that fledglings have a predilection to fly toward certain star patterns," the ornithologists speculate. "Man's lights could be 'super-normal' starlike stimuli that unwittingly convert an adaptive response into a disaster that may threaten the existence of rare species."

A bird of passage may set its eye on the stars, but come to grief in the neon jungle.

Part

Three

WHAT MAKES A
BIRD TICK?

THE ORIGINS

OF BIRDS

Roger F. Pasquier

While we adults often content ourselves with relatively pedestrian questions (what is that bird's name? what is it doing?), children confound us by asking the real questions, such as "What is it like to be a bird?" What would it feel like to be covered with feathers, and what does the world look like (sound like, smell like) to a bird? Are particular bird behaviors—song, for example—inherited, expressed instinctually, or learned? What, in short, makes a bird tick?

Roger F. Pasquier, a longtime student of birds in both field and museum, addresses what is perhaps the first question of all: How long have birds been around, and where did they come from?

Fossil evidence indicates that birds are descended from reptiles, with which they still share many characteristics. Birds, of course, have feathers and are warm-blooded, unlike all modern reptiles, but the two groups have many similarities of bone, muscle and joint structure, blood cells, and egg type. Precisely how birds developed from reptiles remains very much a matter of guesswork, in part because we have so few fossils of the earliest birds. Bird skeletons are fragile, and few birds happened to die in places where their bodies would be covered by the layers of mud or silt necessary to preserve the skeleton or its impression. As you might expect, most of the oldest bird fossils are of water birds that had strong bones and lived in environments where their skeleton had the greatest chance of being preserved.

Several types of now extinct reptiles could fly. Some had wings made of flaps of skin held stretched by the forearm (similar to bats); other lizardlike animals . . . had flattened ribs covered by skin, enabling them to glide, but not flap, like a flying squirrel. However, there is evidence that none of these flying reptiles were ancestors of birds: they lacked the clavicle (wishbone) found in all birds, and they lived at a time when some birds already existed.

The earliest known bird has been named *Archaeopteryx* ("ancient

From *Watching Birds: An Introduction to Ornithology*. Boston: Houghton Mifflin, 1977.

wing"). Its fossils, found in German deposits believed to be approximately 155 million years old, indicate birds . . . with feathers except on the head and neck, short rounded wings with claws, feathers growing down the sides of a long, lizardlike tail, and teeth in the jaws. The skeleton resembles that of a small dinosaur that ran on its hind legs and used its forelegs to grasp prey. *Archaeopteryx* may also have lived on the ground, using its wings mainly to help catch prey rather than for flight, or in trees, using the claws in the wings to help it climb, and gliding from one tree to another. In either case, *Archaeopteryx* was not a very advanced flying machine—it did not have the bones or muscles essential to powerful flight and its bones were not hollow for lighter weight, like those of most later birds.

Feathers are extended reptile scales, but the reasons for their evolution into feathers are open to question. They may have been developed by ancestors of *Archaeopteryx* that gradually did more gliding and less jumping from branch to branch, or flapped their forearms to increase speed while running. Other theories are that some dinosaurs were warm-blooded and originally developed extended scales to keep warm, or that extended, moveable scales developed to keep cold-blooded dinosaurs cool, by shading the body from the sun's rays. In any case, use of these extended scales, or feathers, for flight only came later. Discovery of other early bird fossils will tell us more.

The next oldest known fossils come from the shale beds of western Kansas, once an inland sea. They are all 35 million years more recent than *Archaeopteryx*. One is *Hesperornis* ("western bird"), a toothed, loonlike bird five feet long and highly specialized for swimming. Its wings were reduced to two small bones. Another is *Ichthyornis* ("fish-bird"), the first known bird with wings developed for powerful flight. It was a gull's size and presumably ate fish; whether it had teeth or not is undecided. Neither of these birds has any modern descendants, nor do most of the approximately 33 fossil species dating from this period. (A few specimens resemble modern loons, grebes, and rails, but are not definitely ancestors). The diversity of bird types already present 120 million years ago is impressive.

From about 60 million years ago we have fossils of birds from several modern families, including the herons, ducks, vultures, hawks, grouse, cranes, rails, sandpipers, and owls. None of these species still exist, however. Other fossils represent types that have disappeared, such as *Diatryma*, a flightless, heavy-bodied, seven-foot bird; its fossils have been found in Wyoming, New Mexico, New Jersey, and Europe. It may be distantly related to the rails.

Between 28 and 12 million years ago nearly all the families of larger North American birds developed, and by 10 million years ago there were even some songbirds. These, the passerines, are considered the most recently evolved birds.

One million years ago many species alive today existed, mixed with others that were shortly to become extinct. Since then, the earth has experienced several widespread changes in climate, especially periods popularly known as "ice ages" when large areas became colder and drier. These drastically altered many environments, causing the extinction of many birds that had lived in them, and created opportunities for evolution and expansion of the newer bird families, which took over some of the roles left vacant by the older, highly specialized birds that could not adjust to the changes. By the end of the most recent period of climatic change, about eight thousand years ago, all the birds that exist today had probably evolved.

THE BIRD'S SENSES

Roger F. Pasquier

It has been said that birds are built and programmed to "see and flee."
How acute is a bird's vision, and what part do the other senses play in its
life?

Vision

Vision is the bird's most highly developed sense. Unlike most animals,
they see in color. Nearly all birds find their food by sight, and many
must be visually alert to avoid predators. Birds can distinguish objects
much farther away than can humans, and their vision is in fact the most
highly developed of any animal. Captive birds kept outside have often
been observed looking nervously at the sky, watching a hawk that humans could detect only through binoculars. Similarly, the hawk in the
sky can see and dive on small animals from a distance at which, to a
human, the animal would be invisible.

The eyes of most birds are located on the side of the head, allowing
them to see over a larger area than if both eyes faced forward as ours do.
Most of the area a bird sees is perceived with only one eye; the fields of
vision of the two eyes only overlap in a small area in front. (Penguins
have no overlap at all; they always see two entirely separate images.) A
disadvantage to perceiving an object through only one eye is the difficulty in judging distance, and for this reason you often see a bird cock
its head to carefully focus on an object; likewise, the bobbing up and
down of the head characteristic of many shorebirds may be an effort to
gauge distances. Hawks have a greater overlapping range of forward
vision, since they usually pursue prey in front of them, and owls, with
their eyes in the front of the head, see only forward, the fields of both
eyes overlapping almost entirely. The owl compensates for this limitation of field by being able, unlike other birds, to turn its head completely backward. At the other extreme is the American Woodcock,
with eyes placed so that it can see in a complete circle all around its
head. The woodcock is thus able to see predators approaching behind it,
an important adaptation for a bird that often has its head bent over the
ground while it probes for earthworms. The bittern's eyes are placed so

From *Watching Birds: An Introduction to Ornithology.* Boston: Houghton Mifflin, 1977.

that it can see forward when it "freezes" with bill pointed upward to blend in with the reeds of its marsh environment; when the bill is pointed forward, its normal position, a bittern can see food items directly below.

The eye of a bird is relatively large—the European Buzzard has eyes as large as man's. The two eyes of a bird may, in fact, weigh more than its brain. Beneath the surface, the area covered by the eye is much greater than what is visible externally. The eye's shape varies from group to group; in most passerines it is flattened, in raptors active by day the cornea, or outer surface of the eye, bulges, and in owls it is practically tubular. Bony plates of the sclerotic ring hold the eye in place and affect the amount of bulge in the cornea. Muscles control the curvature of the cornea and the shape of the soft lens beneath it, allowing the eye to quickly change its focus from far to near.

The rear wall of the eye is densely lined with the rods and cones that form the retina, the surface on which images are formed. The rods are sensitive to light, especially at low intensities; the more rods it has, the better a bird is able to see at dusk or at night. Species active at night predictably have more rods than do other birds. The cones function in bright light to form sharp images and distinguish shades of color. Among hawks and eagles, which are generally considered to have the keenest vision of all, the cones may be as dense as one million per square millimeter. (Man has only a fifth as many in the same area.) There is some evidence that hawks may have sacrificed some of their color vision to achieve sharper perception of form, distance, and motion. . . .

Hearing

The number and variety of noises that birds make indicate that their hearing is acute. For most birds, hearing is a way of receiving the communications of other birds; few birds use their ears to warn them of approaching dangers, as do so many mammals, and only owls can locate their prey entirely by sound. Some birds, like robins, may listen for the vibrations produced by movements of their prey underground, but this is not yet proved.

Tests of the hearing ability of birds show that they hear within a range that partially overlaps our own. While man's hearing range is nine octaves, Starlings hear about five octaves, from 650 to 15,000 cycles per second, so that every sound lower-pitched than the C note at 600 cps (two octaves above middle C on the piano) is imperceptible to them. Most small birds have similar hearing ranges, although warblers probably hear notes higher than we can. If you watch certain high-pitched warblers sing, you may see their throat continuing to quiver and their bill remain open after you can no longer hear any sound; presumably the birds hear all sounds they make themselves, as they respond to recordings of their own vocalizations. (Since most small birds therefore cannot hear human voices, the real reason to be quiet while bird watching is so you can hear the birds.) Some larger birds, including waterfowl, hawks, pigeons, owls, and woodpeckers, which all have lower pitched calls, hear lower notes than do most passerines.

Bird ears are not visible, being covered with loosely constructed feathers called auriculars which do not interfere with sound reception. Even some of the bareheaded vultures have a little group of feathers covering the ear. (The "horns" or tufts on certain owls play no role in hearing.) The ear functions very much as our own, but the length and shape of the cochlea, the fluid-filled inner ear, varies in different species; those with complex songs have long cochleas, but what the relationship may mean is not known. Owls, which have very large ear openings and very long cochleas, also have one opening higher than the other, so that by turning its head to make a sound's intensity equal in both ears, the owl faces it directly.

A few birds active at night have developed a form of echolocation less sophisticated than the bat's ultrasonic system. The birds emit certain high clicking notes and judge the distance and shape of objects from the quality of the sounds bounced back, but can only locate obstacles, not food items. Like many bats, these birds live in dark caves; they include the Oilbird of northern South America, a distant relative of the nighthawks which feeds by picking fruit off of trees as it hovers, and certain swifts of the East Indies.

Smell

In most birds the sense of smell is barely developed, the bones of the nasal passages lacking the sensory nerve endings that mammals, for example, have in abundance. Among the few birds with a demonstrated sense of smell are the tubenoses, which are attracted by oily fish scents from far away. Seabird-watching boat trips often pour small amounts of heated fish oil on the water; shearwaters and petrels far out of view will sometimes appear with astonishing speed.

The Turkey Vulture has long been suspected to use a sense of smell to locate carrion, but experimental evidence has been contradictory. Audubon found that vultures could not detect a strong-smelling carcass if it was covered, but would find and attempt to eat his painting of a dissected sheep. The experiments of others have shown Turkey Vultures able to find hidden animal carcasses but not equally strong-smelling hidden fish carcasses, although the vultures will eat fish when they find it. Recent research indicates that Turkey Vultures can detect at least certain scents, but depend more on sight to find food. The related Black Vulture and condors do not have a sense of smell, nor do the unrelated Old World vultures.

The kiwis of New Zealand, flightless birds that feed at night on earthworms, have poor vision, but they have developed the strongest sense of smell of all birds. Unlike other birds, they have nostrils at the tip of the upper mandible, and seem to sniff the ground for concealed food.

Taste

The sense of taste is often closely associated with smell, but we do not know that birds with a demonstrated sense of smell have greater sensitivity to taste. Birds have very few taste buds, usually between forty and sixty, compared with man's approximately ten thousand, and most of their taste buds are not on the tongue, but on the roof of the mouth and in the throat. Some birds also have taste buds on the edge of the mandibles.

Most birds swallow their food quickly, giving little indication of taste discrimination. Insect eaters, however, learn to avoid the Monarch butterfly and a few other insects whose diet of milkweed gives them a bitter taste and some poisonous qualities. At feeders, birds may examine, accept, or reject certain new types of food, but we do not know what role taste has in the decision.

FREE

AS A BIRD?

John and Jean George

"Behavior pattern" is a term dear to modern students of natural history—
and also to the sociologists of today. Much has been learned of the extent to
which both man and the other animals are predictable and of the many
things they "can't help doing." Perhaps it would be helpful and encourag-
ing if more attention were paid to the extent to which man, at least, is also
free to violate these patterns when he is intelligent enough and strong-
willed enough to do so. Perhaps also the difference between him and the
other animals is less absolute than is sometimes assumed. The following
account focuses on the involuntary aspects of bird behavior.

FREE as a bird, we say; yet nearly all birds and most bird watchers
know how mistaken that saying is. The conduct of birds is so rigidly
fixed that they are prisoners to the land they fly over, slaves to the air they
fly through. Once we watched a bird go to his death because he was not
free to fly 700 feet to safety.

We were returning home along the Huron River near Ann Arbor,
Mich., where we were studying birds and mammals, and stopped to visit
a cardinal we had named Red Click because of a special clicking note he
used at the end of his song. We found him stranded on the piece of
property where he lived; the land had been scalped that day by bulldozers
so that only a few stumps and roots remained. As we watched, Red Click
flew about 400 feet, then suddenly back-winged as if he had hit an invisible wall. After flopping to earth he flew off in another direction, only
to smash into another invisible barrier.

"What's the matter with that crazy cardinal?" Jean asked. "He'll be
killed by a hawk or an owl if he doesn't fly to the woods."

"He can't fly to the woods," John said. "His 'territory' is in the middle

From *The Christian Science Monitor*, February 4, 1959.

of the cleared land. The bulldozers have taken away his trees, his bushes, his grasses, but the boundaries of his home that he and his neighbors carefully established in their bird minds are still there and he can't fly through them."

"Perhaps we could carry him to safety," Jean suggested.

"And turn him loose on some other cardinal's territory? He's a prisoner precisely because he is more terrified of intruding on another male's land than he is of remaining here without shelter."

A screech owl called from the wood lot behind us. "Hear that?" John said. "That will probably be the last chapter in the biography of Red Click."

Next morning, at the roots of a maple sapling in the wasted field, we picked up the blood-red feathers of our cardinal.

This devotion unto death to a piece of ground is probably more intense in birds than in any other vertebrate. Strongest during the breeding season, the territory fixation serves to aid in the formation of pairs, to provide shelter for the young and to ensure perpetuation of the species by spreading its population over a wide area.

By simply walking behind chickadees, pushing them around their property in the spring, we were able to map some 200 of their territories in the woods near Poughkeepsie, N.Y. The chickadees would fly to the extremities of their lands, then circle back around the edges, revealing their unseen fences. Sketched on a map, a chickadee community looks like an exurbanite settlement of people, with the size of each property varying according to the "social standing" of the occupant; the older the male, the bigger, the stronger he is, the more land he gets.

Birds which are year-round residents tend to retain the same territory for life; migrants have both summer and winter properties. The birds that stay around your home all winter may seem to be in flocks, and therefore trespassing, but they are not. They are a well-ordered bird society made up of old-timers and young, complete with a leader or "boss bird." In these winter societies the defense of the breeding territory has given way, in certain species, to the common defense of a community territory against neighboring groups of the same species. Birds will tolerate trespassers of a different species on their land, since they are not competing, but not intruders belonging to their own.

Birds' property lines are established by song. If a male bird, returning in the spring, can sing from a tree without being challenged by a neighbor, he has it as his own, to mark the limits of his real estate. If, however, another male comes winging at him and puts him back a tree or two, he knows that this land is already claimed.

By taking the best land he can and as much of it as he is able to defend, he assures himself not only a good food supply but also a mate. Female birds pick their mates by their attractive voices (each bird's voice is as distinctive as your own) and by the quality of the nesting sites in the land they have staked off. The weaker males and the late-comers, pushed into submarginal land, often go through the season as bachelors.

A bachelor song sparrow we called Mike sang so beautifully that Jean couldn't understand why the girls would not set up housekeeping with him. John said, "Your friend's territory is very small and in the woods. Song sparrows like some open fields and brush borders on their property. Getting a female to nest on Mike's territory would be like asking a debutante to live in Siberia."

Territory varies with different species from several square miles, as in the case of the horned owl, to only a square foot or so around the nest, as among the colony nesters such as terns and gulls.

Once boundary lines are settled, the feelings of the bird toward his territory mount with the progress of his nest, until he seems to do desperate things particularly near the nest site. Flying at windows and the shiny grillwork of automobiles is not bird hara-kiri. It is territory defense. His reflection in a window or grille is another male on his property, and he will fight this adversary until exhausted.

Territorial disputes, though constant in the bird world, are normally resolved by singing duels, almost always between males of the same species. Sometimes a disputed territory touches off a breast-to-breast battle in the air; the battlers seem to be rising and sliding down an invisible wall. The fight will usually be brief, and afterward each contestant will fly to a tree limb on his side of the property line and click in agitation. Usually there is a compromise and both birds will sing, in a full and exuberant song.

The female ordinarily stays within the boundaries established by her mate, but occasionally a blundering or frivolous wife can cause trouble. One season we observed a tragi-comedy in a community of vivid indigo buntings. A little female, a first-time mother, had by error built her nest on another male's property. She would fly happily to her nest, expecting her husband to usher her home, only to find that he had stopped at the edge of his territory. There he was, turning around in circles, torn between two powerful impulses: to follow his mate, and to stay off his neighbor's property. Apparently property rights proved stronger than family love. He never once crossed the barrier during the nesting period. When the young hatched, the father would catch insects for the babies, call his mate and give her the offerings. Taking them eagerly, she would return to stuff her bottomless young. We were all (including the frustrated father) greatly relieved on the day the little mother coaxed her fledglings over the border to their father's estate.

A territory boundary is not the only restraint in a bird's life. Even within their own property birds do not fly around their land on any random course, but stick to routes or "sidewalks." A bird will take the same path daily from his night roost to his feeding spot, from his nest to a certain singing post. We once saw impressive evidence that birds can map the fixed routes of other birds in the interest of safety.

A Cooper's hawk in our Michigan area staked off two square miles and soared elegantly around to attract a mate. The presence of this bird-eating intruder threw the small birds into a dither. But soon things quieted down and we wondered what adjustment they had made to the predator. In time we discovered the answer.

The big hawk, too, was a slave of habit. He nested in their woods, but always hunted in a far wood lot. Each morning he took an aerial sidewalk to the wood lot, returning home along another fixed path. The small-bird population figured out his habits, for they used fewer and fewer alarm notes to announce his coming and going. They knew he stayed on his sidewalks and never dipped down into their woods for food.

These invisible sidewalks can easily be noted in any back yard where there is a feeding station. A bird will come to the station every day about the same time from the same direction, and by way of the same sticks and twigs. There is generally a sidewalk in and another one out. We once put up a post on a bird's sidewalk, and he almost struck it, he was so confined to his route.

Each night the bird returns faithfully to his bedroom or roost, which he picks as carefully as his nesting site. In a world teeming with enemies, its loss can mean his undoing.

A woodpecker roosted in a hole in an apple tree outside our window. He went to bed at the same time every night, depending on the amount of light. As the days grew shorter, our clock showed him returning two minutes earlier each night, but our light meter registered exactly the same light value. On cloudy days he came to roost early.

One night a white-breasted nuthatch went into the woodpecker's bed-room a few minutes before he was due home. The woodpecker per-formed his night rituals according to his heritage. He squawked from the top of a maple. He defecated in the same spot he had used for months; he flew to the apple tree, spiraled up it and winged into his hole—where he hit the intruding nuthatch head-on.

Out they both tumbled and fought briefly. The nuthatch departed, with the woodpecker in pursuit. Sometime later we caught a glimpse of the woodpecker. It was late, but probably he could still see to get into his hole. However, he had to repeat the rituals of retirement all over again and so he went back to the maple tree. The night grew cold but the wood-pecker never returned. Now it was very dark, well below his accustomed level of light. He squawked but did not fly to the apple tree. One twilight a few nights later the nuthatch cautiously investigated the empty hole and moved in. He had finally won the contest, probably because he upset the woodpecker's evening retirement habits, and the woodpecker, unable to change, was literally left out in the cold.

Almost all birds live and love and die behind the bars of nature's compulsions. They are captive in cages of their own instincts, from which, with rare exceptions, they cannot—and have no desire to—escape.

LEARNING

IN BIRDS

John K. Terres

Inherited behavior patterns do not account for all of bird behavior. Veteran natural history writer and editor John K. Terres here sums up the part learning (in several guises) plays in the lives of birds.

BIRDS learn in various ways—for example, by *habituation*. The range of objects to which young birds respond is at first large, but this is later reduced by learning in which they become habituated or "used to" certain situations to which they do *not* respond. For example, the young of some birds, soon after hatching, will follow the first relatively large object they see. The young of the European greylag goose, *Anser anser*, do so, and they soon learn the object's behavior characteristics—whether the object is the parent goose, a man, a boat, or some other moving object. This type of learning, known among bird behaviorists as *imprinting*, does not fit neatly into many categories of learning but seems to be related to habituation. It is confined to a definite, brief period early in the individual bird's life when it is narrowing the range of objects to which it responds. . . .

By habituation, birds learn what to fear and what not to fear. Mourning doves are much hunted in the United States, yet, before and after the hunting season, they may be attracted to bird feeders in the garden . . . where they may lose much of their fear of man. Anyone who has found robins nesting or wintering in deep woods must have compared their wild behavior with those that nest in the protection of our dooryards and run about tamely over the lawn. Many birds—blue jays, crows, wood thrushes, and others that were woodland species 50 or 60 years ago—now nest in our towns, villages, and city parks. . . .

However, birds seldom lose their fear of wild predators and they learn to recognize the forms of hawks, owls, snakes, and other predatory enemies. Many birds have precise responses to the appearance of the particular kind of predator most dangerous to them, but may be-

From *The Audubon Society Encyclopedia of North American Birds*. New York: Alfred A. Knopf, 1980.

come habituated to, or learn to ignore, predators that are not a threat to them, or even predators that are a threat to them, simply by recognizing that they are not in a hunting mood. . . .

Birds also learn by *trial and error*, in which their appetitive motor patterns may adjust to changes in their environment. . . . In nature, certain birds—young doves, for example—must learn to drink water, and even the pecking of domestic chicks improves about 30 hours after hatching with an increase in the skill with which they seize and swallow each grain . . . or perhaps in learning *what* to peck at. Simple trial-and-error learning is believed to be very important to birds in their nest building, although there is little doubt that the nest-building motions of birds are innate, or unlearned. . . .

Margaret Nice, in her studies of song sparrows, found that the parents improved their feeding skill of the young as a result of learning. Individual learning by birds is sometimes remarkable. For example, in England, titmice of various species learned to open milk bottles left in the early morning on doorsteps and to reach down into the bottle and drink the milk. Within 30 years the habit had spread among these birds to many parts of England, possibly through those watching and imitating others of their kind. . . .

In the laboratory, trial-and-error learning by birds has been studied by presenting them with puzzle boxes and mazes. House sparrows, blue jays, and a woodpecker learned to open doors by pulling a string . . . , although they apparently did not "understand" the relationship between the string and the door. What the birds did learn was to associate disconnected responses and to perform them in the right order. . . .

House sparrows have learned to run through a maze with ability equal to that of a rat; pigeons can readily learn mazes of various types; and in tests of captive European songbirds, they quickly learned to run through a small maze in from 4 to 6 trials.

Birds also learn by *playing* and there are now sufficiently numerous documented examples to believe that true play is fairly widespread among birds. . . . The play of a captive young turaco included sparring and mock attacks; young gannets in captivity were "as playful and mischievous as a litter of puppies"; young white-necked ravens and silvery-cheeked hornbills and a captive common buzzard (similar to the American red-tailed hawk) were playful, and young European kestrels in the wild, when satiated with hunting, returned to their former breeding territory among sand dunes to play with pine cones, grasses, and roots until the time came for them to start hunting again. . . .

Adult crows, ravens, and magpies are playful, house sparrows play with pebbles . . . and the marsh hawk and other birds of prey, also grebes, are known to play a cat-and-mouse game with their quarry. Woodpeckers often play . . . and in Iceland, eider ducks were seen riding down the waters of a rapids, then climbing the banks to again launch themselves on the stream, apparently for the delight of the swift ride through the swirling waters. . . . About play in birds, W. H. Thorpe wrote: "In whatever category the behaviour comes . . . it may be of physiological value in maintaining and perfecting muscular co-ordination and control; in other words, it is an important element in both motor and sensory learning". . . .

Some birds have much curiosity. House sparrows and crows, which have enormous curiosity, are especially intelligent and adaptable birds . . . which helps them in trial-and-error learning. Some birds also have remarkable memories. Crows, jays, nutcrackers, and ravens remember where they hide nuts and other items . . . and domestic hens and pigeons are said to remember their homes after several years of absence. . . . Pigeons learn local topography around the home loft, which they use with orientation mechanisms in returning . . . and some wild migratory birds return, in part, by memory of known landmarks . . . and learn to remember their nesting territories as a recognizable unit. . . .

Birds also learn by imitation of the behavior and voice of other birds. The call notes of a great many birds seem to be inborn, but there is considerable evidence that many species learn a part or even the whole of their territorial songs from members of their own species. It is claimed that the European song thrush's song is innate, or unlearned, but can be slightly modified by learning, while the skylark's song is wholly learned. . . .

A few birds use tools—the tailor bird uses spider's silk as thread while using its bill as a tool for sewing in building its nests. The satin bower bird uses fibrous material with which to "paint" the sticks of its bower with coloring material from berries and charcoal, a Galápagos finch uses a long cactus spine to pick insects out of crannies and crevices, and N. American brown-headed nuthatches . . . have been seen using a small piece of bark to remove another bark scale on a tree trunk in order to forage for insects. . . .

RAVENS

WORK IT OUT

R.D. Lawrence

It is generally agreed that the corvids—ravens, crows, jays, magpies—are our most inventive and clever birds. As the following piece illustrates, the popular Canadian nature writer R.D. Lawrence has abundant reason to admire Corvus corax, *the northern raven. The cast of characters here includes Tundra, the Lawrences' big malamute, and Matta and Wa, growing wolf pups that Lawrence had bought on the banks of the Mattawa River in northwestern Ontario from an Indian who had killed their mother.*

TUNDRA was quite accustomed to the highly intelligent black scoundrels; he knew how to deal with them. But I didn't think that Matta and Wa had yet experienced close contact with *Corvus corax*, who is, in my considered opinion, the toughest and most intelligent of all the birds in the northland. In the Yukon Territory I have seen them flying nonchalantly, high in the air, when the ground temperature was down to 60 degrees below zero. I have watched them land at a wolf kill while the big predators were busy feeding, the birds biding their time as they strutted through the snow, then darting in to grab some morsel right under the nose of a big timber wolf, who, wise to the ways of the ebon robbers, would essay one swift snap and be content to continue eating when it missed the target.

When everybody else is seeking shelter from the biting cold of the north, it is not unusual to see a raven fly straight down, as though intent on dashing out its brains against the ground, level off a few feet before collision, apply brakes at the last moment, and plop itself into the snow. Seconds later the glossy black head will emerge, followed by the neck and, at last, by the shoulders. Now the wings flap, like a domestic chicken essaying a flight; the snow spatters upward, but it has hardly had time to settle before the raven is off, running with all its body buried in snow; propelled as much by its hidden but flapping wings as by its pumping feet, it will career along for distances of fifty

From *Secret Go the Wolves*. New York: Holt, Rinehart and Winston, 1980.

yards or more, the strange and disembodied inky head sticking up a few inches above the snow. When the run is over, the raven will take a snow bath in the same way that sane birds take a dust bath. Much refreshed, it will flap madly again for a few moments and then climb skyward chortling loudly as though wanting to share its pleasure with all the more craven beings of the northland.

When I was last in the Yukon . . . I watched a raven remove the metal lid from one of our garbage cans. I was writing, but I became suddenly disturbed by a steady, tinny banging. When it didn't stop, I got up and looked out of the window. The sound occurred each time a big raven closed its beak on the edge of the garbage can lid and lifted it with a jerk, then let it fall, making the clang. I had built an off-the-ground, wooden-slatted cage for the garbage containers in order to keep the northern dogs out of the cans; but I hadn't reckoned with the ravens. Interested, but not believing that the robber baron could really remove the lid, I stayed to watch. Unfortunately I didn't time the feat, but I would estimate that it took the bird about two minutes to get the lid off.

That bird had technique! It could not physically lift the lid high enough to remove it in one go, but by lifting and dropping the thing, it gradually bounced off. Having achieved its purpose, the raven hopped onto the edge of the garbage can, gripped tightly with its sturdy feet, dipped forward and downward until only its back and tail showed, and then rose again, carrying in its great beak a half-full grocery bag containing table scraps.

Holding the prize, the bandit paused a moment, perhaps to recover its breath, then rose into the air. When it was some ten feet above my driveway, it opened its beak. Bombs away! The bag burst, scattering its contents all over the place. Now the raider descended and found a tidbit, in this case the remnants of a chicken breast. With that, it flew into one of our lodgepole pines and began to devour its spoils. In the meantime, half a dozen of its eagle-eyed relatives appeared, each from a different direction. Almost regretfully, I went outside to break up the party; I didn't want all the garbage scattered over the driveway. But every one of the latecomers left with a prize in its beak, the last one taking off with a waxed cardboard container that had held honey.

Now, as though gathering for a quick tactical meeting, three of the birds swooped off their perches and landed on the same branch as the fourth member of the gang. Immediately, amid a great deal of bobbing and bowing, untidy crests fully erect, the quartet began to chatter, mixing deep caws with an entire range of glottal variations that ranged from coos and gurgles to slurred squawks. Finished, they all launched themselves out of the tree in near unison, split up in the air, and planed down, each raven landing in a different place, undoubtedly under the premise that it is a good deal more difficult to keep an eye on four scattered individuals than on a grouping of the same number.

Tundra wasn't about to be fooled. He had jousted with these brigands often in the past, and been bested every time. By now, like the wild wolves, he knew it was useless to charge at any one of them; not only would the target bird escape, but while he was charging, one of the others would dart in and grab the prize. As soon as they landed, Tundra lifted one massive paw and plopped it deliberately on the bone he was chewing, sparing the birds but a short, darting glance.

The cubs had yet to learn this particular lesson. One bird, the one I presumed to be the leader and who was certainly the biggest and toughest looking, strutted with stiff gait toward Matta, walking easily on top of snow that had become crusted during the time that the wolves had spent here eating the whitetail. Matta immediately raised her head, ears pricked all the way forward, lips peeled back in a silent snarl. The raven changed direction slightly, now angling toward a point a few feet to one side of the bitch. When the bird was about a yard away, Matta charged, leaping swiftly and fluidly, going from a prone position to a fast run in one movement. But when her gleaming teeth closed shut, all they got was air, the snap of ivory on ivory ringing loud. The object of her anger was already six or seven feet up by the time she collected herself sufficiently to jump for the raven, rearing on her hind legs. But by then the big bird had risen another six feet and was circling around.

While this action was taking place, Raven Two flapped quickly from its position just outside the area of the kill and grabbed Matta's bone, taking off with the prize immediately. Matta turned sharply, took a run at the airborne robber, and thought better of it, returning to dig in the hard snow and to uncover a new bone.

Meanwhile, the remaining birds were individually concentrating on Wa and Tundra. The one that was advancing on the dog, evidently an old hand, was soon able to judge that Tundra was not to be coaxed into a charge. It hopped a few feet into the air and reversed direction, no doubt to see if its buddy needed help; this bird was repeating the technique employed by the first raider, but Wa didn't wait for it to get close. Angry, growling like a tiger, he leaped up and dashed full bore at the raven, thus allowing its companion to make off with the bone.

Twice more did Matta try to kill the ravens, and each time she returned unsuccessful to find her tidbit stolen. After the third time she gave up in obvious disgust, leaving the scene of her defeat and coming to lie down beside Joan. Wa proved himself a little quicker in the uptake in this instance. He lost one more bone, but the third one that he dug up was quickly protected by a big paw. He may have taken his cue from Tundra, or he may have figured it all out for himself. However it was, he, like the dog, now ignored the ravens. The birds, finding that the game was over, started a free-for-all, each raven attempting to corner all the profits. As far as I could make out, the ones that got away with bones hid them somewhere in the forest, then returned to seek more.

BIRDSONG

Christopher Leahy

We tend to think of the instinct/learning issue as an either/or proposition, which may well be misleading. Painstaking lab experiments have shown, for example, that both are involved in the songs birds sing; and Christopher Leahy proceeds to address the question of purpose in song.

To the human sensibility, birdsong is mainly a source of aesthetic delight. . . . From a bird's perspective, of course, the sounds it makes have an altogether different significance. They are practical means of communication and expression which for most species are as necessary for survival as *visual* signals such as distinctive color, pattern, and physical gesture. Bird sounds also help fill the "communications gap" left by birds' negligible (with minor exceptions) senses of smell, taste, and touch.

It is not surprising then that bird sounds are by now highly evolved. Although sound plays an important role in the lives of many insects, amphibians, and mammals, only human speech and perhaps the vocalizations of some cetaceans surpass bird sounds for vocal subtlety and complexity. . . .

HOW BIRDS ACQUIRE THEIR SONGS. The answer to whether birds *inherit* their characteristic repertoire of sounds or *learn* them through imitation and practice appears to be: *both.* Early experiments involving birds hatched and reared in total isolation from any contact with their species have shown that with the passage of time these birds not only know as many songs and calls as their normal counterparts and know when to sing them but also—at least to the ears of the experimenters—give them the same intonations heard in wild birds. . . . Subsequent experiments on different species, however, indicate that young birds hatch knowing a sort of generalized song but must listen to adult birds singing it "correctly," and then imitate them, before they perfect their vocal technique. Such birds deprived of this learning experience may stick with the simple "baby song" or they may invent the missing elements and end up with a full complex song which, however, does not conform

From *The Birdwatcher's Companion: An Encyclopedic Handbook of North American Birdlife.* New York: Hill & Wang, 1982.

closely to the characteristic song of their species. If they are exposed when young to the song of a different species they may "adopt" its song or use elements of it to devise an original composition. How to make particular call notes . . . may be more firmly fixed genetically at hatching, yet untutored individuals may not understand in what circumstances they should be used and must learn this from experience, i.e., by hearing other birds use them in the appropriate situation.

The development of the vocal faculties has as yet been studied in only a relatively few species. Given the different results obtained (even allowing for the foibles of the experimenters) and the great diversity birds exhibit in other forms of behavior, it is not unrealistic to speculate that the proportional influence of nature and nurture in song development varies significantly from species to species.

Passerines typically make "begging" sounds within the first couple of days after hatching, and the first generalized singing may begin as early as the 13th day in some species, but not for 8 weeks in others. . . . Young male Song Sparrows appear to advance gradually—during a period when they are exposed to the adult song of their species—from a nondescript warble to shorter phrases to a recognizable adult song. Males singing on territory their first spring may begin with a rather crude rendition, but improve noticeably as they listen to and conform with the songs of neighboring males. At least in some species, the entire vocal repertoire is completely acquired and "fixed" within the first year. Once this happens birds seem to have an infallible vocal memory and can, for example, reproduce their territorial songs precisely after a winter of silence or even if deafened.

As a class, birds are perhaps the most vocal of animals. The majority of species have an elaborate vocabulary equaled by only a few gregarious mammals and conspicuously surpassed only by ourselves. . . . Anyone who has paid any attention to the sounds birds make is aware of two broad categories of vocalization. The one we call "song" typically contains a series of different notes uttered in a cohesive sequence so that they form a characteristic phrase with a recognizable rhythm and "tune" like a line of music. Some songs, such as the abrupt *chebec* of the Least Flycatcher, don't fit this description very well but are still defined as songs because of their function.

Most of the birdsongs we hear are those of male birds advertising their presence on their territories to prospective mates and to potential rivals of their own sex and species. . . . Neighboring males may engage in singing contests to establish their invisible boundary lines. They may "escalate" their song battles by adding aggressive motifs, but they almost always come to terms vocally without resorting to physical violence. Wandering males are also warned efficiently when they trespass on occupied territory. This territorial song usually continues through the breeding cycle and seems to cement the pair bond after mating. When a similar (or identical) song is sung by a male to communicate with its mate and serves no aggressive or advertising functions, it is sometimes distinguished as a "signal song."

Another type of song, usually very distinct in phrasing from the territorial/signal song, seems to be unrelated to the breeding cycle, but rather to be pure release of energy of the kind that Shelley attributed to his Skylark. "Emotional-release songs" of this kind have been recorded for many passerine species. They usually happen at random; they may be accompanied by an "ecstasy flight" (not to be confused with territorial song flights characteristic of many open-country species); in some species . . . they are likely to be performed at twilight; but they may also be given at night during migration or on the wintering ground. They often contain many improvised elements. The function of this category of song is unclear. But even sober scientists, who eschew anthropomorphism by profession, acknowledge its expressive quality and have even suggested that it contains a germ of artistic invention (!).

HIBERNATION AND
THE POOR-WILL

Edmund C. Jaeger

The correction of one error often leads to another. Thus the belief, current from classical times and well into the eighteenth century, that swallows hibernate under the water of ponds was hardly disposed of before most ornithologists would have been willing to say, "No bird hibernates." That a few of them do is one of the most startling of recent discoveries. Here the tale is told by the man who first observed the strange phenomenon.

WHILE going up through a very narrow, high-walled, almost slot-like cañon in the Chuckawalla Mountains of the Colorado Desert two of my students and I saw on December 29, 1946, a most unusual sight. On the side-wall about two and a half feet above the sand of the cañon bottom was a Poor-will (*Phalaenoptilus nuttallii*) resting head-upward in a vertical rock-hollow, its gray and black, mottled plumage blending so perfectly with the coarse gray granite that we had to look twice to convince ourselves it was really a Poor-will. The shallow crypt, with deepest part above, was just a little more than large enough to hold the bird, hence its back was almost flush with the rock surface. When we had observed the bird quietly for more than ten minutes without noticing any motion, I reached forward and touched the bird without evoking any response. I even stroked the back feathers without noticing the slightest movement. Was our bird dead, sick or just deep in winter sleep? We left the place for awhile, then about two hours later returned. The Poor-will was still in the same position. I now reached forward and picked it up, freely turning it about in my hands. It seemed to be of unusually light weight and the feet and eye-lids when touched felt cold. We made no further attempt to be quiet; we even shouted to see if we could arouse our avian "sleeper." I finally returned it to its place in the crypt; but while I was doing this I noticed that it lazily opened and shut an eye, the only sign I had that it was a living bird. Unfortunately

From *The Condor*. January–February, 1948.

we soon had to leave the place and return home without making further observation.

Ten days later at about ten o'clock in the morning I returned with Mr. Lloyd Mason Smith. To our great surprise and satisfaction the Poor-will was still there in its rock niche, with every indication that it had not moved "even so much as a feather" in the intervening time. I reached forward and as before carefully picked it up. But this time instead of remaining perfectly quiet, it gave several "puffy" sounds as if expelling air from the lungs, opened an eye, and began to make a variety of queer high-pitched whining or squeaky mouse-like sounds. After some moments it opened its mouth widely as if yawning and then resumed its quiet. As Mr. Smith further handled it, it again made the whining notes; then suddenly it raised both wings and held them in rigid, fully outstretched upright position. The eyes remained closed. After the bird had held the wings stiffly upward for several minutes we worked together to put them back in normal position; several times we attempted this but the wings came quickly back high above the head until the tips almost touched. Some five minutes later while one of us still held the bird, we tried again, this time more successfully, for we got the wings at least partially in position. We now put the Poor-will back in its crypt as best we could and left. The morning was cool (42° F.), the sky overcast.

That afternoon while the sky was still gray with clouds we returned for further observations. We had put the bird into its crypt not quite in normal position and with feathers somewhat ruffled and wings askew, and so it was now when we found it after an absence of three hours. Mr. Smith picked up the Poor-will hoping to photograph it while I held it in my hand. But to our great surprise it whipped open its wings and flew out of hand in perfectly normal flight as if it had only been playing 'possum all the time but now had suddenly become alert to danger. It flew about forty feet up-cañon into an iron wood tree (*Olneya tesota*). We walked toward it and again it flew, alighting this time among some rocks high above us and where we were unable to reach it.

On this day there were fresh coyote tracks directly below the Poor-will's roosting site. The position of the foot prints indicated that the coyote had stopped and turned toward the bird. There were fresh feces and claw marks in the sand, all indications that he had remained there a number of minutes. Perhaps he even saw or smelled the bird, for it probably was perching there on the side of the rock at about the level of his eye.

On November 26, 1947, a Poor-will, probably the same bird, was in the same crypt, and again it was lethargic. On December 6 it was banded.

I am not venturing to state any conclusions, but this experience leads me strongly to suspect that one reason that so little is known and written about the winter habits of Poor-wills is because the birds then for the most part hide away and perhaps spend a short period in a kind of somnolence at least somewhat akin to true hibernation. Culbertson (Condor, 48,1946:158–159) found a Poor-will hidden in a rotten log and in sort of a torpid state of low metabolism. I take this as a partial corroboration of my belief that a period of winter inactivity among Poor-wills may be more common than we have supposed.

FEATHER

MAINTENANCE

Robert Burton

"How jolly it would be to have a coat of feathers to keep us warm and enable us to fly!" Children are notorious for immediately seeing presumed advantages in any imagined situation while remaining entirely blind to concomitant disadvantages. Being covered with feathers, as Robert Burton points out, entails a continuing round of maintenance work.

A bird must keep its feathers in perfect condition. If the plumage is in disarray, insulation and waterproofing will be spoiled and flight will be less efficient. It will cost the bird more in terms of energy to keep warm and fly, and labored flight may even cost the bird its life. . . .

A feather is a complex structure, delicately pieced together, so that it must be treated with care. From the central shaft, or quill, there run two rows of barbs which are linked together by overlapping barbules. Maintenance consists of ensuring that the thousands of barbules stay hooked up, because the integrity of the feather is responsible for its unique flexibility and strength, as well as for its waterproofing properties. Air trapped between the barbs increases the surface tension of the feather vane and causes water to pearl into droplets and run off (like the air held between the fibers in tent canvas). In waterbirds, the air trapped in the plumage also increases buoyancy.

Bathing

Most birds bathe, even in cold weather, and starlings have been seen to break thin ice so they could immerse themselves. The typical bathing action gives the bird more of a shower bath than a soaking. Standing in shallow water, it bends down to immerse the belly and vigorously flicks its bill from side to side in the water. At the same time the wingtips are vigorously beaten so that sprays of water are thrown over the body. In heavy rain, drops of water run off the plumage leaving the bird dry, so,

From *Bird Behavior*. New York: Alfred A. Knopf, 1985.

to make bathing effective, the bird ruffles its plumage to allow wetting. But it must not get soaked or it will be unable to escape if danger threatens.

Some birds bathe in the rain. Larks, for instance, squat on the ground with wings outstretched when it rains, and parrots stand with feathers ruffled and wings and tail spread. Hornbills and some other birds bathe by flapping among rain- or dew-soaked foliage. The plunge bath is a feature of the most aerial of birds, such as swifts, swallows, owls, night-jars, kingfishers and hummingbirds, which dip into the water for an instant before continuing their flight.

Preening

After bathing, the bird retires to a safe place to preen. Wetting the feathers before preening helps the spread of preen oil. Most birds have a preen gland at the base of the tail whose contents are smeared over the plumage. The function of the oil is not known for certain. It was once believed to act as a lacquer that helped to increase the surface tension, and hence the waterproofing of the feathers, but ducks treated with a solvent to remove the oil remained waterproof. Neither is there any support for the notion that preen oil contains a substance which is converted into Vitamin D under the influence of sunlight. The oil does seem to keep the feathers from becoming brittle, and it has antibacterial and fungicidal properties.

Several actions involving sensitive movements of the bill are used in preening. The most thorough movements are gentle nibblings of each feather as it is drawn between the tips of the beak. This cleans and rearranges the barbs and barbules. Sometimes the bird digs vigorously at one spot to clear away dirt or remove a parasite; at other times it draws the feather rapidly through the bill. Stroking movements help to smooth the feathers and to dry them. Finally, the bird shivers its body feathers and beats its wings to settle everything comfortably into place.

Dusting, Sunning and Anting

As well as being a frequent visitor to the bird-bath, the house sparrow also indulges in dustbathing, particularly in fine weather. Sandgrouse, bustards and the gallinaceous order—chickens, grouse, guineafowl and others—dustbathe but never bathe in water. These are birds of open, often dry, country where there is plenty of dust but little water. The bird scrapes with its feet and shuffles its wings so that its ruffled plumage becomes filled with dust.

The value of dusting is not clear, and neither is that of sunbathing. At its simplest, the bird sits with its feathers ruffled and wings drooping. At higher intensities, it leans away from the sun with the nearer wing drooping and half-spread, or it lies flat with both wings spread. Pigeons raise the wing nearest the sun over the back, and bateleur eagles perch with their wings spread to catch the sun, like heraldic eagles.

Some birds probably sunbathe to warm their bodies in the morning, but it is noticeable that others sunbathe when the sun comes out even though the air is very warm. They pant at the same time so they are presumably already too hot. Furthermore, a sunbathing bird looks "stupid": it appears to be in a trance and often loses its natural wariness. A possible function for sunbathing in large birds is to assist in feather maintenance. When birds such as vultures, storks and pelicans soar for extended periods, their long flight feathers become bent. These birds sunbathe, whereas large birds that flap—herons, swans and cranes— and those that have short wing feathers, such as albatrosses, do not. It has been found that a twisted vulture feather straightens out in four to five minutes when exposed to the sun, but takes two to three hours in the shade.

Perhaps sunbathing for some birds, as for human beings, is more than a functional pursuit and is positively enjoyable through the sensation of physical well-being. The same may be said for anting. This is an odd performance in which a bird picks up ants, one at a time, and applies them to the underside of the wings, as if oiling the feathers. Then the ants are dropped, or eaten, and the performance is repeated. Some species, notably members of the crow family, squat over the ants, often with wings spread as if sunbathing, and let them swarm over the plumage.

The usual explanation is that the formic acid from the ants may kill or dislodge lice from the feathers, or that other secretions may act like preen oil in preserving the feather structure. There is no evidence that fluid from the ant's body has any beneficial effect on the feathers, however, and anting appears to be something of an addiction. Some birds ant avidly while others seem never to ant. Such is the passion for anting that "addicts" twist their wing and tail feathers against the ground in a way which is hardly calculated to improve the condition of the plumage. Captive birds have anted with such odd things as mothballs, matches and cigarette ends, while starlings and crows occasionally display the same type of behavior over smoke and flames.

Part

Four

FAMILY MATTERS

TYRANNUS TYRANNUS

Louis J. Halle, Jr.

Many birds are exemplary parents and lead ideal family lives. For that reason medieval moralists sometimes cited their example as a reproach to humankind. Modern ornithologists, on the other hand, are insistent upon avoiding "the anthropomorphic fallacy." Birds, they say, are creatures of instinct and perhaps of emotion, but they can't think and they are not conscious of the purpose of their seemingly purposeful actions. Here Louis J. Halle, Jr. makes the point in a vivid account of the family life of a pair of eastern kingbirds.

Does he, one asks, overstate the case—not by stressing the instinctive character of bird behavior but by seemingly making too absolute the contrast with the parallel behavior of human beings? "The kingbird," he writes, "leading the abundant life somewhere in the jungles of tropical America, was not suddenly overcome last spring by the appalling thought that if he and his mates did not act promptly his species might disappear from the earth." How many human children are conceived because their parents were struck by the fear of extinction?

I N most forms of animal life the propagation of the race seems to be a purely unintentional outcome of the sexual impulse, which is directed toward the satisfaction of the moment rather than the population of the future. A physical need exists to be satisfied, and its satisfaction involves remote consequences which were certainly not considered at the moment. Among birds, however, procreation is not the incidental consequence of an impulsive act, but the end of a chain of action that seems to have been deliberately followed with the sole purpose of bringing into being a new generation. There is no trace of capriciousness in the history of their mating. The ruling impulse seems to be the production of a family, and the physical union merely one of several incidental means to that premeditated end. They put as much passion into the choice of a nesting site, the building of the nest, the brooding of the eggs, and the feeding of the young, as into the act of union itself. The male lavishes as much devotion and protecting care on his nest as on his mate, and fights as readily in its defense.

From *Birds Against Men*. New York: The Viking Press, 1938.

Still, I don't for a moment suppose that birds, who are creatures of impulse and incapable of contemplation, can visualize the remote future consequences of their acts. We must not allow the lower forms of life credit for spiritual faculties that even we possess imperfectly. The kingbird, leading the abundant life somewhere in the jungles of tropical America, was not suddenly overcome last spring by the appalling thought that if he and his mates did not act promptly his species might disappear from the earth. He did not think of Duty. He did not think of a nest and a clutch of fertile eggs, of embryonic life stirring, or fledglings trying out their fledgling wings over a neat green lawn some thousands of miles distant. He did not think at all. Nevertheless, he was possessed by an urge, some obscure, unrealized impulse, some restlessness which made him less content to stay where he was, even though there had been no change in his outward circumstances. The jungle still offered the same abundant food and shelter. The sun still shone, flowers bloomed, insects hummed, night and day alternated as usual. Nevertheless, the periodic urge, which scientists have guessed arises from seasonal glandular changes in the body's interior, was there. I suppose it may have been several weeks before it was strong enough to prompt action. However that may be, the time came when he found himself flying northward to alleviate the urgency which he did not understand. It was merely that he felt better about flying north than about flying east or west or south, or remaining where he was. Surely he did not picture that neatly pruned apple tree on the lawn outside our house, even though he may have nested in its immediate vicinity less than a year earlier. I doubt that at any point he saw beyond his actual physical horizon. He embarked on a journey that must have fazed him had he been capable of grasping its magnitude. A man would have to be endowed with exceptional courage to undertake it. But courage is needed only where there is imagination, and the kingbird had no need of it. . . .

The urge that had carried him across land and sea did not leave him when he arrived. But he stopped here now because it no longer satisfied that urge to go farther. Still obedient to his fate, he claimed the apple tree as his stage and waited, knowing (and not knowing) that the solitary first labor of his mission had been accomplished, that from now on he would have a mate to share his duties. And sure enough, within a few days he was joined at his post by another kingbird, who took for granted his presence and his inclinations as he took for granted her arrival. With the apple tree as their chosen setting they played their traditional parts to a single rhythm, for both wills were bent by the same motive, prompted by the same series of momentary inspirations, subject to the same transcending intelligence that both followed blindly.

It is easy enough to conjure up the picture of a pleasant domestic scene to describe the family life of the kingbird—something on the order of the hearth-loving English vicar of the nineteenth century, surrounded by devoted wife, clay pipe, and three affectionate daughters. The early flutterings of mutual love in the respective breasts, the ripening of a maturer affection as family cares impose sobriety—protective affection in the male, devoted and worshipful in his mate. . . . The thing has been done. It was quite the fashion some years ago to draw moral sustenance from the examples of the good life set us by our feathered brethren. This was done chiefly, I believe, by ladies, closet ornithologists who rarely ventured out of sight of their pet canaries, though the literary clergy may also have had a hand in it. But the age of moral elevation has passed, and the feathered brethren, like the unfeathered, have had their manners corrupted by the literature of an irresponsible new age. Times change, birds change. . . .

I cannot conscientiously report that my kingbirds underwent any mystical or moral experience in the process of their union. As far as I could tell it was a purely practical matter. One after another, the female produced four eggs in the interior of her body, and one after another her mate fertilized them, acting exactly as though he had a perfect understanding of the mysterious processes of egg-production and embryogeny. His advances and her acceptances were spaced, as though by intelligence, to fit into the established rhythm of procreation. When, for the first time, she began to spend the night in their nest while he went off alone to roost in the woods, I knew that the spotted eggs had already been deposited in the pocket especially built to contain them.

The kingbird's days of freedom were definitely over. One may assume that his liberty had already been severely qualified ever since that urge which he had first felt in distant lands had taken possession of him. "Free as a bird" is an expression in which a bird might find ironical amusement; especially as coming from man, the only animal who has, in his individual life, succeeded in achieving some measure of independence from the discipline of nature. But now the kingbird's responsibility was embodied in four small white spheroids spotted with umber. He had a concrete treasure to guard. Those fragile shells contained the future of his race, the reason for his long migration, the cause to which he had been dedicated many weeks earlier and thousands of miles away. It was no longer enough to guard his own person from enemies. At last he had a treasure, a treasure which lay in an open nest exposed to enemies who would ravish it at the first relaxation of the vigil he shared with his mate.

Crows, especially, were dangerous. By inherited instinct, if not by experience, the kingbird knew that they would eat his eggs and young if he allowed them occasion, and, following the Napoleonic policy of his species that the best form of defense is an effective offense, he never gave the crows a chance to launch an attack. I don't suppose it was really policy. Again, he seemed prompted by a racial intelligence that was not his own. Whenever a crow appeared on the distant horizon, though he were only passing peacefully by and minding his own business, the kingbird and his mate, with piercing shrieks of anger, would project themselves at him like a pair of missiles shot out of the tree by the force of their own energy. It was unreasonable, but effective. Darting at him from above, and occasionally landing on his back in midflight, they would soon have him plunging like a maddened horse under a swarm of bees, and it was a pretty sure thing that he would make a long detour the next time his business carried him that way. Unreasonable, but extremely effective. The piratical crows were the first to be driven out of our neighborhood when the kingbirds set about establishing their kingdom.

In those early days, however, before the embryos had developed in the eggs, it was enough to guard them from nest-robbers. The constant brooding, to insure the proper temperature for their development, came later. The kingbirds were still free to expend their limitless vitality in exhibition flights, hawking for insects and harassing the neighborhood birds. Occasionally one or the other of them would rest for a while on the eggs, but any excuse to abandon them was good enough.

You might have thought that both birds were expert embryologists from the way they seemed to know just how much brooding was necessary, increasing the amount gradually from day to day. But they had read no book on the prenatal care of birds, attended no course of lectures, studied no diagrams. They did not know the contents of those eggs or the purpose of their brooding. They did not know why they had produced them, or why they had ever built a nest to contain them; or why they now bothered to guard them. Nor could previous experience, rule of thumb acquired through trial and error, have been a basis for their actions, since birds will follow the same established procedure whether or not they are nesting for the first time. I rather think it was the lack of any intelligent comprehension of their own actions that made those actions possible. Calculation would merely have confused the process. Completely devoid, as they were, of the capacity for reasoning, for weighing alternatives, for valuing ends, their natural instincts, shaped over millennia of evolution to the sole end of survival, had no rivalry to their leadership, authority was undivided. They acted blindly because their actions were only reflections of intuition; they acted surely, without hesitation, because only intuition prompted their actions.

The perfect co-operation between the two prospective parents was another indication of the integrity of instinct they shared in common.

When the female had brooded long enough and was ready to leave the nest in search of food or exercise, she did not call her mate into consultation and ask him to take her place. She merely followed her urge and departed. The male would sometimes delay for several minutes after her departure, but you could see that the empty nest concerned him. When the safe time had elapsed, he would fly over and settle down in her place, folding his wings carefully for a long vigil. Gradually the time between watches was reduced, as the developing embryos required more constant warmth, until in the last stages the birds would replace each other immediately.

It will be no surprise to the reader who has followed the history of the kingbirds this far to learn that their eggs did finally split open and bring forth the renewed life of the species in the form of four pink dabs of flesh, with eye-slits for eyes, with ludicrously disproportionate bills and feet, and with wing-stumps that were far from having the aerodynamic perfection of the adults' feathered pinions. And yet, how can it be otherwise than surprising? Here was an achievement out of all proportion to the kingbirds' limited powers; the culminating fourth act of a drama played over two continents, involving the most sweeping action and the most subtle dialogue, by two insignificant actors whose limited powers, placed at the disposal of the unlimited forces of nature, had produced this immortality. By themselves, these two little birds had no powers of generation. They lacked the intelligence and the knowledge to understand the necessary processes. The two kingbirds who had performed this exploit were but the instruments of an inscrutable and disembodied will, a universal purpose heard only in the echo of their own unpondered desires.

The kingbirds themselves were not surprised when they felt the eggs stirring beneath them. As passive instruments of an unfathomable fate they accepted as they had performed, without fear or question. And now the labor of the performance was increased by the necessity of filling those four bottomless gullets. Time was passing. Summer was half gone. Quantities of young robins, bluebirds, phoebes, had taken possession of the countryside and were already feeding themselves. Insects were plentiful. The kingbirds perched on the topmost twigs of the trees adjacent to their nest-tree and every minute or two sallied forth to bring in some new prey. At midday, when the sun beat down with tropical intensity, one or the other of them would stand guard on the edge of the nest, wings spread to shelter the unfeathered young from its rays. In the evening, as the heat began to wear off, the young would grow increasingly clamorous, and both parents would be hard pressed to keep them satisfied with tributes of insects until nightfall.

Up to now the kingbirds had paid little attention to me, evidently not classing my kind with such worthy opponents as crows and hawks.

Along with rabbits, muskrats, groundhogs, and white-footed mice, I was considered harmless. They did not even flatter me by trying to hide their nest or dissemble their concern for it in my presence. All other birds I have been familiar with have at least had some hesitation about approaching their nests (always hidden) when I was observing them. But that was never a kingbird's way. Like the stalwart fighter he is, he has no need of trickery or deception. He builds his nest and rears his young in full view; let anyone approach at his peril. Only when I took advantage of their openness to get some photographs of them did the kingbirds change their estimate of me. That machine I carried raised me definitely to the status of a menace. From that moment I could call the crows my equals. Hovering overhead with shrill staccato shrieks, they took turns in plunging at me, their flaming crests, never displayed except in battle, standing erect on their heads, their bills snapping like the strokes of doom. So fierce was the onslaught that, despite my manifest advantages, I felt something of the terror that must accompany the insect's instant of annihilation. The first plunge brought me to my knees, my arms clasping my head for protection. But they could not drive me away. Eventually the clamor of the young for food forced them to abandon the attack, and I got the photographs I wanted. After that, however, I was a marked man. Camera or no camera, whenever I entered their territory (which was anywhere up to a hundred yards from the tree) they charged me. Other men could come and go as they pleased; I had earned their undying enmity by my invasion of their privacy. They knew now that I, different in that from others of my kind, had taken an interest in their nest and young, and they could not know that my interest was benevolent.

Of course they were right not to take any chance. They were eminently right in everything they did; as witness the fact that the four dabs of flesh grew rapidly in a few days' time to fully fledged reproductions of their elders, and were soon out of the nest. No ceremony accompanied their departure, no ostentation. In fact, it was anything but deliberate. The young birds were literally pushed out into the world by their own growth. They hatched from the nest as they had hatched from those spotted eggs, only when it could no longer contain them. Their reluctance was marked. The first day they merely tried their footing on the edge of the nest and along the adjacent twigs; and by evening all had crowded back into the cradle. One can understand their unwillingness to say farewell to the day of their infancy. But time does not wait on the pleasure of mortals. The next night the four kingbirds roosted all in a row beside an abandoned nest, and in the morning they embarked on their first experimental flights, fluttering across the great open spaces between twig and twig.

I cannot say the parent birds took any pride in the achievement.

From first to last their attitude was strictly businesslike. They maintained the food-supply and kept all enemies at a distance, but I never saw them give their progeny any sign of encouragement or commendation in those first attempts to cope with the problem of flight. The young birds now had to take their share of the responsibility for their own survival. When one of them, weaker and less developed than the others, with a mere stump of tail and inadequate pinions, fell out of the tree in an abortive attempt at flight, he was left to lie where he fell, exposed to all the dangers that creep on the ground. Had it not been for my benevolent intervention, which made me the target of a series of breathtaking attacks, he would never have escaped the universal fate of weaklings. Again the kingbirds were right. According to the strictly practical ethics of nature, the Spartan code which subordinates the individual to the race, the weak must always die so that the strong may survive. But, mere man that I was, a renegade from nature and the child of a decadent humanitarian age, I followed the less practical ethics of my kind, which assume that the kingdom of nature is governed by a Bill of Rights based on the political philosophy of the eighteenth century, assuring, in the mystic name of Justice, the participation of weak and strong alike in the goods of this earth. My fault was human. But the kingbirds were right. The next day that same fledgling fell out of the tree again, and again I replaced him, in the teeth of their violent opposition. I don't suppose he survived the year, however. There are too many pitfalls in the path and only the strong and warlike can hope to hold their place on the program of nature.

I have heard a good many stories about the fierceness of a lioness in the defense of her cubs, but I would set my kingbird up against any lioness, real or legendary. Now that the young were out in the open, exposed to the attack of every passing hawk, he and his mate were transformed into a pair of Furies who anticipated the need of vengeance by harrying the countryside with a fierce, demoniac rage. The smaller birds were unmolested as long as they kept their distance. But an interdict was issued against all greater fowl, especially the hawks, who were proscribed from showing themselves anywhere within the circle of the horizon. No longer was there peace in the land. At any moment the air might be torn by the staccato shrieks of the kingbirds and I would spin about in time to see them go sizzling into the sky like a pair of rockets after a distant speck of a hawk passing through on the way to his feeding grounds. They always attacked from above, and the harassed hawk never made any attempt to meet the challenge except by escape. . . .

I am not much given to hero-worship, but before the summer was over I was persuaded that the kingbird could do no wrong. To a human being, endowed with the intelligence and imagination that distract men from their purpose, confuse their policy, and lead them into a morass of doubts and hesitations, the kingbird's ever-unhesitating choice of the right course could only command admiration. He never wavered between alternatives. He never questioned. He was never uncertain. And he was always amazingly right. The triumph of his sovereignty was inevitable from the first because it was inevitable that he should always use his powers to their best advantage. In the strength of his single-mindedness that little mite, not so big as my first, became a symbol of invincible purpose in nature.

The kingdom which he had come up from the south to establish in our apple tree was now justified by four brand-new princes clothed in the traditional black-and-white of their kind, their breasts immaculate, their tails tipped with white, the feathers of wing and back still fresh and unworn. It had taken them only a few days to learn proper kingbird flight, and now they knew all the tricks: how merely to vibrate their wing-tips for hovering and how to dig deep in the sprints, how to spread their tails for sudden turns, how to change their pace without interval, and how to glide in to their landings on motionless pinions. They accompanied their parents about the countryside in a screaming procession and flew after them to snatch prey from their bills in mid-air. Only the fact that their plumage was now shabby, that their breasts had darkened and the white edges of their wing-feathers worn off, distinguished the parents from their offspring. But the moulting season was at hand, and when the six kingbirds took their separate departures for the tropics there would no longer be any way of telling them apart.

Simultaneously with the development of the young birds' capacity to care for themselves, the inscrutable urge which had driven the kingbird over thousands of miles of land and sea, had prompted him to build a nest and take a mate, and had aroused in him a concern for the fledglings that resulted from the union, lost its strength. When the young birds no longer depended on him they became strangers and possible rivals who might, when the next nesting season came round, be attacked with as much vigor as they had been cherished during their upbringing. His mate became merely another bird whose existence did not concern him. Once more he was free of ties and responsibility.

Almost free, but not quite. As long as mortal beings are subject to the passage of time, the constant revolution of the four seasons, the steady march of days and hours—each minute leaving its faint, ineffaceable mark so that there can be no turning back from the universal end—as long as the earth and all its inhabitants continue to grow older, they can never be quite free. The kingbird's mission had been successfully accomplished, another generation had been produced. But there was some loss: a whole season of life had passed away. In a few more weeks the insects on which he depended for his livelihood would be gone, the leaves would be stripped from the trees, the first wintry frosts would wither the verdure of summer. Again he must move.

With millions of other birds, the majority pursuing their first migration (he no longer recognized his offspring among them), he began to drift southward. He had no vision of the approach of winter, for he could never have experienced it. But now a new urge had taken possession of him, growing stronger with the weeks. His life was once more shaped to a deliberate will which commanded it. That southern course was not new to him, but time had passed since he had last flown it, another year had been taken from the term of his life.

I like to picture my kingbird arriving once more in tropical lands on a warm November evening, after his long flight across the high seas, and resting for the night among the grass-covered ruins of some city of the jungle over which a monarch, centuries dead, had once held sway. It would be only poetic justice for him to enjoy the posthumous hospitality of a vanished empire, while in a bare apple tree to the north a bundle of grasses, tilted more than ever, now, and capped with a little mound of snow, remained as the last monument of his own temporal sovereignty.

COURTSHIP OF THE

HOUSE SPARROW AND

THE PEREGRINE FALCON

A.C. Bent

A.C. Bent's monumental Life Histories of North American Birds—
*its eighteen volumes were published one by one between 1919 and 1968—are
the lifework of a dedicated man. In part a compilation, they draw upon
both printed works and private communications from hundreds of observers. Here are Bent's accounts of the courtship of two American birds, the
ubiquitous and pedestrian house (or "English") sparrow and the scarce and
compelling peregrine falcon (previously called "duck hawk").*

T HE courtship of the English sparrow is more spectacular and
strenuous than elegant. It used to be a common experience to see
a group of these dirty, soot-begrimed street gamins struggling and fighting almost under our feet in our streets and gutters, oblivious to their
surroundings. Charles W. Townsend (1909) thus describes the actions of
the ardent male:

"With flattened back, head held up and tail down (up?), wings out
from the body, the tips of the primaries touching or nearly touching the
ground, he hops back and forth before the coy female as if on springs.
Not one but several dance thus before a lady who barely deigns to look
at them, and then only to peck in feigned disgust at the lovelorn suitors.
These pecks are often far from love pats. At times she stands in the
middle of a ring of males at whom she pecks viciously in turn as they fly
by, all chirping excitedly at the top of their lungs. The casual observer
might think the lady was being tormented by a crowd of ungallant
males, but the opposite is in reality the case for the lady is well pleased
and is showing her pretended feminine contempt for the male sex, who
on their part are trying their best to attract and charm her. At other
times she plants her bill firmly on the head of the suitor, and pecks at

From *Life Histories of North American Blackbirds, Orioles, Tanagers, and Allies.* Smithsonian Institution, Washington, D.C., 1958.

him violently from time to time without letting go her hold. I have seen several such one-sided fights, for the oppressed rarely fights back, where the male seemed to be on the verge of exhaustion, lying panting on the ground, but on being disturbed both birds flew off apparently none the worse. About a year ago I watched two males in fierce encounter on a small grass plot in front of my house. One had the other by the bill and held him back downwards on the grass. They were both using their claws vigorously and bracing with their wings. Occasionally they would roll over, or go head over heels. Breaking apart they would fly up at each other like enraged barn-yard cocks. Although I stood within two feet of them, so intent were they that they did not notice me until I made an incautious movement and they fled to fight elsewhere.

"A disgraceful fight between two female English Sparrows occurred in front of my house one April day. Catching each other by the bills they pulled and tugged and rolled over on the grass. When they broke away the fight was renewed a few inches above the ground in fighting cock style. Three males appeared, and watched the fight. One, evidently scandalized, endeavored to separate the Amazons by pecking at them, but they paid no attention to him and only after some time flew away, one chasing the other."

Claude T. Barnes has sent me the following interesting account of the mating of this strenuous species: "The incredible English sparrow is the best illustration of *furor amatorius*. The male suffers from satyriasis, the female from nymphomania. In the several years that we have observed them breeding, in two instances copulation took place fourteen times in succession, with a stopwatch record of five seconds for the act and five seconds for the interval. In each instance it was the soft *tee tee tee tee tee tee* of the female, sitting with outstretched wings that attracted our attention, and our count one was perhaps in reality two or three. Since other males within 20 feet took no interest, we believe that despite its reputation for promiscuity the domestic sparrow, after earlier imbroglios are settled, actually does mate with at least a short period of fidelity. Once mated, however, the female seems willing to continue the venery beyond the capacity of the male, for in every instance we have observed she continued her fluttering chant until he ceased to respond."

*   *   *   *   *

I N Massachusetts adult duck hawks reoccupy the breeding stations before the end of February, and since the first eggs are not laid

From *Life Histories of North American Birds of Prey*. U. S. Government Printing Office, Washington, D.C., 1938.

before March 25 or April 1, there is a long and interesting courtship. So wonderful are the aerial evolutions of the peregrines during this season that I am inclined to think that no observer can fully appreciate their powers of flight who has not seen them at the nesting site on a windy March day; every movement, no matter how extended, is centered about the home cliff, so that its whole course may be traced, which is not usually the case at other seasons and places.

There is some evidence that it is the male bird that is strongly attached to the cliff—that he returns there first and endeavors to attract a female, but if unsuccessful, remains there throughout the summer, while unmated females apparently roam about from place to place. Whether the duck hawk mates for life, and the female of the previous season returns directly to the cliff, if still alive (as has been generally assumed), I am not yet prepared to say, but I do recall very vividly a little drama that throws considerable light on the initial stages of courtship. This took place at Mount Sugarloaf on March 16 and involved a male peregrine that at that date, some three weeks after his return to the mountain, appeared to be still unmated. I had been watching him for more than an hour as he sat quietly on a dead pine above the cliff and during this whole period had heard no call or seen no such animation as is associated with the courting period. Suddenly, at about 9 o'clock, he launched out from his perch and began to sail back and forth along the face of the cliff, repeatedly giving the *wichew* or rusty-hinge note. A moment later I spotted a large female peregrine coming up the valley from the south, some 200 feet above the mountain. Arriving abreast of the cliff, she began to describe wide circles over the crest, flying very leisurely and seeming to watch the proceedings below her; the tercel redoubled his cries and flew from one shelf to another, alighting for a moment on each one and then swinging along to the next, with every appearance of the greatest excitement. The falcon, having presently completed three or four circles, now straightened her course toward the north, and picking up speed with every stroke of her wings soon disappeared in the haze along North Sugarloaf; the male continued his vain activity, wailing and *wichew*-ing for nearly a minute after she had passed from sight. He then made a short silent sally out over the valley and finally returned to sit hunched up and quiet on his dead tree for many minutes, before leaving on a hunting expedition behind the mountain. This episode introduces several of the elements of the courtship—the flight display, the shelf display, the coaxing *wichew* note —and it remains only to elaborate on their use and to mention the food-bringing routine.

The male assumes an aggressive role throughout the first part of the period, seeming to arouse and lead on the female from step to step of the reproductive cycle. With both birds at a cliff, early in March, the first business of each morning is feeding. Shortly after daylight the falcons will be discovered perched on their favorite dead trees on the upper part of the cliff, watching closely for the passing of some smaller bird suitable for prey. If none appears near at hand the male will sally out at intervals and go far across the valley, returning perhaps at the end of 20 or 30 minutes with a blue jay hanging limp in his talons. He wails while still at a distance, and the female, wailing in return, flies to meet him and receives the bird in the usual way. Or perhaps his search has been in vain, and he suddenly plunges down from a great height, empty-footed, to resume the watch from his perching tree. Perchance a flicker now appears flying up the valley at a considerable height above the trees, but still below the level of the hawks; they both start out from their trees and, stroking steadily, converge on the unfortunate bird with a speed and deadly earnestness chilling to the onlooker. The female takes the lead. The flicker sees its peril too late, and in a trice the falcon snatches it dead in the air and, turning sharply about, heads back for the cliff while her mate convoys her from behind. She lights on her tree, holding the bird against the branch with one foot, and in another moment flicker feathers are drifting down-wind as she eagerly plucks her booty. Meanwhile the tercel sallies forth again over the valley and this time returns with his bird. There are many variations of this morning scene—the birds may go away hunting together, the male may make his kill near the cliff, or the female may miss her stoop, in which case the tercel often stoops at the same bird—but certain parts of the pattern are quite invariable. In general, the female stays closer to home; if they both chase the same bird, the female makes the first stoop; and she eats the first bird whether she kills it herself or the male brings it to her.

Having fed, the hawks are likely to sit quietly for some little time, occasionally wailing to each other, preening their feathers, perhaps lazily stretching first one wing and then the other. At length the tercel starts off his perch and begins to soar and swoop about the cliff, describing a series of figure-eights in the air, sometimes in a horizontal, sometimes a vertical, plane. At times he lights on little shelves and *wichews;* again he returns to his tree and wails, or perhaps he soars higher and higher in the air, farther and farther out across the valley, until at last he shuts his wings to his sides and plunges down in a mile-long swoop that brings him back to the cliff. Sometimes the falcon accompanies him on these flights, but for the most part she is distinctly passive. The culmination of these flight displays depends much on the weather, but eventually the patient watcher will see an exhibition of flying that is literally breathtaking. I have seen it at many nest sites, but never to better advantage than one beautiful spring morning at Black Rock when a rising southerly gale was whipping along the flanks of Mount Everett. We were hidden in the woods below the south end of the cliff, and the peregrines were quite unconscious of our presence at the time; again and again the tercel started well to leeward and came along the cliff against the wind, diving, plunging, saw-toothing, rolling over and over, darting hither and yon like an autumn leaf until finally he would swoop up into the full current of air and be borne off on the gale to do it all over again. At length he tired of this, and, soaring in narrow circles without any movement of his wings other than a constant small adjustment of their planes, he rose to a position 500 or 600 feet above the mountain and north of the cliff. Nosing over suddenly, he flicked his wings rapidly 15 or 20 times and fell like a thunderbolt. Wings half closed now, he shot down past the north end of the cliff, described three successive vertical loop-the-loops across its face, turning completely upside down at the top of each loop, and roared out over our heads with the wind rushing through his wings like ripping canvas. Against the background of the cliff his terrific speed was much more apparent than it would have been in the open sky. The sheer excitement of watching such a performance was tremendous; we felt a strong impulse to stand and cheer.

As March advances, the male peregrine tries more and more to entice the female to certain shelves he has picked out. Between hunting trips and exercising flights above the valley he spends long intervals on these shelves, scratching around in the debris, *wichew*-ing in his most persuasive tones, standing at their front edges breast out to the sun, wailing mournfully now and then, and even flying to the female's roost tree to *wichew* at her in soft conversational tones. At first she pays no attention, nor leaves her tree, but gradually her passivity gives way to mild interest; she flies to the shelf where he is working and lights there; they both walk back out of sight and for a moment there is an outburst of argumentative *wichew*-ing and creaking as she seems to disagree emphatically with all his plans. Either bird may come off first, leaving the other to scratch and dig around, but as a rule they do not both stay. At any time now the female may be seen to return to her tree alone; the male *wichews* excitedly at one or more shelves and then comes off the cliff, flies directly to her with no other preliminaries, and copulation takes place to the accompaniment of a low, conversational, chuckling noise, which is entirely distinct from the usual notes. Coition is more likely to occur near the middle of the day and is usually repeated within an hour or so; it is also repeated on succeeding days until at least two eggs are in the nest.

The interest of the male in nesting shelves now begins to wane in inverse proportion to the female's increasing, though somewhat furtive, activity. While he is away hunting she may be seen going all over the cliff, squeezing into the most inadequate cracks and niches, scratching and scraping with bill and feet, turning round and round to get the feel of tentative nest hollows. At length she chooses the site, apparently with no reference to the male's previous selection, and in the course of a few days makes a smooth well-rounded scrape an inch or two deep. If disturbed at this time she is very likely to pick a new site at once and hurriedly prepare it, and I have several times had the experience of watching a falcon carefully form a nest hollow only to return after a short interval and discover the first eggs in quite a different spot on the cliff. The eggs are laid at intervals of every other day, with often two full days between the third and fourth.

IN DEFENSE

OF THE

PAIR BOND

John James Audubon

Part of the greatness of Audubon lies in the fact that he was both rigidly scientific within the limitations of his time and yet capable both of emotion himself and of recognizing it in birds.

IT is extremely amusing to witness the courtship of the Canada Goose in all its stages; and let me assure you, reader, that although a Gander does not strut before his beloved with the pomposity of a Turkey, or the grace of a Dove, his ways are quite as agreeable to the female of his choice. I can imagine before me one who has just accomplished the defeat of another male after a struggle of half an hour or more. He advances gallantly towards the object of contention, his head scarcely raised an inch from the ground, his bill open to its full stretch, his fleshy tongue elevated, his eyes darting fiery glances, and as he moves he hisses loudly, while the emotion which he experiences causes his quills to shake, and his feathers to rustle. Now he is close to her who in his eyes is all loveliness; his neck bending gracefully in all directions, passes all round her, and occasionally touches her body; and as she congratulates him on his victory, and acknowledges his affection, they move their necks in a hundred curious ways. At this moment fierce jealousy urges the defeated gander to renew his efforts to obtain his love; he advances apace, his eyes glowing with the fire of rage; he shakes his broad wings, ruffles up his whole plumage, and as he rushes on the foe, hisses with the intensity of anger. The whole flock seems to stand amazed, and opening up a space, the birds gather round to view the combat. The bold bird who has been caressing his mate, scarcely deigns to take notice of his foe, but

From *The Birds of America*. New York: George R. Lockwood & Son, 1870.

seems to send a scornful glance towards him. He of the mortified feelings, however, raises his body, half opens his sinewy wings, and with a powerful blow, sends forth his defiance. The affront cannot be borne in the presence of so large a company, nor indeed is there much disposition to bear it in any circumstances; the blow is returned with vigour, the aggressor reels for a moment, but he soon recovers, and now the combat rages. Were the weapons more deadly, feats of chivalry would now be performed; as it is, thrust and blow succeed each other like the strokes of hammers driven by sturdy forgers. But now, the mated gander has caught hold of his antagonist's head with his bill; no bull-dog could cling faster to his victim; he squeezes him with all the energy of rage, lashes him with his powerful wings, and at length drives him away, spreads out his pinions, runs with joy to his mate, and fills the air with cries of exultation.

SHOREBIRD

COURTSHIP

Peter Matthiessen

---

*Most Americans, even those who are active birders, have minimal experi-
ence with any aspect of the shorebird mating cycle, for the simple reason
that the great majority of shorebirds nest only in the bog-and-tundra country of the Far North. That the courtship displays of these birds are both
various and dramatic is made abundantly clear in this summary account
by Peter Matthiessen, one of our most talented contemporary writers.*

IN the great majority of shorebirds, the sexes are scarcely distinguishable in the field, even among those species in which the spring
plumage differs markedly from winter dress. In the Hudsonian godwit,
however, the seasonal red-browns of the male and female plumages are
distinguishable, and the spring male has more white in his back feathers. The phalaropes, too, are sexually dimorphic, though the differences
between male and female are not at all what one would expect; the male
phalarope is not larger and more gaudy than his mate, as in most birds,
but exactly the reverse, a chagrin he shares with the male jaçana.

Because the sexes are similar in most species, the voice is more important than spring plumage as a secondary sex character (the unique primary character, rightly enough, is the gonad), since it reveals not only
individual but sexual identity. In many shorebirds, cock and hen may
both add voices to the din—not surprisingly, since the shorebirds are
notoriously slack in regard to the roles of the sexes, not only in courtship but in nesting.

Certain species, although anxious for a hearing, do not use the syrinx
to achieve their finest sound effects. The lapwing, an occasional visitor
from Europe, uses its wing quills to produce an unmusical "chattering"
effect much to the liking of its females, to judge from the abundance of
this bird throughout its range. . . . The woodcock, with the three stiff
narrow feathers of its outer primaries, and the snipe, with the lateral
feathers of its short tail, produce analogous but dissimilar sounds best
known as "feather music," and the black turnstone is comparably

From *The Shorebirds of North America*. New York: Viking, 1967.

gifted, filling the air over its breeding grounds on the Alaska coast with a mighty *zum-zum-zum.*

As the male woodcock, like a love-struck leaf, flutters earthward for the benefit of its intended, the air forced past its quills produces an eerie quavering; the aerial evolutions of the snipe are accompanied by fantastic loud wild whifflings. In its passion, the snipe may fly short distances upside down, but its most stirring effects are not attained until its high-altitude maneuvers are completed; it now hurtles earthward as if bent on the total destruction of all beneath, traveling with such speed and force that its passage creates an awesome *ZOOM* or *BOOM.* In this sport, the snipe is tireless: one rainy June in the Northwest Territories, in the high moose-and-caribou country north of Ross River, I watched snipe careen through the huge gray skies for long days at a time, waking the heavens with the sound that has caused this shy creature to be known in Europe as the "thunderbird."

Unlike the snipe, knot, and other species which declare themselves on high, the Baird's sandpiper conducts itself discreetly, executing its "butterfly" flight but a few feet over the female's head. Variations on this slow flitting or shivering flight are practiced by most courting shorebirds (though for the Wilson's plover and the buff-breasted sandpiper, no courting flight of any kind has been reported); so is wild zigzag pursuit of one sex by the other. In the killdeer, golden plover, and several other species, both sexes participate in an aerial courtship flight, which, among killdeer at least, may last for an hour or more. There is also a kind of frantic hovering, which reaches its apogee in the Wilson's phalarope and the upland and stilt sandpipers, the last of which, in these exalted moments, permits itself a "donkey-like hee-haw."

The willet, once its passions are engaged, displays a fine high-stepping strut, and it also lifts its brilliant wing in amorous display, a habit shared, in spite of less flashy equipment, by the purple, the Baird's, and the buff-breasted sandpiper. The willet's wing has an auxiliary use as a flocking or flight signal, and the purple sandpiper, it appears, may raise its wing in simple greeting, but the wing display serves ordinarily as a deterrent to other males and as an attraction to the females. That its role as deterrent is the more important of the two is suggested by the behavior of the buff-breast. Like the rest, the buff-breast lifts a single wing, at which point it runs about as if giddy with pride in its silver wing lining. Yet sometimes it displays in perfect solitude, in silence, as if practicing for some dread fray which awaits it in the future, and often it performs for the edification of other males rather than for its females, which customarily pay no attention to it whatsoever.

Similarly, in the avocet, the idle males "stand in little groups and all talk at once. . . . A great deal of bowing and posing and running around each other takes place, and a variety of beautiful attitudes are assumed."

Paired short-billed dowitchers sing sweetly and bill tenderly like pigeons, the cock of the long-billed curlew strokes the hen with his magnificent proboscis, and even the ruddy turnstone, which largely dispenses with display, may "comb" his partner's head feathers with his bill. The sanderling, on the other hand, has no finesse at all. In this species, tender behavior and an attractive voice are replaced by marked pugnacity and a kind of "snarling"; its brusque attitude is impartially extended to mate and enemy alike.

The pectoral sandpiper, over its long evolutionary course, has hit upon a remarkable means to smooth the path of love; it has fitted itself out with a gular sac which, once inflated, transforms an otherwise indifferent voice into an awesome reverberation. The pectoral rises from the ground like a small balloon and, with head thrown back and tail straight down, sets sail across the tundra. Uttering strange boomings as it goes, it descends at last before its mate like a visitation.

SANDERLINGS

IN THE

ARCTIC SPRING

Rachel L. Carson

Rachel Carson was a biologist little known to the lay public until The Sea around Us *became one of the most praised and widely read nature books ever written in the United States. In the following excerpt from another book, she describes in more detail the nesting cycle of a particular shorebird.*

As the patches of earth spread over the snow fields, the sanderlings, plovers, and turnstones gathered in the cleared spots, finding abundant food. Only the knots resorted to the unthawed marshes and the protected hollows of the plains, where sedges and weeds lifted dry seed heads above the snow and rattled when the wind blew and dropped their seed for the birds.

Most of the sanderlings and the knots passed on to the distant islands scattered far over the Arctic sea, where they made their nests and brought forth their young. But Silverbar and Blackfoot and others of the sanderlings remained near the bay shaped like a leaping porpoise, along with turnstones, plovers, and many other shore birds. Hundreds of terns were preparing to nest on near-by islands, where they would be safe from the foxes; while most of the gulls retired inland to the shores of the small lakes which dotted the Arctic plains in summer.

In time Silverbar accepted Blackfoot as her mate and the pair withdrew to a stony plateau overlooking the sea. The rocks were clothed with mosses and soft gray lichens, first of all plants to cover the open and wind-swept places of the earth. There was a sparse growth of dwarf willow, with bursting leaf buds and ripe catkins. From scattered clumps of green the flowers of the wild betony lifted white faces to the sun,

From *Under the Sea-Wind*. New York: Oxford University Press, 1952.

and over the south slope of the hill was a pool fed by melting snow and draining to the sea by way of an old stream bed.

Now Blackfoot grew more aggressive and fought bitterly with every cock who infringed upon his chosen territory. After such a combat he paraded before Silverbar, ruffling his feathers. While she watched in silence he leaped into the air and hovered on fluttering wings, uttering neighing cries. This he did most often in the evening as the shadows lay purple on the eastern slopes of the hills.

On the edge of a clump of betony Silverbar prepared the nest, a shallow depression which she molded to her body by turning round and round. She lined the bottom with last year's dried leaves from a willow that grew prostrate along the ground, bringing the leaves one at a time and arranging them in the nest along with some bits of lichen. Soon four eggs lay on the willow leaves, and now Silverbar began the long vigil during which she must keep all wild things of the tundra from discovering the place of her nest.

During her first night alone with the four eggs Silverbar heard a sound new to the tundra that year, a harsh scream that came again and again out of the shadows. At early dawn light she saw two birds, dark of body and wing, flying low over the tundra. The newcomers were jaegers, birds of the gull tribe turned hawk to rob and kill. From that time on, the cries, like weird laughter, rang every night on the barrens. . . .

When Silverbar had begun to brood her eggs, the moon had been at the full. Since then it had dwindled to a thin white rim in the sky and now had grown again to the quarter, so that once more the tides in the bay were slacker and milder. One morning when the shore birds gathered over the flats to feed on the ebb tide, Silverbar did not join them. Throughout the night there had been sounds in the eggs under her breast feathers, now worn and frayed. They were the peckings of the sanderling chicks, after twenty-three days made ready for life. Silverbar inclined her head and listened to the sounds; sometimes she withdrew a little from the eggs and watched them intently. . . .

Now for the first time an abiding fear entered the heart of Silverbar —the fear of all wild things for the safety of their helpless young. With quickened senses she perceived the life of the tundra—with ears sharpened to hear the screams of the jaegers harrying the shore birds on the tide flats—with eyes quickened to note the white flicker of a gyrfalcon's wing.

After the fourth chick had hatched, Silverbar began to carry the shells, piece by piece, away from the nest. So countless generations of sanderlings had done before her, by their cunning outwitting the ravens and foxes. Not even the sharp-eyed falcon from his rock perch nor the jaegers watching for lemmings to come out of their holes saw the movement of the little brown-mottled bird as she worked her way, with infinite stealth, among the clumps of betony or pressed her body closely to the wiry tundra grass. Only the eyes of the lemmings who ran in and out among the sedges or sunned themselves on flat rocks near their burrows saw the mother sanderling until she reached the bottom of the ravine on the far side of the ridge. But the lemmings were gentle creatures who neither feared nor were feared by the sanderling.

All through the brief night that followed the hatching of the fourth chick Silverbar worked, and when the sun had come around to the east again she was hiding the last shell in the gravel of the ravine. A polar fox passed near her, making no sound as he trotted with sure foot over the shales. His eye gleamed as he watched the mother bird, and he sniffed the air, believing she had young nearby. Silverbar flew to the willows farther up the ravine and watched the fox uncover the shells and nose them. As he started up the slope of the ravine the sanderling fluttered toward him, tumbling to the ground as though hurt, flapping her wings, creeping over the gravel. All the while she uttered a high-pitched note like the cry of her own young. The fox rushed at her. Silverbar rose rapidly into the air and flew over the crest of the ridge, only to reappear from another quarter, tantalizing the fox into following her. So by degrees she led him over the ridge and southward into a marshy bottom fed by the overflow of upland streams. . . .

When Silverbar had led the fox far enough from her young she circled around by the bay flats, pausing to feed nervously for a few minutes at the edge of the salty tide. Then she flew swiftly to the betony clump and the four chicks on which the down was yet dark with the dampness of the egg, although soon it would dry to tones of buff and sand and chestnut.

Now the sanderling mother knew by instinct that the depression in the tundra, lined with dry leaves and lichens and molded to the shape of her breast, was no longer a safe place for her young. The gleaming eyes of the fox—the soft pad, pad of his feet on the shales—the twitch of his nostrils testing the air for scent of her chicks—became for her the symbols of a thousand dangers, formless and without name.

When the sun had rolled so low on the horizon that only the high cliff with the eyrie of the gyrfalcon caught and reflected its gleam, Silverbar led the four chicks away into the vast grayness of the tundra.

Throughout the long days the sanderling with her chicks wandered over the stony plains, gathering the young ones under her during the short chill nights or when sudden gusts of rain drove across the barrens. She led them by the shores of brimming fresh-water lakes into which loons dropped on whistling wings to feed their young. Strange new food was to be found on the shores of the lakes and in the swelling turbulence of feeder streams. The young sanderlings learned to catch insects or to find their larvae in the streams. They learned, too, to press themselves flat against the ground when they heard their mother's danger cry and to lie quite still among the stones until her signal brought them crowding about her with fine, high-pitched squeakings. So they escaped the jaegers, the owls, and the foxes.

By the seventh day after hatching, the chicks had quill feathers a third grown on their wings, although their bodies were still covered with down. After four more suns the wings and shoulders were fully clothed in feathers, and when they were two weeks old the fledgling sanderlings could fly with their mother from lake to lake . . .

Many of the cock sanderlings, who had been gathering in flocks about the fresh-water lakes almost from the time the chicks had begun to hatch, had already left for the south. Among them was Blackfoot. . . .

There came a day in August when Silverbar, who had been feeding with her grown young on the shores of the bay in company with other sanderlings, suddenly rose into the air with some twoscore of the older birds. The little flock wheeled out over the bay in a wide circle, flashing white wing bars; they returned, crying loudly as they passed over the flats where the young were still running and probing at the edge of the curling wavelets; they turned their heads to the south and were gone.

There was no need for the parent birds to remain longer in the Arctic. The nesting was done; the eggs had been faithfully brooded; the young had been taught to find food, to hide from enemies, to know the rules of the game of life and death. Later, when they were strong for the journey down the coast lines of two continents, the young birds would follow, finding the way by inherited memory. Meanwhile the older sanderlings felt the call of the warm south; they would follow the sun. . . .

THE

HOUSE WREN'S

NOTION OF

ARCHITECTURE

Elliott Coues

The wrens are among the relatively few birds who seem to take a genuine and sympathetic interest in men. The bird watcher is likely to find them stalking him for a change, and of course one species (the house wren) gets its name from its preference for the neighborhood of human habitation. No bird is "cuter," but his morals are not of the best and it is said that certain respectable old ladies took down their wren boxes when it was discovered some years ago that house wrens are likely to change mates in the middle of the season. The fanciful may imagine that this giddiness of character explains why they build the messy nests complained of below. Bohemians are notoriously not neat housekeepers.

THE birds seem to be afflicted with an *insanabile construendi cacoëthes* (to borrow a simile from Juvenal), which impels them to keep on building after they have built enough for any practicable purpose. Their notion seems to be, that whatever place they select, be it large or small, must be completely filled with a lot of rubbish before they can feel comfortable about it. When they nest in a knot-hole, or any cavity of inconsiderable dimensions, the structure is a mass of sticks and other trash of reasonable bulk; but the case is otherwise when they get behind a loose weather-board, for instance, where there is room enough for a dozen nests; then they never know when to stop. I witnessed a curious illustration of their "insane" propensities in one case where a pair found their way through a knot-hole into one of those small sheds which stands in the back-yard, with a well-worn path leading to the house, showing its daily use. (It should be premised that a wren likes to

From *Birds of the Colorado Valley*. Washington: U. S. Government Printing Office, 1878.

get into its retreat through the smallest possible orifice; if the entrance be small enough, there cannot be too much room inside; and, when the hole is unnecessarily large, it is often closed up to the right size.) Having entered through a nice little hole, into a dark place, the birds evidently supposed it was all right inside, and began to build in a corner under the roof, where the joists came together. Though annoyed by frequent interruption, the indefatigable little creatures, with almost painful diligence, lugged in their sticks till they had made a pile that would fill a bushel, and I cannot say they would not have filled the whole shed had they not been compelled to desist; for they were voted a nuisance, and the hole was stopped up. The size of the sticks they carried in was enormous in comparison with their own stature; it seemed as if they could not lift them, much less drag the crooked pieces through such a narrow orifice. These coarse materials, it will be remembered, are only the foundation of a nest, as it were; their use in places where there is no real occasion for such a mass of trash is evidently the remaining trace of primitive habits. Inside this pile of material, there is a compact cup-like nest proper, of various fine soft vegetable and animal substances. The birds are extremely prolific, ordinarily laying six or eight eggs; and they will continue to deposit more if the nest be robbed —sometimes to the number of three or four full clutches. The eggs themselves are too well known to require description. As to the sites of the nest, it is almost impossible to speak in specific terms. The old hat Audubon drew has become historic; the sleeve or pocket of a coat hung up in an outhouse—a box in a chaise from which the birds were often ejected, and to which they as often returned—boxes, jars, or gourds set up for Martins—skull of an ox or horse—nest of another bird—are among the odd places the birds have been known to fancy.

ON WATCHING

AN

OVENBIRD'S NEST

Margaret Morse Nice

The ringing song of the ovenbird is familiar to many inhabitants of the bird's wide breeding range, but it is a bird of the woodland shadows, seldom seen except by birders and woodsmen. Margaret Morse Nice, an amateur ornithologist who made great contributions to the discipline through her patient observation of common species, here describes the goings-on at an ovenbird's oven-shaped ground nest.

ONE Monday in July as I wandered through the woods, I was suddenly stopped by loud protestations. Looking about I saw an Ovenbird on a branch with his bill full of grubs while below on the ground beside the Dutch oven of a nest stood the mother bird, staring up at me absolutely motionless. As I walked towards her, she flew up, adding her objections to those of her mate. Inside the nest were two tiny infants, blind and naked. I retired behind a bush twenty feet away, effacing myself as much as possible, but the commotion kept on unabated. All the neighbors came to sympathize or look on—another pair of Ovenbirds, a Black and White Warbler, a Chestnut-sided Warbler, a Black-throated Green Warbler, a Phoebe, and a Chewink.

After awhile father with a moth in his bill descended to the ground, flew up again, scolded and scolded, raising his orange crown and jerking his tail; then he flew down again and ran towards the nest still objecting. His mate became frantic with alarm, on seeing such rash conduct; he reconsidered, flew up above the nest, ate his insect, and devoted himself to reproaches.

Seeing that the situation was hopeless, I moved forty feet away across the brook, seating myself beside a rock and behind a small hop hornbeam tree; with my glasses I could see the happenings at the nest. At once there was peace, and in two minutes mother went to the young to brood them. Soon Father came with a big spider and caterpillar; his mate slipped

From *The Watcher at the Nest*. New York: The Macmillan Company, 1939.

out and waited while he fed the babies, returning to them when he left.

Mother brooded and brooded, then slipped quietly off and walked away. For a long time she stayed away, finally reappearing as stealthily as she had left, bringing with her a large meal. The most striking thing about the routine of an Ovenbird's household is its deliberateness—broodings three-quarters of an hour long, meals sometimes an hour and a half apart—all in marked contrast to the ways of most warblers, whose broodings are short, and who bring food every five to ten minutes.

It seemed as if life stood still for me while I devoted myself to this nest, as if I had endless leisure to look, to enjoy, to think, alone in this pleasant place in the woods. The stately clusters of evergreen wood fern, the sun-dappled water beeches and hemlocks, the tiny waterfall—to these I could give but fleeting glances, for always I had to concentrate on the rocks and brown leaves about the center of activities of mother Ovenbird. A baby tree bowed; I seized my glasses, for any movement in that region was fraught with possible meaning. But the alarm was false. It is curious how one small branch will bend with a breeze that nothing else feels. In these vigils I learned much of the ways of the wind.

Often there was no sound but the tumbling brook. Sometimes there were discordant notes. A soft pattering across the leaves, and suddenly a red squirrel vented his wrath at my presence by the strangest squeaks and squeals, more like those we expect from a toy than those from a real animal. A gray squirrel flirted his handsome tail in quirks and curlicues and then exploded into a snarling, jarring string of vituperations, extraordinary noises to proceed from such a soft and furry little beast.

The birds were pure delight. The Scarlet Tanager threw a wild, proud challenge to the woods in keeping with his gorgeous plumage. The solemn, continuous strain of the Red-eyed Vireo embodied the very spirit of serenity and content. Most beautiful of all was the song of the Hermit Thrush; when heard near by it has a note of courage, of triumph over the difficulties of life; at a distance it expresses ineffable sweetness and peace.

Mother Ovenbird had her notions; she did not mind me looking at her when she was by the nest, but if ever I caught sight of her on her way there, she froze at once, and would not be reassured until I had put down the offending glasses. It was curious that on Tuesday morning, of the five intervals between the meals she brought, four lasted exactly forty-eight minutes each.

That afternoon I noted:

"How pretty mother looks inside her rustic bower! She steps out and views the weather, which is threatening; then withdraws again to shelter."

Father was an almost negligible factor in the home life during the first half of the week, for he seldom came with food, sometimes absenting

himself for an afternoon at a time, and he did not even proclaim his
territory with the loud, insistent *teacher teacher teacher teacher*, as is the
custom of his kind earlier in the season. On Wednesday I was shocked to
see a Hermit Thrush chase him three times, when he had had one of his
rare impulses to bring food to the young.

Although most of the authorities state that male and female Ovenbirds
are identical in appearance, I was glad to find that I could distinguish my
birds, not only by the brighter orange crown of the male, but particularly
by the color of their backs, father's being more golden brown, and
mother's having more of an olive cast.

Mr. Mousley "never once approached the nest" of the Ovenbirds he
was studying; but by choosing my time I could steal across the brook
each day and admire the progress of the babies without the parents being
any the wiser. Although little Ovenbirds are fed so seldom in comparison with most other baby birds, their meals make up in size what
they lack in number. I was repeatedly astonished at the enormous mouthfuls of spiders, caterpillars and moths that were brought to the young.

Thursday afternoon there came a change in the schedule. Mother gave
up brooding and guarded instead, mounting a near-by bush and sitting
quietly for fifteen minutes or so, her handsome black-streaked breast
puffed out—a picture of motherly satisfaction. Father suddenly woke
up to his responsibilities, and for the rest of the week outdid his mate
in bringing food. Instead of meals appearing once every forty-two minutes, they now came at the rate of once in twenty minutes, the difference
being largely due to father's zeal, since mother kept on the even tenor
of her way, hardly hastening her return at all.

On Saturday morning the young had been fed at 10:35 and I was beginning to feel that it was full time they received further attention:
"11:35. A bird flies down two yards from the nest. She feeds; then the
male comes walking over the leaves. She steps aside for him while he
feeds. Strangely enough a gaping, reproachful mouth waves at them
as they leave, like a comic picture of a ferocious snake. Did both large
portions go into one maw?"

On Sunday morning as I neared the familiar spot, I heard mother
scolding very hard and fast. It was plain that something had happened;
I went directly to the nest and found it empty. I had never dreamt that
the precocious little creatures would leave so soon. How could they
have deserted their warm, dry, cozy home for the wild wet woods?

Sadly I returned to my accustomed post; soon it was evident that one
baby was near the nest in mother's charge, while the other was in a bed
of ferns tended by the father. So I watched the family for some time,
not realizing how far a little Ovenbird may travel at such a tender age;
when I went to investigate, mother's babe was far away and well hidden.
The fern bed was a baffling place to search, but all at once I heard a

shrill *peep peep peep;* following the sound I discovered baby looking like a little light brown leaf, the fuzz of down outside his feathers giving him a very odd appearance. His tail had barely sprouted, and his flight feathers were not unsheathed; he could not possibly have flown, but his legs were strong and well developed.

I gently picked him up and he was not a bit afraid; in a few minutes he went to sleep in my hand. Father appeared with a caterpillar, but instead of going through the extravagant demonstration of alarm I expected, merely gave a loud *tchip* and vanished. Baby begin to preen himself, then said *peep* and again *peep.* A mosquito started to bite my hand, and I brought it in front of the little bird as a small tidbit; but he did not peck at it till it flew. Another alighted on his wing and sucked itself full, while I perceived a new bond of sympathy between birds and people.

Presently baby grew hungry and called more and more frequently, so I returned him to his twig and went back to my hornbeam. Louder and more persistent came his far-reaching cries, until I could not help thinking how easily an enemy might find him. It was time for me to go home; as I passed the fern bed I stepped on a dead twig that snapped—instantly there was silence. I do not suppose the little fellow had ever heard this sound before, but something in his inherited make-up told him it spelled danger. I was not able to visit this family again, but I hope they escaped the perils of youth, and journeyed South in safety.

By good fortune the next summer I again discovered an Ovenbird's nest in the Grey Rocks woods in mid-July. The mother flew quietly away from her three eggs, but the following day she behaved differently. While her mate scolded at my approach, she hurried off, then turned back, and ran about in a peculiar attitude with her back hunched, wings dragging, tail spread fanwise and body feathers puffed out. There was no simulation of injury, but she certainly did look strange and conspicuous and well suited to draw the attention of an unsophisticated enemy to herself.

The next morning (which happened to be Monday) two babies had hatched. I settled myself twenty feet away behind a little hemlock, thankful that neither parent had seen me look at their progeny. Before long there was a rustle in the great hemlock to the south and I became motionless while mosquitoes settled over my face. I felt like St. Macarius who, inadvertently crushing a gnat and thereby missing an opportunity of enduring mortification patiently, stationed himself for six months in the marshes of Scete. Fortunately for me, little mother took only three minutes to decide that I was not too alarming a neighbor. She flew to the ground and walked to the nest where she fed the babies and stepped in to brood. Then I began once more on my occupation of reducing the pests of the world.

Mother covered her children for fifty-four minutes, then walked away, but to my surprise returned in ten minutes with another large meal—the other mother had never spent less than seventeen minutes away. This time she waited in the hemlock two minutes and the next time only one, and after that bothered no more about me. How my heart warmed to her for her good sense and devotion!

Her mate, unfortunately, felt differently about me. He came once that morning to bestow a morsel on his offspring, but upon spying me, he started to scold and for one half-hour he protested; then he departed, not to be seen again that day nor the next. In an attempt to calm his nerves, I moved farther away; but even that concession did not reassure him. Sometimes I hear his loud announcement of ownership and very occasionally the ecstatic flight song; but he refused to risk his precious skin by coming near me.

For three days the routine varied very little; long broodings; sometimes long, sometimes short, absences from the nest; ten large meals brought during eight hours the first day, eleven the next, and fourteen the next—and every bit of the work done by mother. Oddly enough there were two intervals of forty-eight minutes on this Tuesday, one of forty-six, and one of forty-four.

Wednesday father appeared with a contribution; but instead of feeding his babies all he did was to reprove me, raise his crest, flutter his wings, and give a curious, soft, three-syllable note to his mate. She, as if in a spirit of bravado to show him the unreasonableness of his fears, did a thing without precedent, for she dropped directly down to the nest from a branch above it. (Every other time she walked from quite a distance to the nest.) Still he remained stubbornly distrustful.

One day I had a philosophic thought; namely, that pleasure was given to three sets of beings by the occasional visits from the biting flies: First, it must seem like a banquet to the flies to discover me still and tasty in the woods. Next, there was a distinct feeling of achievement within me when I dispatched the creatures. And finally the carcass was a boon to the ant that carried it off for a dinner with her sisters. My philosphizings vanished, however, the next day when I was attacked by an army of deer flies. I used to think the etymology of Beelzebub—"king of the flies"—was a prophetic reference to the noxious germs given us by our satellite the housefly, but now I knew better; it was these little demons that were meant.

This year as last, Thursday afternoon showed a change in the home life; but this time the male had no part in it. First, mother gave up brooding; then, instead of walking directly away when leaving the nest as heretofore, she browsed around for a few minutes in front of the nest, finding small insects for herself; twice she flew away instead of leaving on foot; and finally she fed her three children twice as often as before.

The first three and one-half days she had brought meals once in forty minutes on an average; this afternoon she presented them once every nineteen minutes. I looked forward eagerly to what the next day would bring forth, in further variations in her behavior and a possible reform on the part of her mate.

As I watched little mother, I longed to know more of her life. I wished I could have seen the courtship, could have viewed the construction of the quaint little home, and then could have followed the fortunes of the young family after their first venture into the world, and somehow could have known how they found their way on the incredible journeys to South America and back to these Massachusetts woods. A great admiration for this quiet little bird arose in me, for her self-sufficiency, the simplicity of her life unencumbered by the possessions that overwhelm us human beings. Here she was her own architect, her own provider, bringing up her babies independently of doctors, nurses, books, and even her husband, facing unaided the elements and prowling enemies.

Each morning I left a blessing with the brave little bird, and each morning was happy to find all well. But Friday as I walked through the woods, I noticed that big mushrooms that had been standing for several days were now lying low, gnawed by some animal. A sense of foreboding caused me to go straight to the nest as soon as I reached my hemlock; the home was empty and beside it lay five feathers from little mother's wing. I trust the gallant bird had escaped with her life.

THE

GROWING FAMILY

Helen G. Cruickshank

Just as successful courtship leads to mating, which leads to eggs, so success-fully incubated eggs produce nestlings. "Precocial" young—those of grouse and shorebirds, for example—are active and relatively independent upon hatching, but the young of many more species are "altricial," born helpless and requiring extended parental care. Helen G. Cruickshank gives us an overview of the nestling life of these birds.

E VERY species has its own code of signals essential for courtship and the formation of the pair; without the correct signals the birds cannot mate. Signals of a different kind are just as vital to the survival of the young birds, who must indicate to their parents when they are hungry and where to put the food. Many altricial birds, especially songbirds, have brightly colored bills that will fade once they are old enough to care for themselves. White, cream, or yellow skin usually surrounds the gape so that when the bill is opened the inside of the huge mouth looks rather like a bright, diamond-shaped flower. Striking colors line the mouth and point the way to the throat, where food must be placed or the nestling cannot swallow it. Anybody who has ever acted as foster parent to a baby crow knows that putting food near the tip of the bill is useless; it must be pushed deep into the throat until you feel the strong pull of the muscles there as the food is sucked down.

The vivid mouth lining of some horned larks is emphasized by black dots that point the way down, and a few birds have beadlike structures that seem to glow, especially useful in dark nests. House sparrows have tiny knobs in the mouth that reflect light, and a young meadowlark has white hairlike growths on the roof of the mouth that point toward the throat, like the hairs of a pitcherplant leaf. Two large, white-edged projections in the lower jaw seem to say, "Put it here."

No matter what color the mouth lining of the baby birds (red, or-ange, or yellow, or a combination of these colors), or what the added

From *The Nesting Season: The Bird Photographs of Frederick Kent Truslow*. New York: Viking, 1979.

decorations (black, white, blue, green, purple, or opalescent), the sight arouses frantic efforts by the parents. We know that these are special targets to aid the parents in feeding their young because as soon as the youngsters can feed themselves, the bright colors fade and the decorations vanish. In addition to color signals, songbird nestlings attract the attention of their food-bearing parents by stretching their necks as far as they can, quivering their heads, and cheeping furiously.

A female robin incubates her eggs alone, but as soon as they hatch, a deep-seated instinct to feed them is aroused in the male. He stops singing and defending his territory to join his mate in collecting food for the hatchlings. Visits to the nest by both parents follow one another quickly; sometimes both arrive at the same time, each with a bill crammed with earthworms, which are stuffed into the gaping mouths.

A helpless infant robin develops quickly. By the third day its blind eyes begin to open, and at five days it can turn in the nest to face its parents as they arrive with food. When seven days old it exercises legs and wings, and at ten days it preens the unsheathed feathers that began to push through the skin at four days of age. It begins to peck at objects in the nest and sometimes at its nest siblings. By the time the robins are thirteen days old and ready to leave the nest, their birth weight has multiplied many times over. It has been estimated that a young robin can eat fourteen feet of earthworms in a single day. Anyone who has tried to find some earthworms for fishing on a late spring day wonders how the robins find enough of them to cope with the insatiable hunger of four or five demanding nestlings. By the end of two weeks, a robin chick will manage a weak, fluttering flight away from the nest. In those few short days it has changed from a tiny, helpless infant into a bird as heavy as its parents.

We know that birds have the highest metabolism of any creatures in the world and require a great deal of food just to survive. Baby birds must grow rapidly. The chicks of many species eat their own weight in food each day. Because of the enormous amount of food required, young birds usually hatch at a time when food is most abundant; swarms of midges, damselflies, mosquitoes, and other insects often coincide with the arrival of chicks, as does the appearance of seeds, berries, and other fruits. We rarely consider in concrete terms the amount of food young birds consume. Dr. Niko Tinbergen, after studying a large gull colony off the coast of Britain, estimated that at the height of the season in a gull colony of approximately forty-eight thousand growing gulls, about twenty tons of food were transported to the island daily, or almost a pound for each young gull. Often the amounts fed are small, but the frequency of feeding is high. When barn swallows are eight days old they are fed about once a minute. House wrens have fed their young 491 times a day, while phoebes have been known to take food to their young a grand total of 845 times in a single day. It is no surprise that many passerine birds grow so rapidly!

A California condor, however, seldom feeds its single young more than twice a day, and it grows so slowly that it must remain in the nest for four to five months. Golden eagles feed their young only three or four times a day. Both these raptors range widely to find the prey to take to the nest, but probably no bird in the world flies so far to find the needed food as the wandering albatross. Bands attached to their legs prove that these adults will travel up to twenty-five hundred miles from their nests to find food for their slow-growing, infrequently fed, single chicks. White pelicans are tiny and helpless at hatching, but by the time they are sixty days old they weigh from three to five pounds more than their sixteen-pound parents. This surplus weight must be lost before they can make a genuine flight.

Raptors, such as hawks, eagles, and owls, catch their food in their talons and use these same talons to carry the food to the nest. Red-tailed hawks appear to be especially fond of snakes; it is not uncommon to see one of them flying heavily with a large black snake dangling below like the mooring of a balloon. Black snakes eat many young birds; then, in turn, they become food for other nestlings. At first, predatory birds tear their prey apart and place bits in the mouths of the young, but later on, the prey is simply dropped on the nest and the young must tear it apart themselves. The hummingbird female carries nothing visible to the nest, but her crop is filled with nectar and tiny insects. The two young hummingbirds, aware of her approach, open their slender bills wide and she thrusts her bill inside one of the gaping mouths and begins to jab up and down. It is an alarming sight, for it seems certain that she will kill her delicate young. Though her actions appear savage and even deadly, her method of feeding is effective. Gorged at last, the chicks subside and sleep off the nutritious meal.

LEAST TERNS

ON CAPE COD

Henry Beston

Many reproductive efforts are, of course, unsuccessful; most birds' nests are as vulnerable as the eggs they contain are delicate. Nests are predated by mammals and snakes and other birds. They are destroyed—both accidentally and deliberately—by man, his pets, and his vehicles. And, as Henry Beston reminds us in his classic book The Outermost House, *nature's own weather plays culprit as well.*

THE most interesting adventure with birds I have had this summer I had with a flock of least terns, *Sterna antillarum.* It came to pass that early one morning in June, as I happened to be passing big dune, a covey of small terns unexpectedly sailed out at me and hovered about me, scolding and complaining. To my great delight, I saw that they were least terns or "tit gulls," rare creatures on our coast, and perhaps the prettiest and most graceful of summer's ocean birds. A miniature tern, the "leastie," scarce larger than a swallow, and you may know him by the lighter grey of his plumage, his bright lemon-yellow bill, and his delicate orange-yellow feet.

The birds were nesting at the foot of big dune, and I had disturbed their peace. In the splendour of morning they hung above me, now uttering a single alarmed cheep, now a series of staccato cries.

I walked over to the nests.

The nest of such a beach bird is a singular affair. It is but a depression, and sometimes scarcely that, in the open, shelterless beach. "Nest building on the open sand," says Mr. Forbush, "is but the work of a moment. The bird alights, crouches slightly, and works its little feet so rapidly that the motion seems a mere blur, while the sand flies out in every direction as the creature pivots about. The tern then settles lower and smooths the cavity by turning and working and moving its body from side to side."

I have mislaid the scrap of paper on which I jotted down the number of nests I found that morning, but I think I counted twenty to twenty-

From *The Outermost House.* New York: Rinehart and Co., 1928.

five. There were eggs in every nest, in some two, in others three, in one case and one only, four. To describe the coloration of the shells is difficult, for there was a deal of variation, but perhaps I can give some idea of their appearance by saying that they were beach-coloured with overtones of bluish green, and speckled with browns and violet-browns and lavenders. What interested me most, however, was not the eggs, but the manner in which the birds had decorated their nests with pebbles and bits of shell. Here and there along the beach, the "leasties" had picked up flat bits of sea shell about the size of a finger nail, and with these bits they had lined the bowl of their nests, setting the flat pieces in flat, like parts of a mosaic.

For two weeks I watched these "leasties" and their nests, taking every precaution not to disturb or alarm the setting birds. Yet I had but to pass anywhere between them and the tide to put them up, and when I walked south with coast guardsmen, I heard single cries of alarm in the starry and enormous night. Toward the end of June, a sudden northeaster came.

It was a night storm. I built a little fire, wrote a letter or two, and listened to the howling wind and the bursts of rain. All night long, and it was a wakeful, noisy night, I had the "leasties" on my mind. I felt them out there on the wild shelterless beach, with the black gale screaming over them and the rain pouring down. Opening my door, I looked for a moment into the drenching blackness and heard a great roaring of the sea.

The tide and the gale had ebbed together when I rose at five the next morning, but there was still wind and a grey drizzle. At the foot of big dune I found desolation. The tide had swept the beach. Not a nest remained or a sign of a nest, and the birds had gone. Later that day, just south of big dune, I saw bits of bluish-green eggshell in a lump of fresh weed. Where the birds went to, I never knew. Probably to a better place to try again.

Part

Five

BIRDS OF A FEATHER

TURKIES

Thomas Morton

All men are alike, said Montaigne, or we would not know that they were men; all men are different, or we could not tell them one from another. The thing which makes them different is what we call "personality," and no other species has so much of it as man has. Individual men have, in other words, more individuality; individual members of every other species are more like one another. Nonconformity is a conspicuous trait of the human being.

Though ornithologists have recently come to realize that even birds sometimes exhibit more individual personality than used to be supposed and that there are nonconformists sometimes found among them, the fact remains that when we speak of the "character" of this bird or that, we usually mean the character of the species to which it belongs. And how different those characters are! The rigidly scientific object to our saying that eagles have dignity, that wrens are impudent, or that peacocks are vain, but we will go on saying it nevertheless. And the scientist himself will stress the fact that species are sometimes so different from one another that it is only by anatomical and other analyses that we are able to say of, for instance, the penguin and the swift that both are birds.

The present section of this volume deals with a few outstanding personalities among American birds.

We begin with Thomas Morton—something of a character himself—and the wild turkey.

Most early American colonists were little interested in birds beyond their edibility. Thomas Morton was no exception in this respect, but he was an exception in many others. He was so far from being a puritan that he called the settlement of which he became the head Merrymount, set up a maypole there, and thus scandalized his neighbors in Plymouth Colony. Hawthorne immortalized him in Twice Told Tales *but he seems, unfortunately, to have been in fact a rather scurrilous character whose reputation was dubious even before he left England. In the New World he violated the law by supplying firearms to the Indians, and he was at one time sentenced to banishment. His book,* New English Canaan, *published in 1637, was denounced by a rival author as "full of lies and slanders, and full fraught with profane calumnies." However, he seems to have been sound enough on the wild turkey, with the proviso that it would have required two very large birds to reach the figure of forty-eight pounds.*

TURKIES there are, which divers times in great flocks have sallied by our doores; and then a gunne (being commonly in a redinesse), salutes them with such a courtesie, as makes them take a turne in the Cooke roome. They daunce by the doore so well.

Of these there hath bin killed, that have weighed forty eight pound a peece.

They are mainy degrees sweeter than the tame Turkies of England, feede them how you can.

I had a Salvage who hath taken out his boy in a morning, and they have brought home their loades about noone.

I have asked them what number they found in the woods, who have answered Neent Metawna, which is a thousand that day; the plenty of them is such in those parts. They are easily killed at rooste, because the one being killed, the other sit fast neverthe lesse, and this is no bad commodity.

From *New English Canaan*, or *New Canaan*. Printed at Amsterdam by Jacob Frederick Stamm, 1637.

THE

BALD EAGLE

Mark Catesby

One of the important pioneer explorers of the natural history of what is now the United States was Mark Catesby, who came here first in 1712 and returned to England a few years later with what was called the best botanical collection that had ever been made on our continent. He later came back to America, but returned to his native England to work on his Magnum Opus. He died there in 1749 after publishing in two volumes an excellent *Natural History of Carolina, Florida, and the Bahama Islands.*

Here are three of his bird portraits from that work.

This Bird weighs nine pounds: the Iris of the eye white; over which is a prominence, cover'd with a yellow skin; the Bill yellow, with the Sear of the same colour: the Legs and Feet are yellow; the Tallons black, the Head and part of the Neck is white, as is the Tail; all the rest of the Body, and Wings, are brown.

Tho' it is an Eagle of a small size, yet has great strength and spirit, preying on Pigs, Lambs, and Fawns.

They always make their Nests near the sea, or great rivers, and usually on old, dead Pine or Cypress-trees, continuing to build annually on the same tree, till it falls. Though he is so formidable to all birds, yet he suffers them to breed near his royal nest without molestation; particularly the fishing and other Hawks, Herons, etc. which all make their nests on high trees; and in some places are so near one another, that they appear like a Rookery. This Bird is called the BALD EAGLE, both in Virginia and Carolina, though his head is as much feather'd as the other parts of his body.

Both Cock and Hen have white Heads, and their other parts differ very little from one another.

From *The Natural History of Carolina, Florida, and the Bahama Islands*. London: Printed for C. Marsh, in Round Court in the Strand; and T. Wilcox, over-against the New Church, in the Strand, 1754.

THE "SEA-DOTTREL": RUDDY TURNSTONE

THIS Bird has, in proportion to its body, a small head, with a strait taper black bill, an inch long. All the upper part of the body is brown, with a mixture of white and black. The quill feathers of the wings are dark brown; the neck and breast are black; the legs and feet light red. In a voyage to America, in the year 1722, in 31 deg N. Lat. and 40 leagues from the coast of Florida, the Bird, from which this was figur'd, flew on board us, and was taken. It was very active in turning up stones, which we put into its cage; but not finding under them the usual food, it died. In this action it moved only the upper mandible; yet would with great dexterity and quickness turn over stones of above three pounds weight. This property Nature seems to have given it for the finding of its food, which is probably Worms and Insects on the Sea-shore. By comparing this with the description of that in Will. Ornitholog. which I had then on board, I found this to be the same kind with that he describes.

"CARPENTEROS": THE IVORY-

BILLED WOODPECKER

THE Largest White-bill Woodpecker weighs twenty ounces; and is about the size, or somewhat larger than a Crow. The bill is white as ivory, three inches long, and channelled from the basis to the point: the iris of the eye yellow: the hind part of the head adorned with a large peaked crest of scarlet feathers: a crooked white stripe runs from the eye on each side of the neck, towards the wing: the lower part of the back and wings (except the large quill feathers) are white: all the rest of the Bird is black.

The bills of these Birds are much valued by the Canada Indians, who make coronets of them for their Princes and great warriors, by fixing them round a wreath, with their points outward. The Northern Indians, having none of these Birds in their cold country, purchase them of the Southern people at the price of two, and sometimes three buck-skins a bill.

These Birds subsist chiefly on Ants, Wood-worms, and other Insects, which they hew out of rotten trees; nature having so formed their bills, that in an hour or two they will raise a bushel of chips; for which the Spaniards call them *Carpenteros*.

THE

EASTERN

MEADOWLARK

Alexander Wilson

Readers will find an account of Alexander Wilson's life and career in Elsa G. Allen's essay in Part Six of this volume.

Since Wilson concludes this piece by correcting a fellow ornithologist's mistake, we may perhaps be forgiven for pointing out that he himself was quite wrong to assume that our meadowlarks are members of the lark family. They belong, instead, to the blackbird and oriole family.

T HOUGH this well-known species cannot boast of the powers of song which distinguish that "harbinger of day," the Sky Lark of Europe, yet in richness of plumage, as well as in sweetness of voice (as far as his few notes extend), he stands eminently its superior. He differs from the greater part of his tribe in wanting the long straight hind claw, which is probably the reason why he has been classed, by some late naturalists, with the Starlings. But in the particular form of his bill, in his manners, plumage, mode and place of building his nest, nature had clearly pointed out his proper family.

This species has a very extensive range; having myself found them in Upper Canada, and in each of the states from New Hampshire to New Orleans. Mr. Bartram also informs me that they are equally abundant in East Florida. Their favourite places of retreat are pasture fields and meadows, particularly the latter, which have conferred on them their specific name; and no doubt supplies them abundantly with the particular seeds and insects on which they feed. They are rarely or never seen in the depth of the woods; unless where, instead of underwood, the ground is covered with rich grass, as in the Choctaw and Chickasaw countries, where I met with them in considerable numbers in the

From *American Ornithology; or, The Natural History of the Birds of the United States,* in 3 vols. New York and Philadelphia: Collins & Co., 1828.

months of May and June. The extensive and luxuriant prairies between Vincennes and St. Louis also abound with them.

It is probable that in the more rigorous regions of the north they may be birds of passage, as they are partially so here; though I have seen them among the meadows of New Jersey, and those that border the rivers Delaware and Schuylkill, in all seasons; even when the ground was deeply covered with snow. There is scarcely a market day in Philadelphia, from September to March, but they may be found in market. They are generally considered, for size and delicacy, little inferior to the quail, or what is here usually called the partridge, and valued accordingly. I once met with a few of these birds in the month of February, during a deep snow, among the heights of the Alleghany between Shippensburg and Somerset, gleaning on the road, in company with the small snow-birds. In the states of South Carolina and Georgia, at the same season of the year, they swarm among the rice plantations, running about the yards and outhouses, accompanied by the Kildeers, with little appearance of fear, as if quite domesticated.

These birds, after the building season is over, collect in flocks; but seldom fly in a close compact body; their flight is something in the manner of the grous and partridge, laborious and steady; sailing, and renewing the rapid action of the wings alternately. When they alight on trees or bushes, it is generally on the tops of the highest branches, whence they send forth a long, clear, and somewhat melancholy note, that in sweetness and tenderness of expression is not surpassed by any of our numerous warblers. This is sometimes followed by a kind of low, rapid chattering, the particular call of the female; and again the clear and plaintive strain is repeated as before. They afford tolerable good amusement to the sportsman, being most easily shot while on wing; as they frequently squat among the long grass, and spring within gunshot. The nest of this species is built generally in, or below, a thick tuft or tussock of grass; it is composed of dry grass, and fine bent laid at bottom, and wound all around, leaving an arched entrance level with the ground; the inside is lined with fine stalks of the same materials, disposed with great regularity. The eggs are four, sometimes five, white, marked with specks and several large blotches of reddish brown, chiefly at the thick end. Their food consists of caterpillars, grub worms, beetles, and grass seeds; with a considerable proportion of gravel. Their general name is the *Meadow Lark;* among the Virginians they are usually called the *Old Field Lark.*

The length of this bird is ten inches and a half, extent sixteen and a half; throat, breast, belly, and line from the eye to the nostrils, rich yellow; inside lining and edge of the wing the same; an oblong crescent of deep velvety black ornaments the lower part of the throat; lesser wing-coverts black, broadly bordered with pale ash; rest of the wing feathers light brown, handsomely serrated with black; a line of yellowish white passes over each eye backwards; cheeks bluish white, back and rest of the upper parts beautifully variegated with black, bright bay, and pale ochre: tail wedged, the feathers neatly pointed, the four outer ones on each side, nearly all white; sides, thighs and vent pale yellow ochre, streaked with black; upper mandible brown, lower bluish white; eyelids furnished with strong black hairs; legs and feet very large, and of a pale flesh colour.

The female has the black crescent more skirted with gray, and not of so deep a black. In the rest of her markings the plumage differs little from that of the male. I must here take notice of a mistake committed by Mr. Edwards in his *History of Birds*, Vol. VI, p. 123, where, on the authority of a bird dealer of London, he describes the Calandre Lark (a native of Italy and Russia) as belonging also to N. America, and having been brought from Carolina. I can say with confidence, that in all my excursions through that and the rest of the southern states, I never met such a bird, nor any person who had ever seen it. I have no hesitation in believing that the Calandre is not a native of the United States.

THE KING

OF SONG

Edward Howe Forbush

Thoreau once commented indignantly upon the fact that the state of Massachusetts, like most of its citizens, was indifferent to nature except in so far as it affected the pocketbook, and that its only entomological publication was called Injurious Insects—*as though they alone could concern anyone. Perhaps he would have been mollified had he been able to foresee the official publication from which the following description of the northern mockingbird has been taken.*

I HAVE written elsewhere as follows regarding the Mockingbird as a songster: "The Mockingbird stands unrivaled. He is the king of song. This is a trite saying, but how much it really means can be known only to those who have heard this most gifted singer uncaged and at his best in the lowlands of the Southern States. He equals and even excels the whole feathered choir. He improves upon most of the notes that he reproduces, adding also to his varied repertoire the crowing of chanticleer, the cackling of the hen, the barking of the house dog, the squeaking of the unoiled wheelbarrow, the postman's whistle, the plaints of young chickens and turkeys and those of young wild birds, not neglecting to mimic his own offspring. He even imitates man's musical inventions. Elizabeth and Joseph Grinnell assert that a Mockingbird was attracted to a graphophone on the lawn where, apparently, he listened and took mental notes of the performance, giving the next day, a week later, or at midnight an entertainment of his own and then repeating it with the exact graphophone ring. Even the notes of the piano have been reproduced in some cases and the bird's vocalization simulates the lightning changes of the kaleidoscope.

"The Mocker is more or less a buffoon, but those who look upon him only as an imitator or clown have much to learn of his wonderful originality. His own song is heard at its best at the height of the love season, when the singer flutters into the air from some tall tree-top and impro-

From *Birds of Massachusetts and Other New England States*. Published by the Commonwealth of Massachusetts, 1929.

vises his music, pouring out all the power and energy of his being in such an ecstasy of song that, exhausting his strength in the supreme effort, he slowly floats on quivering, beating pinions down through the bloom-covered branches until, his fervor spent, he sinks to the ground below. His expanded wings and tail flashing with white in the sunlight and the buoyancy of his action appeal to the eye as his music captivates the ear. On moonlit nights at this season the inspired singer launches himself far into the air, filling the silvery spaces of the night with the exquisite swells and trills, liquid and sweet, of his unparalleled melody. The song rises and falls, as the powers of the singer wax and wane, and so he serenades his mate throughout the live-long night. One such singer wins others to emulation and, as the chorus grows, little birds of the field and orchard wake just enough to join briefly in the swelling tide of avian melody."

THE

VOLUBLE SINGER

OF THE

TREETOPS

Louise de Kiriline Lawrence

---

*The vireo has a verb for a name—"vireo" is Latin for "I am green." So he
is; but not brilliantly so and that is one of the reasons why the layman who
is not a bird watcher hardly notices him despite the fact that some members
of the genus are among the most abundant of our birds. Nearly everyone
who has ever been in the country has heard a vireo sing, but not one in ten
has noticed him.*

ONE of my favorites among birds is the red-eyed vireo. I know him
well and he appeals to me particularly because in looks and com-
portment he is such a smooth and elegant bird. Slow motion is his spe-
cialty, but sometimes he is brimming with nervous energy and moves
faster than the arrow in a streamlined fashion all his own. I do not think
that the epithet "sluggish," so often used about him, fits him particularly
well. It seems to me that we shall need to find another and a better word,
one that contains the elements of sobriety and fluidity.

About his singing, terms have been used that are not altogether compli-
mentary—monotonous, repetitious, preacher-like—and I was always inclined to question the aptness of these descriptions. Was he as tireless as
his reputation would have him? When in the day did he start singing,
when did he stop? Was there any relation between his manner of singing
and his character which, if known, would dispel the impression of what
might seem monotonous and repetitious? Were his moods, needs, and tem-
perament reflected in the nuances of tone, in the speed and the manner of
the delivery of his songs? What I hitherto knew of the red-eyed vireo's
singing gave only part of the answer to these questions.

From *Audubon Magazine*, May–June, 1954.

When the call came from the British ornithologist, Noble Rollin, to make an all-day study of some special bird activity, I thought this was a fine opportunity to devote to the red-eye. Everything fitted in very well, too, because the day I was able to do the survey was May 27, 1952, a few days after Male A had taken up territory in my study area at Pimisi Bay which, as the crow flies, is about 180 miles north of Toronto, Canada. But at this time my bird was still without a mate and there would, presumably, be few claims upon his attention other than singing and feeding.

Pre-dawn, the most enchanting and mysterious moment in the 24 hours, reigned when I came out at 3 A.M. A soft, misty light prevailed, not enough to see but enough to surmise the outlines of the trees and the opening in the woods through which the trail led, the delicate luminosity of the night. A whip-poor-will called at close quarters, a loud song and passionate of tempo, for he was in the midst of his love-making. I counted 37 whip-poor-wills; then silence. Then he began again.

I walked into the vireo territory, armed with notebook and flashlight and wearing a warm sweater. It was chilly, the temperature was 43 degrees, and the wind light from the west. A faint streak of dawn appeared at the eastern horizon, stealing the light from the stars.

Across my path, two veeries began calling, soft interrogative notes that never waited an answer. Then, muted like a heavenly whisper, the thrushes begin to sing. Penetrating the dusk and hanging deliciously upon the air, these whisperings seemed unearthly, but they represented the most potent reality of these birds' lives. For this was the time when competition between their males was strong, when pairing took place and nesting locations were chosen, when the blood within them ran fast and their sensations were acute.

A purple finch flew over, *tuck*-ed, and gave a burst of song sweeter than honey. His season was a little ahead of the veeries', beyond the culmination of passions, and his song, therefore, was like an afterthought, a reminiscence of what had stirred in him before the nest-building and the laying of the first eggs.

As the light increased, the singing of the veeries became louder and intermingled with the weirdest discordant notes and exclamations, suggesting an excitement which intensified with the approach of day. Startling and strange was this conversation between the thrushes, as it emanated explosively from the depths of the underbrush close to the path where I stood, now here, now over there. Then, all of a sudden, the swish of rapid flight low through the bushes from one place to another. Since their beginning, these rituals and displays, these unanswered and unanswerable queries from one tawny thrush to the other, evolved into the charming game I just now witnessed.

But no vireo was yet awake.

Beyond the valley of the spring, the rose-breasted grosbeak began to sing, songs so deliciously lyrical that the bird himself seemed loath to end such a fine performance and took to his wings the better to enact an accomplished finale. In the top of a green birch, the robin caught the theme of the grosbeak's impassioned utterance, but geared it down to a song modulated to please a mate sitting quietly on well incubated eggs. For at this moment, the robin's song was not of territorial announcement or self-assertion, but one symbolizing the bond between two closely attached creatures.

Light came and at 4 o'clock I could see to write without the flashlight. During the next 22 minutes, the number of birds that had testified to their awakening rose to 20. A pair of yellow-bellied sapsuckers breakfasted on the sap of a white birch before resuming work on their nest-hole. A crow flew over, welcomed by no one, but busy on its own nest and eggs. A porcupine, climbing an aspen for a feed of green bark, sounded to me like a black bear, and a great blue heron flew over my head and croaked so loudly that, weak-kneed, I nearly sat down on the spot.

By this time, had I not known that my vireo was somewhere on this piece of land whereupon I stood, I would have despaired of his intention ever to sing again. But then, surprisingly, because I had waited so long, exactly nine minutes before sunrise, the red-eyed vireo serenely began dropping phrase upon phrase of song into the confusion of all the other bird-voices. With such casual dreaminess did this long-awaited awakening happen that it required some seconds to penetrate into my consciousness, and forced me to start counting his inaugural sets of two and three notes at five.

I found him high in the crown of a trembling aspen. There he wandered about, hopping from twig to twig, looking around, up and down, from side to side. His bill opened and closed, his throat bubbled, and his crest rose lightly and fell with the rhythm of his utterances. He sang, phrase following upon phrase, with just enough interval to mark a disconnection between them. He sang with an aloof intensity and confluence that seemed totally to divorce his performance from any special objectives and reasons. This bird sang simply because self-expression in song was as much a part of his being as his red eye.

In the next 100 minutes, when the birds filled the woods with the greatest volume of music, our vireo achieved all his vocal records of the day. Thus, from 5:00 to 6:00 A.M., he sang the greatest number of songs in any hour—2155 phrases. From 4:22 A.M., just as he began singing, to 5:00 A.M., he attained his highest speed of delivery, an average of nearly 44 songs per minute; from 6:05 to 6:10 A.M., he sang the most songs in any five-minute period of the day, an average of 70 songs per minute.

Yet, breathless would not properly describe the performance of this bird. He continued to sing for the next three hours with a perfectly calm and casual continuance that at the end amassed him a total of 6063 songs, delivered at a speed of 40 songs per minute. During this time, he allowed himself six pauses from one to six minutes each which he divided equally among the three hours. While he sang, he wandered leisurely from one part of his two-acre territory to the other, selecting his way through the foliated crowns of the tallest aspens and birches. Had not his trail been so clearly marked in song, it would have been a problem for me to follow this bird which moved at such heights and blended so well with his surroundings.

Although my vireo often fed while he sang, and sang with his mouth full, more concentrated feeding called for silence, and the important business of preening claimed all of his attention. Once a trespassing vireo, a stranger, interrupted him. Abruptly he stopped singing and, like an arrow released from a taut bow, he shot down from his tall perch directly in pursuit of the intruder. And with that, the incident closed. With his only red-eye neighbor settled on an adjacent territory to the north, our vireo had no altercations. On one occasion during the afternoon, the two happened to come close to their common border at the same time; but from this nothing more serious resulted than that the birds for about a quarter of an hour indulged in competitive singing.

A little before 9 o'clock in the morning, my vireo stopped singing. Up to this time he had spent almost four out of four-and-a-half hours singing continuously. This was a remarkable record as, apart from the need of advertising himself and his territory, nothing occurred to call forth extraordinary vocal efforts on his part. Red-eyed vireos do not always sing as persistently as this bird did, especially during the first days after arrival from the South when leisurely feeding is often the keynote of existence to many of them. Nor do all individuals possess the same capacity for vocal expression. I have known at least one other red-eyed vireo whose total number of songs in a day, even at the most exciting period, probably never reached four figures. As to the pursuit of the strange vireo, I surmised that this was a passing female, because my male *stopped singing* and dashed off chasing it, instead of challenging it by voice and gesture. That nothing came of it only suggests, that for the female, the moment was not auspicious.

The next half-hour my bird spent feeding and preening. He descended from the heights of the tree crowns to the middle strata of the woods where, one may presume, he found more privacy in the secluded leafy niches. Then, once more, he resumed singing. While he still attained a speed of 38 songs when he sang, his average from 9:00 to 10:00 A.M. was only about six songs a minute for the whole hour. This proved to be an interesting fact, because, regardless of his hourly averages, his speed of singing consistently and gradually declined throughout the day. In other words, he sang more and more slowly as the day advanced.

After his hour of rest, the vireo achieved a forenoon peak of singing that lacked only 13 songs in reaching as high a total as that obtained from 5:00 to 6:00 A.M. He worked up to this peak in the hour before noon, but would, I think, have reached it earlier had he not wandered into a grove of trees heavily infested with the forest tent caterpillar. Here he distracted himself with a great deal of flycatching on the wing. If his objective were the eating of the tachanid flies, which prey upon the tent caterpillars, this activity, from a human viewpoint, may not have been useful. But, of course, I could not be sure that these were the insects he caught. As to the caterpillars, my vireo tramped lightly over the masses of them, apparently without recognizing them as food. When, through my binoculars I saw these worms as wriggling shadows on a translucent leaf, then the bird knew instantly what to do with them—he snapped them down, dashed them to pulp on the twig at his feet, and ate them.

From dawn till noon, the vireo reached a grand total of 14,027 songs, but after this time his singing diminished notably. The interruptions between groups of songs became longer and more frequent, even as he sang more and more slowly. From noon until going to roost, he gave only a little more than half as many songs as during the early part of the day. But even this was a remarkable number and his voice continued to be heard when most of the other birds sang but little or were altogether silent. Moreover, compared with the all-day record of 6140 songs of an unmated European blackbird made by Noble Rollin on April 5, 1948, my vireo's afternoon performance alone exceeded this by 2030 songs.

The lesser peak of singing, which occurred during the afternoon, was perhaps partly due to the encounter at the territorial border with the neighboring red-eye to the north. For quite a while, certainly, this stimulated both birds to greater vocal effort. But the time of afternoon rest came in the next following two hours, when my vireo wandered about within a small area, or feeding or sitting on a twig, trimming and polishing every feather in his plumage, and when he sang only a little.

The last hour of his day the vireo spent in the top of a quaking aspen. Here he moved about from perch to perch. I saw the easy opening and closing of his bill and heard his notes drop, one by one, upon the calm air.

All day I had heard him singing thousands of songs, of two to four, seldom five, notes. Monotonous, repetitious, preacher-like? His singing was all this, if an utterance that was so intrinsic a phase of a creature's character, so innate an expression of self, could be any of these attributes. What I had heard all day, set to music, was this vireo's instinctive emotions and preoccupations, the wherefores and the end of his very existence.

Lovely and clear, simple and eloquent, his song and intonations continued to reach me from the top of the aspen. Hitherto his voice had been unaffected by his day-long singing. But now, as if he had reached the end, yet only with reluctance gave in, his songs shortened and were often just softly whispered. Then the sun hid behind alto-cumulus clouds and it grew dusky in the vireo territory, while out yonder, at the edge of the forest, the sun still threw its gold upon the trees and hillsides.

Between 6:00 and 6:13 P.M. my vireo sang 44 songs. Two minutes later, with wings closed, he dropped from the crown of the aspen into a thick stand of young evergreens. From here, like an echo of his day's performance, he gave six more songs. Then he fell silent and was heard no more. Officially, the sun set one hour and 39 minutes later.

Fourteen hours, less six minutes, my red-eye vireo had been awake, and of this time he spent nearly 10 hours singing a total of 22,197 songs. This was his record. But the most important is not the record, but my introduction to an individual bird and the glimpse he gave me of his true character.

OLD

SICKLE WINGS

John Kieran

John Kieran—well known in his day as sports writer, TV personality, and naturalist—went on regular nature walks with a select company. It is no secret that the drama critic who figures in the passage is Brooks Atkinson, one of the few Broadwayites who maintained a passionate interest in doings remote from Times Square. Kieran, again, calls the peregrine falcon by its old American subspecific name, duck hawk.

OUR afternoon record was spotty—just a hawk here and there—but one was a Duck Hawk . . . the Peregrine Falcon of medieval history and romance. It is the avian ace of the air, the fastest thing on wings in our part of the country, a marauder, a fierce and fearless predator for its weight and size. We have seen Duck Hawks swooping at Bald Eagles, apparently just for the fun of it, and Dick Herbert, who keeps a census of all the Duck Hawks that breed along the Palisades, told us that he had seen a Duck Hawk knock down a Great Horned Owl that happened to pass too close to the Duck Hawk's nest.

There is no mistaking the Duck Hawk when it stoops to conquer. It comes down with a lightning plunge on half-shut wings. How fast it drops is a matter of estimate, and some estimates I have seen I believe are much too enthusiastic. The Falconer, when he was a fighter pilot in France in World War I, found himself flying parallel to a Peregrine Falcon as he was returning from a foray over enemy territory in the Champagne sector. He turned to test the speed of the bird and followed it down when it dived to get away from the plane. He knew the speed of which his plane—a Spad—was capable and of this experience he wrote:

"I would say that the Duck Hawk has a cruising speed of about 75 miles per hour and a diving speed of about 150 miles per hour. At least, this one did."

The Dramatic Critic told me that once on a Winter day he was watching a line of ducks winging swiftly northward just a few feet

From *Footnotes on Nature*. New York: Doubleday & Co. Inc., 1947.

above the water of the Hudson River. For some reason the ducks seemed to be in a tearing hurry as he watched them through his field glasses. Suddenly a Duck Hawk, coming from the rear, shot past the line of ducks so fast that, as the Dramatic Critic solemnly stated, it made the ducks look as though they were walking on the water. Once the Medical Student and I went across the Hudson River and along the foot of the Palisades in the hope of seeing a Duck Hawk. It was in early Spring and the ground was muddy, so that walking was a heavy process. We plodded along for hours and saw nothing except a few stray ducks and hundreds of Herring Gulls on the river. By late afternoon we were worn and weary and a cold wind had come up to add to our discomfort. Just as we were going down the slope to take the ferry home in the dusk, the Medical Student grabbed my arm and said: "Look!" I looked and all I saw was a darkish speck shooting downward across the sunset sky with almost incredible speed. There was just one bird in our region that could fly in such fashion—the Duck Hawk! We were dog-tired and our shoes were a mass of clotted mud, but there was a glow of satisfaction in our hearts as we went aboard the ferry. We had seen "Old Sickle Wings" and we were well content.

MASTER

OF

THE WOODS

Robert McConnell Hatch

Clerical bird watchers are common in England. In fact natural history in general owes much to rural clergyman who had the leisure and the inclination to take up sometimes improbable hobbies. One such, Gilbert White, might be called the first English "nature writer"—though of course not the first English naturalist. As the following selection by Bishop Hatch will show, the United States has produced at least one churchman birdwatcher—and a highly placed one at that.

S OMETIMES a bird can cast its spell over a whole countryside. Other birds may live there, but they become mere bit players in the drama. Dominating the scene is a single massive personality.

Such is the case on a wooded hillside in Lancaster, New Hampshire. Far up the hill and tucked deep in the forest is a one-room board camp built by a neighbor of mine when he was cutting logs. His name was Orrin Wentworth, and his wife's name was Lottie. They called the little building Camp Owl, using the first letter in each of their names, O and L, and adding the W for Wentworth. It was a fitting family designation for the camp, but I soon learned that it applied for quite another reason.

On my first overnight visit to the camp I was walking up the trail alone in the dark of the moon. I had reached a murky part of the trail, under some tall fir trees, when the night air was split by a series of eight spine-tingling hoots. The last hoot slurred downward, indentifying its source as a barred owl. I had heard barred owls before, but always at a respectable distance. The proximity of the sudden hoots unnerved me, and I continued up the trail at top speed.

Again and again that summer I heard the barred owl. The woods echoed with hoohoo, hoohoo, hoohoo, hoohooaw. Sometimes the hooting was close to the camp. Sometimes it was so far up the hillside that I could

From *New Hampshire Bird News*, January 1954.

barely hear it. Once in the dead of night the owl awoke me, not hooting this time, but clucking, cackling and snarling from a point directly over the camp. In fact, I still wonder if the owl was not perched on the ridge-pole of the building during this performance.

Other birds inhabit the hillside—black-throated blue warblers, redstarts, black and white warblers, oven birds, hermit thrushes, brown creepers, whitethroats and juncoes, nuthatches and chickadees, hairy and downy woodpeckers, to name only a few. I have eaten supper listening to the music of olive-backed thrushes, and I have breakfasted to the song of black-throated green warblers. I have watched red-tailed hawks circling over the camp, and one day I saw a goshawk as I sat on the porch. But none of these birds, not even the goshawk, could match the owl. Every night the hoots rang through the forest, now from this direction, now from that, until the owl seemed the master of these woods and all the other birds mere satellites.

Finally I resolved to see the owl. I strained my eyes for him at dusk. I tried to catch him in the beam of my flashlight. I craned my neck throughout the day as I searched dense evergreens and looked for cavities in trees. I felt sure that he saw me repeatedly, and I had an uneasy suspicion that I was affording him a summer's entertainment. But, to save my life, I could not find him. I could only hear his hooting in the night.

My vacation came to an end. My last day in New Hampshire was a rainy one. I felt depressed and decided to walk up to the camp, more to relive old memories than anything else. For once I gave no thought to the owl.

I reached the camp late in the afternoon. It was raining hard, and the woods were growing dark. I sat on the porch and dwelt once more on some of the great memories of that summer—the nesting pair of broad-winged hawks I had found, the kestrels in our pasture, the Lincoln's sparrow on the edge of a bog, the white-winged crossbills singing like canaries on the shores of a wilderness pond. They were stirring memories, but they were abruptly shattered! A large bird flew moth-like to the branch of a tree in front of the camp. He relaxed on his perch and gazed at me calmly for what seemed an age. I gazed back, not so calmly. It was the barred owl. I felt as though our long acquaintance had changed into friendship. When at last he flew away I murmured, "So long, old friend! I'll see you again next summer."

And so I did, because barred owls have been known to inhabit a locality for many years. I am at home with him now and because of this I am also at home with the tract of woods that belongs so exclusively to him.

THE

MALIGNED CATBIRD

Elliott Coues

I am intrigued by the basic premise of this piece. I have birded here and there in the gray catbird's breeding range since childhood, and have never encountered human animosity towards the bird. Can it be that an entrenched prejudice such as that described by Elliott Coues has simply died, or does it persist regionally? Coues, incidentally, was a brilliant but controversial birdman; his acerbic manner ruffled many a feather on the early American ornithological establishment.

I T is not easy to account for the vulgar prejudice against this bird. The contempt he inspires cannot be entirely due to familiarity; for other members of the household, like the Robin, Bluebird, and Swallow, do not come under the ban. If his harsh, abrupt, and discordant note were the cause, the croaking Crow and chattering Blackbird would share the same disgrace. Yet the fact remains that the Catbird is almost always regarded unfavorably, not so much for what he does, perhaps, as for what he is, or is not. To eyes polite, he seems to be "off color" in the best society, he is looked upon as *un peu compromis*. There must be a reason for this—the world is too busy to invent reasons for things—for there never was a popular verdict without roots in some fact or principle. It is instinctive; the school-boy despises a Catbird just as naturally as he stones a frog; and when he thinks a thing is mean, no argument will convince him to the contrary.

For myself, I think the boys are right. Like many of the lower animals, they are quick to detect certain qualities, and apt to like or dislike unwittingly, yet with good reason. The matter with the Catbird is that he is thoroughly common-place. There is a dead level of bird-life, as there is of humanity; and mediocrity is simply despicable—hopeless and helpless, and never more so than when it indulges aspirations. Yet it wears well, and is a useful thing; there must be a standard of measure, and a foil is often extremely convenient. The Catbird has certainly a good deal

From *Birds of the Colorado Valley*. Washington: U. S. Government Printing Office, 1878.

to contend with. His name has a flippant sound, without agreeable suggestiveness. His voice is vehement without strength, unpleasant in its explosive quality. His dress is positively ridiculous—who could hope to rise in life wearing a pepper-and-salt jacket, a black velvet skull-cap, and a large red patch on the seat of his pantaloons? Add to all this the possession of some very plebian tastes, like those which in another case render beer-gardens, circuses, and street-shows things possible, and you will readily perceive that a hero cannot be made out of a Catbird.

But to be common-place is merely to strike the balance of a great number of positive qualities, no single one of which is to be overlooked. It is accomplished by a sort of algebraic process, in which all the terms of an equation are brought together on one side, which then equals zero. There is said to be a great deal of human nature in mankind, and I am sure there is as much bird-nature in the feathered tribe. There is as much life in the kitchen as in the parlor: it is only a matter of a flight of stairs between them. We who happen to be above know none too much of what goes on below—much less, I suspect, than the *basse-cour* often learns of the *salon* and the *boudoir*. I sometimes fancy that the Catbird knows us better than we do him. He is at least a civilized bird, if he does hang by the eyelids on good society; if he is denied the front door, the area is open to him; he may peep in at the basement window, and see the way up the back stairs. His eyes and ears are open; his wits are sharp; what he knows, he knows, and will tell if he chooses. His domesticity is large; he likes us well enough to stay with us, yet he keeps his eye on us. His is the prose of daily life, with all its petty concerns, as read by the lower classes; the poetry we are left to discover.

Explain him as we may, the Catbird is inseparable from home and homely things; he reflects, as he is reflected in, domestic life. The associations, it is true, are of an humble sort; but they are just as strong as those which link us with the trusty Robin, the social Swallow, the delicious Bluebird, or the elegant Oriole. Let it be the humble country-home of toil, or the luxurious mansion where wealth is lavished on the garden—in either case, the Catbird claims the rights of squatter sovereignty. He flirts saucily across the well-worn path that leads to the well, and sips the water that collects in the shallow depression upon the flag-stone. Down in the tangle of the moist dell, where stands the spring-house, with its cool, crisp atmosphere, redolent of buttery savor, where the trickling water is perpetual, he loiters at ease, and from the heart of the greenbrier makes bold advances to the milkmaid who brings the brimming bowls. In the pasture beyond, he waits for the boy who comes whistling after the cows, and follows him home by the blackberry road that lies along the zigzag fence, challenging the carelessly thrown stone he has learned to dodge with ease. He joins the berrying parties fresh from school, soliciting a game of hide-and-seek, and laughs at the mishaps that never fail when children try the brier patch. Along the hedge row, he glides with short easy flights to gain the evergreen coppice that shades a corner of the lawn, where he pauses to watch the old gardener trimming the boxwood, or rolling the gravel walk, or making the flower bed, wondering why some people will take so much trouble when everything is nice enough already. Ever restless and inquisitive, he makes for the well-known arbor, to see what may be going on there. What he discovers is certainly none of his business: the rustic seat is occupied; the old, old play is in rehearsal; and at sight of the blushing cheeks that respond to passionate words, the very roses on the trellis hang their envious heads. This spectacle tickles his fancy; always ripe for mischief, he startles the loving pair with his quick, shrill cry, like a burlesque of the kiss just heard, and enjoys their little consternation. "It is only a Catbird," they say reassuringly—but there are times when the slightest jar is a shock, and pledges that hang in a trembling balance may never be redeemed.

"Only a Catbird" meanwhile remembers business of his own, and is off. The practical question of dining recurs. He means to dine sumptuously, and so, like the French philosopher, place himself beyond the reach of fate. But nature, in the month of May, is full of combustible material, and the very atmosphere is quick to carry the torch that was kindled in the arbor where the lovers sat. His fate meets him in the only shape that could so far restrain masculine instincts as to postpone a dinner. The rest is soon told—rather it would be, could the secrets of the impenetrable dark-green mass of *Smilax* whither the pair betake themselves be revealed. The next we see of the bird, he is perched on the topmost spray of yonder pear tree, with quivering wings, brimful of song. He is inspired; for a time at least he is lifted above the common-place; his kinship with the prince of song, with the Mockingbird himself, is vindicated. He has discovered the source of the poetry of every-day life.

THE

NORTHERN SHRIKE

John Burroughs

The most dangerous and relentless of all predators is man himself. Yet he is quick to call "savage" and "cruel" the animal who kills for food and to forget that, with very few exceptions, he alone either takes more prey than he needs, kills for the sake of killing, or calls wanton slaughter of other creatures "sport." As Bernard Shaw once said: "When a man wants to murder a tiger he calls it sport; when the tiger wants to murder him he calls it ferocity."

John Burroughs was too good a naturalist not to know all this and not to know, besides, that without the predator the balance of nature could not maintain itself. Yet the soundest of naturalists is not wholly free from human prejudice, and the reader will find in the following account the telltale language of censure.

Bᴜᴛ let me . . . contemplate for a few moments this feathered bandit —this bird with the mark of Cain upon him, *Lanius borealis*—the great shrike or butcher-bird. Usually the character of a bird of prey is well defined; there is no mistaking him. His claws, his beak, his head, his wings, in fact his whole build, point to the fact that he subsists upon live creatures; he is armed to catch them and to slay them. Every bird knows a hawk and knows him from the start, and is on the lookout for him. The hawk takes life, but he does it to maintain his own, and it is a public and universally known fact. Nature has sent him abroad in that character, and has advised all creatures of it. Not so with the shrike; here she has concealed the character of a murderer under a form as innocent as that of the robin. Feet, wings, tail, color, head, and general form and size are all those of a song-bird—very much like that master songster, the mocking bird—yet this bird is a regular Bluebeard among its kind. Its only characteristic feature is its beak, the upper mandible having two sharp processes and a sharp hooked point. It cannot fly away to any distance with the bird it kills, nor hold it in its claws to feed upon it. It usually impales

From *Locust and Wild Honey*. Boston: Houghton Mifflin Company, 1879, 1895.

its victim upon a thorn, or thrusts it in the fork of a limb. For the most part, however, its food seems to consist of insects—spiders, grasshoppers, beetles, etc. It is the assassin of the small birds, whom it often destroys in pure wantonness, or merely to sup on their brains, as the Gaucho slaughters a wild cow or bull for its tongue. It is a wolf in sheep's clothing. Apparently its victims are unacquainted with its true character and allow it to approach them, when the fatal blow is given. I saw an illustration of this the other day. A large number of goldfinches in their full plumage, together with snowbirds and sparrows, were feeding and chattering in some low bushes back of the barn. I had paused by the fence and was peeping through at them, hoping to get a glimpse of that rare sparrow, the white-crowned. Presently I heard a rustling among the dry leaves as if some larger bird was also among them. Then I heard one of the goldfinches cry out as if in distress, when the whole flock of them started up in alarm, and, circling around, settled in the tops of the larger trees. I continued my scrutiny of the bushes, when I saw a large bird, with some object in its beak, hopping along on a low branch near the ground. It disappeared from my sight for a few moments, then came up through the undergrowth into the top of a young maple where some of the finches had alighted, and I beheld the shrike. The little birds avoided him and flew about the tree, their pursuer following them with the motions of his head and body as if he would fain arrest them by his murderous gaze. The birds did not utter the cry or make the demonstration of alarm they usually do on the appearance of a hawk, but chirruped and called and flew about in a half-wondering, half-bewildered manner. As they flew farther along the line of trees the shrike followed them as if bent on further captures. I then made my way around to see what the shrike had caught, and what he had done with his prey. As I approached the bushes I saw the shrike hastening back. I read his intentions at once. Seeing my movements, he had returned for his game. But I was too quick for him, and he got up out of the brush and flew away from the locality. On some twigs in the thickest part of the bushes I found his victim—a goldfinch. It was not impaled upon a thorn, but was carefully disposed upon some horizontal twigs—laid upon the shelf, so to speak. It was as warm as in life, and its plumage was unruffled. On examining it I found a large bruise or break in the skin on the back of the neck, at the base of the skull. Here the bandit had no doubt gripped the bird with his strong beak. The shrike's bloodthirstiness was seen in the fact that it did not stop to devour its prey, but went in quest of more, as if opening a market of goldfinches. The thicket was his shambles, and if not interrupted he might have had a fine display of tidbits in a short time.

The shrike is called a butcher from his habit of sticking his meat upon hooks and points; further than that, he is a butcher because he devours but a trifle of what he slays.

A few days before, I had witnessed another little scene in which the shrike was the chief actor. A chipmunk had his den in the side of the terrace above the garden, and spent the mornings laying in a store of corn which he stole from a field ten or twelve rods away. In traversing about half this distance, the little poacher was exposed; the first cover going from his den was a large maple, where he always brought up and took a survey of the scene. I would see him spinning along toward the maple, then from it by an easy stage to the fence adjoining the corn; then back again with his booty. One morning I paused to watch him more at my leisure. He came up out of his retreat and cocked himself up to see what my motions meant. His forepaws were clasped to his breast precisely as if they had been hands, and the tips of his fingers thrust into his vest pockets. Having satisfied himself with reference to me, he sped on toward the tree. He had nearly reached it, when he turned tail and rushed for his hole with the greatest precipitation. As he neared it, I saw some bluish object in the air closing in upon him with the speed of an arrow, and, as he vanished within, a shrike brought up in front of the spot, and with spread wings and tail stood hovering a moment, and, looking in, then turned and went away. Apparently it was a narrow escape for the chipmunk, and, I venture to say, he stole no more corn that morning. The shrike is said to catch mice, but it is not known to attack squirrels. He certainly could not have strangled the chipmunk, and I am curious to know what would have been the result had he overtaken him. Probably it was only a kind of brag on the part of the bird— a bold dash where no risk was run. He simulated the hawk, the squirrel's real enemy, and no doubt enjoyed the joke.

On another occasion, as I was riding along a mountain road early in April, a bird started from the fence where I was passing, and flew heavily to the branch of a near apple-tree. It proved to be a shrike with a small bird in his beak. He thrust his victim into a fork of a branch, then wiped his bloody beak upon the bark. A youth who was with me, to whom I pointed out the fact, had never heard of such a thing, and was much incensed at the shrike. "Let me fire a stone at him," he said, and jumping out of the wagon he pulled off his mittens, and fumbled about for a stone. Having found one to his liking, with great earnestness and deliberation he let drive. The bird was in more danger than I had imagined, for he escaped only by a hair's breadth; a guiltless bird like the robin or sparrow would surely have been slain; the missile grazed the spot where the shrike sat, and cut the ends of his wings as he darted behind the branch. We could see that the murdered bird had been brained, as its head hung down toward us.

The shrike is not a summer bird with us in the Northern States, but mainly a fall and winter one; in summer he goes farther north. I see him most frequently in November and December. I recall a morning during the former month that was singularly clear and motionless; the air was like a great drum. Apparently every sound within the compass of the horizon was distinctly heard. The explosions back in the cement quarries ten miles away smote the hollow and reverberating air like giant fists. Just as the sun first showed his fiery brow above the horizon, a gun was discharged across the river. On the instant a shrike, perched on the topmost spray of a maple above the house, set up a loud, harsh call or whistle, suggestive of certain notes of the blue jay. The note presently became a crude, broken warble. Even this scalper of the innocents had music in his soul on such a morning. He saluted the sun as a robin might have done. After he had finished he flew away toward the east.

The shrike is a citizen of the world, being found in both hemispheres. It does not appear that the European species differs essentially from our own. In Germany he is called the nine-killer, from the belief that he kills and sticks upon thorns nine grasshoppers a day

To make my portrait of the shrike more complete, I will add another trait of him described by an acute observer who writes me from western New York. He saw the bird on a bright mid-winter morning when the thermometer stood at zero, and by cautious approaches succeeded in getting under the apple-tree upon which he was perched. The shrike was uttering a loud, clear note like *clu-eet, clu-eet, clu-eet*, and, on finding he had a listener who was attentive and curious, varied his perform-ance and kept it up continuously for fifteen minutes. He seemed to enjoy having a spectator, and never took his eye off him. The observer approached within twenty feet of him. "As I came near," he says, "the shrike began to scold at me, a sharp, buzzing, squeaking sound not easy to describe. After a little he came out on the end of the limb nearest me, then he posed himself, and, opening his wings a little, began to trill and warble under his breath, as it were, with an occasional squeak, and vi-brating his half-open wings in time with his song." Some of his notes resembled those of the bluebird, and the whole performance is described as pleasing and melodious.

This account agrees with Thoreau's observation, where he speaks of the shrike "with heedless and unfrozen melody bringing back summer again." Sings Thoreau:—

> "His steady sails he never furls
>   At any time o' year,
> And perching now on winter's curls,
>   He whistles in his ear."

But his voice is that of a savage—strident and disagreeable.

I have often wondered how this bird was kept in check; in the struggle for existence it would appear to have greatly the advantage of other birds. It cannot, for instance, be beset with one tenth of the dangers that threaten the robin, and yet apparently there are a thousand robins to every shrike. It builds a warm, compact nest in the mountains and dense woods, and lays six eggs, which would indicate a rapid increase. The pigeon lays but two eggs, and is preyed upon by both man and beast, millions of them meeting a murderous death every year; yet always some part of the country is swarming with untold numbers of them. But the shrike is one of our rarest birds. I myself seldom see more than two each year, and before I became an observer of birds I never saw any.

In size the shrike is a little inferior to the blue jay, with much the same form. If you see an unknown bird about your orchard or fields in November or December of a bluish grayish complexion, with dusky wings and tail that show markings of white, flying rather heavily from point to point, or alighting down in the stubble occasionally, it is pretty sure to be the shrike.

THE

AMERICAN DIPPER

John Muir

Perhaps the most famous single passage describing an American bird is John Muir's rapturous account of his own favorite, the American dipper or "water-ouzel." Though it has often been reprinted, the editors of the present volume cannot bring themselves to omit it. Muir was a first-rate naturalist, a daring, lonely explorer, and a brilliant writer. Unlike many contemporary naturalists he saw no reason why he should strive for "objectivity" or to either conquer or conceal his "love of nature." He gloried in his passion for everything which was wild and grand in the natural world and it is the intensity of his emotions which is in part responsible for the greatness of his books. No other native writer of the past or present is more eloquent.

THE waterfalls of the Sierra are frequented by only one bird—the Ouzel or Water Thrush (*Cinclus Mexicanus, Sw.*) He is a singularly joyous and lovable little fellow, about the size of a robin, clad in a plain waterproof suit of bluish gray, with a tinge of chocolate on the head and shoulders. In form he is about as smoothly plump and compact as a pebble that has been whirled in a pot-hole, the flowing contour of his body being interrupted only by his strong feet and bill, the crisp wing-tips, and the up-slanted wren-like tail.

Among all the countless waterfalls I have met in the course of ten years' exploration in the Sierra, whether among the icy peaks, or warm foothills, or in the profound yosemitic cañons of the middle region, not one was found without its Ouzel. No cañon is too cold for this little bird, none too lonely, provided it be rich in falling water. Find a fall, or cascade, or rushing rapid, anywhere upon a clear stream, and there you will surely find its complementary Ouzel, flitting about in the spray, diving in foaming eddies, whirling like a leaf among beaten foam-bells; ever vigorous and enthusiastic, yet self-contained, and neither seeking nor shunning your company.

If disturbed while dipping about in the margin shallows, he either

From *The Mountains of California*. New York: The Century Company, 1894.

sets off with a rapid whir to some other feeding-ground up or down the stream, or alights on some half-submerged rock or snag out in the current, and immediately begins to nod and courtesy like a wren, turning his head from side to side with many other odd dainty movements that never fail to fix the attention of the observer.

He is the mountain streams' own darling, the humming-bird of blooming waters, loving rocky ripple-slopes and sheets of foam as a bee loves flowers, as a lark loves sunshine and meadows. Among all the mountain birds, none has cheered me so much in my lonely wanderings —none so unfailingly. For both in winter and summer he sings, sweetly, cheerily, independent alike of sunshine and of love, requiring no other inspiration than the stream on which he dwells. While water sings, so must he, in heat or cold, calm or storm, ever attuning his voice in sure accord; low in the drought of summer and the drought of winter, but never silent.

During the golden days of Indian summer, after most of the snow has been melted, and the mountain streams have become feeble—a succession of silent pools, linked together by shallow, transparent currents and strips of silvery lacework—then the song of the Ouzel is at its lowest ebb. But as soon as the winter clouds have bloomed, and the mountain treasuries are once more replenished with snow, the voices of the streams and ouzels increase in strength and richness until the flood season of early summer. Then the torrents chant their noblest anthems, and then is the flood-time of our songster's melody. As for weather, dark days and sun days are the same to him. The voices of most song-birds, however joyous, suffer a long winter eclipse; but the Ouzel sings on through all the seasons and every kind of storm. Indeed no storm can be more violent than those of the waterfalls in the midst of which he delights to dwell. However dark and boisterous the weather, snowing, blowing, or cloudy, all the same he sings, and with never a note of sadness. No need of spring sunshine to thaw *his* song, for it never freezes. Never shall you hear anything wintry from *his* warm breast; no pinched cheeping, no wavering notes between sorrow and joy; his mellow, fluty voice is ever tuned to downright gladness, as free from dejection as cock-crowing.

It is pitiful to see wee frost-pinched sparrows on cold mornings in the mountain groves shaking the snow from their feathers, and hopping about as if anxious to be cheery, then hastening back to their hidings out of the wind, puffing out their breast-feathers over their toes, and subsiding among the leaves, cold and breakfastless, while the snow continues to fall, and there is no sign of clearing. But the Ouzel never calls forth a single touch of pity; not because he is strong to endure, but rather because he seems to live a charmed life beyond the reach of every influence that makes endurance necessary.

One wild winter morning, when Yosemite Valley was swept its length from west to east by a cordial snow-storm, I sallied forth to see what I might learn and enjoy. A sort of gray, gloaming-like darkness filled the valley, the huge walls were out of sight, all ordinary sounds were smothered, and even the loudest booming of the falls was at times buried beneath the roar of the heavy-laden blast. The loose snow was already over five feet deep on the meadows, making extended walks impossible without the aid of snowshoes. I found no great difficulty, however, in making my way to a certain ripple on the river where one of my ouzels lived. He was at home, busily gleaning his breakfast among the pebbles of a shallow portion of the margin, apparently unaware of anything extraordinary in the weather. Presently he flew out to a stone against which the icy current was beating, and turning his back to the wind, sang as delightfully as a lark in springtime.

After spending an hour or two with my favorite, I made my way across the valley, boring and wallowing through the drifts, to learn as definitely as possible how the other birds were spending their time. The Yosemite birds are easily found during the winter because all of them excepting the Ouzel are restricted to the sunny north side of the valley, the south side being constantly eclipsed by the great frosty shadow of the wall. And because the Indian Cañon groves, from their peculiar exposure, are the warmest, the birds congregate there, more especially in severe weather.

I found most of the robins cowering on the lee side of the larger branches where the snow could not fall upon them, while two or three of the more enterprising were making desperate efforts to reach the mistletoe berries by clinging nervously to the under side of the snow-crowned masses, back downward, like woodpeckers. Every now and then they would dislodge some of the loose fringes of the snow-crown, which would come sifting down on them and send them screaming back to camp, where they would subside among their companions with a shiver, muttering in low, querulous chatter like hungry children.

Some of the sparrows were busy at the feet of the larger trees gleaning seeds and benumbed insects, joined now and then by a robin weary of his unsuccessful attempts upon the snow-covered berries. The brave woodpeckers were clinging to the snowless sides of the larger boles and overarching branches of the camp trees, making short flights from side to side of the grove, pecking now and then at the acorns they had stored in the bark, and chattering aimlessly as if unable to keep still, yet evidently putting in the time in a very dull way, like storm-bound travelers at a country tavern. The hardy nut-hatches were threading the open furrows of the trunks in their usual industrious manner, and uttering their quaint notes, evidently less distressed than their neighbors. The Steller jays were of course making more noisy stir than all the other birds combined; ever coming and going with loud bluster, screaming as if each had a lump of melting sludge in his throat, and taking good care to improve the favorable opportunity afforded by the storm to steal from the acorn stores of the woodpeckers. I also noticed one solitary gray eagle braving the storm on the top of a tall pine-stump just outside the main grove. He was standing bolt upright with his back to the wind, a tuft of snow piled on his square shoulders, a monument of passive endurance. Thus every snow-bound bird seemed more or less uncomfortable if not in positive distress. The storm was reflected in every gesture, and not one cheerful note, not to say song, came from a single bill; their cowering, joyless endurance offering a striking contrast to the spontaneous, irrepressible gladness of the Ouzel, who could no more help exhaling sweet song then a rose sweet fragrance. He *must* sing though the heavens fall. I remember noticing the distress of a pair of robins during the violent earthquake of the year 1872, when the pines of the Valley, with strange movements, flapped and waved their branches, and beetling rock-brows came thundering down to the meadows in tremendous avalanches. It did not occur to me in the midst of the excitement of other observations to look for the ouzels, but I doubt not they were singing straight on through it all, regarding the terrible rock-thunder as fearlessly as they do the booming of the waterfalls.

What may be regarded as the separate songs of the Ouzel are exceedingly difficult of description, because they are so variable and at the same time so confluent. Though I have been acquainted with my favorite ten years, and during most of this time have heard him sing nearly every day, I still detect notes and strains that seem new to me. Nearly all of his music is sweet and tender, lapsing from his round breast like water over the smooth lip of a pool, then breaking farther on into a sparkling foam of melodious notes, which glow with subdued enthusiasm, yet without expressing much of the strong, gushing ecstasy of the bobolink or skylark.

The more striking strains are perfect arabesques of melody, composed of a few full, round, mellow notes, embroidered with delicate trills which fade and melt in long slender cadences. In a general way his music is that of the streams refined and spiritualized. The deep booming notes of the falls are in it, the trills of rapids, the gurgling of margin eddies, the low whispering of level reaches, and the sweet tinkle of separate drops oozing from the ends of mosses and falling into tranquil pools.

The Ouzel never sings in chorus with other birds, nor with his kind, but only with the streams. And like flowers that bloom beneath the surface of the ground, some of our favorite's best song-blossoms never rise above the surface of the heavier music of the water. I have often observed him singing in the midst of beaten spray, his music completely buried beneath the water's roar; yet I knew he was surely singing by his gestures and the movements of his bill.

His food, as far as I have noticed, consists of all kinds of water insects, which in summer are chiefly procured along shallow margins. Here he wades about ducking his head under water and deftly turning over pebbles and fallen leaves with his bill, seldom choosing to go into deep water where he has to use his wings in diving.

He seems to be especially fond of the larvae of mosquitos, found in abundance attached to the bottom of smooth rock channels where the current is shallow. When feeding in such places he wades up-stream, and often while his head is under water the swift current is deflected upward along the glossy curves of his neck and shoulders, in the form of a clear, crystalline shell, which fairly incloses him like a bell-glass, the shell being broken and re-formed as he lifts and dips his head; while ever and anon he sidles out to where the too powerful current carries him off his feet; then he dexterously rises on the wing and goes gleaning again in shallower places.

But during the winter, when the stream-banks are embossed in snow, and the streams themselves are chilled nearly to the freezing-point, so that the snow falling into them in stormy weather is not wholly dissolved, but forms a thin, blue sludge, thus rendering the current opaque —then he seeks the deeper portions of the main rivers, where he may dive to clear water beneath the sludge. Or he repairs to some open lake or millpond, at the bottom of which he feeds in safety.

When thus compelled to betake himself to a lake, he does not plunge into it at once like a duck, but always alights in the first place upon some rock or fallen pine along the shore. Then flying out thirty or forty yards, more or less, according to the character of the bottom, he alights with a dainty glint on the surface, swims about, looks down, finally makes up his mind, and disappears with a sharp stroke of his wings. After feeding for two or three minutes he suddenly reappears, showers the water from his wings with one vigorous shake, and rises abruptly into the air as if pushed up from beneath, comes back to his perch, sings a few minutes, and goes out to dive again; thus coming and going, singing and diving at the same place for hours.

The Ouzel is usually found singly; rarely in pairs, excepting during the breeding season, and *very* rarely in threes or fours. I once observed three thus spending a winter morning in company, upon a small glacier lake, on the Upper Merced, about 7500 feet above the level of the sea. A storm had occurred during the night, but the morning sun shone unclouded, and the shadowy lake, gleaming darkly in its setting of fresh snow, lay smooth and motionless as a mirror. My camp chanced to be within a few feet of the water's edge, opposite a fallen pine, some of the branches of which leaned out over the lake. Here my three dearly welcome visitors took up their station, and at once began to embroider the frosty air with their delicious melody, doubly delightful to me that particular morning, as I had been somewhat apprehensive of danger in breaking my way down through the snow-choked cañons to the lowlands.

The portion of the lake bottom selected for a feeding-ground lies at a depth of fifteen or twenty feet below the surface, and is covered with a short growth of algae and other aquatic plants—facts I have previously determined while sailing over it on a raft. After alighting on the glassy surface, they occasionally indulged in a little play, chasing one another round about in small circles; then all three would suddenly dive together, and then come ashore and sing.

The Ouzel seldom swims more than a few yards on the surface, for, not being web-footed, he makes rather slow progress, but by means of his strong, crisp wings he swims, or rather flies, with celerity under the surface, often to considerable distances. But it is in withstanding the force of heavy rapids that his strength of wing in this respect is most strikingly manifested. The following may be regarded as a fair illustration of his power of sub-aquatic flight. One stormy morning in winter when the Merced River was blue and green with unmelted snow, I observed one of my ouzels perched on a snag out in the midst of a swift-rushing rapid, singing cheerily, as if everything was just to his mind; and while I stood on the bank admiring him, he suddenly plunged into the sludgy current, leaving his song abruptly broken off. After feeding a minute or two at the bottom, and when one would suppose that he must inevitably be swept far down-stream, he emerged just where he went down, alighted on the same snag, showered the water-beads from his feathers, and continued his unfinished song, seemingly in tranquil ease as if it had suffered no interruption.

The Ouzel alone of all birds dares to enter a white torrent. And though strictly terrestrial in structure, no other is so inseparably related to water, not even the duck, or the bold ocean albatross, or the stormy-petrel. For ducks go ashore as soon as they finish feeding in undisturbed places, and very often make long flights overland from lake to lake or field to field. The same is true of most other aquatic birds. But the Ouzel, born on the brink of a stream, or on a snag or boulder in the midst of it, seldom leaves it for a single moment. For, notwithstanding he is often on the wing, he never flies overland, but whirs with rapid, quail-like beat above the stream, tracing all its windings. Even when the stream is quite small, say from five to ten feet wide, he seldom shortens his flight by crossing a bend, however abrupt it may be; and even when disturbed by meeting some one on the bank, he prefers to fly over one's head, to dodging out over the ground. When, therefore, his flight along a crooked stream is viewed endwise, it appears most strikingly wavered —a description on the air of every curve with lightning-like rapidity.

The vertical curves and angles of the most precipitous torrents he traces with the same rigid fidelity, swooping down the inclines of cascades, dropping sheer over dizzy falls amid the spray, and ascending with the same fearlessness and ease, seldom seeking to lessen the steepness of the acclivity by beginning to ascend before reaching the base of the fall. No matter though it may be several hundred feet in height he holds straight on, as if about to dash headlong into the throng of booming rockets, then darts abruptly upward, and, after alighting at the top of the precipice to rest a moment, proceeds to feed and sing. His flight is solid and impetuous, without any intermission of wing-beats—one homogeneous buzz like that of a laden bee on its way home. And while thus buzzing freely from fall to fall, he is frequently heard giving utterance to a long outdrawn train of unmodulated notes, in no way connected with his song, but corresponding closely with his flight in sustained vigor.

Were the flights of all the ouzels in the Sierra traced on a chart, they would indicate the direction of the flow of the entire system of ancient glaciers, from about the period of the breaking up of the ice-sheet until near the close of the glacial winter; because the streams which the ouzels so rigidly follow are, with the unimportant exceptions of a few side tributaries, all flowing in channels eroded for them out of the solid flank of the range by the vanished glaciers—the streams tracing the ancient glaciers, the ouzels tracing the streams. Nor do we find so complete compliance to glacial conditions in the life of any other mountain bird, or animal of any kind. Bears frequently accept the pathways laid down by glaciers as the easiest to travel; but they often leave them and cross over from cañon to cañon. So also, most of the birds trace the moraines to some extent, because the forests are growing on them. But they wander far, crossing the cañons from grove to grove, and draw exceedingly angular and complicated courses.

The Ouzel's nest is one of the most extraordinary pieces of bird architecture I ever saw, odd and novel in design, perfectly fresh and beautiful, and in every way worthy of the genius of the little builder. It is about a foot in diameter, round and bossy in outline, with a neatly arched opening near the bottom, somewhat like an old-fashioned brick oven, or Hottentot's hut. It is built almost exclusively of green and yellow mosses, chiefly the beautiful fronded hypnum that covers the rocks and old drift-logs in the vicinity of waterfalls. These are deftly interwoven, and felted together into a charming little hut; and so situated that many of the outer mosses continue to flourish as if they had not been plucked. A few fine, silky-stemmed grasses are occasionally found interwoven with the mosses, but, with the exception of a thin layer lining the floor, their presence seems accidental, as they are of a species found growing with the mosses and are probably plucked with them. The site chosen for this curious mansion is usually some little rock-shelf within reach of the lighter particles of the spray of a waterfall, so that its walls are kept green and growing, at least during the time of high water.

No harsh lines are presented by any portion of the nest as seen in place, but when removed from its shelf, the back and bottom, and sometimes a portion of the top, is found quite sharply angular, because it is made to conform to the surface of the rock upon which and against which it is built, the little architect always taking advantage of slight crevices and protuberances that may chance to offer, to render his structure stable by means of a kind of gripping and dovetailing.

In choosing a building-spot, concealment does not seem to be taken into consideration; yet notwithstanding the nest is large and guilelessly exposed to view, it is far from being easily detected, chiefly because it swells forward like any other bulging moss-cushion growing naturally in such situations. This is more especially the case where the nest is kept fresh by being well sprinkled. Sometimes these romantic little huts have their beauty enhanced by rock-ferns and grasses that spring up around the mossy walls, or in front of the door-sill, dripping with crystal beads.

Furthermore, at certain hours of the day, when the sunshine is poured down at the required angle, the whole mass of the spray enveloping the fairy establishment is brilliantly irised; and it is through so glorious a rainbow atmosphere as this that some of our blessed ouzels obtain their first peep at the world.

Ouzels seem so completely part and parcel of the streams they inhabit, they scarce suggest any other origin than the streams themselves; and one might almost be pardoned in fancying they come direct from the living waters, like flowers from the ground. At least, from whatever cause, it never occurred to me to look for their nests until more than a year after I had made the acquaintance of the birds themselves, although I found one the very day on which I began the search. In making my way from Yosemite to the glaciers at the heads of the Merced and Tuolumne rivers, I camped in a particularly wild and romantic portion of the Nevada cañon where in previous excursions I had never failed to enjoy the company of my favorites, who were attracted here, no doubt, by the safe nesting-places in the shelving rocks, and by the abundance of food and falling water. The river, for miles above and below, consists of a succession of small falls from ten to sixty feet in height, connected by flat, plume-like cascades that go flashing from fall to fall, free and almost channelless, over waving folds of glacier-polished granite.

On the south side of one of the falls, that portion of the precipice which is bathed by the spray presents a series of little shelves and tablets caused by the development of planes of cleavage in the granite, and by the consequent fall of masses through the action of the water. "Now here," said I, "of all places, is the most charming spot for an Ouzel's nest." Then carefully scanning the fretted face of the precipice through the spray, I at length noticed a yellowish moss-cushion, growing on the edge of a level tablet within five or six feet of the outer folds of the fall. But apart from the fact of its being situated where one acquainted with the lives of ouzels would fancy an Ouzel's nest ought to be, there was nothing in its appearance visible at first sight, to distinguish it from other bosses of rock-moss similarly situated with reference to perennial spray; and it was not until I had scrutinized it again and again, and had removed my shoes and stockings and crept along the face of the rock within eight or ten feet of it, that I could decide certainly whether it was a nest or a natural growth.

In these moss huts three or four eggs are laid, white like foam-bubbles; and well may the little birds hatched from them sing water songs, for they hear them all their lives, and even before they are born.

I have often observed the young just out of the nest making their odd gestures, and seeming in every way as much at home as their experienced parents, like young bees on their first excursions to the flower fields. No amount of familiarity with people and their ways seems to change them in the least. To all appearance their behavior is just the same on seeing a man for the first time, as when they have seen him frequently.

On the lower reaches of the rivers where mills are built, they sing on through the din of the machinery, and all the noisy confusion of dogs, cattle, and workmen. On one occasion, while a woodchopper was at work on the river-bank, I observed one cheerily singing within reach of the flying chips. Nor does any kind of unwonted disturbance put him in bad humor, or frighten him out of calm self-possession. In passing through a narrow gorge, I once drove one ahead of me from rapid to rapid, disturbing him four times in quick succession where he could not very well fly past me on account of the narrowness of the channel. Most birds under similar circumstances fancy themselves pursued, and become suspiciously uneasy; but, instead of growing nervous about it, he made his usual dippings, and sang one of his most tranquil strains. When observed within a few yards their eyes are seen to express remarkable gentleness and intelligence; but they seldom allow so near a view unless one wears clothing of about the same color as the rocks and trees, and knows how to sit still. On one occasion, while rambling along the shore of a mountain lake, where the birds, at least those born that season, had never seen a man, I sat down to rest on a large stone close to the water's edge, upon which it seemed the ouzels and sandpipers were in the habit of alighting when they came to feed on that part of the shore, and some of the other birds also, when they came down to wash or drink. In a few minutes, along came a whirring Ouzel and alighted on the stone beside me, within reach of my hand. Then suddenly observing me, he stooped nervously as if about to fly on the instant, but as I remained as motionless as the stone, he gained confidence, and looked me steadily in the face for about a minute, then flew quietly to the outlet and began to sing. Next came a sandpiper and gazed at me with much the same guileless expression of eye as the Ouzel. Lastly, down with a swoop came a Steller's jay out of a fir-tree, probably with the intention of moistening his noisy throat. But instead of sitting confidingly as my other visitors had done, he rushed off at once, nearly tumbling heels over head into the lake in his suspicious confusion, and with loud screams roused the neighborhood. . . .

Even so far north as icy Alaska, I have found my glad singer. When I was exploring the glaciers between Mount Fairweather and the Stikeen River, one cold day in November, after trying in vain to force a way through the innumerable icebergs of Sum Dum Bay to the great glaciers at the head of it, I was weary and baffled and sat resting in my canoe convinced at last that I would have to leave this part of my work for another year. Then I began to plan my escape to open water before the young ice which was beginning to form should shut me in. While I thus lingered drifting with the bergs, in the midst of these gloomy forebodings and all the terrible glacial desolation and grandeur, I suddenly heard the well-known whir of an Ouzel's wings, and, looking up, saw my little comforter coming straight across the ice from the shore. In a second or two he was with me, flying three times round my head with a happy salute, as if saying, "Cheer up, old friend; you see I'm here, and all's well." Then he flew back to the shore, alighted on the topmost jag of a stranded iceberg, and began to nod and bow as though he were on one of his favorite boulders in the midst of a sunny Sierra cascade.

The species is distributed all along the mountain ranges of the Pacific Coast from Alaska to Mexico, and east to the Rocky Mountains. Nevertheless, it is as yet comparatively little known. Audubon and Wilson did not meet it. Swainson was, I believe, the first naturalist to describe a specimen from Mexico. Specimens were shortly afterward procured by Drummond near the sources of the Athabasca River, between the fifty-fourth and fifty-sixth parallels; and it has been collected by nearly all of the numerous exploring expeditions undertaken of late through our Western States and Territories; for it never fails to engage the attention of naturalists in a very particular manner.

Such, then, is our little cinclus, beloved of every one who is so fortu-

nate as to know him. Tracing on strong wing every curve of the most
precipitous torrents from one extremity of the Sierra to the other; not
fearing to follow them through their darkest gorges and coldest snow-
tunnels; acquainted with every waterfall, echoing their divine music;
and throughout the whole of their beautiful lives interpreting all that
we in our unbelief call terrible in the utterances of torrents and storms,
as only varied expressions of God's eternal love.

ENNUI

AND THE

COMMON CROW

David Quammen

Much of American nature writing is unrelievedly serious, sometimes op-pressively so. Not so the work of the young magazine columnist David Quammen, who seeks the unexpected, the bizarre in the natural world. Here he plays psychiatrist to "the world's smartest bird," the common—more properly American—crow.

Any person with no steady job and no children naturally finds time for a sizable amount of utterly idle speculation. For instance, me —I've developed a theory about crows. It goes like this:

Crows are bored. They suffer from being too intelligent for their station in life. Respectable evolutionary success is simply not, for these brainy and complex birds, enough. They are dissatisfied with the narrow goals and horizons of that tired old Darwinian struggle. On the lookout for a new challenge. See them there, lined up conspiratorially along a fence rail or a high wire, shoulder to shoulder, alert, self-contained, missing nothing. Feeling discreetly thwarted. Waiting, like an ambitious understudy, for their break. Dolphins and whales and chimpanzees get all the fawning publicity, great fuss made over their near-human intelligence. But don't be fooled. Crows are not stupid. Far from it. They are merely underachievers. They are bored.

Most likely it runs in their genes, along with the black plumage and the talent for vocal mimicry. Crows belong to a remarkable family of birds known as the Corvidae, also including ravens, magpies, jackdaws and jays, and the case file on this entire clan is so full of prodigious and quirky behavior that it cries out for interpretation not by an ornithologist but a psychiatrist. Or, failing that, some ignoramus with a supple theory. Computerized ecologists can give us those fancy equations de-

From *Natural Acts: A Sidelong View of Science and Nature*. New York: Nick Lyons Books/Schocken Books, 1985.

picting the whole course of a creature's life history in terms of energy allotment to every physical need, with variables for fertility and senility and hunger and motherly love; but they haven't yet programmed in a variable for boredom. No wonder the Corvidae dossier is still packed with unanswered questions.

At first glance, though, all is normal: Crows and their corvid relatives seem to lead an exemplary birdlike existence. The home life is stable and protective. Monogamy is the rule, and most mated pairs stay together until death. Courtship is elaborate, even rather tender, with the male doing a good bit of bowing and dancing and jiving, not to mention supplying his intended with food; eventually he offers the first scrap of nesting material as a sly hint that they get on with it. While she incubates a clutch of four to six eggs, he continues to furnish the groceries, and stands watch nearby at night. Then for a month after hatching, both parents dote on the young. Despite strenuous care, mortality among fledglings is routinely high, sometimes as high as 70 percent, but all this crib death is counterbalanced by the longevity of the adults. Twenty-year-old crows are not unusual, and one raven in captivity survived to age twenty-nine. Anyway, corvids show no inclination toward breeding themselves up to huge numbers, filling the countryside with their kind (like the late passenger pigeon, or an infesting variety of insect) until conditions shift for the worse, and a vast population collapses. Instead, crows and their relatives reproduce at roughly the same stringent rate through periods of bounty or austerity, maintaining levels of population that are modest but consistent, and which can be supported throughout any foreseeable hard times. In this sense they are astute pessimists. One consequence of such modesty of demographic ambition is to leave them with excess time, and energy, not desperately required for survival.

The other thing they possess in excess is brain-power. They have the largest cerebral hemispheres, relative to body size, of any avian family. On various intelligence tests—to measure learning facility, clock-reading skills, the ability to count—they have made other birds look doltish. One British authority, Sylvia Bruce Wilmore, pronounces them "quicker on the uptake" than certain well-thought-of-mammals like the cat and the monkey, and admits that her own tamed crow so effectively dominated the other animals in her household that this bird "would even pick up the spaniel's leash and lead him around the garden!" Wilmore also adds cryptically: "Scientists at the University of Mississippi have been successful in getting the cooperation of Crows." But she fails to make clear whether that was as test subjects, or on a consultative basis.

From other crow experts come the same sort of anecdote. Crows hiding food in all manner of unlikely spots and relying on their uncanny memories, like adepts at the game of Concentration, to find the caches again later. Crows using twenty-three distinct forms of call to communicate various sorts of information to each other. Crows in flight dropping clams and walnuts on highway pavement, to break open the shells so the meats can be eaten. Then there's the one about the hooded crow, a species whose range includes Finland: "In this land Hoodies show great initiative during winter when men fish through holes in the ice. Fishermen leave baited lines in the water to catch fish and on their return they have found a Hoodie pulling in the line with its bill, and walking away from the hole, then putting down the line and walking back on it to stop it sliding, and pulling it again until [the crow] catches the fish on the end of the line." These birds are bright.

And probably—according to my theory—they are too bright for their own good. You know the pattern. Time on their hands. Under-employed and over-qualified. Large amounts of potential just lying fallow. Peck up a little corn, knock back a few grasshoppers, carry a beak-full of dead rabbit home for the kids, then fly over to sit on a fence rail with eight or ten cronies and watch some poor farmer sweat like a sow at the wheel of his tractor. An easy enough life, but is this *it*? Is this *all*?

If you don't believe me just take my word for it: Crows are bored.

And so there arise, as recorded in the case file, these certain . . . no, *symptoms* is too strong. Call them, rather, *patterns of gratuitous behavior*.

For example, they play a lot.

Animal play is a reasonably common phenomenon, at least among certain mammals, especially in the young of those species. Play activities—by definition—are any that serve no immediate biological function, and which therefore do not directly improve the animal's prospects for survival and reproduction. The corvids, according to expert testimony, are irrepressibly playful. In fact, they show the most complex play known in birds. Ravens play toss with themselves in the air, dropping and catching again a small twig. They lie on their backs and juggle objects (in one recorded case, a rubber ball) between beak and feet. They jostle each other sociably in a version of "king of the mountain" with no real territorial stakes. Crows are equally frivolous. They play a brand of rugby, wherein one crow picks up a white pebble or a bit of shell and flies from tree to tree, taking a friendly bashing from its buddies until it drops the token. And they have a comedy-acrobatic routine: allowing themselves to tip backward dizzily from a wire perch, holding a loose grip so as to hang upside down, spreading out both wings, then daringly letting go with one foot; finally, switching feet to let go with the other. Such shameless hot-dogging is usually performed for a small audience of other crows.

There is also an element of the practical jokester. Of the Indian house crow, Wilmore says: ". . . this Crow has a sense of humor, and revels in the discomfort caused by its playful tweaking at the tails of other birds, and at the ears of sleeping cows and dogs; it also pecks the toes of flying foxes as they hang sleeping in their roosts." This crow is a laff riot. Another of Wilmore's favorite species amuses itself, she says, by "dropping down on sleeping rabbits and rapping them over the skull or settling on drowsy cattle and startling them." What we have here is actually a distinct subcategory of playfulness known, where I come from at least, as Cruisin' For A Bruisin'. It has been clinically linked to boredom.

Further evidence: Crows are known to indulge in sunbathing. "When sunning at fairly high intensity," says another British corvidist, "the bird usually positions itself sideways on to the sun and erects its feathers, especially those on head, belly, flanks and rump." So the truth is out: Under those sleek ebony feathers, they are tan. And of course sunbathing (like ice-fishing, come to think of it) constitutes prima facie proof of a state of paralytic ennui. . . .

But maybe it's not too late for the corvids. Keep that in mind next time you run into a raven, or a magpie, or a crow. Look the bird in the eye. Consider its frustrations. Try to say something stimulating.

THE

SCAVENGERS

Mary Austin

Mary Austin was not an ornithologist. She was a mystic, a visionary, and, in the opinion of many, a prophetess and seer besides. Born in Illinois, she grew up in Bakersfield, California, fell under the spell of the desert, and there evolved her curious theory of the influence of landscape upon culture. Americans, she argued, were eternally different from the people of the Old World because the land they inhabited was different. They would find their true selves when they learned, as the Indians had learned before them, the lessons this land could teach them.

Of her many books the best was probably The Land of Little Rain *(1903), from which the following selection is taken. The vultures she describes are actual birds that an ornithologist will recognize. But they are also symbols and riddles to be read. They know and they can teach one aspect of the mystique of the desert. Her "buzzard," incidentally, is the turkey vulture, her "vulture" the California condor.*

FIFTY-SEVEN buzzards, one on each of fifty-seven fence posts at the rancho El Tejon, on a mirage-breeding September morning, sat solemnly while the white tilted travelers' vans lumbered down the Canada de los Uvas. After three hours they had only clapped their wings, or exchanged posts. The season's end in the vast dim valley of the San Joaquin is palpitatingly hot, and the air breathes like cotton wool. Through it all the buzzards sit on the fences and low hummocks, with wings spread fanwise for air. There is no end to them, and they smell to heaven. Their heads droop, and all their communication is a rare, horrid croak.

The increase of wild creatures is in proportion to the things they feed upon: the more carrion the more buzzards. The end of the third successive dry year bred them beyond belief. The first year quail mated sparingly; the second year the wild oats matured no seed; the third, cattle died in their tracks with their heads towards the stopped watercourses. And that year the scavengers were as black as the plague all across the mesa and up the treeless, tumbled hills. On clear days they betook themselves to the upper air, where they hung motionless for hours. That year there were vultures among them, distinguished by the white patches

From *The Land of Little Rain*. Boston: Houghton Mifflin, 1903.

under the wings. All their offensiveness notwithstanding, they have a stately flight. They must also have what pass for good qualities among themselves, for they are social, not to say clannish.

It is a very squalid tragedy—that of the dying brutes and the scavenger birds. Death by starvation is slow. The heavy-headed, rack-boned cattle totter in the fruitless trails; they stand for long, patient intervals; they lie down and do not rise. There is fear in their eyes when they are first stricken, but afterward only intolerable weariness. I suppose the dumb creatures know nearly as much of death as do their betters, who have only the more imagination. Their even-breathing submission after the first agony is their tribute to its inevitableness. It needs a nice discrimination to say which of the basket-ribbed cattle is likeliest to afford the next meal, but the scavengers make few mistakes. One stoops to the quarry and the flock follows.

Cattle once down may be days in dying. They stretch out their necks along the ground, and roll up their slow eyes at longer intervals. The buzzards have all the time, and no beak is dropped or talon struck until the breath is wholly passed. It is doubtless the economy of nature to have the scavengers by to clean up the carrion, but a wolf at the throat would be a shorter agony than the long stalking and sometime perchings of these loathsome watchers. Suppose now it were a man in this long-drawn, hungrily spied upon distress! When Timmie O'Shea was lost on Armogossa Flats for three days without water, Long Tom Basset found him, not by any trail, but by making straight away for the points where he saw buzzards stooping. He could hear the beat of their wings, Tom said, and trod on their shadows, but O'Shea was past recalling what he thought about things after the second day. My friend Ewan told me, among other things, when he came back from San Juan Hill, that not all the carnage of battle turned his bowels as the sight of slant black wings rising flockwise before the burial squad.

There are three kinds of noises buzzards make—it is impossible to call them notes—raucous and elemental. There is a short croak of alarm, and the same syllable in a modified tone to serve all the purposes of ordinary conversation. The old birds make a kind of throaty chuckling to their young, but if they have any love song I have not heard it. The young yawp in the nest a little, with more breath than noise. It is seldom one finds a buzzard's nest, seldom that grown-ups find a nest of any sort; it is only children to whom these things happen by right. But by making a business of it one may come upon them in wide, quiet cañons, or on the lookouts of lonely, table-topped mountains, three or four together, in the tops of stubby trees or on rotten cliffs well open to the sky.

It is probable that the buzzard is gregarious, but it seems unlikely from the small number of young noted at any time that every female incubates each year. The young birds are easily distinguished by their size when feeding, and high up in air by the worn primaries of the older birds. It is when the young go out of the nest on their first foraging that the parents, full of a crass and simple pride, make their indescribable chucklings of gobbling, gluttonous delight. The little ones would be amusing as they tug and tussle, if one could forget what it is they feed upon.

One never comes any nearer to the vulture's nest or nestlings than hearsay. They keep to the southerly Sierras, and are bold enough, it seems, to do killing on their own account when no carrion is at hand. They dog the shepherd from camp to camp, the hunter home from the hill, and will even carry away offal from under his hand.

The vulture merits respect for his bigness and for his bandit airs, but he is a sombre bird, with none of the buzzard's frank satisfaction in his offensiveness.

The least objectionable of the inland scavengers is the raven, frequenter of the desert ranges, the same called locally "carrion crow." He is handsomer and has such an air. He is nice in his habits and is said to have likable traits. A tame one in a Shoshone camp was the butt of much sport and enjoyed it. He could all but talk and was another with the children, but an arrant thief. The raven will eat most things that come his way—eggs and young of ground-nesting birds, seeds even, lizards and grasshoppers, which he catches cleverly; and whatever he is about, let a coyote trot never so softly by, the raven flaps up and after; for whatever the coyote can pull down or nose out is meat also for the carrion crow.

And never a coyote comes out of his lair for killing, in the country of the carrion crows, but looks up first to see where they may be gathering. It is a sufficient occupation for a windy morning, on the lineless, level mesa, to watch the pair of them eying each other furtively, with a tolerable assumption of unconcern, but no doubt with a certain amount of good understanding about it. Once at Red Rock, in a year of green pasture, which is a bad time for the scavengers, we saw two buzzards, five ravens, and a coyote feeding on the same carrion, and only the coyote seemed ashamed of the company.

Probably we never fully credit the interdependence of wild creatures, and their cognizance of the affairs of their own kind. When the five coyotes that range the Tejon from Pasteria to Tunawai planned a relay race to bring down an antelope strayed from the band, beside myself to watch, an eagle swung down from Mt. Pinos, buzzards materialized out of invisible ether, and hawks came trooping like small boys to a street fight. Rabbits sat up in the chaparral and cocked their ears, feeling themselves quite safe for the once as the hunt swung near them. Nothing happens in the deep wood that the blue jays are not all agog to tell. The hawk follows the badger, the coyote the carrion crow, and from their aerial stations the buzzards watch each other. What would be worth knowing is how much of their neighbor's affairs the new generations learn for themselves, and how much they are taught of their elders.

So wide is the range of the scavengers that it is never safe to say, eyewitness to the contrary, that there are few or many in such a place. Where the carrion is, there will the buzzards be gathered together, and in three days' journey you will not sight another one. The way up from Mojave to Red Butte is all desertness, affording no pasture and scarcely a rill of water. In a year of little rain in the south, flocks and herds were driven to the number of thousands along this road to the perennial pastures of the high ranges. It is a long, slow trail, ankle deep in bitter dust that gets up in the slow wind and moves along the backs of the crawling cattle. In the worst of times one in three will pine and fall out by the way. In the defiles of Red Rock, the sheep piled up a stinking lane; it was the sun smiting by day. To these shambles came buzzards, vultures, and coyotes from all the country round, so that on the Tejon, the Ceriso, and the Little Antelope there were not scavengers enough to keep the country clean. All that summer the dead mummified in the open or dropped slowly back to earth in the quagmires of the bitter springs. Meanwhile from Red Rock to Coyote Holes, and from Coyote Holes to Haiwai the scavengers gorged and gorged.

The coyote is not a scavenger by choice, preferring his own kill, but being on the whole a lazy dog, is apt to fall into carrion eating because it is easier. The red fox and bobcat, a little pressed by hunger, will eat of any other animal's kill, but will not ordinarily touch what dies of itself, and are exceedingly shy of food that has been manhandled.

Very clean and handsome, quite belying his relationship in appearance, is Clark's crow, that scavenger and plunderer of mountain camps. It is permissible to call him by his common name, "Camp Robber": he has earned it. Not content with refuse, he pecks open meal sacks, filches whole potatoes, is a gormand for bacon, drills holes in packing cases, and is daunted by nothing short of tin. All the while he does not neglect to vituperate the chipmunks and sparrows that whisk off crumbs of comfort from under the camper's feet. The Camp Robber's gray coat, black and white barred wings, and slender bill, with certain tricks of perching, accuse him of attempts to pass himself off among woodpeckers; but his behavior is all crow. He frequents the higher pine belts, and has a noisy strident call like a jay's, and how clean he and the frisk-tailed chipmunks keep the camp! No crumb or paring or bit of eggshell goes amiss.

High as the camp may be, so it is not above timber-line, it is not too high for the coyote, the bobcat, or the wolf. It is the complaint of the ordinary camper that the woods are too still, depleted of wild life. But what dead body of wild thing, or neglected game untouched by its kind, do you find? And put out offal away from camp over night, and look next day at the foot tracks where it lay.

Man is a great blunderer going about in the woods, and there is no other except the bear makes so much noise. Being so well warned beforehand, it is a very stupid animal, or a very bold one, that cannot keep safely hid. The cunningest hunter is hunted in turn, and what he leaves of his kill is meat for some other. That is the economy of nature, but with it all there is not sufficient account taken of the works of man. There is no scavenger that eats tin cans, and no wild thing leaves a like disfigurement on the forest floor.

CALL TO

A TRUMPETER

Sally Carrighar

Sally Carrighar, a gifted and indefatigable observer in remote northern lands, developed a personal and original approach to the problem of describing the intimate life of birds and other animals. Like Ernest Thompson Seton, her aim is to make us realize that they do actually "lead lives" rather than merely "exhibit behavior patterns," and to establish in this way an empathy between them and us. Walking carefully between the Scylla of mere behaviorism and the Charybdis of the anthropomorphic, she is astonishingly successful in making the subjects of her accounts humanly understandable without attributing to them exclusively human traits.

THE late, yellowing sun shot its rays through the willow brush. The willows grew out of the water in clusters like giant fistfuls. They met at the top in a wide glinting blur. Below was the lucent brown gloss, now frosted lightly with autumn dust. In flowing water the dust had wrinkled against the stems. On sheltered bays swimming animals had left shining paths.

The Trumpeter Swan was gliding beneath the wilderness of the brush. Where the overhead boughs spread apart, his breast broke a pale blue sheen. Under the leaves that joined, he was scattering green-gold flakes. He was crossing reflections of the stems, red with a violet bloom on the bark. But all the willows were not bursts of color. Among them were dead thickets, bare and silvered by the sun so that they looked ice-coated, tangles with the crystal magic of winter. Any day the sheaths of ice would become real, and the tremulous water no longer would yield to a white feathered bow.

Here the willows became so dense that the Swan must keep swinging to wind among them. He paddled faster, with his throat tensely upright. He could not relax when he felt so enclosed, although he was more

From *One Day at Teton Marsh*. New York: Alfred A. Knopf, 1947, 1954.

concerned for his family, following him, than for himself. A moose and her calf were browsing near on the leaves. They were out of sight, but the plunge of their hoofs was disquieting. And he could hear their talk, rough murmurs that may have seemed a violence to the Swan, whose own voice was a ringing clear channel for his emotions.

The thickets beyond were spaced thinly, and he came out on a small lagoon. His throat fell into a flow of curves, a tranquil sway forward and back over his wings, a lift to capture a mayfly, a downward folding to layer a feather, a revolving to scan the shoreline. The fly and feather and shore may have been only excuses for the elegant pleasure of motions so slowly graceful. He seemed more quiet than if he had not moved at all.

Now, late in the afternoon, little wind touched the responsive water. It was a stillness quick to stir, like the Swan's awareness. But a flock of mergansers splashed into the bay. They were learning how to drive fish to the shallows. The one they pursued dodged away to the willow canals, and several of the ducks dived. The Swan returned to the willows himself. Mergansers, with their habit of swimming underwater, made him nervous. For no one could tell where they would come up again. The Swan had a poise so sensitive, controlling such immense power, that lively animals often were subdued by it. Much of the time he lived in a peace he partly created; but no duck respected it. Nor did the winds. And the snows would not, and even more disastrously human beings had entered it.

He was leading his family to the beaver pond, a width from which they could rise in flight. Since the day drew to its end, his mate might follow him into the sky, if she ever would. Rounding a thicket, he missed the silent movement behind, of the others. He strengthened the stroke of one foot to pivot, and paddled back. His three cygnets had stopped to dabble for insects in floating leaves. Their mother was not with them.

The Swan was patient. He held his place with a weaving pressure of one web and the other and watched the fledglings. Their winter plumage was nearly complete. At first they had been all violet-gray, but their heads now were pinkish rust. Their bills were violet, mottled with rose. And did their colors please their father, whose eyes could distinguish them but were used to adult swans' vivid white?

The cygnets were two-thirds grown, larger than ducks but doubtless small to him. Their necks were shorter-proportioned than they would be later, and their heads were fluffier. One was beating his wings, a stretching that half-lifted him into the air, with his olive-brown feet patting the water. The other two also began to flap—little mimics still. In many ways they were not mature, needing yet to be watched. See how heedlessly they are switching their bills through the leaves, concerned only with food. They have not learned a swan's exquisite caution. At their age most birds were meeting the world by themselves, but in those species the new generation numbered thousands, even millions. The Swan was protecting his cygnets as if he had known that less than a hundred new broods of trumpeters had hatched this year, throughout the world.

Their mother should not expose them to danger by lingering so. Surely she was not far behind, concealed by the brush, but why not here? Her manner lately had made the Swan uneasy. She had seemed separate, most of the time near the family but not careful to guard the cygnets on one side while he guarded them on the other, not balancing her moves with his, with a matching grace as harmonious as a single swan's; not coming into the air with the others, not once since the young had begun to fly.

The mother had not been in the air since the flightless weeks of her summer molt. But the Swan's own wing feathers were grown out now; hers should be too. This was the season when swans should be making expeditions around the valley, around the peaks cupping the sky, up the Snake to its highest rill. Always on other years he and his mate had taken their young on autumn flights.

A swan's nature widened as the fall of leaves widened horizons. And these short family tours were the only ones they would make. No trumpeters anywhere migrated southward now. Once they did; even the grandparents of these two had been in the spindrift of wings scudding down the continent to the marshes that do not freeze. But human beings had come to those marshes to shoot swans for their down. And some of the ponds had been drained. Wildness was gone from the south—knowledge that older swans seemed to have given the recent ones. This Jackson Hole pair never had seen the devastation of the wintering grounds; yet their impulse to go was checked.

Actually human beings had stopped killing trumpeters everywhere. They had found that their spirits were lifted by the resonant voices and the great translucent wings. And so they had made a law that no one might destroy these birds. But how could that news be conveyed to the wild discouraged instincts?

The birds' down kept them warm in the northern winters, but too often their food was lost. They would stay on the narrowing ponds until the underwater plants were glazed over completely; then would starve. So quickly a species can die: of the immense flocks of trumpeters less than a thousand birds, anywhere, now remained alive.

These two had been fortunate. They had been reared on the Red Rock Lakes, where there was permanent open water. Then on one of their fall flights they had found this Teton Marsh, even warmer, and had stayed. Men had come here to kill ducks however, and some of their shot had fallen into the shallows. The mother swan had found several and had swallowed them, believing them snails perhaps. By this time the shot had eroded away, but she was sick of lead poisoning—sick of civilization really, as much as the swans who starved.

The father and the cygnets rounded the island and walked up into the sedges. The mother stayed in the water. She no longer spent the nights on their hillock; that was one of her strange new ways. The young ones let themselves down on the spongy roots. Sleepiness soon dazed their eyes. The Swan too folded his feet beneath him. He plucked a few sedge seeds and turned his neck backward so that his head lay at the upper edge of one wing. Most of his bill was under the feathers, but his eyes were out.

His mate appeared tense. He raised his head, for she was pushing against the island. With fumbling, broken motions she was trying to come ashore. But her legs were not strong enough to support her, and she sank back in the water.

She slept. For a long time the Swan stayed awake, watchful and now with a deep uneasiness. The sky was a merging of faded daylight and coming moonlight, a bright dust that anywhere might be stars. The yellow and green of the shoreline grasses still faintly showed. Their reflection was touched by the shine on the pond, which gave them the delicacy of grasses in spring, when they were tremulous, with their stirrings yet uncertain. Below the vertical blurs the water was mauve and blue-silver, the shades in the sky. A dragonfly passed, drained of his color. The grasses grayed. Overhead then was only a dark immensity, pricked by stars.

As soon as the sun was up, the cygnets began to stir. Piping a soft impatience, they slipped down in the water and filed away toward the willow thickets. Their father overtook them; more slowly their mother followed. The family passed other sedge hillocks and a corner of the meadow. The sun, coming in levelly, filled the grasses with light, and glanced off the water, striking the swans' plumage twice.

Even the father's own feeding was an aid to his young. The willow channels were ice-bordered this morning, but he paddled along the open center, watching the liquid brown depths. Some plants grew too deep, but finally he found a bed of clasping-leaf pondweed that he could reach. He swung down his head and first raked in the muck. The sensitive skin on his bill touched a dragonfly nymph. He nibbled it up and probed for more. Meanwhile, in brushing between the rippled leaves, he had broken off some of them. They floated up, nourishment for the cygnets. And when he pulled up a whole spray, waterboatmen and scuds were dislodged, and the young swans caught them. Several ducks—mallards and the consistent little thieves, baldpates—sped up to share the food. The Swan did not object. He cleared the channel of the weeds, satisfying his own hunger, the cygnets', and that of various smaller birds.

When the meal was finished, the cygnets paddled off to the meadow.

They were sleepy, climbed out into the grass, and cuddled down. Their mother had stayed in the willows, but their father joined them.

He laid his head between his wings and closed his eyes. He also wished to sleep, for his day's vigilance had begun too early. Late in the night the beaver had been moving with sounds that were harmless, but toward morning a slap of his tail had sent a warning over the marsh. Peering up from the sedges, the Swan had discovered an otter.

The enemy swam about, underwater or sculling through the surface. Moonlight silvered his wakes, and the ripples swished into the sedge blades of the swans' roost. Finally he went away, but he might return. The Swan had felt too alarmed to relax again.

Even now, in the reassuring light of day, he could not sleep. For the weather was making all the creatures restless. It made the swans, too, nervous, but they did not hop, flutter, or call continually, or fight. They showed their discomfort by letting the others' movements unsettle them. The cygnets were aroused by a varying hare, thumping her own tension.

At once they wished to be somewhere else. The Swan was disturbed at the prospect of taking them out alone. He called to his mate, but she did not come. Perhaps he could lead the young ones to the backwash, usually a quiet place. No; they would go past the dam. Two parents might have distracted them. They ignored their father's urging. He paddled faster and swung in advance.

Beyond the dam was the wooded bank with the beaver's canal cut into it and his house built against it. The adult swans never had brought the young here; an enemy could steal toward them too secretly through the grove. Now the cygnets swung up the shore, piping their pleasure in the new place. They stopped near the canal and jabbed for water-skaters in the debris drifted against the bank.

The current, draining toward the dam, was a swifter movement against the Swan's feet than the flow in the sedge beds or thickets. But his webs could detect another, uneven surge, no doubt stirred by the otter. An otter might swim up under a cygnet and pull it down. He was likely to do it only if he could find no fish, and this pond fairly swayed with fish; yet an otter's caprice was not to be trusted.

The Swan's eyes strained across the pond. The otter was submerged and not visible through the surface, dazzled with sunlit ripples. The smallest cygnet, a female, sensed her father's alarm. She showed the first stilling of her impulsiveness, the first touch of a swan's caution. While her brothers hunted more insects, she moved farther along the shore, where she could take flight more easily.

The heavy irregular surge became stronger. No more waiting; the father must take his young ones into the air. He called and had made the first leaping strokes with his feet when a marsh hawk swung over the grove.

The Swan could outdistance the hawk in flight, but the cygnets could not. Here then they must stay. The harrier had seen them. He would torment them—a prospect that put a more sensuous grace in his wing-beat. This was one of his great days. The swift wind had given him opposition, and that he loved. Here could be more of it.

With a shrill cry he turned down and straightened out, hanging above the young female. His yellow claws dropped. His hovering face would be terrible to a cygnet; ruffed and flat, it combined the look of a hawk and an owl.

The father was down-wind of the harrier. He could rise only by turning his back on the cygnets. He paddled instead to the little one's side, whipping a violent spray with his wings. The hawk cried another taunt, and the Swan replied with a louder warning. His neck was drawn back and his beak was open, ready for a murderous lunge if the hawk should drop lower.

At a sag in the wind the harrier swayed, lost his position, and circled above the pond to advance again over the cygnet. With that brief break the father sped into the wind, was soon off the water and pursuing the hawk. The harrier swept away, across the meadow and river and on over the sagebrush plain. The Swan was close behind, calling threats. The harrier went into a steep dive, a winding ascent, and another dive—sinuous turns that the larger Swan could not closely follow. But in fleeing, the hawk had admitted that he was vanquished. The father hastened back toward the pond and the greater threat of the otter.

The young ones had been subdued by their fright. Now they would be obedient. The marsh no longer beat with the otter's swimming, but the family filed to the sedge beds and their roost. There, secluded behind the tall, upright blades, they would wait out this tumultuous morning.

Soon after noon the wind blew down a dead tree that anchored the beavers' dam. It crashed on the pond with the high, metallic clatter of shattered water. Ducks exploded from the surface. The pelican sailed away. The great blue heron flopped up with a *quonck* in a loud collapsing voice. And out from the willows, like mosquitoes from beaten grass, rose smaller birds, incredible numbers seen together, of magpies, and mourning doves, belted kingfishers, yellow warblers, mountain and black-capped chickadees, pink-sided juncos, and tree swallows. Only the swans did not fly. Over their hillock the white and gray wings briefly waved; then were folded.

Soon the fears, too, were folded. The boldest birds came down, each leading a flock of excited followers.

The storm was close to Jackson Hole. Now the winds whirling around its center had passed on east. The water lay heavy and still, repeating with darkened colors every shoreline twig and root, every russet, cream, or brown-striped breast of a floating duck.

The Swan's mate spread the clearest outline on the surface. Below her perfectly was reflected the white sway of her side. It ended in the black knob of her knee, high because her legs were pulled up in discomfort. The Swan came off the roost to float beside her, and the cygnets followed. The family drew together, seeming to sense a crisis. A strange new sound was roughening the air.

The first hint of its meaning came to the Swan when he found that his toes touched the muck. They never had done that here. Now his webs were flat on the bottom, and he stood. Then the cygnets' feet touched, as their mother may have seen, for she lowered her own webs. At once she started toward the pond. Not being able to walk, she must stay on water deep enough so that she could paddle. She stopped at the outer border of the sedge beds, and the others with her. But she soon had to move again.

The dam had not been visible from the sedge roost. When the swans came out into the pond they discovered a break in the beaver's masonry. Around the roots of the upset tree the water was pouring down to the creek below. This was the reason for the roar they were hearing. The shores of the pond were drawing inward; its size was shrinking. Behind the swans were channels and slopes of bare mud.

Several times the family let the shallow water drive them on. Then they went to the center of the pond and huddled there near the end of the fallen tree. The father was facing the backwash, but into his sidewise vision a shadow flowed. It was the otter, topping the dam with his lilting step.

The mother too saw him. They swung together, enclosing the cygnets. The otter dived in the pond. But he emerged and began to tour the borders. No switch of his tail-tip and no toss of his arrogant head was missed by the eyes of the Swan.

The otter tumbled and swam in the draining pond. He rode the cascade through the break and caught a fish and climbed up on the prostrate trunk of the tree to eat it. The swans went out on the open surface.

A second otter came. The lively creatures were splashing together. The swans turned toward the shore, then back on the pond again, for the otters went out on the silt. The father Swan shifted about, tense and frantic.

Over the earth swept a sudden darkening, and a quick wind stirred the leaves. The air was oppressive. It lay in the Swan's lungs so heavily that each breath must be pushed out. Limpness lowered the arch in the mother's throat.

Down from the sky fell a soft tumult of snow. The flakes dissolved on the water; on the shores, the dam, and the brush they spread a cover. The downy mist thickened. An enemy could pounce from it. The swans heard the otters' cries but they could not see them. They could not see, in fact, to the other side of the pond. They heard also the brutal hoarse-ness of ravens, brawling over something, somewhere out there in the close white shower.

But loudest for the father may have been the calls of competing instincts. Surely he should be loyal first to his sick mate. He should stay here and protect her, helpless, needing him so desperately. His devotion to her was a lifelong emotion; his concern for the cygnets would pass before another brood could hatch.

Yet his full care of the young ones, recently, had strengthened his sense of responsibility for them. To save them, he should leave this vanishing marsh. He should take them to a new home, probably on the Red Rock Lakes, where he had spent his own years as a cygnet. Safety and food depended on water, and soon apparently none would be here.

To protect his mate or his fledglings—both calls rose from the deepest instincts in his nature. And the conflict may have been no less an anguish because conscious reasoning did not weigh it. Decided either way, one almost-irresistible urge must be denied.

He knew which call he would answer when he felt his wings lift. Into the dense enveloping snow he sped. He trumpeted to the cygnets and then slowed his flight, listening for the skitter of their feet, the air thrashed by their wings. When all three were aloft, a different note came into his voice. It spoke to his mate, though not with a summons. He was aware now that she could not rise. But he sent down his cry, for her to understand if she could. Twice he led the cygnets in low circles above the marsh, trumpeting to the white bird, so quiet upon the black pond. Finally her throat straightened, her bill lifted upward, and she trumpeted one answering call.

He turned his course west toward the Teton slope. Along the base of the mountains was a row of lakes, familiar enough so that he could find them in blind flying. He held his speed to the cygnets' and constantly urged them on, so that none would be lost. He was taking them to the smallest lake, on Mount Moran, near the northern tip of the range. It could not be a home, for these lakes froze from shore to shore. But on its breadth were the tops of several muskrat lodges. One would be a roost where the family could await the end of the storm.

He still was awake when the storm broke up. The mountain and the long range south took shape. The overhead thickness began to lift and shred. For a while clouds, luminous with moonlight, continued to cross the frosted blue of the dark night sky. Their shining passage seemed the only happening, now that the earth was covered by the wide monotony of the snow. As smoothly as swans the clouds appeared from over the Teton crest, to stream above the valley and beyond the eastern range. With a lingering hold one pulled away from another . . . lost the touch . . . moved on alone. Two united . . . blended . . . started to separate

. . . clung . . . tore apart. Always they were changing, but their world did not change. It was a world of inviolate wildness.

A new wind swept the clouds away, and in the sky was only the moon, a hanging ball of light that dimmed the stars.

The bugling of an elk awakened the cygnets in the morning. He stood on a granite cliff above the lake and sent his challenge over the valley with a rising flow of notes almost as clear and vibrant as the Swan's.

The early light was coloring the snowy peaks with the nacreous pink of sea shells. Coming down the slope, the sunshine gilded the ivory crown upon the elk's head. It passed the pines and spruces at the shore and stretched back over the misty surface of the lake to the lodge.

The Swan allowed the cygnets to feed for a brief time. Soon he called them and rose from the pond to start their flight to the Red Rock Lakes. The sky felt crisp and electric, for with the storm's departure ozone from above the stratosphere was raining earthward. The pressure of the air was heightened, heightening in turn each animal's vitality. Never had the cygnets flown so swiftly.

Everything seemed changed, and for the better. That may have been the reason why the Swan reversed his course. Or possibly the danger to his mate was, after all, the stronger call. He circled back at the head of the valley, turning south instead of north. Setting an almost-adult speed for the young swans, he was following the Gros Ventre crest.

The indigo river shone between the white flats of the valley floor. One of its curves, there, held the marsh. The pond was smaller than before the tree fell, but it was not empty. The Swan was spiraling down.

His glide along the water stopped him near the dam. During the night the beaver partly had repaired it, and the inflow of the brook had filled the marsh up to the level of the dam's unfinished top. The willow channels still were drained, but the surface spread back past the sedge beds, past the Swan's roost. Floating near the hillock was his mate.

He hastened toward the roost, so eagerly that now the ripples did not melt out from his sides but splashed away. The cygnets stopped at a bed of milfoil, which the lowering of the pond had brought within their reach.

The mother watched her family's return. Her eyes were more intense this morning, with a more accessible look. And there were other proofs that she was slightly stronger. Her wings lay higher on her back, and her throat was swinging slowly. Her head was turning in the sunlight. If she had swallowed more of the shot, she might not have recovered. She might not if the weather had remained depressing. But its most invigorating benefits had come together at her crisis. She would live, though never again to mother cygnets, for the poison had made her barren.

As the Swan approached, he thrust his head beneath the surface, tossed it back with a shower of crystal drops upon his wings. He beat the wings and half-rose from the water. Slowing the stroke, he let himself down but again reared, framed in his wings' great pulsing gleam of white.

The motion may have been stirred by instinct's memory of the autumn when they plighted their devotion. The ritual had been a kind of dance, in which the two, advancing toward each other, lifted from the water, breast to breast. This later day his mate could only once and briefly raise her wings—the merest opening along her sides, yet a wish expressed.

He tilted his bill as if to trumpet, but swung it down and glided closer to her. Both birds turned their attention to the sunny day, the cygnets, and the life that they would share once more, beginning with this new and silent clasping of their spirits.

TITANIA

AND OBERON

George Miksch Sutton

Roger Tory Peterson says that the question he is most often asked by visiting naturalists is, "Where can I see the big cuckoo that runs on the ground?" The answer is, "In the arid Southwest," and the bird in question is the famous greater roadrunner, the cockiest and most impudent as well as the strangest bird of our American deserts. He does not look like a member of the cuckoo tribe—he is almost chicken size and he waves his long tail up and down to express his emotions. Neither does he have the reprehensible habits of the European cuckoo, since he is a good family man. His favorite foods are snakes (even rattlesnakes) and lizards, which he chases madly and captures expertly. No bird is more at home in the desert, and it is easily tamed. Here a distinguished American ornithologist describes his intimate experience with this rather unbirdlike bird who, incidentally, can fly if necessary but much prefers to use his legs.

THE stories that Texans tell to Yankee newcomers in their midst are blood-chilling stories of rattlesnakes, coiled ready to strike; of water moccasins that line the shaded banks of streams; of death-dealing coral snakes, ringed with scarlet, gold and black; of scorpions, lightning-quick of tail, that dart from the roadside; of tarantulas, emerald-eyed and steel-fanged, that leap from every clump of cactus; of foot-long centipedes, with formidable pincers, that lie in wait for passers-by in caves. "Should one of these crawl over you," I was told, "your flesh will rot and fall from your bones!"

These impressive lectures, delivered in an awed and ominous voice, served to make my every walk an adventure. Armed with a stout club, I was ready to meet death at any turn.

Of all the descriptions of prairie creatures, that of a certain bird charmed me most. This was the Road-Runner, a blood-thirsty killer whose eyes were "flaming red," and whose speed was the speed of a race

From *Birds in the Wilderness*. New York: The Macmillan Company, 1936.

horse. He was known by such colloquial names as Chapparal Cock, Ground Cuckoo, and Snake Killer. He was the ancient foe of the rattle-snake, round whom he built walls of cactus and whom he fought to the death. What prowess, what strength, what craftiness must be the Road-Runner's, I thought, as I longed to see this terror of the sandy wilderness. I was not anxious, however, that our first meeting should be intimate.

This meeting was inevitable. Walking across the prairie, I entered a ravine whose nearer bank was covered with bushes and vines. Instantly, hearing a sharp rattle, I halted. Was I in a snake's den? Turning cautiously I saw a bird, about two feet long, with coarsely streaked plumage. For a second he looked at me, then raised his high, steel-black crest, disclosing a red-orange, featherless patch back of his eye. Again I heard the arresting rattle as his mandibles clapped together. He bounded with unbelievable ease over some low bushes, then, spreading his short wings which were obviously unfit for sustained flight, soared down the gully, dropped into the maze of gray-green, and was gone. I had met the Road-Runner! I had been close enough to ascertain that not his eyes, but the bare patches *back of his eyes* were red, and that his tail was very long. His perfectly calculated leaping haunted my memory for days.

During the following care-free years I was to learn much about this famous bird. I saw him often. I found his nest. Finally, I took it upon my-self to raise two young from early infancy.

One day in late April, 1914, while pushing my way through a dense, cobweb-hung thicket, I spied not far in front of me a crude mass of twigs. Instantly on the alert, I wiped the caterpillar silk from my eyelashes and looked at the unshapely structure more closely. A hopelessly lopsided, poorly anchored nest it was, but above it, parallel with a supporting branch, was the long, iridescent tail of a bird. In moving, I disturbed a small vine. At once there peered over the rim an angular face with lifted crest and blazing eyes. There was a flash of scarlet then, with scarcely a rustle of leaf or tremor of tendril, the muscular creature slid away. There was a soft thud as strong feet touched the ground. A thin form faded into the weeds. Wings unspread, the mother Road-Runner had bounded clear of the dense tangle.

There was a weird nestful. Crouching beside a soiled egg were five ugly youngsters whose dark-skinned bodies were sparsely covered with long, white hairs, and whose beaks were tipped with the hard egg-tooth of babyhood. Their flabby feet, two toes pointing forward, two backward, were dull blue. Their eyes were gray-brown, with steel-blue pupils and a reptilian stare. Pinfeathers had just begun to appear on the edge of the wings. Were these four-inch, greasy-looking, uncouth things really baby birds? Though I had no experience in caring for such charges I de-cided to take two of them home.

As I stood there I wondered what I was to feed these infant dragons.

Accidentally I touched an upturned beak and four great mouths, wabbling uncertainly on scrawny necks, rose in unison. I jerked back my hand—the pink-blotched lining of those mouths had an almost poisonous appearance. From the depths of the small frames came a hoarse, many-toned buzzing which gave the impression that a colony of winged insects had been stirred to anger.

Puzzled by the motionlessness of one of the young I examined him more closely and was startled at finding an inch of the tail of a large lizard protruding from his mouth. He had been fed enough to keep his digestive apparatus busy for some time; for, as the gastric fluids would make assimilable that part of the lizard which had entered the stomach, he had only to swallow a little more to prolong his meal. For a four-inch Road-Runner a lizard nine inches long should furnish an enduring repast.

I had learned at least that my pets were carnivorous. At home my long-suffering family gathered round the unattractive pair, exhibiting all the enthusiasm at their command, and wondering, no doubt, when this gathering of crawling, creeping, buzzing and squeaking creatures was to end. We found an old bucket, lined it with dry grass, and placed the birds in their new nest. It took them but an instant to adjust themselves. Once they had assumed their normal attitude they began buzzing for food. For the following two weeks this clamor was almost incessant. It greeted us early in the morning; the merest human whisper or footfall near the bucket roused it instantly. I was to learn much, sometimes to my annoyance, about the rapidity with which young Road-Runners digest their food.

At first my charges could not stand; they merely lay on their bellies, bills upraised, ready to beg for food. Soon, however, they began toddling about in the bucket, jostling each other, and raising their bodies unsteadily when in most importunate mood. Pinfeathers began to burst, each glossy vane tipped with the fragile white hair of babyhood. The young Road-Runners were becoming pretty.

No complete record was kept of the thousands of grasshoppers and other insects, lizards, mice, and small snakes which were endlessly thrust into those insatiable gullets. My friends at school learned that I needed help and it was not unusual to see a small troop of boys approaching our house with mice in pasteboard boxes, or snakes and lizards dangling from their hands. Most of these creatures the birds swallowed entire, head first. An eighteen-inch snake could not be consumed at one gulp, to be sure, but it disappeared soon enough, once it was well started. Although bones, fur, feathers, and scales were swallowed indiscriminately, no pellets of indigestible material were tossed up; the powerful juices of the stomach dissolved all arrivals.

When they were strong enough to stand on their toes, the stub-tailed birds were allowed to wabble about the yard. The bare patch back of the eye was now brightening to orange, and about the round pupil appeared a narrow pale ring, giving to the fully lashed eye a fierceness which checked most admirers at a respectful distance.

The young adventurers found the world exciting. Vultures soaring in the distant sky roused at once their interest and suspicion. Floating milkweed-down they eyed with gravity. Strange voices sent them scuttling to a familiar retreat. The warm light penetrated their loose plumage; yielding, they spread their wings, fluffed out the feathers of their backs and shoulders, and took long sun-baths. They bathed in dust also, but never in water. They recognized me as their protector and provider, and followed me, when they could, wherever I went. If I lay on the grass they ran about over my body, toying with my clothing and seeking the highest perch they could reach, not failing of course to beg for food.

Since they were now so personable and were attracting so much attention—they even had visited the Fort Worth Public Library, where they were shown to a hundred wide-eyed children—my family decided they should receive names. Our final choice was Titania and Oberon, though the harsh-plumaged, athletic creatures did not even remotely suggest fairy royalty, nor had I the faintest knowledge of their sex. But we thought these names were pretty and that they reflected good literary taste.

The pets were called by their euphonyms only when visitors were to be properly impressed; consequently, they paid no attention to the meaningless titles. To a snap of the fingers, a whistle, the shutting of a door, or the calling of a homely, but honest "Birdie, Birdie!" however, they came with an overwhelming rush.

After three weeks they became sturdy enough to catch part of their own food. With patient coaxing they were taught to pick up grasshoppers tossed to them, and finally to run after and capture crippled insects. Content at first, perforce, with sluggish, wingless nymphs which were abundant, they stole about through the weeds, wings pressed neatly against their slender bodies, snapping up the insects as fast as they could find them. Grasshoppers, often still alive and kicking, they swallowed with a toss of the head and a hollow gulp. Large green or gray cave-crickets which lived in piles of boards, or in damp, shadowy places, were especially prized. When a yellow- or coral-winged grasshopper rose noisily from the path, the birds crouched in momentary fear, but soon began to mark the return to earth of the clackety aeronaut and to steal up behind tufts of grass, intent upon a killing.

Finally they learned to capture the biggest, noisiest, and wariest grasshoppers on the prairie. They would watch a coral-wing in his courtship flight and, running stealthily, wait until the performer dropped to the ground. With a bound over low weeds, a dart across the open, and a final rush with outspread wings and tail they would frighten their prey into the

air, leap nimbly after him, nab him unerringly with their bills, and descend gracefully on outspread wings to beat him to insensibility with a
whack or two on a stone.

Once they had learned to capture grasshoppers, their food problem was
largely solved and, since they showed no inclination to run away, they
were at liberty most of the time. They ran about the yard, playing with
each other, or catching insects. In the heat of mid-day they sought shelter
of broad, cool leaves, and sprawled in the sand. Daily, often many times
daily, I took them for a walk across the prairie. Following me closely or
running at my side, they watched the big world with eyes far keener
than my own. Grasshoppers which I frightened from the grass they captured in side expeditions. If I paused near a flat stone, they urged me on
with grunts, bit gently at my hands, and raced back and forth in an ecstasy
of anticipation.

I entertained misgivings concerning these flat stones. What savage creatures might not they conceal! Could young Road-Runners manage swift-
tailed scorpions, sharp-toothed mice, or poisonous spiders? Under the first
stone there were scorpions. The Road-Runners hesitated an instant, as if
permitting an untried instinct to take possession of their brains, then
rushed forward, thrust out their heads, and attacked the scorpions precisely at their tails. Perhaps these venomous tails received more than the
usual benumbing blows, but the scorpions were swallowed with gusto.

I had not supposed that a Road-Runner would capture and devour a
tarantula. One day, however, we paused at the tunnel of one of these big,
furred spiders. Somewhat in the spirit of experimentation, and following
the method known to all Texas boys, I teased the black Arachnid from
her lair by twirling a wisp of grass in her face. She popped out viciously
and jumped a good ten inches to one side. With a dash one bird was upon
the monster before she had opportunity to leap a second time. A toss of
the bird's head and one of the eight legs was gone. Free again, the spider
leaped upon her captor. The other bird now entered the combat, snatched
up the spider, and sliced off another leg. One by one the legs went down,
and finally the two birds pulled apart and gulped the sable torso.

Tarantulas were now our prey. Whenever we came upon a burrow the
birds ran about wildly, looked longingly at the hole, begged noisily for
food, then rushed back and forth flashing their tails. Imagine my delight,
my wonder too, one day, at seeing one of the birds pick up a tiny pebble
and, after creeping up slyly, drop it into the neat orfice.

The pretty race-runner lizards which lived along the roads tantalized
the birds almost to a frenzy. These reptiles were at first too wary and
too speedy to be caught. Day after day the birds gave chase only to return with hang-dog expression, shaking their heads sadly, grunting half-
heartedly, and begging penitently for food. One day we surprised a lizard
and had the advantage of being close to him at the start. Running as

rapidly as I could, I headed him off, and in the twinkle of an eye one of the Road-Runners had him by the tail. We were all surprised, upon examining our quarry, to find a tail, twitching and wriggling in the road— but no lizard! *Sans* tail, which had broken off at the proper instant, the lizard was now safe in his den. The birds seemed in doubt as to whether they should consume so mysterious a morsel. Within a week or two these exceedingly nimble lizards were captured every day; and now and then we saw a tail-less one making off in mad haste.

To the comparatively sluggish though well-armored horned lizards, which were to be found in grassless areas, the birds paid no attention unless they were very hungry. A horned lizard, confronted by his foe, would flatten out, rise high on his legs, and sway back and forth as if about to leap or inflict a dangerous bite. But Road-Runners are not to be bluffed. Grasping their tough victim by the head or back they beat him against a convenient stone. Thirty or forty blows were sometimes needed to render him sufficiently quiescent for ingestion. I felt a tightening at the throat as I watched these reptiles being swallowed. But the birds evinced no pain or discomfort. Occasionally, indeed, horned lizards were swallowed while yet quite alive, and had to be coughed up for further battering.

The conquest of certain individual animals became an obsession with the redoubtable pets. There was, for instance, an old scaly swift lizard whose fortress and sunning place was a lumber pile not far from the house. Attempt after attempt was made to surprise, head off, or corner this sage veteran, but he was always too quick. There were too many convenient crevices into which he could dive, and his favorite sunning spots were so prominent that he could survey his surroundings with ease. He was so handsome and he matched his wits so successfully with those of his feathered tormentors that I grew rather fond of him. One day I saw one of the birds stealing upon him from behind a huge burdock plant. That day might have been his last had I not thrown a stone which popped sharply on a board sending him pellmell into one of his retreats.

There was also a round-bodied cotton rat which had a nest in a rough stone wall that extended along one side of our property. Two or three times a day he scurried across a gap in the wall, and the birds came to look upon him as a possible meal. At first his speed and considerable size kept the enemy at a safe distance, but their interest sharpened daily, and eventually they formed the habit of loitering near the runway. One day I heard a squeal of terror and ran up in time to see the bewildered animal running this way and that, trying to escape the two lightning-quick demons who never really held him, but pinched him, tossed him, dealt him blows, buffeted him, made him weary with fighting for life. Over his limp form the Road-Runners had an argument. He was heavy. No sooner would one bird start to swallow than the other would be tugging at the hind foot or tail, and down he would drop. I finally cut the rat in two.

From the first of our foraging expeditions the birds had killed with ease the small snakes which we found under rocks. Now having attained full size, they were ready for combat with their traditional foe, the rattle-snake; but I never saw them actually killing a large snake of any kind.

Large dead snakes were frequently given to the birds, however, and their attempts to swallow a four-foot meal were vastly amusing. Having beaten the dead reptile's head on the ground to make assurance doubly sure, they engaged in a spirited wrangle to settle ownership. Sometimes one Road-Runner actually got the head-end of the snake swallowed and stood awkwardly gasping for breath while the other bird tugged at the tail-end. What futility! The scales of a snake's skin are so constructed that it would be almost as easy for a snake to move backwards through the grass as for a bird to swallow it tail first.

After they had worn themselves down to a state of philosophical acceptance of their physical limitations, I usually cut the snake into three or four pieces and let them while away the hours in swallowing. At such times they wandered unhappily about, mouths agape, the fore part of their meal safely down and being digested, but the latter part annoyingly in the way, awaiting its hour of engulfment. The unswallowed portion usually hung from one side of the mouth for half an hour until the bird, tiring of this attitude, would step over and about the dangling meal, shifting it to the other side of his mouth, and exhibiting in every movement a mighty determination to keep it from slipping out.

My six-year-old sister, Evangel, was frankly afraid of these pet Road-Runners. While wearing a certain pair of brown sandals she once kicked in self-defense at a bird which ran at her, begging for food. This bird, recognizing that he had the upper hand, rushed at the little girl whenever she wore those sandals. She came screaming into the house one day, a Road-Runner flopping about her neck, his hard bill grasping firmly the lobe of her ear.

A neighbor's small dog seemed to derive immense pleasure from chasing the birds. They never really had to run to out-distance this noisy pest, but he was persistent. Tired of being chased, they would slip under the porch through an opening in the foundation which the dog could not enter. Here, at last, was an animal too large to swallow!

On an interurban car track not far from our house, lizards were wont to sun themselves on the hot ties, and grasshoppers to perform their courtship flights. The birds frequently visited this rich preserve. When a car approached they did not flee in terror but stood their ground, then, bounding from tie to tie, raced just ahead of the roaring, swaying monster. Often they ran thus for a hundred yards or more, when, panting with the unusual exertion, they shot off to one side to rest in the shade of the weeds.

Life on the prairie was pleasant and eventful. Each dawn promised new conquests; each expedition along the roads had its excitement and rewards. But these happy days were numbered. In July, when the birds were almost three months old, we moved to northern West Virginia. I was exceedingly fond of my pets, and feared that leaving them behind would mean their early death. We made a wire cage, covered it with cloth, and took them with us on the train.

The trip was hot and unpleasant. The birds were so frightened that they jumped about, injuring their bills and breaking their feathers so badly that their tails had to be cut off. I was constantly afraid the poor captives would raise such a commotion that they would be sentenced to the baggage car. They ate raw beefsteak; but their appetite was far from normal.

Arrived at our destination, a hamlet sequestered among cool hills, I thought first of all of the Road-Runners. Chilled by fog, sick from lack of exercise and improper food, and, worst of all minus their handsome tails, they were forlorn indeed as they walked about sedately on the cement walks and neat lawn of the college campus. Titania and Oberon! For the first time the names seemed significant and fitting! Smitten with remorse at having brought these sun-dwellers to a hostile land, I was determined to get food for them—grasshoppers, snakes, birds—anything but beefsteak.

By noon the birds and I felt better. The beneficient sun had drawn off the fog, and a few grasshoppers were to be found on the baseball diamond. Furthermore, the creek which threaded the hills was teeming with watersnakes. These fields were not the windy prairies to be sure; but life was endurable so long as there was food for the Roadrunners.

The odd, bobtailed birds soon became popular, especially with children, who wanted to chase them or to watch them eating. Every day snakes or mice were brought to them, and their usual sprightliness returned.

The birds evidently foresaw that they would have to conquer new kinds of prey, for they began to take unusual interest in the English Sparrows which fed about the college buildings. Within a few days they captured the birds with little difficulty. Walking about with a non-committal air that was comically suggestive of the chickens which fed near by, they gradually drew nearer to a sparrow, then, with a dash to one side, and a tremendous leap, snatched the fleeing victim from the air! It was odd that the usually sagacious sparrows did not, as a community, learn to fear these new enemies; instinct, however, seemed to warn them only against prowling cats, or hawks which always attacked from above.

In September the campus hummed with the return of students. Frosty mornings with their lavender-colored asters and scarlet maple leaves heralded a winter which would be difficult indeed for the aliens. I was so busy that I could not properly care for my pets, which now ran hither and yon through the countryside. For a week or two I saw little of the Road-Runners, though daily I heard reports of strange birds seen here and there along the roads sometimes some distance from town.

Winter in West Virginia is rarely severe; but it is damp, and there is little in the way of food for Road-Runners. I made plans for sending them back to their Texas prairie. I considered feeding and keeping them indoors for winter. But when I tried to locate them, they were not to be found. I spent many hours, day after day, in searching. Through likely meadows, now rank with iron-weed and strewn with silken milkweed balloons, I wandered in the morning, or after school hours, eager to glimpse a familiar slender form, or to hear the sharp rattle of mandibles. But I failed to find the birds.

One afternoon, when I returned from college, my mother told me of a dead bird, wrapped in newspaper, brought by a man who had heard I was interested in collecting specimens. Two odd creatures had rushed up to him from the roadside, he had said, fluttering their wings as if they were baby birds, begging for food; and he had killed one of them with a stick.

I did not need to unwrap the slender package, for I saw a familiar foot sticking out at the end. I should not have known, anyway, whether it was Titania or Oberon who had been returned to me.

THE

GREAT

HORNED OWL

Edward Howe Forbush

It is no wonder that owls were among the first birds to strike strongly the imagination of Western man. Their eerie cries, their great, glowing eyes, the silence of their flight, and the very fact that most species, unlike us, are creatures of darkness rather than of light has surrounded them with an air of mystery. It is still difficult not to think of them as fascinatingly sinister and possibly even wise in some esoteric way. Actually, of course, they are first of all neither philosophers nor evil spirits but mousers, and hence among the most economically useful of birds. The great horned owl, common over most of the United States and Canada, is one of our larger species. Here is a strictly light-of-common-day account of this nighttime predator.

EVERY living thing above ground in the woods on winter nights pays tribute to the Great Horned Owl except the larger mammals and man. Ordinarily when there is good hunting this owl has a plentiful supply of food, and when there is game enough it slaughters an abundance and eats only the brains; but in winter when house rats and mice keep mostly within the buildings, when woodchucks and skunks have "holed up" and when field mice are protected by deep snow—then if rabbits are scarce and starvation is imminent, the owl will attack even the domestic cat, and usually with success. A farmer brought me a Great Horned Owl one winter day that had killed his pet tom cat on the evening of the previous day. The cat was out walking in the moonlight on one of his usual expeditions in search of unattended females, when the farmer heard a wail of mortal agony and opening the door saw Mr. Cat in the grasp of the owl. Before he could get his gun and shoot the bird the cat was no more. Its vitals had been torn out. Usually the noiseless flight of the owl enables it to take the cat by surprise and seize it by the back of the neck and the

From *Birds of Massachusetts and Other New Engand States.* Published by the Commonwealth of Massachusetts, 1927.

small of the back, when all is soon over; but if the cat is not taken by surprise and is quick enough to turn on the owl, the episode is likely to have a different ending. Sometimes the owl "wakes up the wrong customer" as the following incident related to me by Mr. J. A. Farley clearly shows:

"Mr. Zenas Langford, for many years superintendent of streets in the southern part of Plymouth, tells me that a few years ago in the Pine Hills, he came upon a Horned Owl in trouble with a black snake. As he went along the cart road, the two suddenly 'fell into it.' Plainly the owl had caught the snake, but the reptile had twisted itself around the bird so that it was unable to fly, and fell to the ground with its prey. Mr. Langford says that the owl had grasped the snake about six inches below its head, but the part of the snake below the owl's talons had twisted itself around the bird tightly. There was at least one light turn around the owl's neck. Mr. Langford could not see that the snake had bitten the owl, which however, was nearly exhausted. The owl nevertheless had not relaxed its hold on the snake. Neither of the creatures had given up. Mr. Langford killed the snake, which measured 4 feet. The owl was so weakened and helpless that it could not fly; it seemed to have been choked. Mr. Langford wrapped it in a blanket, took it home, kept it for a week and then let it go." The porcupine, also, does not yield up his life, without doing all the harm possible. Witness the Horned Owl, liberally besprinkled with porcupine quills, which was shot in the Province of Quebec in December 1907, and reported by Rev. G. Eifrig.

Horned Owls kill and eat many skunks, and seem to care little for the disagreeable consequences of attacking these pungent animals. Many of the owls that I have handled give olfactory evidence of the habit. They kill both wild and domesticated ducks, picking them up skillfully out of the water at night, and no goose is too large for them to tackle. Occasionally, however, the owl comes to grief in its attack on some water-fowl. At Lanesboro, Massachusetts, in February, 1918, one was found floating dead in a pool with a duck that it had killed. No one knew the details of this midnight tragedy. It may be that the owl was weakened by hunger and was unable to rise from the water. Where hens, chickens and turkeys are allowed to roost at night in the trees, many fall victims to this owl, which is said to alight on the branch beside its chosen prey, crowd it off the limb and then strike it in the air. Some guinea hens roosting in trees on my farm disappeared in some such manner. Usually the owl does not stop to eat his victim on the spot but bears it away.

Mr. A. A. Cross of Huntington informed me that in December, 1918, one of his neighbors left a live guinea hen in a sack and it disappeared. The next day he found the remains of the fowl in the orchard. The sack had been torn open and about half of the bird had been eaten. Two traps were set near it and the next night a splendid specimen of the Great Horned Owl was taken.

In eating its prey this owl usually begins at the head and eats backward. The birds are plucked, but small mammals such as mice and rats are swallowed whole, head first. Mr. E. O. Grant says that he saw an owl strike a Ruffed Grouse in a bush and bear it away without even checking his flight. "The owl flew up a stream with a stream of feathers trailing in his wake. I think," says Mr. Grant, "that he must have had that bird pretty well plucked before he had gone 60 rods." The Horned Owl is no respecter of persons. It kills weaker owls from the Barred Owl down, most of the hawks and such nocturnal animals as weasels and minks. It is the most deadly enemy of the Crow, taking old and young from their nests at night and killing many at their winter roosts. Game birds of all kinds, poultry, a few small birds, rabbits (especially bush rabbits), hares, squirrels, gophers, mice, rats, woodchucks, opossums, fish, crawfish and insects are all eaten by this rapacious bird. It is particularly destructive to rats. Mr. E. O. Niles tells of a nest of this owl on his farm containing two young owls and several dead rats. On the ground below the nest were the bodies of 113 rats, recently killed, with their skulls opened and the brains removed. When we find young in the nest of one of these owls, they are well supplied with game. Mr. H. O. Green writes that he found remains of a skunk, a Crow and a Pheasant at one nest and Mr. Joseph Peters says that the parent birds that supplied another nest brought black ducks, rabbits, rats, snakes, a Red Phalarope, a Virginia Rail, two Woodcocks, a Bob-white, a Northern Flicker, a Pheasant and some small birds. In eating their food the fierce young birds grasped the game firmly in the talons and tore at it with their beaks. They began their feast on the larger birds and mammals by consuming the head and then working backward through the carcass. Of 127 stomachs of Great Horned Owls examined by Dr. A. K. Fisher, 31 contained poultry or game birds; 8, other birds; 13, mice; 65, other mammals; 1, a scorpion; 1, fish; 10, insects; and 17 were empty.

In the wilderness the Great Horned Owl exerts a restraining influence on both the game and the enemies of game, for it destroys both and thus does not disturb the balance of nature.

"SNAKE BIRDS":

THE AMERICAN ANHINGA

William Bartram

---

*One of the main attractions of Everglades National Park in southern
Florida is the American anhinga or, as it is sometimes appropriately
called, the snakebird, from its long, writhing neck; and sometimes most
inappropriately the water turkey—for no good reason. This creature
strikes the most casual visitor as somehow queer, and its queerness is no
doubt due to the fact that it is a very ancient bird and in many ways
archaic. Though perhaps distantly related to the cormorants, anhigas are
not sea birds, and the few species are usually put in a group by themselves.
Fossils suggest that they are descended from an extinct group of which bones
have been recovered from Eocine sediments something like eighty million
years ago.*

*William Bartram observed them during his late-eighteenth-century ex-
ploration of Florida, called them snake birds, and noted their remote simi-
larity to the cormorants. The more dignified appellation, anhinga, comes
from a native Amazonian word.*

HERE is in the river and in the waters all over Florida, a very curious
and handsome bird, the people call them Snake Birds, I think I
have seen paintings of them on the Chinese screens and other India
pictures: they seem to be a species of cormorant or loon (*Colymbus
cauda elongata*) but far more beautiful and delicately formed than any
other species that I have ever seen. The head and neck of this bird are
extremely small and slender, the latter very long indeed, almost out of
all proportion, the bill long, straight and slender, tapering from its ball to
a sharp point, all the upper side, the abdomen and thighs, are as black
and glossy as a raven's, covered with feathers so firm and elastic, that
they in some degree resemble fish-scales, the breast and upper part of
the belly are covered with feathers of a cream colour, the tail is very
long, of a deep black, and tipped with a silvery white, and when spread,
represent an unfurled fan. They delight to sit in little peaceable com-
munities, on the dry limbs of trees, hanging over the still waters, with
their wings and tails expanded, I suppose to cool and air themselves, when

From *Travels through North and South Carolina, Georgia, East and West
Florida*. Printed by James & Johnson, Philadelphia, 1791.

at the same time they behold their images in the watery mirror: at such times, when we approach them, they drop off the limbs into the water as if dead, and for a minute or two are not to be seen; when on a sudden at a vast distance, their long slender head and neck only appear, and have very much the appearance of a snake, and no other part of them are to be seen when swimming in the water, except sometimes the tip end of their tail. In the heat of the day they are seen in great numbers, sailing very high in the air, over lakes and rivers.

I doubt not but if this bird had been an inhabitant of the Tiber in Ovid's days, it would have furnished him with a subject, for some beautiful and entertaining metamorphoses. I believe they feed entirely on fish, for their flesh smells and tastes intolerably strong of it, it is scarcely to be eaten unless constrained by insufferable hunger.

WINGS

OF THE

STORM

Robert Cunningham Miller

The Greeks thought that the Halcyon, or kingfisher, nested on the sea dur-
ing a season of unusual calm. It doesn't, and neither does any other bird,
though we still use the phrase "Halcyon days" to describe a time of unusual
tranquillity.

As happens in the case of so many exploded myths, there are even more
wonderful truths to take its place. Many sea birds do incredible things, such
as wandering over millions of square miles of ocean, spending almost their
entire lives above or on the water, coming to land only to nest. Food is
abundant; but why do they not, like the Ancient Mariner, cry in despair,
"Water, water everywhere, nor any drop to drink?" Physiologists long
pooh-poohed the notion that they could drink sea water. No kidney is
capable of removing so high a concentration of salt. We now know that sea
birds have well-developed salt glands which separate out and excrete the
dissolved salts from the water.

O F all the habitats available to birds, the wide and lonely reaches of
the open sea might appear to be one of the most inhospitable. Yet
there are birds that are just as much at home over vast and turbulent
waters as is the red-winged blackbird in a marsh, or a robin on a lawn. So
completely are they adapted to the marine environment that they may
go weeks or months without sighting land, and indeed have no need of
the land whatever except for nesting, which is carried out on remote
oceanic islands. If all the land on earth were to be submerged beneath
the sea, years after the human race had become extinct there would
still be birds winging their way about this global ocean, able to live out
their normal life span completely at home in a world of water.

Nine persons out of ten, asked to name a bird of the ocean, would

From *Pacific Discovery*. September–October, 1955.

promptly reply "sea gull," or name one of the numerous species of gull. Even as good a sea-faring man as John Masefield might not win a prize on this quiz program, for in "Sea-fever" he refers in one breath to "the gull's way and the whale's way," although the paths of gulls and whales only occasionally and accidentally cross. Gulls by and large are not birds of the ocean, but birds of the shore and even of inland lakes.

To a person spending a summer at the seashore, the gulls, with their attractive plumage, wheeling flight and plaintive cries, are likely to be a memorable part of his seaside experience. But as a matter of fact, and with no disrespect to either, they are a good deal like himself. They like the sea shore and the sea wind, and enjoy beach-combing, but they don't care for too much salt water. An exception is the kittiwake, one of the smallest and most maritime of the gulls. In our book this little gull is really a sea-faring bird.

But when we speak of birds of the open ocean, we mean primarily storm petrels, shearwaters, fulmars, and albatrosses. All belong to a single order, the Tubinares, or tube-nosed swimmers, characterized by nostrils which open well forward along the sides of the beak. This article, in case you haven't guessed, is about albatrosses, and more specifically a common albatross of the North Pacific. The fulmars and shearwaters are essentially just smaller versions of the albatross, and though they are remarkable birds in their own right, to whom we would like to return in future, they will be mentioned here only in passing. But the storm petrels are so different and so remarkable that we cannot pass them up without comment.

The name petrel is derived from that of St. Peter who, according to the Gospel of Matthew (xiv:29), walked on the water. Moreover, the scientific name of the family to which the petrels belong (*Hydrobatidae*) means the same thing; it is derived from two Greek words meaning "one who treads on water." Petrels are little sea birds, smaller than a robin, who wing their way across some of the stormiest waters of the world. They fly close to the surface of the sea, and look like tiny, storm-tossed paper kites at the mercy of wind and wave. But each time a wave sweeps up and threatens to engulf them, they let down their slender legs with broad webbed feet and skip lightly along the surface of the water. Thus by an amazing combination of flying and skipping that keeps the onlooker breathless with excited admiration they negotiate the roughest seas.

Albatrosses apparently never use their feet in this manner, but they do make a great deal of use of their feet in taking off and landing. When alighting on the water they drop their legs like the landing gear of an airplane, spread out their webbed feet and thrust them forward to act as a brake when they strike the water. When taking off, they face into the wind, spread their long wings, and kick the water vigorously with both feet, once, twice, thrice or more, until they are airborne, leaving a wake of splashes a yard or two apart, visible for a few moments until they are blotted out in the endless movement of the ocean.

The lighter the wind, the more difficulty the albatrosses have in taking off, and the harder and longer they have to kick their feet. Robert Cushman Murphy, in *Oceanic Birds of South America*, recounts an instance in which, in a calm and fog, he encountered numerous albatrosses sitting on the water. As his boat approached them, they would swim away, or splash away kicking with their feet for as much as a hundred yards before taking to the air. This situation was complicated by the fog, so that it is not entirely clear whether it was the calm or the fog that discouraged the birds from taking off. But some observers believe that albatrosses require wind for flight, and are unable to fly in a dead calm.

My own observations do not entirely bear this out, as I have seen albatrosses take off from a calm sea in nearly still air and flap along heavily like oversize gulls. But they do not go far in this manner, and many observers have noted that in calm weather albatrosses give up flying and spend their time sitting on the water. It is an interesting thought that these masters of flight are so much creatures of the wind that they find themselves at a disadvantage without it. In fact, it is not an unreasonable theory that the tropic belt of calms is an important barrier in preventing albatrosses from moving freely back and forth across the equator. The species found in the northern and southern hemispheres are altogether distinct, and only rarely does a stray turn up in the wrong hemisphere.

In 1860 a black-browed albatross, native to the southern hemisphere, appeared in the Faeroe Islands, midway between Scotland and Iceland, and was seen regularly in this vicinity for 34 years, until it was shot in 1894.

Most species of albatross are found south of the equator, where the great southern ocean that encircles the globe between Antarctica and Australia, South Africa and South America provides the conditions of almost perpetual wind and swell in which these great birds are most at home. There is no albatross in the North Atlantic, its place there being taken in large part by the fulmar. But the North Pacific has its complement of albatrosses, whose flight is just as impressive as that of the wanderers of southern seas. So much has been written of the flight of the wandering albatross, the largest in its wing expanse of any existing bird, that we are inclined to underrate the other albatrosses, especially those we can find nearer home.

Once there were three species of albatross in the North Pacific—the short-tailed albatross, the Laysan albatross, and the black-footed albatross.

The first of these is apparently extinct, through the raiding of its nesting sites many years ago for the feather trade. Not a single individual of the short-tailed albatross has been definitely identified in recent years. The Laysan albatross is still moderately common in mid-Pacific, and occasionally strays to the Pacific coast of North America. It is the only white-bodied albatross to be seen off our coast. The black-footed albatross is happily still abundant, and may be seen in off-shore waters all the way from North America to Japan.

This dark brown albatross, with the whitish forehead and rump patch, and occasionally some other light feathers in its plumage, is known to sailors as the "gooney." Its nondescript appearance is unlikely to arouse any excitement in a seasick voyager. But it is really a magnificent bird, its seven-foot spread of wing not being exceeded by any North American birds except the eagles and the California condor. In powers of flight it is second to none.

Its long knife-like wings, with an aspect ratio (ratio of length to width) of around eleven to one, are especially adapted to horizontal gliding, and to maneuvering in the "bumpy" air that occurs over the surface of the ocean when a sea is running. Each wave or swell has an invisible counterpart in the air immediately above it; the albatross rides these waves of air, adjusting instantly to every draft, and taking maximum advantage of the upward component.

Maneuvering (from the Latin via the French, meaning "to work with the hands") is in fact a particularly apt word in describing the flight of the albatross. The bend of the wrist comes a little more than one-third of the distance in from the tip of the wing. The portions of the wing corresponding to the upper arm and forearm provide a gliding surface; but it is the outer section of the wing, corresponding to the human hand, that "feels" the wind and adjusts to every changing gust. There is even a certain amount of finger movement; the alula or bastard wing, corresponding to the human thumb, carries several stiff feathers which can be moved independently to raise or lower a section of the leading edge of the wing.

If you would like to imagine yourself a black-footed albatross, stretch out your arms as far as possible and think of them as being further extended to a total span of seven feet, and transformed into narrow wings, about eleven times as long as they are wide. Next think of your body size being reduced till your total weight is somewhere around seven pounds. Now, except in small matters of detail (no puns, please), you are a working model of an albatross, and ready to take off in a high wind.

While the albatross is the best of all known gliders, we must remember that it is not only a glider, but a combination of glider and light airplane, able to switch on the engine in an instant to pull itself out of any difficulty. I have seen albatrosses glide for long periods of time with scarcely any visible motion of the wings; but under conditions a little less favorable I have seen them swinging in mile-wide arcs astern of a steamer, flapping the wings once or twice at the end of each long glide. If one attributed human psychology to albatrosses, he might think they were trying to live up to their advance billing by slipping in a few surreptitious flaps now and then when too far away from the ship to be readily observed. Actually they are doing whatever comes naturally to them. As the wind dies down they flap more and more, and at last, as stated above, they give up flying and settle down on the water.

Black-footed albatrosses are seldom seen closer to shore than fifteen or twenty miles. Occasionally they will venture a short distance into wide inlets, like Monterey Bay, the Strait of Juan de Fuca, or Dixon Entrance. There are no records for San Francisco Bay. They can be seen any day from the deck of a trans-Pacific steamer; but the only way to really get to know them is to go well off shore in a fishing boat or other small craft. . . .

When a vessel is hove to for hauling nets or handling oceanographic gear, albatrosses would settle down on the water near by and wait hopefully for hand-outs from the galley. They have an inordinate appetite for pancakes, either with or without syrup. They feed at the surface of the water, or occasionally turn bottoms-up like the nondiving ducks and reach as far down into the water as they can stretch their necks. They never dive. Although they are wild birds and maintain a good deal of wariness, by judicious baiting they can be lured within camera range.

These hours of fraternizing with albatrosses in a calm sea, over pancakes or crusts of bread, are all too brief and infrequent. When the wind freshens and the sea comes up, and it becomes too rough for oceanographer or fisherman to work, then the albatrosses take to the air and give a truly magnificient demonstration of their powers of flight. In many months at sea over a period of twenty-five years, I have never seen weather so rough that the albatrosses seemed to be in the least difficulty. The cold, wet seafarer aboard a small vessel laboring through heavy seas in a full gale, gazes with admiration and envy at these majestic birds, and inevitably thinks of them in terms of the title of this article.

Part

Six

BIRDS AND PEOPLE

UNFAMILIAR SONG

Joseph Wood Krutch

Essayist and literary critic Joseph Wood Krutch was not an avid birder when, as an adult, he moved from New England to the Southwest; even so, he was chagrined to discover that something as presumably unimportant as background birdsong could make him feel a stranger in his native country.

THE birds too, of course, are different, and so far I have learned to recognize only the most obvious—the cactus wren who builds his messy, sparrowlike nest among the murderous spines of the cholla a few yards from the front door; the hooded oriole who wears the obligatory orange-and-black livery of his family; the Arizona cardinal, more brilliant than his southeastern cousin; and the woodpeckers who have excavated two or three holes in every saguaro. As I awake in the morning the first thing I am aware of, the first thing which reminds me that I am not in a familiar bed, is some unfamiliar bird voice. At home I would have murmured sleepily "Robin," or "Phoebe," or "Jay" or "Tanager" and gone back to sleep. Here I am aware of something halfway between interest and annoyance, for there is something like mocking challenge in the sound of an unknown bird. I am not one whose imagination accepts very easily the articulate phrases into which the more fanciful translate bird language. A whippoorwill does say "whippoor-will" and a quail does say "bob white," but that is about as far as I am prepared to go. Here they all say only "Youdontknow whoiam, youdontknow whoiam."

From *The Desert Year*. New York: William Sloane Associates, 1951.

WILDERNESS

MUSIC

Sigurd F. Olson

Modern man is heavily visual in sense orientation; our senses of hearing and smell, so important to most other mammals, have retrenched. Sigurd F. Olson, for decades the eloquent voice of northern Minnesota's canoe country, suggests something of the cost of our auditory dullness, and, in counterpoint to Krutch's experience, points to the power of familiar birdsong in a foreign land.

L AST night I followed a ski trail into the Lucky Boy Valley. It was dark and still, and the pines and spruces there almost met overhead. During the day it had snowed, and the festooned trees were vague massed drifts against the stars. Breathless after my run, I stopped to rest and listen. In that snow-cushioned place there was no sound, no wind moaning in the branches, no life or movement of any kind.

As I stood there leaning on my sticks, I thought of Jack Linklater, a Scotch-Cree of the Hudson's Bay Company. In such a place he would have heard the music, for he had a feeling for the "wee" people and for many things others did not understand. Sometimes when we were on the trail together he would ask me to stop and listen, and when I could not hear he would laugh. Once in a stand of quaking aspen in a high place when the air was full of their whispering, he dropped his pack and stood there, a strange and happy light in his eyes. Another time, during the harvesting of wild rice when the dust was redolent with the parching fires on the shores of Hula Lake, he called me to him, for he felt that somehow I must hear the music too.

"Can't you hear it now?" he said. "It's very plain tonight."

I stood there with him and listened, but heard nothing, and as I watched the amused and somewhat disappointed look on his face I wondered if he was playing a game with me. That time he insisted that he could hear the sound of women's and children's voices and the high quaver of an Indian song, though we were far from the encampment. Now that the years have passed and Jack has gone to the Happy Hunt-

From *The Singing Wilderness*. New York: Alfred A. Knopf, 1956.

ing Grounds, I believe that he actually heard something and that the
reason I could not was that this was music for Indians and for those
whose ears were attuned.

One night we were canoeing on the Maligne River in the Quetico on
a portage trail used for centuries by Indians and voyagers. The moon
was full, and the bowl below the falls was silver with mist. As we sat
listening to the roar of Twin Falls, there seemed to be a sound of voices
of a large party making the carry. The sound ebbed and swelled in
volume with the ebb and flow of the plunging water. That night I
thought I heard them, too, and Jack was pleased. Wilderness music?
Imagination? I may never know, but this much I do know from traveling with Jack: he actually heard something, and those who have lived
close to nature all of their lives are sensitive to many things lost to those
in the cities.

We send out costly expeditions to record the feelings, expressions,
and customs of primitive tribes untouched by civilization, considering
such anthropological research to be worth while because it gives us an
inkling of why we moderns behave as we do. We recognize that a great
deal has been lost to us during the so-called civilized centuries—intu-
itive awarenesses that primitives still possess. Children still have them,
but they soon disappear. Some individuals retain them as long as they
live. All, however, have a need and hunger for them, and much of the
frustration and boredom we experience is no doubt due to our inability
to recapture these forgotten ways of perception.

While most of us are too far removed to hear the wilderness music
that Jack Linklater heard, there are other forms—not so subtle, perhaps,
but still capable of bringing to our consciousness the same feelings that
have stirred human kind since the beginning of time. Who is not stirred
when the wild geese go by, when the coyotes howl on a moonlit night,
or when the surf crashes against the cliffs? Such sounds have deep appeal because they are associated with the background of the race. Why
does the rhythmic tom-tom beat of drums affect us? Because it, too, is
primitive and was part of our heritage centuries before music as we
know it now was ever conceived. Wilderness music to me is any sound
that brings to mind the wild places I have known.

Once during a long absence from the north I heard the call of a loon,
the long, rollicking laughter that in the past I had heard echoing across
the wild reaches of the Quetico lakes. It was in Tennessee that I heard
it, but the instant I caught the first long wail, chills of gladness chased
themselves up and down my spine. For a long time I stood there and
listened, but I did not hear it again. While I waited, the north came
back to me with a rush and visions of wilderness lakes and rivers
crowded upon me. I saw the great birds flying into the sunsets, groups
of them playing over the waters of Lac la Croix, Kawnipi, and Batch-

ewaung. I saw the reaches of Saganaga in the early morning, a camp on some lonely island with the day's work done and nothing to do but listen and dream. And then in the recesses of my mind the real calling began as it had a thousand times in the past, the faintest hint of an echo from over the hills, answered before it died by a closer call and that in turn by another until the calling of the loons from all the lakes around blended in a continuous symphony.

There were other times that also came back to me, times when the clouds were dark and the waves rolling high, when the calling reached a pitch of madness which told of coming storm; mornings when the sun was bright and happy laughter came from the open water; nights when one lone call seemed to embody all the misery and tragedy in the world. I knew as I stood there waiting that when once a man had known that wild and eery calling and lost himself in its beauty, should he ever hear a hint of it again, no matter where he happened to be, he would have a vision of the distance and freedom of the north.

One day in the south of England I was walking through a great beech wood on an old estate near Shrivenham. There was a little brook flowing through the woods, and its gurgle as it ran through a rocky dell seemed to accentuate my sense of the age of those magnificent trees. I was far from home, as far away from the wilderness of the north as I had ever been. Those great trees were comforting to me even though I knew that just beyond them was open countryside.

Then suddenly I heard a sound that changed everything: a soft nasal twang from high in the branches, the call of a nuthatch. Instantly that beech grove was transformed into a stand of tall, stately pines; the brown beech leaves on the ground became a smooth carpet of golden needles, and beyond this cared-for forest were rugged ridges and deep, timbered valleys, roaring rivers and placid lakes, with a smell of resin and duff in the sun. The call of the nuthatch had done all that, had given me a vision of the wilderness as vivid as though for the moment I had actually been there.

How satisfying to me are the sounds of a bog at night! I like to paddle into a swampy bay in the lake country and just sit there and listen to the slow sloshing-around of moose and deer, the sharp pistol crack of a beaver tail slapping the water, the guttural, resonant pumping of a bittern. But the real music of a bog is the frog chorus. If they are in full swing when you approach, they stop by sections as though part of the orchestra was determined to carry on in spite of the faintheartedness of the rest. One must sit quietly for some time before they regain their courage. At first there are individual piping notes, a few scattered guttural croaks, then a confused medley as though the instruments were being tuned. Finally in a far corner a whole section swings into tremulous music, hesitant at the start but gradually gathering momentum and volume. Soon a closer group begins, and then they all join in until there is again a sustained and grand crescendo of sound.

This is a primeval chorus, the sort of wilderness music which reigned over the earth millions of years ago. That sound floated across the pools of the carboniferous era. You can still hear it in the Everglades: the throaty, rasping roar of the alligators and, above that, the frightened calls and screams of innumerable birds. One of the most ancient sounds on earth, it is a continuation of music from the past, and, no matter where I listen to a bog at night, strange feelings stir within me.

One night in the south of Germany I was walking along the River Main at Frankfurt. It was spring and sunset. Behind me were the stark ruins of the city, the silhouettes of broken walls and towers, the horrible destruction of the bombing. Across the river was a little village connected with the city by the broken span of a great bridge. In the river were the rusting hulls of barges and sunken boats. The river gurgled softly around them and around the twisted girders of the blown-up span. It was a scene of desolation and sadness.

Then I was conscious of a sound that was not of the war, the hurrying whisper of wings overhead. I turned, and there against the rosy sky was a flock of mallards. I had forgotten that the river was a flyway, that there were still such delightful things as the sound of wings at dusk, rice beds yellowing in the fall, and the soft sound of quacking all through the night. A lone flock of mallards gave all that to me, awoke a thousand memories as wilderness music always does.

There are many types of music, each one different from the rest: a pack of coyotes and the wild, beautiful sound of them as they tune up under the moon; the song of a white-throated sparrow, its one clear note so closely associated with trout streams that whenever I hear one, I see a sunset-tinted pool and feel the water around my boots. The groaning and cracking of forming ice on the lakes, the swish of skis or snowshoes in dry snow—wilderness music, all of it, music for Indians and for those who have ears to hear.

EMBLEM BIRDS

OF THE

LONG-LEGGED HOUSE

Wendell Berry

Familiar music in a strange land depends for its power on associational values. The extent to which particular birds may become the spirits of our particular places on earth became clear to Wendell Berry—farmer, poet, distinguished essayist—as he settled into a family house perched on stilts over the uncertain banks of the Kentucky River. Berry's "sycamore" warbler is the yellow-throated warbler.

WHEN I began tearing down the old Camp a pair of phoebes was nesting as usual under one of the eaves. Four eggs were already in the nest. I took an old shutter and fixed a little shelf and a sort of porch roof on it, and nailed it to a locust tree nearby, and set the nest with its eggs carefully on it. As I feared, the old birds would have nothing to do with it. The nest stayed where I had put it for another year or so, a symbol of the ended possibilities of the old Camp, and then it blew away.

As I wrote through the mornings of the rest of that summer, a green heron would often be fishing opposite me on the far bank. An old willow had leaned down there until it floated on the water, reaching maybe twenty feet out from the bank. The tree was still living, nearly the whole length of it covered with leafy sprouts. It was dead only at the outer end, which bent up a few inches above the surface of the river. And it was there that the heron fished. He stooped a little, leaning a little forward, his eyes stalking the river as it flowed down and passed beneath him. His attention would be wonderfully concentrated for minutes at a stretch, he would stand still as a dead branch on the trunk of his willow, and then he would itch and have to scratch among his feathers with his beak. When prey swam within his reach, he would crouch, tilt, pick it deftly out of the water, sit back, swallow. Once I saw

From *The Long-Legged House*. New York: Harcourt, Brace and World, 1969.

him plunge headlong into the water and flounder out with his minnow
—as if the awkward flogging body had been literally yanked off its
perch by the accurate hunger of the beak. When a boat passed he did
not fly, but walked calmly back into the shadows among the sprouts of
the willow and stood still.

Another bird I was much aware of that summer was the sycamore
warbler. Nearly every day I would see one feeding in the tall sycamores
in front of the house, or when I failed to see the bird I would hear its
song. This is a bird of the tall trees, and he lives mostly in their highest
branches. He loves the sycamores. He moves through their crowns,
feeding, and singing his peculiar quaking seven-note song, a voice passing overhead like the sun. I am sure I had spent many days of my life
with this bird going about his business high over my head, and I had
never been aware of him before. This always amazes me; it has happened to me over and over; for years I will go in ignorance of some
creature that will later become important to me, as though we are
slowly drifting toward each other in time, and then it will suddenly
become as visible to me as a star. It is at once almost a habit. After the
first sighting I see it often. I become dependent on it, and am uneasy
when I do not see it. In the years since I first saw it here and heard its
song, the sycamore warbler has come to hold this sort of power over
me. I never hear it approaching through the white branches of its trees
that I don't stop and listen; or I get the binoculars and watch him as he
makes his way from one sycamore to another along the riverbank, a
tiny gray bird with a yellow throat, singing from white branch to white
branch, among the leaf lights and shadows. When I hear his song for
the first time in the spring, I am deeply touched and reassured. It has
come to be the most characteristic voice of this place. He is the Camp's
emblem bird, as the sycamore is its emblem tree.

FATHER

OF AMERICAN

ORNITHOLOGY

Elsa G. Allen

The first great American ornithologist was not Audubon but his older contemporary, the Scotsman Alexander Wilson, whose reputation has always been blighted by the shadow of his famous contemporary. Born in 1766 and growing up in poverty, Wilson was one of those obscure Europeans who came alone and unsponsored to the New World, not to seek their fortunes, but to see for themselves its natural wonders and beauties. For ten years he supported himself in the United States by schoolteaching until a meeting with William Bartram marked the turning point of his career. The first volume of his American Ornithology *was published in 1808 and the eighth was in the press when he died in 1813. Of his work Elliot Coues wrote: "Probably no other work of ornithology of equal extent is equally free from errors; and its truthfulness is illumed by a spark of the divine fire."*

BACK in 1794 in Old Philadelphia, adjacent to Peale's Museum, a zoological garden was founded. The principal attraction was an eagle with this sign on his cage—"Feed me well and I'll live a hundred years." I think of this fine old bird as a cynosure of American ornithology, a science which was indeed reared and fledged in Philadelphia, and which later, when it came of age, spread throughout the land.

Seventeen ninety-four was also the year that brought to our shores the immigrant Scot, Alexander Wilson, who became America's first ornithologist. He had space on the deck of the American ship, Swift, sailing from Belfast for Philadelphia on May 23, and he took his young nephew, William Duncan, with him.

Times had been hard for Wilson in Paisley, his native town. At thirteen, soon after his mother died, he was taken out of school and bound apprentice and servant to a weaver. For three long years he rebelled against

From the *Atlantic Naturalist.* November–December, 1952.

this unnatural confinement and finally, when the indenture expired and he was free, he wrote these feeling lines:

> "Be't kent to a' the world in rhime
> That wi right meikle wark and toil
> For three lang years I've ser't my time,
> Whiles feasted wi' the hazel oil."

Yet, so limited was young Wilson's education that he had to continue at weaving, and he stooped over the webs another four years. He was then twenty years of age, and loath to face another year of weaving, he took to the road with a pack on his back, and a few of his poems in his pocket. He had decided to study nature and write verse.

Two slender little volumes of his poetry came out with indifferent success, and another, a humorous ballad called *Watty and Meg*, with a homely and witty philosophy on marriage, was published anonymously. It was popular at once, and thousands of copies were sold. The beloved poet of the people, Robert Burns, was thought to be the author, but instead it was the humble and dissatisfied weaver, Alexander Wilson.

Wilson's early twenties were divided between the weaver's craft and the journeyman's uncertain lot. When he was weaving, his employers complained of his indifference to his work and his constant scribbling, while his customers along the road cared little for his wares or his poetry.

Though Wilson could write feelingly of the beautiful Scottish landscape, he could not refrain from using his bitter and sarcastic wit against the political and industrial ills of the times, and finally, in a personal attack on a certain manufacturer in his poem, *The Shark*, he was found guilty of libel. It was the repercussion of this unfortunate incident, with his imprisonment, his trial, his fine and at last his sentence requiring him to burn his offensive lampoon on the steps of the Tolbooth, that determined him in his plan to go to America.

Accordingly, he took leave of his few good friends the last of April, 1794, and after fifty-three days at sea, he and his young companion arrived at New Castle, Delaware. Here they disembarked with their guns and luggage, and walked thirty-five miles to Philadelphia, although the ship was bound for that port.

The first bird that Wilson saw was a red-headed woodpecker. He shot it and made a skin of it, and he thought it the most beautiful bird he had ever seen.

Wilson's Early Years in America

A new world spread out before him; strange birds, new trees and flowers stirred his love of nature; and life at once was full of promise. He scanned the landscape and settlements for possible employment, ruefully aware that weaving was the only trade he knew. Duncan got a job at the looms of James Robertson, of Philadelphia; Wilson took one in a copper-plate print shop, abandoned it, and returned to weaving, in the service of Mr. Joshua Sullivan, of Pennsypack Creek, ten miles from the city.

But the birds were on his mind; he had arrived at the height of the nesting season and he could not forget the abundant whistling cardinals so striking in their red plumage nor the wood thrushes with their lovely morning and evening singing, and many lesser songsters of the roadside. In a few weeks he was a peddler again, carrying a pack of silk and cotton fabrics. He reasoned that in this way he could at least study birds and he set out for Virginia, settled for a few months at Sheppardstown, then up to Bustletown, Pennsylvania, where he served as a country schoolmaster. Finally he went to Milestown, Pennsylvania, where he lived for several years.

Here Wilson began his self-education and worked at mathematics, surveying, German, drawing, and music. He became much interested, too, in American politics and on the day of Jefferson's inauguration March 4, 1801, he delivered at Milestown an *Oration on Liberty*, in which he displayed an amazing command of English.

"Pedagoging" was his scornful way of referring to school teaching, and he liked it little better than weaving. He had to study hard at night to keep ahead of his pupils, and during his week-ends, he worked at surveying to help out the wretched pittance he was paid as schoolmaster. He hated the community and branded the village as a settlement of canting, preaching, praying, ignorant Presbyterians. His general unhappiness was augmeted by an unfortunate love affair in the summer of 1801, that caused him great anxiety. He wrote to his intimate friend, Charles Orr, a writing master of Philadelphia: "Do come," he said; "your friendship and counsel may be of the utmost service to me. I have no friend but yourself and *one*, whose friendship has involved us both in ruin, or threatens to do so. You will find me at the schoolhouse." In another letter Wilson says:

> "Of all the events of my life nothing gives
> me such inexpressible misery as this.
> O, my dear friend, if you can hear
> anything of her real situation, and
> whatever it is, disguise nothing to me."

He concludes his letter to Orr thus:

> "I have no company and live unknowing and
> unknown. I have lost all relish for this
> country and if Heaven spares me, I shall
> soon see the shores of Old Caledonia."

Who the woman of Milestown was we cannot learn from any of Wilson's letters, but she apparently was married and the situation for him was hopeless, except that this love enriched his life and matured his writing. He turned more and more to poetry, studied the Scottish pastoral poets, Pope, Thomson, Shenstone, Ramsay, and Fergusson, and yearned to make his own name live among the Scottish bards. To Orr again he unburdened his heart:

> "The idea (of poetry) is transporting and such a
> recompense is worth all the misfortunes
> penury and deprivations here that
> the most wretched sons of science have ever suffered."

He was torn between two desires: to write poetry and to study nature. Could he combine these two absorbing interests to produce poetical writings of lasting worth? The answer seems clearly to be *no*. His poetic craftsmanship could not plumb the deep wells of human feeling, but remained on the surface—purely objective.

In the field of prose, however, Wilson came a long way both by native ability to observe, combined with his inherent love of nature, and by the long schooling he gave himself with the out-of-doors. To all his prose writing he was able to bring an originality of expression, and a real facility with words. This quality, however, is entirely lacking or very rare in his verse. Nevertheless, after the unhappy affair in Milestown, Wilson gave much attention to verse-writing and published several pieces in newspapers and magazines, but he could not earn a living at it, and soon returned to teaching.

By application to the trustees of Union School in the township of Kingsessing, Wilson was assigned to the school at Gray's Ferry, only four miles from Philadelphia.

Although in his own words he resumed "that painful profession with the same sullen resignation that a prisoner re-enters his dungeon, or a malfactor mounts the scaffold," his life took a definite turn for the better by this change. In a few weeks he was a neighbor of the famous naturalist, William Bartram, and a warm friendship grew up between them.

The Schoolmaster at Gray's Ferry

The poverty and bitterness that had distorted his outlook and that is so clearly reflected in several of his American poems were softened in the pleasant atmosphere and surroundings of the Bartram home. This was a charming stone dwelling set in eight acres of ground, that sloped down to the Schuylkill River. The elder Bartram, John, father to William, had assembled gardens of great interest from his travels in quest of rarities for British and continental horticulturists. It was a simple Quaker home, but because of its gardens, it was also a Mecca for visiting naturalists from abroad, as well as other travelers, and Wilson at last could mingle with the learned and the cultured.

There were books in the Bartram library with which he spent long hours, especially Mark Catesby's two-volume *Natural History of Carolina, Florida and the Bahama Islands* (1731), and George Edwards' four-volume *Natural History of Birds* (1751), both full of accounts and plates of American birds. Wilson already, from his long pedestrian journeys, could detect many errors in these earlier works.

He discussed his findings with William Bartram and all the daylight hours he could spare from his school work he spent in the field, gradually adding new specimens to his little collection that he had been building up since the day he shot the red-headed woodpecker.

At the Bartram home he met a fellow-countryman, Alexander Lawson, an artist and engraver, who offered to teach him how to etch. The English ornithologists Catesby and Edwards, had done their own etching, and Wilson thought he, too, could learn. Soon he had, as he expressed it, an "insatiable itch" to draw birds, and as fast as he accumulated a few drawings, he sent them to Bartram for criticism and begged that he mark them in pencil with the proper names. Bartram became his mentor and Lawson his instructor in his study of the delineation of American birds, and gradually he conceived the plan of portraying all the common American birds in a manner suitable to their great interest and beauty. Poetry was slipping to a second place in his affections and birds became his consuming passion. But the irksome task of "pedagoging" was still his only source of a livelihood.

It was 1804—ten years after his arrival in America. Wilson's school was prospering; it was even crowded with pupils. After school he studied his lessons first, then drew pictures of birds by candlelight. Poetry, too, was not yet abandoned, for to this period belong some of his better efforts: *The Solitary Tutor* and *The Rural Walk*, both published in the *Literary Magazine*, and several poems on birds, for example, *The Bluebird*, *The Osprey*, and *The Tyrant Flycatcher*.

But drawing was uppermost in his mind and as his finished plates increased in number, he envisaged a monumental work, *The American Ornithology*. Birds from the St. Lawrence to the mouth of the Mississippi and from the Atlantic to the interior of Louisiana were his goal. To his engraver he said, "Do not throw cold water on my notion, as Shakespeare says, quixotic as it may appear. I have been so long accustomed to the building of airy castles and brain windmills that it has become one of my earthly comforts, a sort of rough bone that amuses me when sated with the dull drudgery of life."

The Trip to Niagara Falls

Wilson furthered this ambitious plan by making a foot journey from Philadelphia to Niagara Falls in 1804—a fantastic undertaking at that time; his companions, William Duncan and a young friend, Isaac Leech. He took note of every incident and minutely described the changing scene the whole way, all of which he transposed into a long poem *The Foresters*, consisting of 2210 lines of heroic couplets. This epic of hardship has small literary value, yet Wilson entertained high hopes of literary fame accruing from it. It was published serially in the magazine *Portfolio* which at that time was taking an interest in American scenery, but Wilson, struggling for a bare living, received nothing for this, his major effort in verse.

The entire distance traversed was upwards of 1200 miles, but his companions could not match either Wilson's endurance nor his enthusiasm, and left him on the return trip. The expedition took fifty-nine days and the last day Wilson walked forty-seven miles, arriving back in mid-December, 1804.

While at Niagara he had sketched the Falls, and returning via the Mohawk River, he collected two birds unknown to him. He introduced drawings of these birds against the background of the Falls, and sent the whole picture to President Jefferson. The reply received from the President, expressing his appreciation and offering queries on other birds delighted Wilson, and encouraged him to apply for an assignment as collector on the Zebulon Pike Expedition to the sources of the Mississippi River, which was then being organized.

This letter to the President was apparently not received, for Wilson did not hear from him. He was disappointed, but by no means crushed, as some commentators have interpreted the incident. On the contrary, his letters of this period indicate a healthy sense of potential accomplishment with plans for study and travel. He was scarcely home from Niagara when he expressed hope of a southeastern journey for he felt sure that many undescribed birds were to be found there. However, he wisely deferred it.

Wilson in Philadelphia

Hard upon the failure of his letter to secure him the Pike assignment, he was offered a position as assistant editor on Rees New Cyclopedia. This tribute to Wilson's ability was almost transporting. He resigned his teaching position and took up his residence in Philadelphia in April, 1806. We may imagine the difficult change, immured as he was among books with nothing to look at but walls and chimneys and the noise of the city in his ears. His flute and violin were comforting and by getting up at dawn he could dash to the outskirts of the city after birds.

The new work was quite exacting, for not only ornithology but the whole field of zoology, with also botany and geology, were to be revised. In addition to this, Wilson served as tutor to the two young sons of Mr. Samuel E. Bradford, the publisher, yet he did not abate his efforts to accumulate a series of bird plates and a knowledge of the haunts and habits of common species.

In fact, it seems probable that Wilson welcomed his call to the staff of a publishing house, not only for the substantial stipend of $900.00 per annum, but also as a possible outlet for his own work on ornithology.

After a year at his new post, the *American Ornithology* rapidly took form. Bradford agreed to publish it, and as early as 1807 a prospectus of all the proposed ten volumes was ready for distribution. A copy went at once to William Bartram for criticism, and Wilson received a letter of approval in three days.

Launching the American Ornithology

The first volume came out in September, 1808. At the same time Wilson set out on his first soliciting trip, a sample copy of his book in one arm and his faithful fowling piece across his shoulder. "Like a beggar with his bantling," he said. Yet he preserved a friendly, dignified, and sophisticated interest in all persons who examined it. Writing from Boston to a friend October 10, he said he had heard "nothing but expressions of the highest admiration and esteem." Passing through Pennsylvania on his return trip, however, he met a certain judge who bluntly refused to examine his work, which he said was "undemocratic" and "too good for the commonality." In the face of this rebuff, Wilson stuck to his guns. To a friend he wrote: "If I have been mistaken in publishing a work too good for the country, it is a fault not likely to be soon repeated." These were prophetic words, but Wilson forged ahead in his plans, making useful contacts throughout his journey, "so that," as he put it, "scarcely a wren or tit would pass from York to Canada but I shall get intelligence of it."

By a study of the prefaces of Wilson's volumes, one can learn much about the author's hopes, plans and difficulties in connection with the publication of the *American Ornithology*.

In Volume 2, for instance, with swiftly-developing pride in things American, he tells of some beautiful pigments from the laboratory of Messrs. Peale and Son, of the Peale Museum, which he substituted in place of certain French products, with excellent soft results. Here, also, he solicits specimens and correspondence from interested persons, and gives detailed directions for the care of birds in the flesh and for making

skins. He sought to cultivate the study of birds on the American side of
the Atlantic, for it seemed to him humiliating to be obliged to apply to
Europe for an account of the fauna of his adopted country.

The second part of his soliciting journey took him through the
coastal cities and down to the deep South. After three months he had
obtained his goal of two hundred and fifty subscribers and was encouraged by favorable comments on his work in the southern paper,
Republican.

The environs of Charleston and Savannah and the dark cypress swamps
of the Santee River took him back in thought to his predecessor, Mark
Catesby, who had roamed that area some eighty years earlier. Though
aware that Catesby's knowledge of plants and trees was far better than
his, he was proud of his own better knowledge of the birds, and bent
every effort to get a good collection of southern species.

The people, however, were disappointing to Wilson with his Spartan
outlook on life. Said he of the persons he wished to interview: "At nine
they are in bed, at ten, breakfasting, dressing at eleven—gone out at
noon and not visible til ten the next morning." In Savannah a fever
attacked him, but since he intended to return to New York by ship, he
said with a gibe at his indisposition: "I hope the sea air and sea-sickness
will carry it off."

But the privations of this southern journey and his persistent careless-
ness about his health, combined to undermine his general condition.

Wilson's journals of his American experience have never been found,
although his biographer, George Ord, makes frequent reference to them.
However, we have another source in Wilson's letters to his friends,
where we can follow his travels and business contacts, and gather his
impressions of many parts of the United States. On return, Wilson
plunged into his double job, his writing for Rees Cyclopedia and the
preparation of other volumes on American birds. As soon as two were
ready, he wrapped then carefully and sent them to his father by an acquaintance returning to Paisley.

The Trip Down the Ohio River

Only a few months elapsed before Wilson was deep in plans for his
long-contemplated trip down the Ohio River. The journey to Pittsburgh
in Western Pennsylvania he made on foot and his expenses he limited to
a dollar a day. To this rigorous excursion Wilson in all good faith invited
his friend, William Bartram, a man twenty-seven years his senior, and a
home-loving man who could not even be lured to the Chair of Botany by
the University of Pennsylvania.

So once again Wilson set out alone. Many stops were made for collecting birds and soliciting subscriptions—Lancaster, Hanover, Chambers-

burg, Shippensburg, Greensburg, and Pittsburgh. Four days in Pittsburgh secured him nineteen subscribers from the city's most prominent residents. Here he purchased his small skiff, which he christened, "The Ornithologist." Then he laid in his modest stores of biscuit and cheese, tucked in a gift bottle of cordial and a tin can for bailing the boat. In high hopes of rich collecting and flouting all advice against going alone, the intrepid oarsman launched downstream for Cincinnati. With difficulty he dodged the floating masses of ice, but in a day's voyage toward the south, these quite disappeared.

Wilson was happy in his solitary journey, the hazards of which were great, but he seemed equal to every emergency. Starting on February 24th, 1810, he suffered every discomfort, but felt rewarded by the magnificent scenery and the opportunity to study the settlers and their hardworking way of life. Above all, he valued his increasing knowledge of American birdlife, and dreamed and planned about the volumes he was going to write after returning home. At Big Bone Lick he encountered his first paroquets and besides securing several for his collection, he wing-tipped one, which became his little companion.

Seven hundred and twenty miles the ornithologist voyaged downstream before the lights of Louisville, Kentucky became dimly visible. He then moored his skiff securely to a large Kentucky boat in Bear Grass Creek above the rapids of the great river, and by the time he had groped his way across a swamp, carrying his satchel, his gun and pet paroquet, it was late when he arrived at the Indian Queen Tavern and asked for a room.

Wilson had four letters of introduction to prominent persons in Louisville, and lost no time in fitting in these calls during the next few days of bird-hunting. He dropped into other places, too, if they seemed to hold promise of a subscription, and by a strange coincidence, he entered the store of John James Audubon, then an obscure merchant of this frontier town. This man, who twenty years later published the famous *The Birds of America* in "Elephant Folios" was, in 1810, having but indifferent success.

Audubon had started an importing business with his partner, Ferdinant Rosier, but the Embargo Act of President Jefferson in 1807, which prohibited traffic in foreign goods, had greatly curtailed his business.

Naturally Wilson had no letter of introduction to this little-known shop or its owner, so he came quickly to the purpose of his visit, laid his books on the counter, explained the scope of the work, and asked Mr. Audubon if he would care to subscribe. The price was $120.

Audubon leafed it through without much comment and, taking the pen from the counter, was about to sign the subscription list. Just then his partner Mr. Rosier, speaking French from the adjoining room, interrupted him. His words according to Audubon's account of the incident were to the effect that since Audubon's drawings were superior and also since his knowledge of American birds must be better than this gentleman's, why should he subscribe?

Always susceptible to praise, Audubon laid down the pen.

Wilson, until that moment feeling safe in the uniqueness of his enterprise, was stunned. Not much of a French student, he had nevertheless gathered Rosier's meaning and managed to ask if Audubon had drawn many birds.

He had, and he reached for a large portfolio of his work which lay on an upper shelf in his shop, and proceeded to show his drawings to the astonished Wilson.

Many European birds which Audubon had drawn as a youth in France, before he took up his residence in America in order to engage in business, and also many American species were among the beautiful and striking portraits.

In October 1808, a year and a half previously, Wilson had said that a work such as his own was not likely to be soon repeated.

Yet here before his eyes he was outdone.

In spite of this heavy blow not a word about this meeting escaped his lips or his pen. We search in vain in his letters of this period and his accounts of birds for some mention of Audubon. He seems sedulously to avoid it but writes in detail of many other events and incidents. Only in George Ord's biography of Wilson published in 1828, nearly eighteen years after the meeting of the two ornithologists, do we find two entries supposedly from Wilson's Journal which can be construed as referring to Audubon:

> March 19—Rambling about town with my gun. Examined
>   Mr. ——'s drawings in crayons—very good.
>   Saw two new birds he had: both motacillae.
> March 21—Went out this afternoon shooting with Mr. A.
>   Saw a number of sandhill cranes. Pigeons numerous.

These journal entries and a few others are put in between quoted letters and are chronologically out of place, without bearing on the letters, and they are without comment by Ord except in that they are offered as samples of Wilson's "unstudied narratives."

Ord's biography of the ornithologist is told largely by quoting his letters so that the student learns little that he does not already know if he has read the letters, and he is left with the feeling that Ord intentionally withheld enlightening information.

Be this as it may, we cannot in the space of this account go into the welter of conjecture and biased published material about the professional rivalry of these two men. So far as can be learned Wilson never broke his sardonic silence on the subject and although Audubon told him in his shop that he had no plans to publish, Wilson of course knew it was only reasonable that eventually Audubon would bring out his work.

Two days after this historic meeting Wilson left Louisville crushed with disillusionment. He sold his boat, parted with his paroquet to the innkeeper and took off southwardly into the wilderness on horseback. We can judge of the impact of Wilson's discovery of Audubon by the desperate concentration with which he went at his work from 1810 on.

The southward course of his journey to New Orleans, his ultimate destination, took him through the Chickasaw and Choctaw territory, a very difficult stretch of wilderness and swampland, where Wilson, in truth, broke his health.

He happened to stop one night, 72 miles south of Nashville, at the house of a Mrs. Grinder, where the famous explorer, Captain Meriwether Lewis had died. His grave lay neglected by the trail, and Wilson, though sick and poor, gave money for a post fence around it. But many nights he slept where darkness forced him to stop, and in a letter to his brother, David, he confessed to spending weeks in the wilderness three hundred miles from a white settlement and so reduced in strength as scarely to be able to stand, or even ride his horse. Friendly Indians told him to live on raw eggs and wild strawberries, and this diet partly restored him.

In spite of all this misfortune Wilson continued to collect and draw birds, and sent home many which were intended for his third and fourth volumes. This parcel was lost in the mail, however, and consequently his work was retarded at a very critical time.

Philadelphia Again

He returned to Philadelphia by ship from New Orleans August* 2, 1810, and faced the task of bringing out the balance of his ten volume work, only two of which had been published. While deep in southern swamps, badly nourished and infected by contaminated water, he had suffered several attacks of dysentery. But he never would, nor could he, in such isolation, take time to get well. The great body of work before him in such a weakened condition caused him to reduce the proposed ten volumes to nine. It is significant that the next four volumes came out during 1811 and 1812. This had entailed another hard journey in 1812—up the Hudson River, across rough mountain country to Lake Champlain and north to Burlington, Vermont. At Haverhill he was taken for a Canadian spy and arrested, but after explaining his travels in the interest of science, he was released.

Returning to Philadelphia, he was heartened by the favorable reception accorded the published books, but at the same time, he was thwarted and

* *Several accounts say Sept. 2.*

dismayed by the loss of all his colourists. He could not pay them. He could not even pay Lawson properly for his engraving. Wilson worked incessantly to collect the birds, write the text and make and color the drawings, himself.

He was having a race with death.

The rest of his short span was spent in several trips to the New Jersey coast after water birds with his new friend, George Ord, later his biographer, a man fifteen years his junior, highly educated, wealthy, and very prominent in Philadelphia.

The work on the water birds was difficult for Wilson. Most of the ducks breed in central and northern Canada; hence it was impossible to familiarize himself with their complete life histories and the same is true of nearly all the shore birds. However, to balance these lacks, Wilson studied the European accounts and he made many dissections which he incorporated in the eighth volume. It is impressive to see the well-organized information set forth with such care, 'ere he forever laid down his pen and brush.

So near was he to the completion of his task that his collapse in August, 1813 evokes profound sorrow.

A bird he had long wanted to possess, he chanced to see one day while talking with friends. He went after it at once and secured it, but suffered complete exhaustion, from which he did not rally, and he died on August 23rd. His friend Ord was not in Philadelphia at the time, but Mr. Jones, with whom Wilson lived, provided the burial site in the churchyard of the old Swedish Church, Gloria Dei, where Wilson had attended services.

George Ord, by previous understanding with Wilson, completed the eighth volume, for which Wilson was doing the coloring when he died. Ord likewise brought out the ninth volume on water birds in January 1814, although Wilson had completed only a few of the plates. To this Ord added a biography of the author, and as long as he lived he sought to bring Wilson recognition for his copious and authoritative studies of American birds.

Wilson's Accomplishment

Wilson drew from life or from freshly killed specimens 320 portraits of American birds, of which 39 were new to science. They were meticulously skinned, numbered, and presented to Peale's Museum in Philadelphia. A few specimens went also to Trowbridge's Museum in Albany. But both of these repositories, after a struggling existence, closed their doors, the collections were divided and sold, and some were destroyed by fire. A very few of Wilson's specimens still exist at the Academy of Natural Sciences of Philadelphia.

The deterioration of Wilson's scientific collection must go down in the pages of history, but in the hearts of American naturalists and bird lovers, six birds that bear his name will always call: the Wilson plover and the Wilson snipe from the sandy beaches and wet meadows of New Jersey; the Wilson phalarope from coastal marshes; the Wilson petrel from all oceans save the Pacific; and the Wilson warbler and Wilson thrush from the cool woods of our northern states and Canada.

Though Wilson did not live to enjoy the plaudits of fame, which he ardently yearned for, and though he was not able to lift himself out of poverty, he did attain certain honors, which must have solaced him in his final years.

He was elected to the Society of Artists of the United States in March 1812 and was chosen a member of that distinguished group of Philadelphia scientists who in 1812 were founding the Academy of Natural Sciences of Philadelphia, but he did not live to sign the register. The honor which he valued most of all was his election to the American Philosophical Society in April, 1813, four months before his death.

WHITE HOUSE BIRD WATCHER

Bates M. Stovall

Theodore Roosevelt, ardent naturalist and great conservationist, was also a mighty hunter whose exploits were satirized by some and aroused the anger of others. The fact remains that Roosevelt was, more than any other one man, responsible for our national parks, and he never ceased to work for the preservation of wildlife. To Frank M. Chapman he once wrote: "When I hear of the destruction of a species I feel as if all the works of some great writer had perished."

CLOSE by Theodore Roosevelt's grave at Oyster Bay is a bird fountain. And near it stands a rock on which one reads that the fountain was erected by the National Association of Audubon Societies as a memorial to "Theodore Roosevelt, Friend of the Wild Birds."

This is no mere flattering phrase, for the late President was a born nature lover who made birds a part of his life. And with the information obtained about them through his prolific reading and from his close friendship with ornithologists of repute, he combined a rare knowledge of the subject gleaned from observations in the field. His powers of observing natural objects were remarkable. Nothing escaped his notice, whether elephant or hummingbird.

His interest in birds was evidenced at the age of nine, when he noted in his diary that several hundred swallows had descended upon a house in which he was staying near Tarrytown, N.Y. They swarmed about the place. Many got inside. One even attached itself to his pants. He caught some of them and put them out the windows.

By the time he was fourteen, he had a fair knowledge of American birds and had taken lessons in taxidermy. Also, with two of his cousins, he had begun what the three described as the Roosevelt Museum of Natural History. When his parents took him and their other children to Egypt, he was careful to take along a supply of printed pink slips labeled "Roosevelt Museum." They were to be used in marking specimens.

The Egyptian trip marks the beginning of his serious attention to collecting as a student of natural history. He took along a taxidermy

From *Frontiers Magazine*. February 1955.

outfit and his father gave him a shotgun. At Cairo he obtained a book with descriptions of Egypt's birds. He had plenty of opportunity, for the elder Roosevelt hired a boat in which the family spent two months on the Nile. The boy scoured the river's vicinity, collecting ibis, plover and other birds. His father trailed along behind through bog and over solid ground, being hard put to keep up.

Many specimens obtained in Egypt and Palestine eventually reached the Smithsonian Institution in Washington. Others found their way to the American Museum of Natural History, New York.

When living as a ranchman in the West, Roosevelt didn't let cattle interfere with his interest in bird life. Although he found many of the western birds, especially in the river bottoms, representative of those in the East, similarities were hardly ever absolute. In some cases the difference was in the songs; in others in the markings.

Sagamore Hill, his Long Island home, was a fertile center of bird life, though the winged population was not as large as that around Washington. During one period of twenty-four hours, the owner of Sagamore Hill counted forty-two different kinds of birds in its vicinity.

While President, he was frequently found early in the mornings rambling about the White House grounds with his wife. Sometimes he carried field glasses with him, the better to examine the skies and the tops of tall trees.

"The people who saw me gazing up into a tall tree like one demented," Roosevelt afterward said, "no doubt thought me insane."

To which his wife added: "Yes, and as I was always with him, they no doubt thought I was the nurse who had him in charge."

Among the visitors to the White House grounds were warblers. The various kinds, with their differences in color and song, perplexed even experienced ornithologists. But Roosevelt knew most of them.

John Burroughs was one of his closest friends. Burroughs said that although he had given his whole life to ornithology, Roosevelt knew almost as much about it as he did.

While the two were in Yellowstone National Park they heard a distant call like someone blowing in an empty bottle. It came from the spruce woods above their camp. They concluded the noise was made by a bird, but were unable to decide what kind. Roosevelt, who was President at the time, exclaimed: "Let's go run that bird down!"

So they crossed a stream and hot-footed it over a snow-streaked plain. When they got into the woods they discovered their quarry high up in a tree. Burroughs imitated the creature's call and caused it to turn toward him. But they still couldn't make out its species.

"You stay here and keep that bird treed, and I'll fetch the glasses," said the President.

So he rushed off to camp, got the field glasses and returned. And with their help, it was found that the feathered object was a pygmy owl. "I think the President was as pleased," said Burroughs afterward, "as if he had bagged some big game, for he had never seen the bird before."

Though Roosevelt loved to hear birds sing, he pointed out it is hard to be an impartial observer of their music. The listener's mood, his keenness of sense and the surroundings, all have a part in the attractiveness of the song.

On one occasion near Nashville, he spent the night in a room with windows overlooking a large magnolia tree. It was spring-time; the magnolia was bathed in the light of a full moon. A mockingbird serenaded Theodore the live-long night. He was enthralled, afterward declaring the bird poured forth such a rapture of ringing melody "as I have never listened to before or since."

. . . To hear the bird songs of England about which he had read, Roosevelt took a long walk through the Valley of the Itchen and through the New Forest. He had Sir Edward Grey, a bird enthusiast, for a guide.

At one point in a flooded lowland, the two had to walk through breast-deep water. While they were drying themselves in the sunshine shortly afterward, the musical notes of a bird sounded. Teddy beamed. "Of all the songs we have heard today," he exclaimed, "that is the only one which resembles in any degree an American song bird."

"That," said Sir Edward, "is the goldencrested wren."

Afterward, Teddy became curious as to the accuracy of his companion's statement, so he asked a bird expert in the British Museum about it. In reply, he was told the song was the only one they could have heard on such a walk which was like that of an American bird.

During their walk, conversation often went somewhat like this:

Grey: "Did you hear that?"

"Yes: what bird is it?"

"A blackcap."

"So that is the song of the blackcap."

Roosevelt didn't have to ask further about the bird. He knew the rest.

Though he thought the blackcap warbler to be the most musical songster heard during the walk, it was the blackbird which impressed him most of the birds he came across in England. Its habits and appearance, he found, were greatly like that of an American robin.

It was during his administration as President that national bird reservations became realities, and when he retired there were more than fifty scattered through our country and its possessions.

PRESIDENTIAL

BIRD

WATCHER

Richard L. Scheffel

Theodore Roosevelt may have been the only American President whose earliest ambition was to be a professional naturalist, but Thomas Jefferson had considerable interest in the subject. He "took all knowledge for his province," and like more than one country gentleman in England he recorded in a diary many observations, not only of his crops, but of every natural phenomenon which came under his wide-ranging scrutiny.

I T had been an average spring. The days had warmed and the hills were green until now it was the 8th of June, 1790. At Philadelphia it already seemed like summer; on that day the season's first peas and strawberries appeared in the markets.

He may have been writing, or calling on friends at the time—we do not know. But we do know that on the evening of that same June 8, Thomas Jefferson heard the insistent call of the whip-poor-will for the first time that year. These simultaneous entries on the stage of spring struck Secretary of State Jefferson as curious and he immediately wrote to his daughter, Mary, asking when these signs of the season had appeared in Virginia.

"Take notice hereafter whether the whip-poor-wills always come with the strawberries and peas," he advised her.

Mary Jefferson replied that the peas at home had been ripe since May 10, and those few strawberries that had survived the late frost had been ready for picking on May 17.

But Mary had to admit to "Dear Papa" that ". . . as for the whip-poor-wills, I was so taken up with my chickens that I never attended to them, and therefore can not tell you when they came, though I was so unfortunate as to lose half of the chickens."

Our third President was, it seems, a dedicated, if amateur, naturalist. He

From *Audubon Magazine*. May–June, 1961.

meant it when he said there is "not a sprig of grass that shoots uninterest-
ing to me, nor anything that moves." He was constantly alert to life
around him and kept prodigious records of his observations. If he saw his
first robins on February 28 in Philadelphia, it prompted him to wonder
when they had returned to Monticello. His letters to his daughters are, as
a result, filled with his observations and requests for information in order
that "we shall be able to compare the climates of Philadelphia and Monticello."

He eventually concluded that the purple martin could be expected at
Monticello sometime between March 18 and April 9, just about the time
the first asparagus should be ready in his kitchen garden each spring.
And he came to expect the whip-poor-will's arrival in Albemarle County
during the first three weeks of April while redbud and dogwood still
glowed from the hills—more than a month before the bird showed up
in Philadelphia.

Nor were Jefferson's thoughts devoted exclusively to affairs of state
while he crossed the Atlantic in 1784 to take up his new duties as
Minister to France. His personal log of the voyage tells us he spent
a good deal of time scanning sea and sky. He kept a record of the
shearwaters and petrels, sharks and whales he sighted, as well as of passing
sails.

While in Europe, Jefferson left his post long enough to tour southern
France and the Italian Riviera where he wrote enthusiastically of the
superb climate and the great numbers of nightingales, beccaficos, ortolans,
quail and other birds. Of these, he said, he would have liked especially
to bring back to America the pheasants and partridges of France, though
he never was able to.

He probably imagined them in the extravagant park he had pictured,
as a young man, surrounding his hilltop mansion. For young Tom
Jefferson had written of a plan for a park which should harbor peacocks,
guniea hens, pheasants and partridges. It would also include feeding stations to attract squirrels and rabbits, deer and "every other wild animal
(except those of prey)." And, besides a buffalo, he wanted to "procure a
buck elk, to be, as it were, monarch of the woods; but keep him shy,
that his appearance may not lose its effect by too much familiarity."

The buffalo and elk, unfortunately, eluded Jefferson, but Isaac, one of
his former slaves, has assured us that partridges were especially abundant
at Monticello. And a French visitor has left us an idyllic picture of
Jefferson strolling over his grounds of an evening with his score or so of
tame deer coming up to take Indian corn from his hands.

Like many other Americans visiting Europe, Jefferson was smitten by
the nightingale. What a bird it would be in America!

"We must colonize him thither," he wrote.

To his daughter, Martha, he described his thrill at sailing on the canal of Languedoc with "cloudless skies above, limpid waters below," while a row of nightingales sang from each bank. He told her of the fountain of Vaucluse, where water gushed from a secluded mountain valley, and Petrarch's chateau perched on the cliff above.

"To add to the enchantment of the scene," he recalled, "every tree and bush was filled with nightingales in full song."

Not that America couldn't do as well, of course. Notice the nightingale's song, Jefferson advised Martha, and remember it for comparison with the mockingbird's song back in America. The mockingbird "has the advantage of singing through a great part of the year, whereas the nightingale," he added, "sings but about five or six weeks in the spring, and a still shorter term, and with a more feeble voice, in the fall."

The mockingbird seems to have been Jefferson's special favorite. While congratulating Martha one spring on the songster's return to Monticello, he added that he hoped all the new trees and shrubs becoming established around the house would attract more mockingbirds ". . . for they like to be in the neighborhood of our habitations if they furnish cover." He even suggested that Martha teach her children to venerate the mockingbird "as a superior being in the form of a bird, or as a being which will haunt them if any harm is done to itself or its eggs."

One mockingbird actually became Jefferson's personal pet. Margaret Bayard Smith, whose husband was editor of Washington's first newspaper, described Jefferson's pet mockingbird as a "constant companion" who followed him about in the White House. It often perched on his couch to serenade him as he napped and would even land on his shoulder and take food from his lips.

Birds, however, were more than just playthings to Jefferson. He considered a man's education incomplete if it did not include study of Alexander Wilson's "American Ornithology."

He also was well acquainted with Mark Catesby's mammoth two-volume work, "The Natural History of Carolina, Florida and the Bahama Islands." In fact, he commented that Catesby's "drawings are better as to form and attitude than color."

He was, after all, the president who organized the Lewis and Clark Expedition. Even before negotiations for the purchase of the vast Louisiana Territory had been completed, Jefferson had secured an appropriation from Congress to finance the expedition by Meriwether Lewis and William Clark.

In three years of explorations up the Missouri, across the Rockies and down the Columbia to the Pacific, Lewis and Clark sent hundreds of herbarium specimens, skins, skeletons and seeds to Jefferson. They even sent him a live prairie chicken and four magpies.

Many species were entirely new to science, and it was Jefferson who filled the vital role of assembling records and distributing specimens among qualified scientists for study, for the expedition discovered hundreds of unknown plants and varieties of wildlife.

Jefferson's other contribution to our knowledge of birds appeared in a work called "Notes on the State Virginia," the only book he ever published. It was inspired by a series of questions submitted to him by the Marquis de Marbois, Secretary of the French Legation at Philadelphia, who was gathering information on the American states for dissemination in Europe.

Jefferson took advantage of this opportunity to organize his vast file of notes and memoranda, "which I did in the order of Mr. Marbois' queries, so as to answer his wish, and to arrange them for my own use." The result was a book that has been called the most important scientific work, except for Benjamin Franklin's on electricity, published in America up to that time. It included information on the geography, climate, commerce, laws and the plants and animals of Virginia. Several pages of the "Notes" are given over to a listing, by both scientific and common names, of over 100 of the birds of Virginia, qualified by the comment that there were "doubtless many others which have not yet been described and classed."

It is an impressive list but not enough, of course, to establish Jefferson as an expert ornithologist. Some people have exaggerated his accomplishments in this field. Elsa Allen, historian of American ornithology, has analyzed his list critically, pointing out its many weaknesses and errors along with its strong points, in order to dispel the legend.

We have to agree with Mrs. Allen that Jefferson was not an ornithologist, although even this strict critic concedes "he had a tolerable familiarity with some 60 or 70 birds."

But whether he knew 70 or 100 species is not of monumental importance. What is intriguing is the fact that this busy and learned statesman considered bird study one of his major secondary interests.

Only a man of intense devotion to wildlife would take the time, for instance, to observe and write of the "chattering plover or killdee" as it flew down the lane ahead of him at Monticello.

This Founding Father enjoyed an intimate kinship with nature which he liked to describe as an "interest or affection in every bud that opens, in every breath that blows."

THE POPULAR
NAMES OF BIRDS

Ernest Thompson Seton

In most branches of natural history the instructed amateur is likely to call animals or plants by their official Latin names. For some reason or other, bird students as well as mere bird lovers seldom do. They say "house wren" instead of "Troglodytes aedon" and "yellow-bellied sapsucker" instead of "Sphyrapicus varius." This does very well for common birds, but it leads in the end to precisely the sort of confusion which the Linnaean system was invented to avoid. The same species gets different names in different regions and the same name is given to different species in different parts of the country.

Hence the continuing attempt on the part of the American Ornithologists' Union to standardize popular names; in effect, to make them "scientific" rather than popular. The attempt has met with considerable success, though of course regional "popular" names hang on. In a letter to the editors of The Auk *in 1885, one of the most popular of American naturalists examines the problem and comes to some interesting conclusions.*

To the Editors of *The Auk:*

The "powers that be," I understand, are preparing a "Check List" and revising the scientific and popular names of our birds.

There is no doubt that scientific names are entirely in the hands of scientists, but it seems to be overlooked that popular names are just as completely in the hands of the people. Scientists may advise, but not dictate on this point. A short analysis of the principle of common names may place the matter in a new light.

A bird's name, to be popular, must be distinctive, and in accordance with the genius of our language. Examples of such are Thrush, Rail, Heron, Hawk, Crane, Nightjar, and many others. These are truly popular names, evolved originally out of description, handed down and condensed and changed until they have assumed their present terse, abrupt,

From *Ernest Thompson Seton's America*, edited by Farida Wiley. New York: Devin-Adair, 1954.

and to a foreign ear uncouth forms, but, nevertheless, forms in accordance with the pervading spirit of the Saxon tongue; or, in other words, they are *really* popular.

On the other hand, look at the so-called popular, but really translated, scientific, spurious English names given to our birds, taking as examples the following: Baird's Bunting, Leconte's Sparrow, Wilson's Green Black-capped Flycatching Warbler, Bartram's Sandpiper, Sprague's Lark, Wilson's Thrush, Black Ptilogonys, Semiplamated Tattler, Fascinated Tit, Florida Gallinule.

Surely, the gentlemen whose names are applied to these birds have not so slight a hold on fame as to require such aids as these to attain it, if indeed aids they be, which I question; for such nomenclature *cannot* stand the test of time.

If you show an "out-wester" the two birds mentioned above as Baird's Bunting and Leconte's Sparrow, and tell him that these are their names, he will probably correct you, and say one is a "Scrub Sparrow," and the other a "Yellow Sparrow." Convince him he is wrong, and in a month he will have forgotten all but the names he formerly gave them; they are so thoroughly appropriate and natural that they cannot be forgotten. The next name in the list above is clumsy enough to strangle itself with its own tail. A lad on the Plains once brought me a *Neocorys spraguei*, and asked its name. I replied it was Sprague's Lark. Soon afterward he came again; he could not remember that name; so I told him it was a "Skylark," and he never forgot that. On the Big Plain that seed was sown, and not all the scientists in America can make, or ever could make, the settlers there call that bird anything but "Skylark." And I consider that lad precisely represented the English-speaking race; he rejected the false name, and readily remembered the true one, and was aided by that which was apt and natural. No better illustration could be given of the fact that phraseology may be the life or death of a cause, according as it is happy or unfortunate.

A similar instance is the case of the "Bartram's Sandpiper." Ever since Wilson's time this name has been continually thrust into the face of the public, only to be continually rejected; "Upland Plover" it continues to be in the East, and "Quaily" on the Assiniboine, in spite of Bartram and Wilson, and will continue so until some name, answering all conditions, is brought forward; for here, as elsewhere, the law of the survival of the fittest rigidly prevails. As an example of the fit ousting the false, note how, in spite of the scientists, "Veery" is supplanting "Wilson's Thrush" throughout the length and breadth of the land.

The spurious English names scarcely need comment, they so evidently contain in themselves the elements of their own destruction. Imagine a western farmer being told that a certain songster was a "Ptilogonys."

In spite of the books, the three examples cannot hold ground against "Willet," "Ground Wren," and "Waterhen," respectively.

The purpose of a check list that includes English names is, I take it, not to attempt the impossible feat of dictating to our woodmen what names they should give their feathered friends, but rather to preserve and publish such names as are evolved in the natural way—names which are the outcome of circumstances. Only in cases of egregious error is a common name to be superseded; and in doing this it must be remembered that no name can be popular unless true to the principles of the English tongue. It must be short, distinctive, and, if possible, descriptive. Of this class are Veery, Junco, and Verio. These are the only successful artificial names that I can at present recollect. Among natural English names for American birds are Bobolink, Chewink, Kingbird, and many others. Such as these not only more than hold their own, but are as great aids to the spread of knowledge as the Ptilogonys kind are hindrances; while such as Wilson's Thrush can only be accepted as provisional, until better knowledge of the bird and its surroundings shall result in the evolution of an English name founded on true principles.

Ernest E. T. Seton
of Manitoba

Glen Cottage, Howard Street,
Toronto, March 21, 1885

SENSING

AND

NAMING

Walt Whitman

The very fact of naming is controversial. Some see naming as the beginning of knowledge, others as the death knell for appreciation (and perhaps for knowledge as well). The poet Walt Whitman's approach to nature was sensual rather than analytical; as the following passage makes clear, he "soaked up" the natural world. From Whitman—as from early Wordsworth—we get the Romantic notion that naming and science are inimical to a loving and sympathetic relationship to nature.

JUNE 19TH, 4 to 6½ P. M.—Sitting alone by the creek—solitude here, but the scene bright and vivid enough—the sun shining, and quite a fresh wind blowing (some heavy showers last night,) the grass and trees looking their best—the clear-obscure of different greens, shadows, half-shadows, and the dappling glimpses of the water, through recesses—the wild flageolet-note of a quail near by—the just-heard fretting of some hylas down there in the pond—crows cawing in the distance—a drove of young hogs rooting in soft ground near the oak under which I sit—some come sniffing near me, and then scamper away, with grunts. And still the clear notes of the quail—the quiver of leaf-shadows over the paper as I write—the sky aloft, with white clouds, and the sun well declining to the west—the swift darting of many sand-swallows coming and going, their holes in a neighboring marl-bank—the odor of the cedar and oak, so palpable, as evening approaches—perfume, color, the bronze-and-gold of nearly ripen'd wheat—clover-fields, with honey-scent—the well-up maize, with long and rustling leaves—the great patches of thriving potatoes, dusky green, fleck'd all over with white blossoms—the old, warty, venerable oak above me—and ever, mix'd with the dual notes of the quail, the soughing of the wind through some near-by pines.

From *Specimen Days and Collect*. Philadelphia: Rees Welsh and Company, 1882–83.

As I rise for return, I linger long to a delicious song-epilogue (is it the hermit-thrush?) from some bushy recess off there in the swamp, repeated leisurely and pensively over and over again. This, to the circle-gambols of the swallows flying by dozens in concentric rings in the last rays of sunset, like flashes of some airy wheel.

A JULY AFTERNOON BY THE POND. The fervent heat, but so much more endurable in this pure air—the white and pink pond-blossoms, with great heart-shaped leaves; the glassy waters of the creek, the banks, with dense bushery, and the picturesque beeches and shade and turf; the tremulous, reedy call of some bird from recesses, breaking the warm, indolent, half-voluptuous silence; an occasional wasp, hornet, honey-bee or bumble (they hover near my hands or face, yet annoy me not, nor I them, as they appear to examine, find nothing, and away they go)—the vast space of the sky overhead so clear, and the buzzard up there sailing his slow whirl in majestic spirals and discs; just over the surface of the pond, two large slate-color'd dragon-flies, with wings of lace, circling and darting and occasionally balancing themselves quite still, their wings quivering all the time, (are they not showing off for my amusement?)—the pond itself, with the sword-shaped calamus; the water snakes—occasionally a flitting blackbird, with red dabs on his shoulders, as he darts slantingly by—the sounds that bring out the solitude, warmth, light and shade—the quawk of some pond duck—(the crickets and grasshoppers are mute in the noon heat, but I hear the song of the first cicadas;)—then at some distance the rattle and whirr of a reaping machine as the horses draw it on a rapid walk through a rye field on the opposite side of the creek—(what was the yellow or light-brown bird, large as a young hen, with short neck and long-stretch'd legs I just saw, in flapping and awkward flight over there through the trees?)—the prevailing delicate, yet palpable, spicy, grassy, clovery perfume to my nostrils; and over all, encircling all, to my sight and soul, the free space of the sky, transparent and blue. . . .

May 14.—Home again; down temporarily in the Jersey woods. Between 8 and 9 A.M. a full concert of birds, from different quarters, in keeping with the fresh scent, the peace, the naturalness all around me. I am lately noticing the russet-back, size of the robin or a trifle less, light breast and shoulders, with irregular dark stripes—tail long—sits hunch'd up by the hour these days, top of a tall bush, or some tree, singing blithely. I often get near and listen, as he seems tame; I like to watch the working of his bill and throat, the quaint sidle of his body, and flex of his long tail. I hear the woodpecker, and night and early morning the shuttle of the whip-poor-will—noons, the gurgle of thrush delicious, and *meo-o-ow* of the cat-bird. Many I cannot name; but I do not very particularly seek information. (You must not know too much, or be too precise or scientific about birds and trees and flowers and water-craft; a certain free margin, and even vagueness—perhaps igno-rance, credulity—helps your enjoyment of these things, and of the sen-timent of feather'd, wooded, river, or marine Nature generally. I repeat it—don't want to know too exactly, or the reasons why. . . .)

A LISTER IS

(WITH QUALMS)

BORN

Joseph Wood Krutch

Few bird watchers (and no birders) have followed Whitman's advice. The burgeoning field guide literature is one indication of our determination to identify—to put proper names to—the birds we see. Accurate naming often leads to listing—keeping records of the species one finds on one's property, in one's county or state or region or country or continent or. . . . Some birders embrace listing with joyful abandon; others, like Krutch, sidle up to the sport with second thoughts.

WILL Cuppy once remarked that the ability to distinguish one kind of sparrow from another was a gift which seemed to be hereditary in certain New England families. Not belonging to such a family, I am not surprised that I am not at all good at this particular art, science, or diversion. Nevertheless, I have long been a little ashamed that a professed lover of most animal creatures should know as little as I did about the birds. Many people begin, indeed many people also stop, with them. But a turtle or a lizard, even an unfamiliar bug, was surer to get my sympathetic attention. I knew by sight and sound the commoner birds of the lawns and gardens, but that was almost all.

For this perversity I have offered myself various excuses. For one thing, the birds seemed determined to elude me. They were always flying away or hiding behind leaves when I wanted to see what they looked like. Old-fashioned bird lovers, like Audubon, used to blaze away with a gun when this situation arose, and some still do. But I have a sentimental disinclination to shoot a passer-by just to find out who he is. In fact, once he was dead I don't think I should very much care. And so the birds and I went about our respective business.

Moreover, the loss was, I think, exclusively mine since there is probably some truth as well as some exaggeration in the opinion recently

From *The Desert Year.* New York: William Sloane Associates, 1951.

expressed in print that—when all the "collecting," photographing, and experimentation is taken into consideration—the best friend of the birds is often the one who pays no attention to them. A winter handout of suet and seeds is no doubt often appreciated, but what starts that way often ends quite differently.

Had I stayed at home in New England I should perhaps never have made a start. One does not like to begin learning one's letters at fifty and more. But in a new environment ignorance is nothing to be ashamed of. All the commoner birds which haunt the open desert itself —thrashers, cactus wrens, white-winged doves, road-runners and Gambel's quail—thrust themselves upon my attention. They appreciated the dish of water I put out for their benefit; they got into the habit of paying me regular visits; and there were no leaves for them to hide behind.

Nothing so difficult as sparrow-distinguishing was called for, and at least this company of a dozen regular visitors was soon as familiar as the robin and catbird. Armed with one of the modern field guides which are so much better adapted to the needs of the beginner than the old bird books used to be, I was soon wandering down the canyons, along the washes, and even into the pine forests of the higher mountains, looking for species which have no great fondness for the cactus and the sand. Before I knew it, I was equipped with a better pair of binoculars than I had ever owned before and, murmuring an occasional apology to Thoreau who boasted that he was well along in life before he consented to use a "spy glass," I was engaged in that sometimes ridiculed enterprise called "compiling a life list."

This game, which consists merely in seeing how many different birds one can identify, is played on the side by some "serious" ornithologists, but it is also often despised both by the ultrascientific on the one hand and by the ultrapoetical or philosophical on the other. The more advanced form, which consists in keeping the score for a year or even a single hectic day, has been derisively called "ornithogolf," but it is at least harmless even to the birds, most of whom do not seem to mind being peered at through binoculars. Simple listing seems to me rather more like stamp collecting than like golf, but as long as one competes with nobody except oneself it affords the elementary pleasures associated with "making a collection" of anything. One is easily pleased with one's own achievements as long as no anxious comparisons are made, and what does not grow very fast at least never goes backward.

I felt quite pleased when my list had reached forty, though now that it numbers one hundred and thirty-eight—including a few California species—I look back with tolerant amusement upon the ignorant satisfaction of a few months ago. For an eastern community, one hundred and thirty-eight would be quite good for a tyro; but it is less impressive out here, where the number of different birds is much greater. In the entire United States there are said to be about six hundred and fifty species. A census taken by a group one Christmas day turned up one hundred and seventeen within a circle fifteen miles in diameter with its center at Tucson. A similar count at Brownsville, Texas, yielded one hundred and sixty-four. And since I have wandered over a much larger area and also had the advantage of a whole cycle of the seasons, my record would not interest the virtuosos—among whom are such prodigies as Ludlow Griscom who is said to be able to recognize five hundred birds by their songs alone. But I am not competing with anyone except that dead self which thought forty quite a respectable number.

Fortunately for such as I, a surprising number of the southwestern birds are bright-colored and strikingly distinctive. We, too, have our sparrows; but many of them are quite easy to tell apart, and the more difficult ones are not necessary to fill out a respectably long list. Moreover, if my collection has not done anything else for me, it led to the discovery of a charming nook I would probably not otherwise have found.

THE

BIG DAY

Roger Tory Peterson

*A special event in most listers' lives is the "big day," usually scheduled in
May during the height of spring migration, when a group of birders attempts to identify by sight or sound as many species as possible in a predetermined geographical area. The much-honored birdman and conservationist Roger Tory Peterson describes one such big day in New Jersey. If the
number of species bandied about here seems impressive, it may interest you
to know that, in the winter of 1986, a team of birders in Kenya posted a
new world record big day total of 342 species!*

At three o'clock in the morning a large open touring car parked just
off the highway in the hills of northern New Jersey. After switching off the ignition and the headlights, the driver relaxed while the other
occupants of the car leaned out and listened. Two state police saw the
suspicious-looking automobile. The six silent, roughly dressed men within
appeared to be a hardboiled and dangerous lot.

"What do you gents think you are doing?" inquired one of the patrol-
men.

"Listening for the whip-poor-wills," replied the driver.

"Wise guys!" retorted the officer.

It took these men a full hour to convince the skeptical police that they
really were listening for whip-poor-wills. Furthermore, they were trying
to find as many birds as they could within a twenty-four hour day. They
were starting with the night birds; that is why they had parked in this
lonely place.

Some years ago, when the star of the field-glass ornithologist was
rising and it was no longer necessary to check every observation over the
sights of a shotgun, some fellow with good legs and sharp eyes found he
could list over 100 species of birds in a day. In the north this would be in
mid-May, at the time the spring migration was at flood tide.

From *Birds over America*. New York: Dodd, Mead & Company, 1948.

This all-out May-day tournament was something I had never heard of before I came into contact with the birdmen of the big cities along the East coast. New Yorkers and Bostonians call it the "Big Day"; the New Jerseyites the "Lethal Tour"; Philadelphians the "Century Run," and Washingtonians the "Grim Grind." One museum man, with a note of scorn, has dubbed it "ornithogolfing." Lately it has become tradition, planned for weeks in advance. Each hour is mapped out so that the most productive places are visited at the most opportune time. From dark to dark the field-glass forces invade the realm of the birds with military thoroughness. Crossing a field, they deploy their ranks on a wide front so that no bird slips by. Fast travel between strategic areas, with a tankful of gas and good brakes, is part of the tactics.

A dozen pairs of eyes are better than one pair, or two; and although there is dead wood in every Big Day party, the larger the group the better the list. In Massachusetts, half a dozen of us usually went together, led by our commanding general Ludlow Griscom. I remember particularly the day we piled up a grand total that broke all previous records for New England.

The evening before we held a council of war over the telephone. Griscom had studied the weather maps and the tide tables. He had outlined where we would stop and when, but each of us offered amendments. Even though the trip was planned as precisely as a train schedule, we left some room for flexibility. In migration, birds seemed to gather in "pockets." It is a waste of time to linger where not much is stirring.

I got my gear together before I went to bed, so there would be no delay. My trousers were of a sort that could not be ripped easily on barbed wire. I prefer sneakers to boots when the weather is warm for they let the water out as well as in, and they dry quickly. I dug out a hat with a good brim to shade my eyes from the sun. Although I had a pair of 12-power glasses, I decided to use my eights. They had a very wide field and were better for warblers and other small birds than the larger glass. Griscom would have his Zeis telescope, with its three rotating oculars, so if we saw any shore birds on a bar too distant to identify them with our glasses, we could magnify them as much as forty times if need be.

My alarm went off at two that morning. Although I hate alarm clocks and choose to ignore them, suffering as I do from some sort of compulsion complex, at the sound of the bell this morning I jumped from bed like a fighter from his corner. At the diner, three blocks away, I gulped my coffee and scrambled eggs while little gray mice played among the boxes of breakfast food on the shelf. I do not know what birdmen would do without diners! They are as much a part of early-morning bird trips as the robin chorus and the rising sun.

I met Griscom and the others at Harvard Square, in Cambridge. Al-

though it was black as pitch, Griscom said there was no time to lose. We
had to reach Boxford, thirty miles down the turnpike, to listen for owls
before it got light. We made only one stop. Pulling to the side of the road,
we turned off the engine and listened. The sound of the motor still
hummed in our ears and at first we could hear nothing. Then Griscom
announced. "There it is—number one!" We strained, and faintly above
the chorus of the spring peepers came a nasal *beezp!* It was a woodcock,
the first bird of the day. A moment later came the chirping whistle of its
wings as the "timber-doodle" took off on its aerial song-flight. Higher
and higher it climbed against the descending moon; until, reaching the
zenith, it spilled forth its ecstatic bubble-pipe-like warblings and twisted
headlong back to earth. All was silent again as we climbed back into the
car. We did not wait to hear the performance again nor did we search out
the singer. A bird heard is as good as a bird seen, and there were other
night birds to be recorded before dawn rolled back the darkness.

We turned off the main highway onto a dirt road, went as far as we
could, parked, and walked down the narrow path leading to Crooked
Pond. Faint lisps and chirps dropped from the blackness above us, a good
sign that meant there would be a flight. It is almost impossible to be sure
of these tiny night voices beyond identifying them broadly as warblers
or sparrows, but the thrush notes are quite distinctive. There was no
doubt, either, about the whip-poor-will that lashed out with its nocturnal
chant. It went down on our list as number two.

Griscom, leading the party single file through the dew-drenched grass,
stopped abruptly as a strange call came from the second-growth woodland
to our left. Dove-like yet frog-like, we could not place it. "Long-eared
owl," Griscom announced finally. "It had me guessing for a minute." The
rest of us had never heard that note before, so we could not dispute the
verdict. Yet we had not expected the long-ear. The real reason we were
walking down this trail was to try for the pair of barred owls that lived
near the pond. Owls won't "talk" every morning, but that day we were
favored; a few hoots from Griscom in his best strixine falsetto brought
a muffled answer. The second bird gave moral support to the first, and
we left Crooked Pond with both owls whooping and caterwauling at the
tops of their lungs, in defiance to the strangers who had invaded their
wilderness.

By the time we reached the car, the east was streaked with light. The
robin chorus was in full voice and, although we had not yet seen a
single bird, our list had already passed twenty. Song sparrows, field sparrows and catbirds announced themselves. A pheasant squawked. We had
to hurry. Marsh birds are at their best around sunrise, and if we did not
reach the Lynnfield Meadows early, we might miss the rails.

Dawn on a marsh is the most vocal time of day—even on a New England marsh, which is, at best, a pale reflection of the teeming duck marshes

further west. Following the high dry cinder bed of the railroad, the one way in and out of the Lynnfield Meadows, we were soon in the heart of the great swamp. Patches of fog still clung to the sodden earth, or, stirred by the dawn wind, drifted off in milky wisps. Chilled, we could have done with a second cup of coffee, but this would have to wait. Our luck at Lynnfield would have much to do with the success of the day. Perhaps we might pick up a rarity—a king rail, big and rusty, or even the small elusive yellow rail. In this we were disappointed. Lynnfield was particularly poor. We heard the bittern's hollow pumping, and detected both marsh wrens: the long-bill gurgling in the cattails and the short-bill stuttering from the more grassy part of the swamp. We heard the grunting of the Virginia rail but once and missed the whinny of the sora entirely. Usually these little chicken-like birds sound off all over the swamp in the early morning. We laid their silence to the cool breeze that had sprung up, rattling the sabers of the reeds.

We had already picked up a large number of small land birds in the sparse groves at the edge of the swamp, but we placed our biggest hopes for these on Nahant, a narrow-waisted headland that juts out into the ocean. There on the spacious estates would parade the warblers and other migrants, concentrated in this natural bird trap by the barrier of the sea. We found buffy-breasted Lincoln sparrows and smart-looking white-crowns on the lawns, as we had hoped, but we had not expected the flock of ten purple sandpipers that scrambled over a dripping, tide-exposed rock. These hardy junco-colored sandpipers are uncertain enough on these barnacle-encrusted boulders, even in winter. In May, they were a genuine surprise for us. We were doing well, but it looked as though our luck would taper off; it was beginning to rain.

Mount Auburn Cemetery, in Cambridge, was our last stop before starting on the long run to the Cape for shore birds. By the time we entered the wrought-iron gates the drizzle had stopped and the gray clouds were breaking up. This famous old cemetery, where ornithologists have hunted warblers among the tombstones since the days of William Brewster, was full of birds, brought in by the southwesterly wind of the night before. Quickly we rounded out our list of warblers, adding the Tennessee, Blackburnian, Canada, Wilson's and bay-breast. Our warbler list alone was twenty-two, not bad for New England, although twenty-five or even more, is a possibility.

Our total list had reached eighty by 8:00 A.M.; a hundred by 10:00 A.M. But this furious pace slowed down to a walk by noon. New birds were harder to find; our limbs had become weary from the ten-hour grind; eyelids were heavy and heads nodded in the back seat, while the driver doggedly held to the endless ribbon of concrete unwinding toward the Cape. We went by way of Carver to take in a colony of purple martins, one of the few breeding colonies of this big glossy swallow in eastern Massachusetts. A detour at Wareham gave us the hermit thrush, singing beside a cranberry bog in the barrens, and three bald eagles, lured by the myriads of shad that swarmed into the inland ponds to spawn and die.

Nothing is duller for birds than most pine-barren country, so we spent little time on it. The outer Cape was a long haul, and it was late in the day before we reached Chatham, with its white houses and wind-swept silver poplars. There we changed into a hired beach wagon with low-pressure balloon tires for gripping the loose beach sand.

There were not more than two hours of daylight left when we started down Monomoy, the long peninsula of sand dunes and mud flats that stretches southward for ten miles or so into the Atlantic from the crooked elbow of Cape Cod. Here we hoped to wind up the day in a burst of glory. Nor were we disappointed. Shore birds swarmed the flats like sand fleas on a beach. There were a thousand ruddy turnstones all in high rufous breeding plumage with orange legs and harlequin-like head markings. We estimated 300 black-bellied plovers, 3000 sanderlings and countless numbers of the smaller "sand peeps." Our shore-bird list rose to fifteen species.

In the surf bobbed belated groups of those rugged sea ducks, the scoters. All three species were in sight and among them six American eiders, males with white backs, stragglers from the great flocks that make Monomoy their winter headquarters.

Like a magician, plucking rabbits from a hat, Griscom pulled out the two "fanciest" birds of the day. Ordering the driver to stop, he put his glasses on a lone bird swimming beyond the surf. Quickly appraising, he called out "Brunnich's murre." The telescope was brought to bear on the piebald swimmer and without a hint of chagrin, Griscom retracted the first guess. "Sorry!" he apologized, "just an old-squaw." Even Griscom makes mistakes, but he is usually the first to correct them.

We had hardly gone several hundred yards further down the beach when another lone swimmer caught our attention. Griscom squinted, hesitated and blurted "Brunnich's murre." We respectfully reserved judgment while he tensely hauled out the telescope again. In a moment he relaxed. "Don't you believe me?" he queried. "Look for yourselves!" We did. There was no doubt about it; the bird was a murre, that black-and-white sea bird that reminds one so much of a penguin. It was in changing plumage and the proportion of the bill and the light-colored mark along the gape showed it to be a Brunnich's! This curious coincidence did much to increase our ever-growing awe of Griscom. No one but he would have dared cry "Brunnich's murre" again so soon after making a blunder.

The pay-off came a short distance further down the beach when a third lone sea bird was spotted, bobbing up and down in the wave troughs. With hardly a moment's deliberation Griscom electrified us with

"Atlantic murre!" That was too much! To get both murres in one day was an extremely rare event in Massachusetts even in the dead of winter. It was next to impossible in May. Surely Griscom was getting tired—probably he had too much sun. But the telescope backed him up. The bird *was* an Atlantic murre in winter plumage. The thin pointed bill and the dark line behind the eye left no doubt about it.

At the tip of Monomoy we found the usual great congregation of gulls and terns resting on the high crown of the shell-studded beach. Facing in one direction, into the wind and the setting sun, rested five kinds of gulls and four of terns. Besides the tiny least terns with yellow bills and the familiar common tern with black-tipped vermilion bills, there were a number of roseates with blackish bills, and a few arctics, grayer than the others, with bills blood-red to the tip. This is one of the southernmost spots in America where the arctic tern can be depended upon. Indeed, I know of no better place anywhere to study the several most confusing terns side by side. An hour with these birds at the tip of Monomoy is worth months of experience with them elsewhere.

With the sun setting in a coppery haze on the horizon, we sped up the beach, satisfied with Monomoy and with ourselves. We were blissfully pleased but tired—faces windblown, eyes bloodshot and hair filled with sand. Griscom, always a martinet, said we would not stop for food until we had done one thing more—not until we had tried for the great horned owl back in the barrens.

We got not only the great horned, which was obliging enough to hoot once or twice in stentorian tones, but also a screech owl that timidly answered my bad imitations of its lonely wail. Four kinds of owls in one day was not bad. We had done about all we could, and we were hungry!

Dinner never tasted so good. When the apple pie had been followed by coffee and we had taken out our check-list cards, we counted the day's total. It came to 148! This was a new high for Massachusetts and for all New England.

Riding home, we put our trust in our driver while we dozed and fitfully dreamed of murres with blood-red bills, like those of Arctic terns. At midnight we reached Boston. We had been on the go for twenty-two hours, but we had hung up a record.

For a decade, no one bettered that score in Massachusetts. But on May 20, 1945, after three cold rainy weeks in which the May migrants had become dammed up, a platoon of bird-watchers found 160 species—all in Essex County! Three years later, on May 23, 1948, with identical freak weather conditions in our favor, we nosed out this short-lived record by one species. Late at night the cooperative barred owls of Crooked Pond responded to Griscom's whoops just as they had done on nearly every Big Day for the past fifteen years, and thus became No. 161 on our list.

Among the most famous of all Big Day trips were those which the late Charles Urner organized in New Jersey. Starting in the swampy Troy Meadows before daybreak, running up to the mountain ridges near Boonton for migrating warblers and down through the pine barrens to the southern New Jersey coast for shore birds, Urner's itinerary resembled that of the excursion I have described in Massachusetts. Urner's lists, however, were larger, seldom fewer than 150, once as high as 173. There were more participants, also, sometimes fifteen or twenty; as a result, hardly anyone came within ten of seeing every bird in the day's total. Some of the less experienced men complained it was a dog-eat-dog affair, that once a bird was ticked off no one would wait for the slower fellows to find it.

In the Lower Rio Grande Valley, I think it would be possible to upset Urner's record, if a man had some knowledge of the country. Lists of 200 in one day should be possible in this strategic bird paradise where east meets west and Mexican bird life laps across our border.

A variation of the Big Day is the "Roundup." In this there are no restrictions on distance or number of parties, providing they start from the same point. A number of lists are combined at the end of the day. At St. Louis, Missouri, a "Roundup" recorded 187 species in one day, while the Delaware Valley Ornithological Club checked off 214 between the mountains and the New Jersey shore.

These ornithological sprees do not allow one fully to enjoy the birds or to spend much time watching them. But there are values beyond the excitement of the chase. If exact numbers of each species are kept, a year-to-year comparison gives a hint of increases or declines. Redstart-*common* does not mean much, but redstart-58 does. The conscientious field-man keeps a diary of the outstanding behavior of the birds, his impressions of the sweep and movement of migration and the weather.

No one would want to engage in one of these endurance tests every week end, but once or twice a year it is great sport, a test of the skills acquired by months and years of bird watching. We are waiting for the inevitable day when someone will try by airplane or helicopter.

THE

BIG YEAR

Alan Pistorius

The trouble with sporting pastimes (and dares) is that someone is always upping the ante. Probably you have already guessed that the big day would not be the last word in the mad world of ornithogolf.

W HEN the state Big Day no longer seems sufficiently challenging, it's time to move up to the North American Big Year or even to the World Big Year, which provide more time and geographical scope. Probably the North American Big Year will never be a very popular participatory event, simply because few people can afford to spend most of a year traveling and birding. Big Year records, however, which used to stand for years, toppled regularly during the 1970s as a result of the expanding listing mania, a burgeoning where-to-find-rare-birds literature, a growing bird-tour business, more and better telephone rare-bird alerts and hotlines, and increasing attention on the part of Big Year birders to strategy and the exploitation of local birding expertise.

Kenn Kaufman proved you don't absolutely have to be rich to participate. In 1973, Kaufman, long-haired and jobless, a veteran birder at nineteen, hooked up in a Big Year competition with Floyd Murdoch, an "establishment" graduate student in his thirties. While Murdoch traveled, birded, ate, and slept conventionally—that is to say, expensively—Kaufman hitchhiked around North America, spending under $1,000 for the entire year's living and traveling expenses. (Murdoch spent more than that on airplane tickets alone.) Kaufman grubstaked himself by cashing in his life insurance; when that money ran out he sold his blood. During hard times he subsisted entirely on dried pet foods (he recommends Little Friskies and Gravy Train).

As a seasoned hitchhiker, Kaufman knew the year would not be without incident. It was not. In a brief article he wrote about the experience (called "Under My Thumb but Almost Over My Dead Body," *Birding*,

From *The Country Journal Book of Birding and Bird Attraction*. New York: W.W. Norton, 1981.

May/June 1974), he alludes to the usual "hair-raising rides with trau-
matic drunks," the "disgusting perverted characters I had to punch
out," and the "grillings by suspicious cops." He was not prepared, however, for the two-day stint in a Virginia jail (for hitchhiking), or for the
"pleasantly insane young widow" who kidnapped him in Maryland.

The trouble with any Big Year effort is that it pays increasingly diminished returns. The magic number in 1973 was 650 species, and both
Kaufman and Murdoch had reached 550 by the end of spring migration.
From then on the pool of new birds becomes, like the birder, increasingly exhausted. The two ran into one another on a pelagic trip off the
coast of Washington State on October 7. Murdoch had recorded 666
species, Kaufman 656. They thought about declaring a tie and hanging
it up. But too many people were involved—scouting, advising, pushing,
or just looking on—and they had no choice but to carry on. November
ended with Murdoch leading 668 to 665. And then December—time for
the last push. Murdoch traveled a desperate 12,000 miles, but added only
one new bird, a blue tit discovered in Ontario. (It was later concluded
that the bird was more likely an escapee than a wanderer, and hence not
countable.) Kaufman, meanwhile, dropped into Baja California (which
the American Ornithologists' Union considers part of North America,
while the American Birding Association excludes it), adding five new
species.

When it was all over, the two men had birded from the Dry Tortugas
off the tip of Florida to St. Lawrence Island, in the Bering Sea within
sight of Soviet Siberia. Floyd Murdoch had traveled over 100,000 miles
and had birded in forty-seven states. His tentative list of 669 species was
a new ABA North American Big Year record. Kenn Kaufman had recorded just over 80,000 miles of travel, 69,200 of them by hitchhiking
(some thousands of which he drove himself, without benefit of driver's
license). His tentative list of 670 species set a new AOU North American Big Year record.* (A friend of mine remembers bumping into Kaufman shortly after the ordeal was over, and Kenn said he'd like to go
around again and take time to see what all those birds looked like.)

The 1973 Big Year is yet to be surpassed in terms of dramatic interest;
many birders thought the records coming out of it couldn't be surpassed either. They were wrong. In 1979 a forest-management consul-
tant named Jim Vardaman, a self-styled intermediate birder, set out to
break 700 species, or nearly seven-eighths of all the birds that have *ever*
been identified in North America (including several that are now extinct). That list includes 116 "accidentals," birds such as shy albatross,
Chinese egret, white-tailed eagle, paint-billed crake, Temminck's stint,

---

* Some species from both lists were subsequently disallowed, and the ABA record
going into 1979 was Scott Robinson's 1976 total of 657 species.

jungle nightjar, Bahama woodstar, hoopoe, eye-browed thrush, melodious grassquit, and ant palm swift, exotics that have showed up once or twice (presumably under their own power) somewhere in North America. Only seven birders have been able to record 700 species in North America in their entire lives; Vardaman describes a 700 Big Year as the equivalent of a 3:30 mile.

Vardaman began to plan his assault in the fall of 1977 with the help of a brain trust of seventy-five hard-core birders and a six-man insider Big Year Strategy Council (one of whom was Kenn Kaufman). They determined where and when one had the best chance of finding every possible North American bird, and laid out a detailed itinerary for the year. An expert local birder was set to squire Vardaman at every stop; a widely disseminated periodic newsletter urged birders all over the continent to call him collect immediately (code name: Birdman) upon discovery of a rare bird. He would, he said, go anywhere at any time for a "visitor" or an "accidental."

The Big Year started off on a sour note, as the *Sports Illustrated* writer sent to cover the assault died of a heart attack. Vardaman was not to be deterred. He and his Florida guide were out on New Year's Eve. They camped under bird No. 1, a barn owl, and counted it one second into 1979. By the end of January he had birded in five time zones and had traveled over 12,000 miles. His sighting ledger—he counted only those birds identified by himself and at least one witness—had been signed 294 times.

The Big Year proceeded nicely, and Vardaman broke the standing North American Big Year record with an ironically common American woodcock—bird No. 658—found in a ditch outside Chicago. He birded everywhere—sneaking up on grouse leks in Colorado, beating the bush in Minnesota, watching for Asiatic strays from remote Attu in the Aleutian chain, cruising both oceans in rented planes and boats for pelagics. The numbers mounted, and by the time the bulk of fall migration was over, he had logged 690 species. Only ten birds to go, and three months in which to track them down. But only strays were left to be counted, and you can't track strays; you sit back and wait for one to turn up somewhere, and hope you'll hear about it if it does.

Early December. Vardaman and his south Texas guide find a white-collared seedeater, a tiny Mexican ground finch, along the Rio Grande. Bird No. 698, and three weeks to go. But the phone isn't ringing, and Vardaman is getting desperate. He puts out the word to the south Florida press: a $100 reward for a confirmed sighting of a blue-gray tanager. Nobody responds. He spends a quiet Christmas with the family. Too quiet. Then, with New Year's looming, a last flurry. A great skua has been sighted off the Maryland coast. A Middle American golden-crowned warbler has appeared in Brownsville, Texas. And a stripe-headed tanager has found its way from the Bahamas to Miami. Vardaman charters a plane and goes after the skua, a species on which he has already spent over 1,000 miles of searching by plane and boat. This time he gets it. He is on his way to Brownsville by way of Miami when he gets the bad news—both tanager and warbler have gone. It is New Year's Eve. He says the hell with it and goes to bed.

Vardaman's record 699-bird North American Big Year cost him over 160,000 miles of travel (mostly by plane, but including 20,000 miles by car and over 3,000 miles by boat) and enough money to buy a house. He says it was worth it. (One recalls Kenn Kaufman's comment summing up his Big Year: "It was a ridiculous amount of effort, but anything can be fun if taken to extremes.") What the media people gathered around Vardaman wanted to know was what he planned for an encore. He was thinking, he replied, about planning for an all-out World Big Year. The goal would be 5,500 species, more birds than anyone has ever recorded in a lifetime. His wife, Virginia, says he'd better be kidding. As she put it to a reporter: "I don't know how he'll be able to afford the trip and the alimony, too."

THE

HARRIS'S SPARROW'S

EGGS

George Miksch Sutton

Occasionally the elements of sport and competition play a major role in scientific endeavor. Here George Miksch Sutton—ornithologist and bird painter—narrates in the first person the 1931 epic search for the undiscovered eggs of Harris's sparrow.

I F you are not an ornithologist you probably never have heard of a Harris's Sparrow. And if you have never heard of a Harris's Sparrow you cannot be expected to know that it took us learned scientists almost a hundred years to find its eggs; that the long search ended in two weeks of warfare between the Americans and the Canadians; and that the final, decisive battle of this conflict was won by the Americans.

The Harris's Sparrow is a handsome member of the finch tribe. It is considerably larger than an English Sparrow. It has a pink bill; black crown, face, and throat; streaked back and sides; and white underparts. It inhabits the middle part of North America, nesting in the stunted spruce woods at the edge of the Barren Grounds, migrating across south central Canada and our midwestern States, and wintering in Kansas, Oklahoma, and Texas. It was discovered, in 1837, by a young naturalist named Thomas Nuttall, who described it three years later, naming it *Fringilla querula*, the Mourning Finch. A few years later the famous ornithologist-artist, John James Audubon, rediscovered the bird, bestowing upon it, in honor of his excellent and constant friend Edward Harris, Esq., the common name it now bears. Ornithologists since the time of Nuttall, Audubon, and Maximilian, Prince of Wied, have been observing it, tracing its routes of migration northward, hoping to find its summer home. Its breeding grounds were discovered in 1900, or thereabouts; but even so recently as [1931] its eggs were yet unfound and undescribed.

From *Birds in the Wilderness.* New York: Macmillan Company, 1936.

On June 16, in [that year], a few minutes before nine o'clock in the morning, the Harris's Sparrow's eggs were discovered. They were in no way extraordinary in appearance. In size, shape, and color they were much like the eggs of several closely related Fringilline species. They were very light greenish-blue, heavily blotched with brown. A complete description of them appeared in our leading ornithological journals. . . . But the story of finding these eggs—of the battle waged at the edge of the tundra between the Americans and the Canadians—this story has never been published. I purpose to tell this story here, although I have no desire to disturb the peace that has so long existed along our northern boundary line.

The story begins a good many years ago. As a boy of fifteen I dreamed fond dreams of discovering the Harris's Sparrow's eggs. As I read in my bird books such statements as "the eggs of this sparrow are unknown," I squirmed, felt strange stirrings inside me, and pondered. Where would the nest of such a sparrow be—on the ground, under a thick bush, in a tree? Would it be hidden away in some shadowy place, or would it be at the tip of some high, cone-bearing bough? And how many eggs would be in it?

In the early fall of 1930, while returning from my year with the Eskimos of Southampton Island, I had occasion to wait some days at Churchill, Manitoba, for the train that would carry me south. There at Churchill, on the west coast of Hudson Bay, I for the first time encountered the Harris's Sparrow on its breeding ground. I did not see much of it, to be sure, for I had little opportunity to walk through the country which it preferred to frequent. But I could see that it had nested thereabouts, and the idea of finding the unfound eggs took fresh hold upon me.

I talked the matter over with my good friend JB.[1] Characteristically enthusiastic over the prospect of such a quest he decided to organize an expedition to Churchill the following Spring. "We must be there early," I advised. "The nest has been found, remember, and the young birds have been described; so we must be there early enough to get the eggs!"

We got there early enough, all right. Alighting from our comfortable Pullman on that evening of May 24, 1931, we found ourselves standing in snow two feet deep. A strong wind from the Bay struck us full in the face. The drifts along the ridge just to the north of us were, we learned, over twenty feet deep. Springtime indeed! The Churchill River was frozen shut miles back from the mouth. The Bay was a vast field of ice chunks that rose and sank with the tides. Husky dogs were pulling sledges to an encampment on the opposite side of the River. Our thin, short

[1] John Bonner Semple

topcoats and shining oxfords were ridiculous in this Arctic land. But we were there!

There were four of us: our good friend J.B., he of the eagle's eye and unquenchable enthusiasm; Sewall Pettingill, at that time my fellow graduate student at Cornell, and an expert photographer; Bert Lloyd, an ornithologist who had collected birds extensively and who knew the Churchill region from personal experience; and myself.

We were eager as fox terriers. Each of us dreamed of discovering those eggs. We didn't give voice to our inner feelings in the matter, but there was an ardent glitter in every eye. True, the River was covered with ice four feet thick. True, the Harris's Sparrow had not yet returned from the south. But Spring would come. The tamaracks would turn green with the sinking away of the snow, the ptarmigan would doff their winter garb, and the tundra lakes would thaw. And somewhere out in those silent, all but colorless, half-buried spruce woods there would be a Harris's Sparrow's nest. And in that nest there would be eggs. And one of us, one of us four men, would find them!

We piled our luggage on a tractor-truck, picked our way across the winter-bound construction camp to some lighted windows, and interviewed the Department of Railways and Canals. We were, we explained, strangers in a strange land. We had come to study birds. We had the necessary permits from the government. We hoped to be able to establish camp somewhere near the mouth of the River. We would not be in anybody's way, we promised, nor cause any disturbance.

The Department of Railways and Canals contemplated us a full moment, cleared his throat with a bark, and informed us that he would find us beds for the night; that he would get a tent for us on the morrow, that we could take our meals with the sixteen hundred workmen if we wanted to, but that we'd have to be at the mess hall on time and clear out when we were through. Thanking the Department for his courtesies and creeping off like thieves caught in the act we went to bed. I am not sure that my three confreres felt as I did. As for me, I felt myself wholly unwanted at Churchill—decidedly a *persona non grata*. But what about those Harris's Sparrow's eggs? Could they be found without me?

And next morning we felt better. We were at breakfast at the appointed hour—six o'clock. The food was good and there was plenty of it. We were hungry. A long day was ahead of us. We tried a little conversation between the first mouthfuls, but gave that up. Our "pleases" and "thank yous" drew frowns. We were not there to talk. We were there to stoke our furnaces. And stoke we did. The flapjacks were grand, and easy to manage. We got them down almost without chewing or swallowing. Prunes took more time because the pits had to be discarded somehow. And bacon rinds slowed us up. But in the first three minutes we learned from our hosts how to spread butter on a slice of bread and pour canned milk with the other. In the next three minutes we learned to stuff cookies and oranges into our pockets while gulping coffee. And at the end of the next three minutes we were rising, wiping our mouths with our sleeves, and "clearing out." Breakfast that morning must surely have taken us all of nine minutes. Our hosts finished long before we did. Though I am breaking the strict continuity of my story in telling you this, we learned in time to eat more rapidly.

Churchill was an incredible place. It was not a town, for there were only one or two dwellings and one or two women. It was an enterprise. Huge dredges were gouging away the river bottom. A vast cement grain elevator was rising. Under the snow about us lay a network of narrow-gauge tracks over which "dinkey engines" were soon to pull cars filled with gravel, workmen, and water. On the higher ground between the River and the Bay stood row upon row of barracks, a little hospital, some mission buildings, one or two banks, a motion picture palace of sorts, the headquarters of the Royal Canadian Mounted Police, and a wireless station. Churchill, an ocean port in the making!

We got our big tent and J.B.'s little silk tent up that day, built ourselves a worktable, unpacked our equipment, and unrolled our sleeping bags. And Bert Lloyd and I, eager to make certain that the sparrows were not ahead of us, walked six miles upriver to the spruce woods, wallowed for hours through slushy drifts, dark-brown muskeg streams, and waist-deep, ice-filmed pools. The sparrows had not come. We saw some Snow Buntings and Lapland Longspurs, a few Pipits and Horned Larks, and three Pintail Ducks. We got back just in time for dinner—dead tired. At dinner we stoked again.

On May 27, the Harris's Sparrow arrived from the south. We had beaten him by three days. We thought he looked a bit disconsolate, but the notes of his whistled song reassured us that Spring was on its way.

We continued to eat at the mess hall, but we usually missed the noon meal. Walking six miles in order to begin our day's work took time and energy. We were glad when the gravel trains began running. We became acquainted with the engineers and firemen and sometimes had a chance to bum a ride. By the time we got back from our day afield we were half-starved. Our evening meal, large as it invariably was, invariably made us sleepy. Existence was simple. We rose, dressed, stoked, walked or rode six miles to the spruce woods, tramped the tundra, woodlands and muskeg for hours, walked or rode six miles back from the spruce woods, stoked, undressed, and went to bed. Here and there during this busy program of nest-hunting we found time to prepare birdskins, write notes, make drawings, and take photographs.

Whenever we four men conversed we usually conversed about the Harris's Sparrow, though there were other interesting birds in the region. Bert Lloyd, as we learned, had once found what he thought was a Harris's

Sparrow's nest. This nest had been under a little bush. Yes, it had been the right size for a Harris's Sparrow. No, it hadn't been completely hidden by leaves and moss. Yes, it had been made of grass. But Bert had had no chance to identify the parent birds. So, in the last analysis, we knew next to nothing about a Harris's Sparrow's nest. We were prepared for anything. The fact that the one or two nests on record had been described thus and so didn't help us much. At night I was wont to say to my companions: "We must look everywhere—on the ground, under bushes, in trees, in holes in the ground—everywhere. And we must watch the birds constantly. The easiest way to find some nests is to watch a bird that has a wisp of grass, or a feather, or a twig in its bill."

We came to an agreement concerning our procedure in the event a nest was found. If a full set of eggs were discovered, these were to be collected immediately, lest in our absence from the nest they be destroyed by some Whiskey Jack, weasel, or other predatory creature. We wanted photographs of the first nest if possible, to be sure, but the important thing was to collect and preserve those eggs so that an adequate description of them might be published. By the end of our first week we were somewhat fagged by our exertions, puzzled by our failure to find what we felt to be mated pairs, annoyed at our inability to distinguish male and female birds in the field (their coloration was almost precisely the same), and more fervently, desperately, even frantically eager than ever. Personal pride was at stake by this time. There were reputations to uphold. J.B., the oldest of our party, was also the sharpest eyed—an exceedingly keen observer with an enviable record as a rifle, shotgun and revolver shot. Sewall Pettingill was a youngster, a grand chap too, who felt that his name would flash in electric lights across the land if only he could find that nest. Bert Lloyd had been in the Churchill region before. He had become familiar with the summertime ways of the Harris's Sparrow, and what was more, thought he had already seen a nest. As for me, I was half mad, half downright crazy. I'd dream, quite literally dream at night, about sparrows as big as cows, with huge black eyes and long white lashes. That sort of thing. The less we say about it the better.

And then came the Canadians! One week after our arrival, almost to the minute, on the very train that had brought us, came four stalwart Canadians from the Province of Alberta—four men quite as capable and quite as eager as ourselves, each one of them just as determined as each one of us to be the first to find the Harris's Sparrow's eggs.

We were in bed when the Canadians came. In fact, we were asleep, dreaming about sparrows with long eyelashes. All at once we heard a booming voice outside our tent. The Canadians were making a call. We did out best at wakening, half sat up, rubbed our eyes, and tried to talk. No, we hadn't found a Harris's Sparrow's nest. Oh yes, there were lots of Harris's Sparrows about, dozens of them, but we weren't even sure these birds were mated yet. I fail to remember whether we rose to light a candle or not. I think we didn't. We weren't very hospitable, I fear. And J.B., our indomitable leader, was nettled. "These Canadians!" he was saying as soon as they left. "What do they mean by trying to spoil our game? We came up here to do this thing ourselves and they haven't a right to bust in this way!" There was quite a bit of muttering from the little tent in which J.B. slept. We all felt a good deal the same way, I guess, but Sewall, Bert and I didn't mutter. We lay in our sleeping bags with eyes wide open, wondering how we could beat these unexpected, unwelcome newcomers. If only they'd play fair and go to bed and not begin their search until the morrow!

Next morning there was a new light in our eyes. We four men were no longer pitted against each other. We were pitted against a new, a formidable, a mighty foe—the Canadians.

We three younger men, generous creatures that we were, had decided amongst ourselves that if we possibly *could* do so we'd let J.B. find the first nest. There is nothing written down in black and white to prove this, but I am telling the truth. J.B. had been a good scout. Finding the nest would be a sort of peak in his ornithological career. We younger men could do something else some time that would win us renown. In our inner hearts we hoped that Fate would somehow force us to find that first nest, but our tongues spoke phrases that were as unselfish and altruistic as any ever spoken.

The coming of the Canadians changed all this. The contest was a free-for-all now. And come what may, America must win. We had been the first on the ground. We had made the greater sacrifice in getting there. Feeling ran high.

The egg-hunting tactics of the Canadians were different from ours. Armed with what must have been dishpans, sections of stove-pipe, tin trays and canes they marched through the spruces making the wildest sort of noise. Their purpose was to frighten the mother sparrows from the nests. We laughed as we listened, but scowled as we laughed. This was a silly, childish procedure—a ridiculous method of bird study—but what if it worked! After all, *we* had not found a nest. Our irreproachable methods had thus far failed. We went on with our quiet, determined, methodical searching, but the sound of the enemy's drums made us nervous. Perhaps at this very moment they are finding the nest, we would think. Perhaps a bird is flitting out from under their feet—and in her flitting is giving away the century-old secret! Each and every evening we talked about our experiences of the day, and wondered if the enemy had won. We did not go to see them. They did not come to see us. We had no friendly symposiums of the habits of Harris's Sparrows. We were on speaking terms, yes; but we were uncomfortable whenever we met each other. Occasionally, out on the tundra, we ran into them face to face.

At such times we conversed about the weather (and there is weather to talk about at Churchill); about the interesting birds we had been seeing; and about the methods of bird-skinning. Sooner or later, of course, the matter of *the nest* was sure to come up, and at this juncture we blushed and fidgeted and looked afar off and did our doomed-to-failure best to appear uninterested and casual. The enemy continued to tell us that they had not found the nest. We wondered if they were telling us the truth. They may have had similar doubts concerning us.

The enemy was encamped in a freight car that stood on a siding at the edge of the construction camp. Here they slept and ate and prepared their specimens. We passed the place at least twice a day, sometimes more frequently. But we never called. And we rarely saw them.

The precious days passed. By June 10, I began to be genuinely and deeply worried. Unless we found the nest before the summer waned there would be young birds, not eggs. We had heard the male birds singing day after day. We felt that by this time they must surely have chosen their nesting-territories. But we had found no sign of a nest.

On the evening of June 15, Sewall (by this time we were calling the lad "Sewall the Beautiful" and "Sewall the Cruel") drew me aside to tell me that he had seen a Harris's Sparrow with grass in its bill; that he had watched the bird for hours; and that he had found a nest! Sewall was excited, to say the least. He was fairly shaking. And when I looked upon him and listened to his words a pang shot me through. What right had Sewall, unlettered, callow, inordinately smug youth that he was, to find the nest! "Do you think we'd better say anything about it to the others?" he was asking in a wobbly whisper. "The nest is down under the moss, at the end of a sort of burrow. I watched the bird for a long time, and followed it on hands and knees—but I saw it with grass in its bill only once."

That nest (poor, beautiful, downcast Sewall!) proved to be the nest of a mouse.

And then came the morning of June 16. That morning a strange, in fact very strange, thing happened—something in the nature of an omen. I had walked to a favorite part of the section of woodland I had been studying most closely. I was watching a pair of Harris's Sparrows, wondering as usual which was the male and which the female, when all at once one of the birds flew across a clearing to an old box that had been tossed aside by the men who had built the railroad through the woods. As the bird sat on the box it began to sing. I watched it with my binocular and chanced to note that there were large black letters on the box. Looking at the letters one by one I found to my complete amazement that the word HARRIS was printed there. It was a box in which bacon or ham had been shipped from the Harris Abbatoir, a Canadian meatpacking firm.

I fairly gasped when I realized that a fine male Harris's Sparrow was perching there in front of me on a box that was labeled HARRIS. I rose with the determination of a Perseus or a Columbus and marched through the woods. I cannot very scientifically explain my feelings, but I knew that a sign had been given.

At a little before nine o'clock, while marching across an all but impassable bog, I frightened from a sphagnum island underfoot a slim, dark-backed bird. It made no outcry, but from the explosive flutter of its wings I knew it had left a nest. I searched a moment, parting with my hand the tough, slender twigs of flowering Labrador tea. And there was the nest—with four eggs that in the cool shadow had a dark appearance. The mother bird, by this time was chirping in alarm. I looked at her briefly with my glass. A Harris's Sparrow! I raised the gun, took careful aim, and fired. Marking the nest, I ran to pick her up. Upon my return, the male appeared. I shot him also, for I knew the record would not be complete unless I shot both parent birds. To say that I was happy is to describe my feelings all too tamely. I was beside myself. Shooting those important specimens had taken control. I had been so excited I had hardly been able to hold the gun properly. As I knelt to examine the nest a thrill the like of which I had before never felt passed through me. And I talked aloud! "Here!" I said. "Here in this beautiful place!" At my fingertips lay treasures that were beyond price. Mine was man's first glimpse of the eggs of the Harris's Sparrow, in the lovely bird's wilderness home.

Then I began to wonder how many other nests had been found that morning. The enemy! My comrades! Had they, too, been favored by Heaven with a sign? I had a wild desire to gather everybody about me—friend and foe alike—so that we might work together, compare notes, make plans, take photographs. I looked at my watch. Perhaps some Canadian had found a nest at eight o'clock! Perhaps several nests had been found before nine o'clock that morning! I fired my shotgun loudly as I could (have you ever tried this?) three times, and was a little surprised, as the echoes died, that no familiar form of friend nor unfamiliar form of foe materialized. I fired again. There was no answer.

So, happy in a way that was quite new to me, but dubious as to the priority of my achievement, I hippity-hopped across the bogs. I wasn't much of an ornithologist those next few hours. I was too gay for Ornithology. At a little before noon I chanced to see Bert Lloyd ahead of me. I started to call him—then decided not to. A wild fear seized me. Perhaps all this happiness of the last three hours was unwarranted. Perhaps all this had been some weird hallucination. I knelt on the moss, opened my collecting creel, got out those two specimens I had shot at the nest, and looked at them closely. Yes, they were Harris's Sparrows, there could not be the slightest doubt of that. They were not White-crowned Sparrows, nor Fox Sparrows, nor Tree Sparrows. No, there was nothing wrong with me this time.

"Bert!" I shouted, trying to keep my voice normal. And Bert turned and came. "What luck?" I asked. And Bert gave me the usual report—plenty of birds, mated pairs too, but no nest. Queer that he couldn't see how boiling over I was with excitement.

So I told him. And Bert's response was the response of a good friend, a good sport, a good ornithologist. His words were cordial and the exultant delight that shone from his face was genuine. I showed him the specimens. And from that time until the reunion of our party that evening, two of us wondered how many other nests had been found that day.

To be perfectly honest, I was hoping that nobody else had found a nest. In a vague sort of way I wanted my good friend J.B. to have the thrill of it all—but he had been successful in so many ways that I felt this purely ornithological triumph might quite justly be mine. And Sewall —well, if Sewall had found a nest before nine o'clock that morning he was just too lucky for tolerance. But the Canadians!

Bert and I got back about six o'clock. We were a little late at the mess hall. The workmen frowned as we came in, for they knew the cook would be angry, and we were wet and dirty. But we didn't care. Let them frown. Let them despise us. We were above being despised. J.B. and Sewall were busy stoking—almost too busy to notice us. We sat down. When there was a clatter of departing workmen I leaned toward J.B. and said, "Did you find the nest today?" J.B. said he hadn't. "I found one—with four eggs in it," I rejoined. And the stoking stopped.

I have never, neither before nor since, seen J.B. look as he looked at precisely that moment. He may have been wishing that he had found the nest. He may have been as jealous as a successful, vigorous, fair-minded, generous sportsman can at times be. He may quite possibly have hated me for my insolence. But I think he was happy. For I know he felt, as I did, that beating dishpans in the woods was no way to study birds; that our Harris's Sparrow was a bird of rare discernment; that in this hectic battle of the past sixteen days it was only right that the Americans should win.

SNOBBER—

SPARROW DE LUXE

Edwin Way Teale

Some students of animal behavior scorn pet owners and their observations, which they dismiss as usually anthropomorphic and overinterpreted. In actual fact, however, close association with human beings often brings out unexpected potentialities in the animal very much as they appear in a "savage" who has received a civilizing education. An English book, Len Howard's Birds As Individuals, *so astonished professional bird students with its accounts of the varying "personalities" of tame birds of the same species that Sir Julian Huxley undertook a personal investigation of Miss Howard's pets and testified that her surprising observations deserved full credit. No story of a civilized and humanized bird is more remarkable than that of a house sparrow who regularly entered an apartment house window more than 130 feet above the sidewalk to spend the evening studying with his young friend.*

IN Vineland, N.J., last summer, pedestrians were astonished when an English sparrow darted down from the branches of trees, alighted on their shoulders, and peered intently into their faces. Housewives were equally amazed when the same bird flew in at their open windows. It fluttered about, examined their rooms, and flew out again. The mystery grew for several days. Then the following advertisement appeared in the *Vineland Times-Journal:*

"Lost. Tame female English sparrow. Reward. Call 1291J."

That advertisement brought about the return of a remarkable pet. It also revealed a boy-and-bird companionship which is as interesting as it is unusual. The boy is Bennett Rothenberg; the sparrow, Snobber. They were visiting the boy's uncle near Vineland when the bird became lost.

The boy and the sparrow live on the eleventh floor of a great apartment building across from the Planetarium, on Eighty-first Street in New York City. The bird is never caged. It is free to come and go. At will, it flies in and out of the apartment-house window more than 130 feet above

From *Audubon Magazine*, November–December, 1944.

the street and the Planetarium park. Each night, it sleeps on top of a closet-door left ajar near Bennett's bed.

On rainy days, the sparrow makes no effort to mount upward along the sheer cliff of brick and glass to Bennett's apartment-window. Instead, she rides up on the elevator! Flying in the front entrance of the apartment-house, Snobber alights on the shoulder of the elevator operator, Frank Olmedo. When they reach the eleventh floor, Olmedo rings the bell at the apartment and when the door opens, the sparrow flies, like a homing pigeon, to the boy's bedroom. A year ago, during a month when Bennett was away at a summer camp, Olmedo cared for the the bird and the two became fast friends.

It was in the spring of 1943 that Bennett, then fourteen years old, found a baby sparrow in Central Park. He carried it home and installed it in an empty robin's nest in his room. With the aid of a medicine dropper and a pair of tweezers, he fed it at hourly intervals. On a diet of flies, bits of worms, water and pieces of eggbiscuit, it grew rapidly. It gained weight and the whitish fuzz on its body developed into scores of strong and glossy feathers. A snobbish tilt of its beak when it had had enough food gave it its name.

The boy taught Snobber to fly by placing it in low trees, offering food, and chirping to it. The sparrow now recognizes his chirp and will fly up to the apartment window from the trees below when he calls. To the uninitiated, all sparrows seem to chirp alike. But not to Bennett. He says he can recognize Snobber's chirp in a tree full of sparrows. By the sound, he can tell whether she is angry, curious, or excited. When they go for walks together, they often seem to be carrying on a conversation, chirping back and forth, as the sparrow darts ahead from tree to tree. On reaching Eighty-first Street, Snobber flies on ahead and then waits—like a dog—at the entrance of the apartment-house for Bennett to cross the street.

A friendly bird, she often is much in evidence when the boys of the neighborhood are engaged in playing games. In the middle of a baseball game, she sometimes alights on the shoulder of the batter or settles down directly on the baseline to attract attention. At other times, when the boys are flipping playing cards in local version of "pitching pennies," Snobber will dart down, grasp one of the cards in her bill, and fly away with it. Any small, shiny object instantly arouses her interest. When she finds a dime on Bennett's dresser, she picks it up and darts this way and that, flying until she is tired. Two marbles in a small metal tray on the boy's desk keep her occupied for a quarter of an hour at a time. She pushes them about with her bill, apparently delighted by the jangling sound they make.

Her interest in bright-colored objects prevented Bennett, last fall, from keeping track of the position of Allied armies by means of colored pins on a large wall-map. No sooner did he put up the pins, placing them carefully to show the location of the lines, than they would disappear. He would find them lying on his bed, the dresser, his desk. Snobber, fluttering like a flycatcher in front of the map, would pull out the pins with her bill. Red-headed pins seemed her first choice with yellow-headed pins coming second. She became so interested in this game that she would perch on Bennett's shoulder, or even his hand, while he inserted the pins. Then she would pull them out as soon as he had finished his work. When he substituted tiny flags in place of pins, her interest rose to an even higher pitch. In the end, Bennett had to give up his efforts and the game ended for Snobber.

One August, in Central Park, one of the eminent ornithologists of The American Museum of Natural History—a scientist who had journeyed as far away as Equitorial Africa to observe bird-life—was surprised to see something entirely new to his experience. A sparrow darted down, perched on a boy's shoulder, and began to eat ice cream from a cone. The sparrow, of course, was Snobber and the boy was Bennett.

Ice cream, pieces of apple, and small bits of candy are delicacies of which the bird is passionately fond. Boys in the neighborhood share their candy and cones with her when she alights on their shoulders. As soon as she sees a piece of candy, she begins to chirp and flutter about. Bennett and a companion sometimes play a game with her for five minutes at a time by tossing a piece of cellophane-covered candy back and forth. Like a kitten pursuing a ball, Snobber will shuttle swiftly from boy to boy in pursuit of the flying candy.

Along Eighty-first Street, pedestrians are often as surprised as were the people of Vineland to have a sparrow swoop down and alight on their shoulders. The reaction is varied. One woman jerked off a fur neck-piece and swung it around in the air like a lasso to ward off the supposed attack. Several persons have made a grab for the sparrow. But, always, Snobber is too quick for them.

One day, last summer, an elderly gentleman, stout, near-sighted and wearing a derby hat, was walking down the Planetarium side of Eighty-first Street reading a newspaper held close to his face. In his left hand he clutched an ice cream cone from which he absent-mindedly took a bite from time to time. Snobber was perched on the lower limb of a tree. She cocked her head as he went by; she had spotted the ice cream. Swooping down, she alighted on the cone and began nibbling away. Just then, the man put the cone to his mouth abstractedly to take another bite. The cone bit him, instead! Or, at least, that was the impression he got when Snobber pecked him on the lower lip. Unable to believe his eyes, he peered near-sightedly at the cone and bird. Then he began to wave the cone in circles in the air. Like a pinwheel, the cone and the pursuing sparrow whirled above his head.

Seeing the commotion, Bennett ran across the street to explain and to catch Snobber. But in the process he accidentally knocked the cone from the man's hand. Thinking he was being set upon from the air and the ground simultaneously, the nearsighted gentleman clutched his newspaper in one hand and his derby hat in the other and sprinted, puffing, down the street. At the end of the block, he stopped, turned, shook his fist, and hurried around the corner.

Indoors, when Snobber gets hungry she perches on a seed-box as a signal to the boy. Two of her favorite foods, aside from seeds and bits of biscuit, are cornflakes and maple sugar. She gets greens by eating pieces of leaves from time to time. If the sash is down when she wants to fly out the window, she will dash about the room in a special manner which Bennett has learned to understand.

As might be supposed, the sparrow had difficulty at first in picking out the right window among the vast number which pierce the masonry of the great apartment-house. Once, after Bennett had chirped with his head out the window he was called back into the room and when he looked out again he was just in time to see the sparrow come flying out of a window on the floor below. As a guide, he has tied a ribbon to the iron bar of a window-box outside his bedroom. Before dusk, Snobber always returns to the apartment. The only time she has spent the night outdoors was during the days when she was lost near Vineland.

From the beginning, Bennett determined that if she ever wanted to go free, he would not try to restrain her. The train-trip to Vineland, last summer, was one of the few times when she has been locked in a cage. The ride was bumpy and she disliked it, chirping most of the time. Bennett spent his time during the journey explaining to interested passengers about the sparrow in the cage. At his uncle's farm, Snobber was ill at ease. She had never seen a rocking chair before and the unstable perch it provided when the boy was sitting in it, disturbed her still further.

On the second day there, she dashed from an apple tree in pursuit of two wild sparrows, flew too far, became confused, then hopelessly lost. Four days later, when Bennett recovered her through his advertisement, she was several miles from his uncle's farm in the direction of New York City. She recognized the boy in an instant and flew chirping to his shoulder. A small American flag in the window of the house where she was found resembled the ribbon tied to the window-box of the apartment-house and may have influenced her in choosing that particular place. When chasing among the trees, with wild sparrows of the Planetarium park, she seems to prefer Bennett's companionship to that of any bird. She is always slightly suspicious of other sparrows. When dusting herself with others of her kind, she always stays on the edge of the group. If one of the birds becomes too familiar, she will charge it with lowered head and open beak. Bennett once brought home a young sparrow to keep her company. She refused to have anything to do with it. He then placed a canary in the bedroom as a playmate for Snobber. When he returned to the room to see how they were getting along, he found her holding the hapless bird by the bill and swinging it around in the air. The next day, she lured the canary out on the window-ledge and then chased it away down the street. After that, the boy ceased trying to find a bird companion for her and Snobber is well content to let matters rest as they are.

This spring, although she had not mated, Snobber was overcome by the impulse to build a nest. Tearing up a robin's nest and a song sparrow's nest, which Bennett had in his room, she used the material to create a nest of her own. She was busy with this task for days, sometimes flying about the room with straws fully a foot in length. In the nest, she laid two eggs. Neither hatched and one now rests on cotton batting in a small box which bears this notation on the lid: "English Sparrow Egg Laid By Snobber."

When Bennett is doing his homework, during winter months, Snobber often perches quietly on his book or on the desk beside him. And, at night, when the boy is sleeping in his bed, the sparrow is lost in slumber on the top of the closet door, its head tucked in its feathers. Often, it sleeps on one leg. At such times, it has the appearance of a ball of ruffled feathers, with one leg sticking down and a tail sticking out at right angles to the leg.

As soon as it is daylight, Snobber is awake. Bennett doesn't need any alarm clock. He has Snobber. She hops down, perches on his head, begins tugging at individual hairs. If he doesn't wake up, she often snuggles down near his neck for an additional nap herself. If he disturbs her by moving in his sleep, she gives him a peck on the chest. As a consequence, Bennett often keeps moving back toward the far side until when he wakes up he is lying on the edge and the sparrow is occupying most of the bed.

On the floor of Bennett's bedroom, there is a shiny spot six or seven inches in diameter. This is where the sparrow takes her imaginary dust-baths. Alighting at this spot, she squats down, fluffs up her feathers, turns this way and that, goes through the motions of taking a real dust-bath by the roadside.

Like Mary's famous little lamb, Snobber sometimes tries to follow Bennett to school. He rides to and from classes on the subway. Winter mornings, he always tries to leave the apartment-house without the sparrow seeing him. But the bright eyes of the little bird miss little that is going on. Several times, just as he was sprinting into the entrance of the subway a block from his home, he has heard a lively chirping behind him and Snobber has fluttered down on his shoulder. Twice he has had to explain to teachers that he was late for classes because a sparrow delayed him! At the school he attends, however, both teachers and pupils know all about Snobber. In fact, whenever Bennett gets an extra good grade, his classmates have a standing explanation: Snobber has helped him!

BIRD INVASION

Edwin Way Teale

A rare or disappearing species naturally attracts our sympathy. On the other hand, any bird which is too numerous and too successful is likely to be looked upon with disfavor. The house sparrow used to bear the brunt. Samuel Johnson said he could love anybody except an American, and I have known bird lovers who felt the same way about this immigrant whom we blame on England though it is actually European. Nowadays the European starling, which has spread rapidly from the east coast to the Pacific and bred in such numbers that flocks sometimes almost "darken the skies," is with some equally unpopular.

During the nineteenth century, attempts were made to introduce many exotic birds. Luckily nearly all of them failed. Oddly enough the starling introduction looked at first like another failure. But in 1891 a leader of the American Acclimatism Society liberated a certain number—no one is sure just how many—in Central Park. This time the "innoculation" took. Many people are anxious to know how to attract birds. Possibly even more would now like to know how to discourage starlings. Incidentally it is another significant fact that nearly all successful introductions are of birds which had already learned how to live either in cities or in the neighborhood of cultivation.

D URING the early days of a recent winter, the deepest snow in more than half a century lay on the fields around my home. In that time of crisis for many birds, a flock of starlings demonstrated the versatile resourcefulness that has enabled them to invade America and spread from coast to coast in less than sixty years.

Starlings are primarily ground feeders. Yet during these days we saw them probing in bark crevices like nuthatches. We saw them hovering on fluttering wings like humming birds to obtain suet from a feeding stick. We saw them bracing themselves with stiffened tails on tree trunks, like woodpeckers. We even saw them pulling apart a squirrel's nest, high in a maple tree, hunting for spiders and other edible creatures hibernating in the mass.

Sometimes starlings catch insects on the wing like flycatchers. They

From *Days without Time*, New York: Dodd, Mead and Company, 1948.

have been observed scooping beetles out of the air while in full flight in the manner of swallows. And, like cowbirds, they often follow cattle and sheep across a pasture to feed on the small creatures that the grazing animals stir out of the grass.

In a tree near my study window, a starling once darted upward from a branch and snatched a piece of bread from the mouth of a surprised blue jay on the limb above. On another occasion, a starling on the ground walked up to a crust of bread where an English sparrow was feeding. Grasping one edge in its bill, and with the dogged sparrow hanging on, it swung the crust and sparrow in a crack-of-the-whip half-circle through the air. Aggressive, omnivorous, resourceful, the starling is well fitted to survive under many conditions of life. In spite of man's antagonism, it has increased and spread in America. Its conquest of this country probably is the greatest, the most dramatic bird invasion recorded in natural history.

The story of the invasion begins in the spring of 1890 when a liner from Europe steamed into New York Harbor to discharge its passengers at a pier on lower Manhattan. Sixty of those passengers rode ashore in cages. They were dark, chunky birds with yellow bills. The vessel was the *Mayflower* of the starlings.

Every one of America's untold millions of these birds, according to Dr. Frank M. Chapman, has descended from one hundred immigrants —the sixty that arrived in 1890 to be set free in Central Park and forty more that reached New York the following year. Their coming was the result of one man's fancy. That man was Eugene Schieffelin, a wealthy New York drug manufacturer. His curious hobby was the introduction into America of all the birds mentioned in the works of William Shakespeare.

Skylarks, chaffinches, nightingales, as well as English sparrows and starlings, rode across the Atlantic in cages consigned to Schieffelin. He even organized a society for the importation of foreign birds and incorporated it in Albany. Today, partly in consequence of lessons learned from his activity, no foreign bird or animal can be imported without special permission from the United States Department of Agriculture. Schieffelin was only one of several to introduce the English sparrow; but he, alone, is responsible for the starling. His skylarks and nightingales soon died out but his starlings flourished like weeds of the air.

The somewhat dubious honor of being the site of the first starling nest in America belongs to the American Museum of Natural History. Soon after the original birds were released in Central Park, a pair nested in an opening under the eaves of one of the wings of the museum. That, however, was only the beginning. The starling is one of the first birds to nest in spring. It has two broods in a season—and sometimes even three—each producing four or five new birds. The first brood is often out of the nest before many birds have laid their eggs. Moreover, starlings set up housekeeping close together, as many as five pairs of birds nesting in the knotholes of a single tree.

In the matter of nesting material, the starling has an advantage over many other birds. It uses common and easily obtained lining for its nest. And it displays an instinctive thrift in employing such material. Unlike numerous birds, if it drops the dry grass it is carrying in its bill, it stops to pick it up again. Malcolm Davis, of the National Zoological Park, in Washington, D.C., tells of a remarkable instance of the kind in a note published in *The Auk* for October, 1946. "While walking along one of the busy streets of Washington, D.C.," he writes, "I observed several starlings carrying nesting material. One with a mouthful of dry grasses flew across the street. In mid-street, it accidentally dropped the nesting material. The grass floated down upon a passing truck. Immediately, the bird dived down upon it, falcon style, recovered the grasses from the speeding truck, and flew in the direction of the nesting site. Any factor," Davis adds, "small as it may be, that contributes to the firm establishment of a species in a certain area may be well worth considering. This small display of persistent economy may be a contributing factor to the establishment of this species."

Another and paramount factor is the fertility of the starling, its early nesting and its double broods. Each year, the multiplication of these birds is something to make the ears of the fecund rabbit droop in frustration. It was not long after they were introduced before the compound interest of this fertility began to show results.

Starlings overflowed into the suburbs of New York, onto Long Island, across the Hudson into New Jersey. In the following years, Bridgeport, New Haven, Boston, Philadelphia, Washington reported the appearance of a few starlings, then many starlings, then far too many starlings. The newcomers were driving native birds—swallows, martins, flycatchers, flickers, blue-birds—from their nesting sites. They were pushing their way into feeding grounds. They were upsetting the whole balance of nature. A bird invasion was on in full force. By that time, nothing could stop the advance of the starlings.

Not that a good many people didn't try. They are still trying. People fired shotguns into trees where the birds roosted at night and were showered with falling starlings. They doused the birds with fire hoses; they set off Roman candles; they clanged bells; they stood around beneath the trees and slapped long boards together to produce artificial thunderclaps. They set out stuffed owls, electrically-charged dummy owls, aluminum owls with eyes that would shine at night, imitation owls re-enforced with explosive charges. One man painted a live starling pure white in the belief that such an abnormal bird would frighten the others away.

In Milwaukee, Wisconsin, an ingenious janitor smeared axle-grease over the grillwork at the courthouse windows so the alighting birds skidded, bumped their noses, did flipflops and generally discouraged themselves from choosing the building as a roosting place. Molasses paste was used in some places for catching the birds. In Decatur, Illinois, an estimated twenty thousand starlings were killed in the course of a two-months' campaign. And in Washington, D.C., Government men spent their evenings jiggling strings to which were attached rubber balloons containing dried peas. The peas in the balloons produced a hissing rattle that scared the starlings out of their wits—for a time.

But all these were relatively unimportant skirmishes on a long battle line. The starlings continued to advance. They followed the Great Lakes west. They spread down the Mississippi Valley. They penetrated beyond the Rockies. They crossed the line into Canada. They flew over the Rio Grande. Today, after only slightly more than half a century of rapid multiplication, the starling occupies the country from Maine to Oregon and from Mexico to Churchill, on the Hudson Bay. It is a permanent part of our bird family. Schieffelin has given America the starling—for better or for worse.

The bad side of this bird is easy to see, particularly in fall and winter. At those seasons, old and young gather together in immense flocks. They settle in the later afternoon in treetops or on the ledges of city buildings for a social hour before going to bed. The din is tremendous. I remember walking past the White House, in Washington, one October dusk and hearing a continuous, almost deafening clamor from the starlings in the treetops. In New York City, one bridge, not far from Grant's Tomb, is the roosting place of as many as forty thousand starlings. In troops and straggling bands, they come flying across the Hudson from New Jersey, across the East River from Long Island, down from Westchester feeding grounds, as sunset nears.

Another favorite starling roost in New York City is on the Metropolitan Museum of Art on Fifth Avenue. As short winter days near an end, starling flocks stream toward this structure, sometimes flying down the streets lower than the rooftops, turning corners like soldiers on parade. In Lancaster, Pennsylvania, and Paterson, New Jersey, so many starlings perched on the hands of the town clocks that the timepieces were put out of order. During one cold February, starlings were found to be keeping their feet warm by roosting on the small electric bulbs of a theater sign in the heart of Boston. In my neighborhood, the birds sometimes fly down to perch on the tops of warm brick chimneys during the coldest weeks of winter.

Along the seacoast, wherever there are stands of the high, plumed Phragmites, the starlings find a safe roosting place. A solid mass of these cane-like plants extends for a hundred yards along one edge of the swamp at the foot of my Insect Garden. Here, from miles around, the starlings congregate as winter evenings approach. Once, as I was walking down the hillside, a Cooper's hawk shot from between the apple trees and streaked low along the slope, a starling leading it by a rapidly diminishing distance. The dark little bird gained the haven of the Phragmites clump and the hawk rose in a swift wing-over and returned to the orchard. As it curved upward, a sound as of a great wind sweeping through the Phragmites reached me. The clump was alive with roosting starlings; they all had moved on their dry supports at the sudden approach of the hawk.

In Europe, some starling roosts have been used by the birds continuously for more than a century and a half. The fact that these birds stick pretty close to man and often flock in the downtown districts of a city make their garrulousness and gregariousness the more annoying. During fall and winter months, "starling awnings" sometimes have to be put over the entrances to public buildings as a protection against the droppings of the assembled birds. Eleven tons of droppings were cleared off the Capitol roof in Springfield, Illinois, after starlings had been roosting there for years. To some people, the odor of starlings, in the mass, is objectionable. Add to these facts a few other considerations and the causes of the starling's unpopularity are obvious. In many localities the aggressive newcomer has displaced such old favorites as the bluebird and the martin. Moreover, its appetite for ripe cherries is so great that when a starling flock alights in a tree the pits seem to rain down and the branches are stripped in a single afternoon. The starling, in many ways, comes close to being the bird that nobody wants.

But whether we want it or not, we have got it. It is here to stay. And, fortunately for us, the starling, for all its faults, has a good side.

Even the mockingbird of the South hardly excels the starling as an accomplished mimic. When I started to write this, I knew of twenty-seven different birds that the starling imitates. Now I know twenty-eight. I have just heard one of these birds, perched on a lamppost, imitate the high, trilling call of the cedar waxwing. In the yard of a friend at Stamford, Connecticut, starlings gather each autumn to feed on the ripe berries of various bushes. One old male, after dining plentifully, is in the habit of expressing the pleasures of a full stomach by going through his whole repertoire. With hardly a pause, but with many a jerk of tail and twitch of wings, it will imitate the songs of the bluebird, the wood peewee, the red-winged blackbird, the meadow lark, the bobwhite, the Carolina wren, the blue jay, the whippoorwill and the flicker.

A small boy in my neighborhood was in the habit of giving a peculiar whistle when calling his chum. Soon the chum was coming out of his house, called by the whistle, when his friend was nowhere to be seen.

He discovered that a starling, balancing itself on a telephone wire, was imitating the sound. In some instances, these birds have mimicked the barking of dogs and the peeping of baby chicks. W. H. Hudson, the English naturalist, tells of a starling he encountered in a Hampshire village that cackled like a hen whenever it brought food to the nest.

In its own right, the starling has little that can be termed truly a song. It squeaks and chatters and gives rasping cries of alarm. During breeding season, the males sometimes indulge in faint little "whisper songs," produced with the bills apparently closed. The nearest a starling comes to singing is a pleasing, long-drawn whistle that sounds like "Fee-you!"

In 1826, when John James Audubon visited England, he noted in his journal that the starlings he saw reminded him of the American meadow lark. And well they might. For although an ocean separated the two, they have many traits in common. Both walk instead of hop when on the ground. Both fly in the same manner, alternately flapping and sailing. Only the starlings, however, gather together in immense flocks to perform the aerial evolutions that are a regular feature of their autumns. In great clouds, like swarming bees, thousands of birds rise and fall, turn and circle, wings moving together, individuals lost in the coordinated mass movement of the whole. From a distance, they look like wind-blown smoke. "These aerial evolutions," Dr. Frank M. Chapman, the noted bird authority of the American Museum of Natural History, once wrote, "constitute the chief claim of the starling to a place in the Birds' Hall of Fame."

From a practical point of view, however, another side of the starling's activity is even more important. This is its consumption of insects. All during its unusually long nesting season, it is searching for insects to feed the four to six ravenous baby birds that hatch from the pale bluish or whitish eggs. Cutworms, weevils, grasshoppers, crickets, beetles, caterpillars, millipedes and spiders are thrust hastily into the wide-open mouths and immediately the parent birds are off again, hunting for another course in the day-long, continuous dinner.

Government scientists who examined the stomachs of hundreds of starlings report that this unwelcome immigrant must be classed, on the basis of its food habits, as a beneficial species. Its destruction of immense numbers of injurious insects far outbalances the loss from the cherries it eats. An increase in the number of starlings in certain parts of England is given as the explanation for the disappearance of the great "cockchafer years" of former times. During such years, the beetles appeared in immense numbers, stripping the oaks of their leaves in midsummer.

In the eastern part of the United States, where the Japanese beetle has been spreading rapidly, the starlings have developed an appetite for these insects. They take them both young and old, as grubs and as adult beetles. I have watched starlings going over the leaves of roadside plants, picking off the Japanese beetles. I have also seen them probing lawns with their long pointed bills, seeking out the buried larvae.

One striking instance of the value of these labors occurred in Connecticut. For several years, the birds came regularly to the yard of a friend of mine to search for beetle grubs. Marching in a straggling line across the grass, they would probe the ground. Then, one spring, a cat was added to the household and the starlings were frightened away. Before the second summer was over, the consequences became dramatically apparent. Working unseen and unhindered in the ground, the grubs of the Japanese beetle sliced their way through the grassroots, killing whole sections of the lawn. This snipped-off turf could be rolled up almost like a carpet. No other bird I know is as effective in combating such injurious grubs as the starling.

In all the world, there are ninety-odd species of starlings. In the United States, there is only one—the one that Eugene Schieffelin's fancy turned loose the last years of the past century.

HOW TO

GET ALONG

WITH BIRDS

Robert Cunningham Miller

While your ordinary bird lover may jest about trivial things like politics, love, and religion, his feathered friends are sacred.

The present author, however, says that the problem is not how to attract birds but how to protect your garden and how to get a reasonable quota of early-morning sleep. "The poetry of earth is never dead," wrote Keats, who then went on to praise the grasshopper for taking up when the birds leave off at midday. Dr. Miller says in effect that the poetry of earth may also be described as an unceasing, infernal racket. Since he has devoted his life to the study of nature he probably feels differently most of the time but it was doubtless a relief to get this charming if rebellious protest out of his system.

H UNDREDS of books and magazine articles have been written on how to identify birds, how to study birds, how to attract birds, how to encourage them to take up residence about the house and garden. There are reams of literature on how to build bird houses, bird baths, and feeding trays, and how to plant your back yard so that birds for miles around will gather to admire it. But hardly anybody has dealt with the problem of how to get along with birds after you have them.

The first and worst thing to be noted about birds is that they get up too early in the morning. This in itself would not be so bad if they didn't make so much noise about it; but like other early risers they act as if

From *National League for Women's Service* Magazine, March 1950.

nobody else had a right to sleep. They start greeting the dawn before the night is much more than half over, and one is tempted to think they don't know the difference between Aurora and aurora borealis.

If you live in the country you awaken to the crowing of roosters, the cackling of hens, and the quacking of ducks. If you dwell in a suburban retreat, the robins gather round and join their voices in a rousing matutinal chorus. If you live in the city, the sparrows and house finches take over. These categories, moreover, are not mutually exclusive. If you select your habitat with sufficient care, you can have every one of these avian voices, plus a lot of others, greeting your ears in the pale, chill dawn.

There is a common rural expression about "getting up with the chickens," and you might as well do just that if you live within two hundred yards of a flock of poultry, for they are not going to let you sleep if they can help it. One of Aesop's fables tells of a maid who wrung a cock's neck because he was instrumental in waking her up at a given time every morning. Thereafter her mistress, with no rooster to act as an alarm clock, took to rousing the maid at all hours of the night, so she was worse off than before. Anybody who has ever raised poultry will agree that this is a fable, because roosters, far from being accurate in their timing, crow *ad lib* anywhere between midnight and morning. For this they deserve to have their necks wrung, which is not the moral, if any, that Aesop intended to draw.

Happily, most birds are more regular in their habits. Chaucer, it is true, remarks:

> *And smale foules maken melodye*
> *And slepen all the night with open ye.*

But doubtless he referred to nightingales. With a few noteworthy exceptions, birds restrain their paeans until at least the first faint streaks of dawn are visible on the eastern horizon. This at all events brings the problem within bounds, and makes it slightly easier to cope with.

Let us digress at this point to consider the question of why birds sing at all. Maybe you think it's because they are happy, but that is not to be taken for granted. Bear in mind that morning song commences before it is light enough for the birds to see to begin feeding. Some of the finest bird music is produced on an empty stomach, and it is hard to see how even a bird can be that happy at breakfast.

Scientists have come up in recent years with a new explanation, one that is not at all romantic, not on first thought very convincing, and possibly not even true. Anyway this is the theory: birds sing to enforce their property rights—to announce that possession has been taken of a certain area, and to warn other birds of the same species to keep out.

As a rough analogy, let us suppose that your neighbor has been taking a shortcut through your yard, trampling down your peonies and wearing a path across the lawn. Instead of arguing or quarreling with him, or putting up "No trespass" signs, or building a fence, you climb a tree, sit on a branch and sing "O Sole Mio" at the top of your lungs, starting at dawn and continuing at intervals till after sundown. This is guaranteed to produce results of some kind. It will probably be effective in keeping your neighbor off the property, at least until you are committed to an institution.

Well, whether birds sing because they are happy, or hungry, or real estate minded—sing they do; and they are going to keep right on singing in the early hours of the morning when even their best friends and sincerest admirers prefer to sleep. It's no use to turn and toss and raise your blood-pressure, much less go out and throw rocks at them when it is still too dark to see. There are only two courses to pursue. One is, again to quote Chaucer, "To maken vertue of necessite"—to get up and dress and pretend you like it, thinking meanwhile of all the old maxims on the advantages of early rising. The other, and better, is a technique I learned from a friend in college, who used to set his alarm clock an hour early just for the fun of turning it off and going back to sleep.

I have a robin who takes up a stance outside my bedroom window and warbles stridently in the pale gray dawn: "Get up, get up—you better get up, you better get up—see?" He varies this at intervals with a stacatto "Beep, beep, beep, beep, beep" in a descending scale. He does everything except honk like an automobile or whistle like a train. Do I allow myself to be annoyed? No. I just say, "Pfui! my fine feathered friend, go chase a worm." Then, with a deep sense of comfort and well being, I turn over for another snooze, thankful I *don't* have to get up with the birds.

Now about this matter of attracting birds, so you can properly enjoy your beauty sleep, the books all say to plant pyracantha, cotoneaster, toyon, and sun-flowers. These may be all right for certain places; but everyone who has ever tried it knows that the real way to attract birds is to plant a vegetable garden. The moment you walk out in the yard with a spade they begin to gather round, and they follow the progress of events with increasing interest and enthusiasm. Robins work the place over looking for worms, and flickers go over it again looking for ants. As tender shoots begin to appear above the soil, the white-crowned sparrows feel a sudden urge to get their vitamins. Finally the quail come out and snuggle down and dust themselves in what remains of the lettuce patch.

There are again two ways to look at this. You can practice psychology and try to feel glad that you have been able to assist our little feathered friends. Or, if you want to raise a garden, you can take some practical steps. Most damage by birds is done to the tender shoots, before the vegetables are one inch high. If you can get them two inches high they are practically immune. This can be accomplished by covering your vegetables with paper caps, either the commercial variety known as "hotcaps" or just plain waxed paper propped up in the middle and staked out along the rows. Such procedures not only give protection from birds, but offer the advantage of a little temporary hotbed.

Probably the best of all possible ways of protecting a vegetable garden from birds is that developed by Italian fisher folk. Get old fishing nets and spread them around over your garden, with suitable supports two or three feet high. The vegetables will grow and thrive. The birds may feel frustrated, but that is *their* problem. You can enjoy both ornithology and gardening, once you learn to get along with birds.

AN ADVENTURE

WITH A

TURKEY VULTURE

George Miksch Sutton

Dedicated field birders inevitably find themselves, on occasion, in, well, tight fixes. George Sutton recalls one such close encounter of the harrowing kind.

I N Texas we lived in a big white house that stood on a hill southwest of the city of Fort Worth. About us stretched the rolling prairies, gay in Summer with red and yellow daisies and the tall spikes of blooming yucca, and studded with clumps of prickly pear cactus and feathery mesquite trees.

Not far to the south of us the Trinity River slipped through a dense, low woodland. Here I spent much of my time, eager to watch, and capture if possible, the strange and interesting creatures which lived thereabouts. Flying squirrels built their globular nests of twigs high in the slender pecan trees. Chuck-will's-widows fluttered up from the leaves like gigantic moths. Raccoons and opossums searched for food along the banks of the slow-flowing streams, leaving their neat lacy track-patterns in the mud.

In the pale far sky drifted wide-winged, sable-coated Turkey Vultures, their pinions motionless for hours at a time as they ascended in slow spirals, breasted the wind, or swung low to the level of the tree tops. I never ceased to marvel at their clean-cut outline, and the ease with which they handled themselves in flight. . . .

Walking one day in the depths of the woodland, near a stagnant pool, I came upon a huge, partly decayed, hollowed log. Instinctively curious, I peered cautiously into the darkness, half expecting to discern the taut form of a wildcat crouched for a spring, or the lazy, pulpy coil of a water moccasin, white-mouthed and venomous. I could see nothing, though I strained my eyes. I went to the other end of the log, lay upon

From *Birds in the Wilderness*. New York: The Macmillan Company, 1936.

my side, and peered through. From this position I could see light at the other end. The dim interior became more sharply defined. What was that strange shape? Was there a movement, just the slightest movement? Did I hear a noise? My back stiffened.

Then it dawned upon me that I was gazing at the silhouette of a Turkey Vulture—a mother bird, probably, sitting upon her eggs. Eager, fairly breathless, I dragged two large stones to one end of the log, closing the opening there, and instantly sprang to the other end of the log, half expecting to be greeted by a rush of wings. Assured that the bird was still within, I sat down. For a moment I pondered. The log was almost twenty feet long; I could not make the bird come to me by punching it with a stick, and there was danger of breaking the eggs. I could not smoke it out, because I had no matches and I doubted my ability to start a fire by twirling a pointed stick against a piece of wood. My course was plain. I would have to go through the log.

I entertained certain misgivings. Could I force my way through the dark, moist tunnel? What would I encounter there? Would the mother vulture try to pick out my eyes?

Nevertheless I started, to find at once that the aperture was not so large as it had appeared to be. Arms outstretched in front, hair and face scraping the musty wood, I inched forward, my toes digging doggedly into the earth. Within a short time the entire length of my body was inside the log. My face pressed against the wet wood; my body ached with the strain of the unnatural position, but I could not bring my arms back because there was no room for such movement.

Perhaps, after all, I should not attempt this strange tunneling! In a panic I tried to back out, only to find myself powerless. It appeared that in my toes, which could push me forward, was my only propellent power. I was doomed to stay, or to go ahead! I breathed hard, spent with exertion. There did not seem to be enough air in the place. My ribs were crowded. But I must go ahead! Digging my fingers in the soft wood, shoving forward with all the force of my feet, I made slow progress. A flake of wood somehow got into my eye. I could do little more than shed tears over this unfortunate happening, for my arms were so long that I could not reach my face with my fingers. And my handkerchief was in my trousers pocket!

I realized now, without question, that I should have not come into this log, that freedom of movement and plenty of fresh air were really all I had ever desired in the world. But I could not go back. Perhaps I remembered, in that dark moment, certain lines of Joaquin Miller's poem on Columbus. At any rate I squirmed on. I heard dull sounds as the buttons of my shirt gave way. My trousers stayed on only because of the strength of the leather belt, the straps of cloth which held it, and the endurance of my pelvic bones. The slipping downward of my shirt did not improve matters any. Wads of cloth seemed to be knotted all about my body.

I found myself wondering how much more an imprisoned, half-suffocated, tortured boy, miles from home, could endure, when suddenly I realized that the mother vulture and I were not the only inhabitants of this hollow log.

Tripping ever so daintily, his fine leg-threads just brushing the surface upon which he trod, came a grand-daddy longlegs, disturbed in his noonday sleep. A grand-daddy longlegs, considered impersonally, is an interesting creature. His legs are amazingly long and thin; his airy body is a strangely plump hub for those eight filamentous spokes which mince along so questioningly. I do not mind having a grand-daddy longlegs walk across my hand, in fact.

But to have a grand-daddy longlegs, and perhaps four hundred of his companions, suddenly decide to wander all over my face, neck, and back is another story. The first tickle of the advance guard's feet upon my nose drove me nearly frantic. I plunged my face into the wood, crushing my adversary. The odor of his body was unpleasant. Already his companions were bearing down upon me. I writhed and shuddered in exquisite torture. By waiting a moment, then wiping my face deliberately across the damp wood, I could kill or disable whole squadrons at a time. The situation was not improved by the fact that I could see only imperfectly in the dim light and because of the bit of wood in my eye.

Gradually the queer spiders learned that they were safer when they moved toward the light. I could see their dancing, trembling forms slowly withdraw from me. Nervous, full of reproach for my foolhardiness, I tried to relax, to think of something besides the vise in which I was fixed.

Was this soft thing my hand felt a fluff of milkweed down? Was it a bit of silk, so oddly out of place in this nether world? It was the nest of a pair of white-footed mice—dainty, bright-eyed little creatures whose noses quivered with terror, whose bodies shook with dread, as they felt rude fingers upon their nest. Frantically they rushed forth. Instinctively they leaped for the darkest crevice they could find. Owing to the effective stoppage of my end of the log, those havens of refuge were naturally near me. Trim, sharp-clawed feet raced over my back, under my shirt, about my neck. Can mice run nimbly? Can they use their toes in holding on? Do they learn of the unknown in the darkness through touching objects with their silken whiskers? The answers to these questions, and to many more, I learned within our hollow log. I was half afraid the jewel-eyed gnomes would bite my face or that one of them would pounce into my mouth as I strove to get a deep breath of air. Could all this torture be actual? Was I having a nightmare? Would it never end? One of the mice crawled between my body and the wood. I gave my shoulder a frantic shrug; there was a tiny squeak, and the sharp nails which had been digging into my skin instantly went limp. The other mouse lodged himself somewhere in a fold of my trousers. Poor little creatures! They had sought only the safety of darkness. They could have harmed hardly a living thing. But I am sure they wrecked a thousand nerve cells in my quivering body.

Again shoving forward violently with my toes and digging my fingers into the soft structure of the tree, I pressed onward. The passageway became larger; I moved more freely. It was heavenly to be able to rest my weary body, and to breath more deeply.

But I was yet to meet my most amazing, my most uncomfortable adventure! Suddenly the mother vulture stood up, hissed, coughed a little, and began vomiting decayed flesh she had eaten earlier in the day. I had somehow forgotten the vulture. I found myself wishing with all my heart that I had not sealed up the other end of the log. Summoning courage, and wriggling forward as rapidly as I could, I struck the great bird an awkward blow. She hobbled off, hissing hoarsely and leaving a new object exposed.

I could not see very well; but I had enough strength and interest in my strange expedition to permit me to realize that I was face to face with a lovely newborn creature—a baby vulture, no more than a few hours old. It was downy white, its legs and naked head were gray, its infant eyes had no expression. Breathing evenly, quietly, it rested beside a large egg which was of soiled white splotched with blackish brown.

The mother continued to cough and hiss, but she could not produce any more food. I was thankful that the digestive process in birds is so rapid that food does not, as a rule, stay long in the crop or gullet!

Lifting the young vulture as well as I could, and rolling the big egg ahead of me, I wormed my way onward. The dusky parent retreated. At the end of the log I grasped her by the feet, pushed the obstructing stones away as well as I could, and breathed the fresh air in deep gasps. Nearly worn out, I trembled from head to foot. Most of my shirt was somewhere in the log; the underclothes which had covered my shoulders and chest were wound in tatters about my trousers. I was scratched up considerably, and bleeding in several spots. It must have taken me fifteen minutes to get out of the log, for the exit was small.

When I finally reached the outer air I sank to the leaves, awkwardly tied the vulture to a sapling, using a shred of torn underclothing, and panted and trembled as I picked grand-daddy longlegs from my hair, eyes, and neck, and a dead mouse from my clothing. The belt had dug deep into the skin and had worn raw grooves all about my waist. But I was free! I could breathe the air, the cool, fresh air of heaven!

I hobbled over to the pool. In the rustic mirror I could see that I was no lovely vision. I washed my face and hands, smoothed back my hair, and pinned my torn clothing together with a thorn or two.

Then I returned to my captives. Somehow the little white baby seemed pitiably friendless in this bright world of the open. The eyes of the mother were hard and fierce and frightened. The egg was infertile. I could hear the liquid contents slopping about inside when I shook it.

Had I been less weary or had my predatory instinct been more keen, I might have killed the mother vulture and tossed her aside; or I might have carried her home. But I couldn't bring myself to take that woods baby away, or leave it there an orphan. I put it back in the damp shadow of the hollow log. I rolled aside the stones I had brought for sealing the opening. And then I put the mother back beside the cottony infant, which by this time was peeping faintly. The mother bird did not attempt to rush away. Mouth open, she eyed me impersonally. I moved off through the woods quietly, hoping that my retreat would not frighten her, or that if she did fly away she would return to her charge.

I was famished and exhausted when I reached home. I mounted the stairs to my room with stiff and weary feet. When I took off my trousers a bright-eyed mouse whisked out of a pocket and scampered behind the bookcase.

THE "MIRACLE"

OF THE

GULLS

Hubert Howe Bancroft

The age of skepticism began soon after what is now the United States was colonized. We have not, therefore, so many legends about birds as the Europeans have. Perhaps the most famous of ours is the "miracle" of the gulls which appeared from nowhere to save the crops in the new Mormon settlement in Utah. Descendants of these California gulls may still be seen on the nearby Great Salt Lake.

THE spring saw everybody busy, and soon there were many flourishing gardens, containing a good variety of vegetables. In the early part of March ploughing commenced. The spring was mild and rain plentiful, and all expected an abundant harvest. But in the latter part of May, when the fields had put on their brightest green, there appeared a visitation in the form of vast swarms of crickets, black and baleful as the locust of the Dead Sea. In their track they left behind them not a blade or leaf, the appearance of the country which they traversed in countless and desolating myriads being that of a land scorched by fire. They came in a solid phalanx, from the direction of Arsenal Hill, darkening the earth in their passage. Men, women, and children turned out en masse to combat this pest, driving them into ditches or on to piles of reeds, which they would set on fire, striving in every way, until strength was exhausted, to beat back the devouring host. But in vain they toiled, in vain they prayed; the work of destruction ceased not, and the havoc threatened to be as complete as that which overtook the land of Egypt in the last days of Israel's bondage. "Think of their condition," says Mr. Cannon—"the food they brought with them almost exhausted, their grain and other seeds all planted, they themselves 1200 miles from a settlement or place where they could get food on the east, and 800 miles

From *History of Utah* (1540–1887). San Francisco: The History Company, 1891.

from California, and the crickets eating up every green thing, and every day destroying their sole means of subsistence for the months and winter ahead."

I said in vain they prayed. Not so. For when everything was most disheartening and all effort spent, behold, from over the lake appeared myriads of snow-white gulls, their origin and their purpose alike unknown to the new-comers! Was this another scourge God was sending them for their sins? Wait and see. Settling upon all the fields and every part of them, they pounced upon the crickets, seizing and swallowing them. They gorged themselves. Even after their stomachs were filled they still devoured them. On Sunday the people, full of thankfulness, left the fields to the birds, and on the morrow found on the edges of the ditches great piles of dead crickets that had been swallowed and thrown up by the greedy gulls. Verily, the Lord had not forgotten to be gracious!

To escape the birds, the crickets would rush into the lake or river, and thus millions were destroyed. Toward evening the gulls took flight and disappeared beyond the lake, but each day returned at sunrise, until the scourge was past.

EAGLE

MAN

Ted Shane

If we may believe the many articles in the better magazines, the problem of the retired businessman who doesn't know what to do with his "golden years" is widespread and serious. Unfortunately, the solution is not usually as easy or as satisfactory as it proved to be in the case of retired banker Charles Lavelle Broley. Most men of sixty would not take kindly to the suggestion that they should become eagle watchers and learn to climb into nests high in swaying treetops. But Mr. Broley was already a confirmed bird watcher, and he promptly specialized in eagles with the results detailed below.

E n route from Winnipeg, Canada, to Florida in January 1939, Charles Lavelle Broley stopped at the headquarters of the National Audubon Society in New York. Crowding 60, he had just retired as a bank manager; as a confirmed bird watcher, he wondered if he could put his new leisure to use for the society.

Wildlife custodians were worried about the bald eagle, our national symbol, which was in danger of extinction. Little was known about its migratory and personal habits, and it was being shot on sight as a common chicken thief.

Richard Pough, now chief of conservation for the American Museum of Natural History, gave Broley a few aluminum identification tags, and suggested he try banding eagles. Only 166 of the birds had been banded; their eyries were perched dizzily in tall trees or other inaccessible places. "Naturally you won't be able to do any climbing," Pough said. "Get a boy for that, and you can do the easy part—the banding."

In the Tampa Bay area of Florida, it was then common to see the big white-headed birds soaring regally over the shorelands. Broley found himself a brash 16-year old and went eyrie-hunting. They sighted Nest One in the deep-tangled flatlands back of Gibsonton. From a distance it looked like a clump of Spanish moss. Up close it was as big as a small

From *Lifetime Living.* January 1953.

car, cup-shaped, near the top of a sturdy pine whose lowest branch was 40 feet from the ground.

The ex-banker was slightly nervous. There were no handbooks on banding eagles, and Broley's equipment was homemade. Would Mama and Papa Eagle interfere? How do you catch a falling boy?

Broley, an old lacrosse player, took aim and threw a lead weight tied to a fishline over the 40-foot limb. As he hauled up a rope ladder via the line, two eagles zoomed up from the nest. The lad mounted the swaying ladder and pulled himself up into the huge stickpile. Broley heard a yell, saw him seize a stick from the nest and begin fencing with an unseen adversary. Then a young bird backflipped from the nest into the underbrush 500 feet away.

Broley found the eaglet cowering under a saw palmetto. It was a magnificent dark-brown youngster, about 11 weeks old but still unable to fly. When he grabbed the bird's legs, it slashed out with its scimitar beak and its big talons hooked deeply into his hand. Painfully he pried them out with his banding pliers and lugged the bird like a chicken back to the tree. There he found his assistant, white-faced and bleeding. Wrestling the eaglet, they got it banded and into a canvas bag for the return trip to the nest.

Broley hadn't shinned up a tree in 45 years, but since the shaking boy was in no condition to go, he began the giddy climb up the rope ladder. In the nest he found another eaglet. He approached with caution, but this baby did not protest when he banded it.

As he runged down the quivering ladder he was sweating, and he was bloody. "But," he says, "I had banded my first eagle. And I knew I was going to like it."

After that, Broley did his own climbing. He ran out of bands and telegraphed for more. Pough sent them with the reminder, "Don't let your boy take unnecessary risks."

When the nesting season slacked off in March, the ex-banker had banded a total of 44 young eagles. He had lost 15 pounds, had thrown away his outdoor glasses, and had never felt better in his life. He was also learning that the eagle is a much-libeled bird. Not one adult had attacked him, and he has yet to see an eagle toting anything but the food it normally eats—large fish. [Of 800 nests he has examined, he has found chicken bones in only two.]

While Broley spent that summer at his home in Ontario, one of his bands was "recovered" near Poughkeepsie, N.Y., 1100 miles from Florida; its wearer had died for alleged chicken theft. Another band was found in New Brunswick, Canada; a third on Prince Edward Island. Like any tourist, the Florida bald eagle appeared to summer in the North.

The following winter, provided with a gross of bands and a U. S.

Fish and Wildlife badge, Broley returned to Florida and found so many eyries he had to number and map them. Citizens began phoning the police to report a crank who was climbing trees. Three times Broley was clapped in jail for "molesting birds." Back-country folk, suspecting he was a "revenooer," lit brush fires while he was aloft, to burn his car and maroon him.

His 1940 Florida score was 76 bandings. That summer he tackled 20 eyries in the elms of Ontario—some of them 110 feet up. He tied two ladders together to reach lower branches 60 feet high, then steeple-jacked himself into the penthouses to find them tenanted by northern cousins of his Florida babies—slightly larger, and equally sharp-clawed and spirited.

What had begun as a casual hobby was now a new life. Broley began tackling the 115-foot Florida cypresses, wading waist-deep through the swamps with his 65 pounds of ladders, ropes, tools, cameras and snake-bite juice poised atop his bald head, marking his way in and out with the skill of an Indian.

In 1946 Broley became the Babe Ruth of banding—tagging 150 eaglets, 14 in one day. That report alarmed Richard Pough. His protege was 67 now, an age when elderly gentlemen climb into rocking chairs, not eagle roosts. He tried to get him to quit. "What would I do, play shuffle-board?" inquired Broley. "I don't know how."

His banding trips are mostly lone affairs, but recently some have become public events, with as many as 1000 spectators. Fan mail has found him which was addressed simply: "Eagle Man, Tampa, Fla."

As Broley accumulated eagle lore, he set out to correct public misunderstanding. At schools and club meetings, on radio and TV, he has plugged for preservation of our national bird. Watching his splendid slides and movies of eagle life, his audiences have done more falling than he. "I fell out of every tree you climbed!" one woman gasped at him.

He has had some close calls. When one nest gave away beneath him, he saved himself by grabbing an overhanging branch. Next day he came back and jacked up the nest with two-by-fours. Another time, a limb he was standing on snapped under him. His sickening plunge was stopped short when his pants caught on a branch stub. "I felt foolish," he admits, "just hanging there. It took me an hour to squirm around and rip my pants open, then slide down the trunk. I was lucky to get home even in a barrel."

"What brings my heart to my mouth," Mrs. Broley says, "is seeing him stand on a branch 80 feet up, nonchalantly toss a rope over a higher branch, and climb that. I don't like it when he has to pull the ladder up after him to get into very high nests. That means he has to come down with the ladder not fastened at the bottom at all, and he swings and sways dizzily, especially if there's a high wind."

Broley never knows what he'll find when he steps into an eagle's nest. The great horned owl, a militant character with a six-foot wing-spread and murderous claws, often takes over an eyrie. Last year Broley was nearly knocked out of an eyrie when a mother owl swooped in noiselessly on her down-lined wings. He has been besieged by hornets and by irate flying squirrels.

Ornithologists agree that Broley hasn't climbed in vain. He has proved that the Florida eagle practices "reverse migration"—it nests *before* it goes north—and travels as far northwest as Lake Winnipeg, 2400 miles away. . . . The $500 fine for shooting the bald eagle or taking its eggs and young from the nest for commercial zoos stems from the publicity Broley has given the monarch of the air.

Nevertheless the number of birds shows a steady, tragic decline. Since the 1946 peak, Broley's score for bandings has dwindled alarmingly each year. Ten percent of the 1200 birds he has banded have been shot. The way things are going, ornithologists gloomily predict, the bald eagle may be extinct by the year 2000. Here and there eagle lovers have chipped in and bought eyrie trees, and recently W. K. Vanderbilt set aside 12,000 acres near Venice, Fla., as a sanctuary.

Today, at 73, Broley is a lithe and sinewy 150-pounder of medium height. He opens his day with a dozen hoists on a chinning bar, eats only breakfast and dinner, doesn't smoke or drink. Radiating physical and mental health, the Eagle Man has proved that retirement can be just the beginning of life. "When you sit in a treetop and look out over the world," he explains, "it does something to your point of view."

BIRD DOCTOR

Paul H. Fluck

Tending sick or injured birds is a ticklish business, and often futile into the bargain. Still, a sprinkling of "bird doctors"—some with veterinary training, others experience-taught amateurs—labors across the continent, their successful rehabilitations usually their only thanks.

I HAVE two Doctor's Degrees. The first was presented to me twenty years ago at a graduation ceremony at the Academy of Music in Philadelphia. That diploma hangs on the wall of my office. It is printed on sheepskin and awes my medical patients into paying my fees. My other Doctor's Degree was presented to me by a blue-eyed freckled child. That diploma was written in pencil on a scrap of notebook paper. It came wrapped around a box that contained a battered robin. It read:

Dear Bird Doctor:
My robin is dying. Mother said you could save it if I brought it to you. Please do.
Carol.

I did save it. Carol's letter made me an *amateur* Bird Doctor. I waited almost ten years for another scrap of paper to make me a *professional*. It was a check for ten dollars, drawn on a bank in Hatboro, Pennsylvania. Written in the lower left corner were the words: "For the Care of One Sparrow Hawk."

It makes no difference that I never received another fee for such services. That check, duly cashed and listed on my income tax return, made me a *professional* Bird Doctor.

There are thousands of doctors, and all kinds of them, but I suspect there are fewer "paid" Bird Doctors than any other physicians.

From *Nature Magazine*, June 1956.

Looking back now over ten years of aiding birds, I see that I always intended to be a Bird Doctor. I knew it that first day, when I held a crippled blue jay, her bill completely snipped off by the washing-machine motor. Holding the bird in my hand, I dashed to my medical kit for a piece of oxidized cellulose to stop the bleeding. I held the cellulose over her bloody face for almost half an hour, while the phone jangled in vain with calls from human patients. When the bleeding stopped, I snipped off most of the cottony stuff and looked hopelessly at my patient. The bird's eyes sparkled behind the bloody clot, and her tiny tongue flicked in and out, in pain. I considered putting the jay in a box with some chloroform on cotton. But my wife said "No."

I said, "How will she eat?"

My wife said, "We'll see about that when the time comes."

When the time came, my wife chewed up food, and the bird picked it from between my wife's lips. For three weeks the bird ate everything in that way. Then she began to eat mashed potatoes and milk by herself, and finally her bill grew back far enough to cover her tongue.

While the jay was getting well her recovery was making news, and the door-bell was ringing. Children were bringing in crippled grackles, robins and sparrows. A policeman brought in a heron and a duck, and I was finding injured birds along the highway and in the park. The bird doctor business was booming. Birds were in boxes, in cages, in the bathroom, and in closets. If I had stopped to look ahead, I would have seen the impossibility of keeping up with the crippled bird business. For Humans a ration of one doctor for every seven hundred patients is about average. But there are said to be seven billion birds in these United States, and I was the only practicing Bird Doctor in the Delaware River Valley.

Besides being the lowest-paid profession in the world, bird-doctoring is the most demanding, physically. I have carried a flicker around from ant hill to ant hill for hours on a hot August day when the thermometer stood at 100. I have chased grasshoppers and leaf-hoppers during July, August and September to feed a kingbird and a scarlet tanager. For fifteen months I drove eight miles every day to stuff a pound of perfectly good beef liver down the throat of a blind barn owl, which never hunted a mouthful for himself all the time he was in my care. After the owl passed on, a rowdy red-shouldered hawk took his place, and for a year I drove the same eight miles to stuff more fifty-cent-a-pound beef liver down his throat. Every day I came home with blood oozing from my hands, and many evenings in my office I could not give a hypodermic injection with my bandaged fingers.

But bird-doctoring pays off in a big way. If you have the stamina to take it, and enough closets, and bird cages, and bathrooms, and back porches to house them, birds make the best patients on earth. They never complain. They never hire lawyers to sue you. They never sign hospital releases and go home. And while it is true that a get-well rate of 50 percent is hardly ever obtainable, you can be sure that you will spend some of the most interesting hours of your life when bird-doctoring.

I feel sorry for people who have unintelligent parakeets and canaries for pets. These have been reared in captivity and deprived of the urge to be free. Wild birds are part of Nature. Many flow north with the spring and south with the fall as unhinderable as water pouring over a waterfall. They roost, eat, fight, drink, sing, bathe, and scheme escapes. Some of the most unforgettable hours of my life I have spent with a red-tailed hawk on my arm. The most affectionate friend I ever had was a blue jay. The most beautiful thing I ever had in my hand was a bluebird dying of footpox. If I sound like I am a bit soft in my head, mull this over in your own. Barney, the blind barn owl who lived in the old house in Washington Crossing Park, drew crowds of hundreds of people every Saturday and Sunday afternoon. Many drove more than a hundred miles to just stroke the feathers on his ugly head for a few seconds. In those fifteen months Barney did a job for conservation. His fans came in sleet, snow, fair weather, and during the terrible Delaware Valley Flood of August, 1955. Barney appeared on TV, and he got fan mail. Some real tears are shed when I tell visitors that the owl died on Halloween.

Actually, here and now, *and with emphasis*, let me make it clear that bird-doctoring is a ninety per cent unnecessary profession. Most small birds with broken wings make out far better if they are left to fend for themselves in a thicket of honeysuckle or blackberry briars near a spring or a brook. I have cold-heartedly released as many as a dozen birds that could not fly from wing injuries, in snow and sleet, in such locations. And in six instances I have recaptured those birds again. The bands on their legs proved that they were the cripples—completely recovered!

One song sparrow flew weakly from my hand and collapsed under a spice bush. I worried about it all night. At dawn I got up and spread enough bird seed around that bush to feed a hundred canaries. I did not see that bird again, for two years, and blamed myself for letting him go in the snow. Then one day I picked him out of a bird trap, and read his band. I thought I was seeing things. I read the number over again, and had two friends read the number. That little scamp came back every day for a month or so. He had so much zip that I could not handle him. I still think that on that first afternoon he was playing "possum," and that if I had kept him overnight he would have died!

Again I say, the best thing for an untrained bird doctor, and that probably means you, to do with a bird that cannot fly is to let it go at once, in the safest place you can find.

Most of the bird patients I have treated have been special patients, large birds like hawks and owls; blind birds; birds with hemorrhages, birds with diseases that might have infected wild birds. It made no difference how hopeless the case looked, I treated every bird exactly as I would have treated a human patient. Then I put the bird in a dark closet, except for owls, which I place in a lighted closet, and I wait twelve hours, or as much as twenty-four. Then I can predict the outcome. Dead birds are buried, or given to a taxidermist to mount. Live birds are treated exactly the same as well birds. Just as it is with chronic patients among people, birds that can never get well, or never care for themselves again, are the most difficult problems. But there is a place even for them.

At the bird programs at Washington Crossing Park my crippled birds pinch-hit for me on days when birds refuse to go into banding traps, or when rain or sub-zero weather makes banding too uncomfortable. From the reaction of the 35,000 people who have come to the bird programs in the Park in the last four years, I am sure that many like the crippled birds best.

Peanut, the scarlet tanager, will never fly again, but he can drink Coca Cola from a straw! Rosie, my helpless rose-breasted grosbeak, has posed for more Kodachromes than any grosbeak on earth. Saucy, my eleven-year-old blue jay with the deformed bill can dance like a strutter at the Mardi Gras. Unlike too many chronic human patients, birds do not give up. They keep on trying to get well. They keep on learning new tricks because new tricks mean more attention.

I have seen a red-shouldered hawk knock itself out two weeks in a row, becoming violently impatient as he waited his turn to be carried outside for the crowd to see. Barney, the blind barn owl, would limp over to the attic door, and wait to be carried outside at exactly 4 o'clock every Saturday and Sunday. On weekdays he always remained in his box in the corner.

Birds under my care are rarely given medicine. Although I can calculate a dose of almost any drug for a newborn baby, I am completely licked by the mathematics involved in figuring a dose for a two-ounce bird. Even whiskey I have found to be too strong as a stimulant for most songbirds. Vitamin drops are essential to almost all wild birds in captivity. I put the vitamin drops in the water dish daily.

Splints for broken wings are useless in most instances. Wing injuries, if they are not hopeless from the start, usually heal themselves in seven to ten days. Occasionally when the wing is dragging on the ground, a doll's sock, or a child's sock with the toe cut off can be slipped over the bird, and two holes can be cut out for the legs. But, after ten years of bird-doctoring, I am inclined to do less splinting.

Small cages cause birds more suffering than almost any ailment. A storeroom, a bathroom, a screened-in porch, or a packing carton, make far better quarters for crippled birds than canary and parrot cages. A few birds do well in cages, but only a few. If you must put a wild bird in a cage, be sure to cover the top of the cage, and the sides if necessary. Pine needles in the bottom of the cages make cleaning an easy task. And the pine needles are almost ideal for birds' feet.

My most ungrateful bird patients have been herons. Great blue herons and night herons have long, dangerous bills, which you have to get a grip on first, before you can feed them or give them a diagnostic looking-over. Feeding a heron calls for patience and a nose clamp. I usually use smelts, and work them all the way down the heron's neck. It is like squeezing mud out of a garden hose. But finally the smelt slips inside, and you turn your back to pick up another. Then you suddenly discover your first smelt lying there, ready for another try.

The best place for herons is in a safe, secluded pond or brook where there are plenty of fish and tadpoles, and no dogs, or children. Taking care of crippled herons is a dangerous and smelly business. The next time I treat one, I am going to have a galvanized bucket on my head with holes cut for my eyes.

Many visitors to Washington Crossing Park will recall the old crow that suffered with asthma. He was one of the few birds who had his own medicine bottle. A few drops would relieve his gasping, but the crow despised the medicine so much he hopped out of an open window one day, and even though he was almost completely blind with cataracts, and had one wing completely shot off, he managed to disappear in the woods and we never found him again.

Few birds have to be destroyed to end their suffering. Usually all that is necessary is to put the dying bird in a tightly covered box, in a completely dark closet. The suffering bird reacts exactly as any bird (except an owl) reacts to night. He will remain absolutely quiet. If men could die as easily as birds, narcotics would be almost unnecessary.

In spite of the low fees, and the dubious future of bird-doctoring, I will be a bird doctor forever. Or until I become hard-hearted enough to send a child on her way with a box containing a dying robin.

THE CARE

AND FEEDING

OF

WILD BIRDS

John K. Terres

Many people who would never attempt to set a broken bone or treat a bird for viral hepatitis find themselves from time to time foster-parenting apparently healthy nestlings, often discovered and brought home by youngsters. John K. Terres here offers advice on how to raise these birds to the age of independence.

RULES for becoming a successful foster-parent:
Every year, bird's nests are blown out of trees by violent storms and newly-hatched, or half-grown young birds, scattered on the ground. If the nest and fledglings can be replaced in the tree or bush, it is far better to do so and let the bird-parents go on with an exacting job for which they alone are best suited. But if you enjoy being a foster parent, the experience of establishing a nursery for young birds can be rewarding. When the nest has been destroyed, and the youngsters seemed doomed to perish without your care, take them in if you are prepared to devote yourself to the task of feeding them at 15-minute intervals for at least 12 hours during the day. Here's how one of our correspondents, an expert at caring for baby wild birds, does it.

If the nest has been destroyed, she puts the helpless young birds in a box in a substitute nest, perhaps of grass, lined with soft cloth or cotton so that the birds' feet have something pliable to push against. She keeps them warm by covering them with a cloth and protecting them from drafts. If the fledglings are old enough to perch, she puts them in a large cage, or better, gives them the freedom of a room in which they can learn to fly.

Young birds should be handled as little as possible and not fed too much at a time. Feed them only during daylight hours, but feedings should be frequent, two or three times an hour. . . . Young birds are like our own children; they demand all the attention they can get, but regularity of feeding gives the best results.

Foods and Feeding

Feeding is common sense, with a dash of ingenuity. Many people try to feed foundling wild birds simply on bread, even offering it to owls and grebes.

Our correspondent's basic food for very young songbird nestlings, other than hummingbirds, is equal parts of finely-mashed yolk of hard-boiled eggs and finely-sifted bread crumbs, *slightly* moistened with milk or cod-liver oil. This mixture will agree with starlings, blue jays, cardinals, towhees, robins, catbirds, orioles, sparrows and other small birds. Good supplementary foods are canned dog-food, bits of grapes, cherries, bananas, or soft apple pulp, pieces of earthworms that have been "squeezed out," and bits of scraped or finely chopped meat. One woman with an orphaned yellow-billed cuckoo got a supply of insects for it each night by attracting insects to a light in her window.

At first, older fledglings may not eat. To forcefeed them, hold the bird by enclosing its body and closed wings in your left hand, and with your forefinger and thumb, gently pry open the bill at its base. In your right hand hold a medicine dropper, or an improvised narrow wooden spoon, or better, a small paint brush to pick up food on the tips of its bristles. Poke the food down the bird's throat, but not too much at once or it will choke. In a short time the youngsters will learn to open their bills for food. Continue the feeding until the bird's crop is full, and it should be especially full at nightfall, just before the bird goes to sleep.

To supplement her basic diet, our correspondent includes chopped nasturtium and watercress, rich in calcium and vitamins, and cottage cheese for added protein.

Most seed-eaters—cardinals, grosbeaks, and finches—also need fine gravel and charcoal, crushed seeds, chopped greens, fruits, mealworms and insects.

Young woodpeckers eat a mixture of dog-food and the basic finely-mashed egg yolks.

For baby hummingbirds supply a syrup in equal parts of sugar and water fed with a medicine dropper. After about 10 days, our correspondent feeds the hummers their first protein—dried dog-food very finely-sifted and thoroughly mixed with the syrup.

Young hawks and owls require meat, preferably meat with the fur or feathers on it which aids the digestion of raptorial birds. Feed them on freshly-caught rats and mice, or poultry and raw beef sprinkled with cod-liver oil, with which chicken feathers may be mixed.

Water and Sunshine

Small birds are quickly killed by forcibly giving them water. Before they learn to drink, they receive sufficient water for their needs from their food. When they are old enough to sit on a perch, water may be offered in a shallow dish. You may also dip their bills into a water-cup until they learn to drink by themselves. Young birds must have some sunshine too, but they should be shaded from the heat of the mid-day sun. Birds, like humans, welcome a cool retreat in hot weather.

When the Bird Grows Up

No matter how attached we may become to the birds we have raised, we must remember that we have been their protectors, not their captors; that wild birds belong to the State. As soon as a bird is strong enough, it should be allowed to forage for itself and should be turned loose as soon as it is able to fly. If the foundlings are not encouraged to return to a wild, free life, they will learn to depend upon human assistance which may bring them disaster when they are suddenly thrown upon their own.

Part

Seven

EXTINCTION AND CONSERVATION

AND I

OUGHT TO KNOW

Will Cuppy

The late Will Cuppy, otherwise known as the Hermit of Fire Island, could never seem to make up his mind whether he was a nature lover or, like Samuel Johnson, Sydney Smith, and Charles Lamb, a nature hater. His various books dealing with natural (and unnatural) history are pretty sure to delight any reader but none so much as those who know enough about both to appreciate fully the curious facts, deliberate fallacies, and puckish comments which he blended in a version which was his alone. One of his best pieces is this one from a section in a book appropriately called How to Become Extinct. *It contains among much other curious matter some comments on the ambivalence of ornithologists who, when they know that a species is threatened with extinction, are torn between the desire to keep it going and the urge to get as many stuffed specimens and skins as possible into the museums.*

THE last two Great Auks in the world were killed June 4, 1844, on the island of Eldey, off the coast of Iceland. The last Passenger Pigeon, an old female named Martha, died September 1, 1914, peacefully, at the Cincinnati Zoo. I became extinct on August 23, 1934. I forget where I was at the time, but I shall always remember the date.

The two Great Auks were hit on the head by Jon Brandsson and Sigurdr Islefsson, a couple of Icelandic fishermen who had come from Cape Reykjanes for the purpose. A companion, Ketil Ketilsson, looked around for another Great Auk but failed to find one, naturally, since the species had just become extinct. Vilhjalmur Hakonarsson, leader of the expedition, stayed in the boat.

The main reason why these particular fishermen went birding that day is part of history. It seems that bird lovers and bird experts everywhere were upset over the disappearance of the Great Auk from its accustomed haunts and its extreme rarity even in its last refuge, the little island of Eldey. Since there was grave danger that it would soon

From *The Great Bustard and Other People*. New York: Rinehart & Company, 1941.

become entirely and irrevocably extinct—as dead as the Dodo, in fact— it looked as though something would have to be done and done quickly.

Well, something was done. As always, one man rose to the occasion. Mr. Carl Siemsen, a resident of Reykjavik and quite an ornithologist on his own, hired Jon and Sigurdr and the rest of the boys to row over to Eldey and kill all the Great Auks they could find, in order that they might be properly stuffed and placed in various museums for which he acted as agent and talent scout. And of course that was one way of handling the situation. It was pretty tough on the Auks, though, wasn't it?

I don't say the museum people themselves would have hit the Great Auks on the head, or even that they would have approved such an act. I do say that ornithologists as a class, so far as I have been able to observe them, generally from a safe distance, do seem to suffer from a touch of split personality when faced with a dwindling species of bird. They appear to be torn between a sincere desire to bring that bird back to par, at any cost to themselves and to certain well-to-do persons whose names they keep in a little black book, and an uncontrollable urge or compulsion to skin a few more specimens and put them in a showcase at the earliest possible moment. I don't pretend to follow their line of reasoning, if such it may be called. To do that you have to be a Ph.D. in birdology. It takes years of hard study, and I guess you have to be that way in the first place.

Right here I might offer a word of advice to the Ivory-billed Woodpecker, now the rarest bird on the North American continent and one that is going to come in for more and more attention. Keep away from bird lovers, fellows, or you'll be standing on a little wooden pedestal with a label containing your full name in Latin: *Campephilus principalis*. People will be filing past admiring your glossy blue-black feathers, your white stripes and patches, your nasal plumes in front of lores, your bright red crest and your beady yellow eyes. You'll be in the limelight, but you won't know it. I don't want to alarm you fellow, but there are only about twenty of you alive as I write these lines, and there are more than two hundred of you in American museums and in collections owned by Ivory-billed Woodpecker enthusiasts. Get it?

Yes, I know that many ornithologists are gentle, harmless souls without a murderous thought in their whole field equipment. I should like to remind them, though, that even a bird has a nervous system, and I am thinking especially of the Roseate Spoonbill, one of our few native birds with a bill shaped like a soup ladle. It can't help the Roseate Spoonbill much to go chasing over hill and dale practically twenty-four hours a day, aiming binoculars at it from behind every bush—as if it didn't know you were there!—clicking your cameras, watching every move and that sort of thing. There must be Roseate Spoonbills who haven't had a decent night's rest in years. No sleep, no nothing. And you wonder why they're neurotic.

I should like to add that the habit of climbing up into trees and rubber-stamping the eggs of birds threatened with extinction in order to warn wandering collectors away from the nests might well be abandoned in the interests of whatever remnants of sanity may still be left among our feathered friends.

Coming back to the Great Auk, if I may, I am rather surprised that I brought up the subject at all, for it is not one of my favorite birds of song or story. I lost interest some years ago when I learned that it was only as large as a tame Goose, and some say smaller—the Great Auk, mind you! When I think of the precious hours I once wasted thinking how wonderful it would be to see a Great Auk, I could sue.

Besides, it was one of those birds that lost the power of flight through long disuse of their wings, and surely that is no fault of mine, to put it no closer home. I am always a bit impatient with such birds. Under conditions prevailing in the civilized world, any bird that can't make a quick get-away is doomed, and more so if it is good to eat, if its feathers are fine for cushions, and if it makes excellent bait for Codfish when chipped into gobbets. Such a bird, to remain in the picture, must drop everything else and develop its wing muscles to the very limit. It does seem as though that should be clear even to an Auk.

Flightlessness alone, however, does not explain the fate of this species to my satisfaction, since it is a well-known fact that fish do not fly, either—that is, most fish. By the way, there are grounds for believing that the Great Auk regarded itself as more of a fish than a bird, for it made its annual migrations to Florida by water, and largely beneath the surface at that. Still and all, it didn't work out in the long run. I cannot avoid the feeling that birds migrating under water is something Mother Nature will stand just so long and no longer.

I'm afraid the Great Auks were pretty foolish in other ways, too. Like Dodos, they had a tendency to pal with just anybody. Whenever they noticed some one creeping up on them with a blunt instrument, they would rush to meet him with glad little squawks of welcome and stick out their necks. Both species did this once too often. Maybe you never heard that duodo, the earliest version of Dodo, is Portuguese for simpleton. You didn't know the Portuguese had a word for that, eh?

We should now be in a position, if we're ever going to be, to form some opinion on why the Great Auk became extinct. It would be too easy, and not very scientific, to say that it happened merely because Jon Brandsson and Sigurdr Islefsson were running amuck on the morning of June 4, 1844. But why were there only two Great Auks left on Eldey? What had been going on in this species? Just how far had *Alca impennis* evolved, whether rightly or wrongly? As Richard Swann Lull states in

Organic Evolution, "Extinction in phylogeny has two aspects, each of which has its equivalent in ontogeny." And two aspects is putting it mildly.

Let's not be too quick to blame the human race for everything. We must remember that a great many species of animals became extinct before man ever appeared on earth. At the same time it is probably true that when two husky representatives of *Homo sapiens,* with clubs, corner the last two birds of a species, no matter how far they have or have not evolved, both the phylogeny and the ontogeny of those birds are, to all intents and purposes, over. For the present I shall have to leave it at that.

Since I mentioned two other extinct individuals in the first paragraph of this article, my readers may expect me to bring them into the story. To the best of my knowledge and belief, Martha, last of the Passenger Pigeons, is now one of the treasures of the Smithsonian Institution. After life's fitful fever she can do with a good rest. No more of those incredible, sky-darkening flights amid general uproar and pandemonium. No more dodging bullets. No more roup. Martha was far from a Squab when she left us in 1914, having reached the age of twenty-nine. Her name, by the way, is no whimsical invention of mine. She was really Martha, as anybody will tell you who knew his Cincinnati around the turn of the century.

We are not quite sure why the Passenger Pigeon became extinct as a species. Some say that all the Passenger Pigeons in the world—except Martha, presumably—were caught in a storm and perished during their last migration southward over the Gulf of Mexico. The weakness of this theory is that Passenger Pigeons never went near the Gulf of Mexico on any pretext, let alone made a habit of flying over it in a body. I grant you there have been some bad storms over the Gulf, but that also holds true of other bodies of water.

My own view is the economic one. The food supply of those birds probably gave out, and there they were. Only the other day I came across the statement that the chief food of the Passenger Pigeon was beech-mast, a commodity which could never have been abundant enough in this country to last them forever. I never even heard of it myself except in this connection. I do think our scientists, instead of spinning picturesque yarns about the disappearance of the Passenger Pigeon, mere guesswork for the most part, might well devote themselves to the question: Whatever became of the beech-mast? Then we might get somewhere.

So much for *Ectopistes migratorius.* Nevermore, alas, will they alight in our forests by the billion, breaking down and killing the trees for miles around by the weight of their untold numbers, destroying the crops for thousands of acres in every direction, wrecking havoc and devastation upon whole counties and leaving the human population a complete wreck from shock, multiple contusions, and indigestion. People miss that sort of thing, but you needn't look for any more Passenger Pigeons. They have gone to join the Great Auk, the Labrador Duck, the Eskimo Curlew, the Carolina Parakeet, the Heath Hen, and the Guadalupe Flicker. You won't find any of them. They're through.

What is more, sooner than we think we may see the last of the California Condor, the Everglade Kite, the Trumpeter Swan, the Whooping Crane and the Limpkin, not to mention some of the Godwits, which haven't been doing any too well here lately. It's enough to made Donald Culross Peattie go and hang himself.

But look, Mr. Peattie, only last June a thing called a Cahow, supposed to be extinct, turned up in Bermuda as chipper as ever. It wasn't extinct at all. Does that help any? And I honestly don't think we need worry about the Whooping Crane. There will always be people who will see to it, if it's the last thing they do, that there are plenty of Whooping Cranes around. Life has taught me that much at least.

If I may close on a personal note, I'm sorry but there seems to be some doubt whether I became extinct on August 23, 1934, or whether the date will have to be moved ahead a few years. That day was one of my birthdays and it was not my twenty-first or my thirtieth—or even, I am afraid, my fortieth. And it got me to thinking. Since then I have had more birthdays, so things haven't improved much in that respect. I find, however, that it is technically incorrect to call anybody extinct while he is still at large. I must have made a mistake in one of the minor details. Some day that can be fixed in a jiffy by changing a numeral or two, and then everything will be right as rain.

Anyway, you can see how the thoughts of a person who fully believed himself to be extinct, even if he had talked himself into it, could be a bit on the somber side. Yet I had my moments, for I assure you that becoming extinct has its compensations. It's a good deal like beating the game. I would go so far as to say that becoming extinct is the perfect answer to everything and I defy anybody to think of a better. Other solutions are mere palliatives, just a bunch of loose ends, leaving the central problem untouched. But now I must snap out of all that. According to our leading scientists, I am not yet extinct, and they ought to know. Well, there's no use crying about it.

As I look back over the period since 1934, I guess I didn't go into the thing quite thoroughly enough. I never really classed myself with the Dodo, a bird we always think of as the ultimate in extinction, though I suppose the Dodo is no more extinct than anything else that is extinct, unless it's the Trilobite. Maybe I'm more like the Buffalo, which seems to be coming back now in response to no great popular demand that I can see. Did I ever tell you what happened to the Buffaloes that time? The moths got into them.

THE

PASSENGER

PIGEON

John James Audubon

Perhaps no story about birds has been more often told than that of the passenger pigeon, which once roamed in flocks of incredible size over eastern North America. Perhaps its disappearance was inevitable, not only because it was recklessly slaughtered, but also because the clearing of the forest deprived it of the immense food supply necessary to such prodigious numbers. The fact remains that the extinction of the species, like the loss of some great work of art, is absolutely irretrievable. And it is startling to realize in how short a time the irretrievable loss can occur. In 1813 Audubon saw passenger pigeons passing hour after hour, sometimes at the rate of 163 flocks in 21 minutes. Just 101 years later the last living specimen died in the Cincinnati Zoological Garden.

THE Passenger Pigeon, or, as it is usually named in America, the Wild Pigeon, moves with extreme rapidity, propelling itself by quickly repeated flaps of the wings, which it brings more or less near to the body, according to the degree of velocity which is required. Like the Domestic Pigeon it often flies, during the love season, in a circling manner, supporting itself with both wings angularly elevated, in which position it keeps them until it is about to alight. Now and then, during these circular flights, the tips of the primary quills of each wing are made to strike against each other, producing a smart rap, which may be heard at a distance of thirty or forty yards. Before alighting, the Wild Pigeon, like the Carolina Parrot and a few other species of birds, breaks the force of its flight by repeated flappings, as if apprehensive of receiving injury from coming too suddenly into contact with the branch or the spot of ground on which it intends to settle.

I have commenced my description of this species with the above account of its flight, because the most important facts connected with its

From *Birds of America*, Vol. 5. Published by George R. Lockwood and Son, 1870.

habits relate to its migrations. These are entirely owing to the necessity of procuring food, and are not performed with the view of escaping the severity of a northern latitude, or of seeking a southern one for the purpose of breeding. They consequently do not take place at any fixed period or season of the year. Indeed, it sometimes happens that a continuance of a sufficient supply of food in one district will keep these birds absent from another for years. I know, at least, to a certainty, that in Kentucky they remained for several years constantly, and were nowhere else to be found. They all suddenly disappeared in one season when the mast was exhausted, and did not return for a long period. Similar facts have been observed in other States.

Their great power of flight enables them to survey and pass over an astonishing extent of country in a very short time. This is proved by facts well known. Thus, Pigeons have been killed in the neighbourhood of New York, with their crops full of rice, which they must have collected in the fields of Georgia and Carolina, these districts being the nearest in which they could possibly have procured a supply of that kind of food. As their power of digestion is so great that they will decompose food entirely in twelve hours; they must in this case have travelled between three and four hundred miles in six hours, which shows their speed to be at an average of about one mile in a minute. A velocity such as this would enable one of these birds, were it so inclined, to visit the European continent in less than three days.

This great power of flight is seconded by as great a power of vision, which enables them, as they travel at that swift rate, to inspect the country below, discover their food with facility, and thus attain the object for which their journey has been undertaken. This I have also proved to be the case, by having observed them, when passing over a sterile part of the country, or one scantily furnished with food suited to them, keep high in the air, flying with an extended front, so as to enable them to survey hundreds of acres at once. On the contrary, when the land is richly covered with food, or the trees abundantly hung with mast, they fly low, in order to discover the part most plentifully supplied.

Their body is of an elongated oval form, steered by a long well-plumed tail, and propelled by well-set wings, the muscles of which are very large and powerful for the size of the bird. When an individual is seen gliding through the woods and close to the observer, it passes like a thought, and on trying to see it again, the eye searches in vain; the bird is gone.

The multitudes of Wild Pigeons in our woods are astonishing. Indeed, after having viewed them so often, and under so many circumstances, I even now feel inclined to pause, and assure myself that what I am going to relate is fact. Yet I have seen it all, and that too in the company of persons who, like myself, were struck with amazement.

In the autumn of 1813, I left my house at Henderson, on the banks of the Ohio, on my way to Louisville. In passing over the Barrens a few miles beyond Hardensburgh, I observed the Pigeons flying from northeast to south-west in greater numbers than I thought I had ever seen them before, and feeling an inclination to count the flocks that might pass within reach of my eye in one hour, I dismounted, seated myself on an eminence, and began to mark with my pencil, making a dot for every flock that passed. In a short time finding the task which I had undertaken impracticable, as the birds poured on in countless multitudes, I rose, and counting the dots then put down, found that 163 had been made in twenty-one minutes. I traveled on, and still met more the farther I proceeded. The air was literally filled with pigeons; the light of noonday was obscured as by an eclipse; the dung fell in spots, not unlike melting flakes of snow; and the continued buzz of wings had a tendency to lull my senses to repose.

While waiting for dinner at Young's inn at the confluence of Salt River with the Ohio, I saw, at my leisure, immense legions still going by, with a front reaching far beyond the Ohio on the west, and the beechwood forests directly on the east of me. Not a single bird alighted; for not a nut or acorn was that year to be seen in the neighbourhood. They consequently flew so high, that different trials to reach them with a capital rifle proved ineffectual; nor did the reports disturb them in the least. I cannot describe to you the extreme beauty of their aerial evolutions, when a Hawk chanced to press upon the rear of a flock. At once, like a torrent, and with a noise like thunder, they rushed into a compact mass, pressing upon each other towards the center. In these almost solid masses, they darted forward in undulating and angular lines, descended and swept close over the earth with inconceivable velocity, mounted perpendicularly so as to resemble a vast column, and, when high, were seen wheeling and twisting within their continued lines, which then resembled the coils of a gigantic serpent.

Before sunset I reached Louisville, distant from Hardensburgh fifty-five miles. The pigeons were still passing in undiminished numbers, and continued to do so for three days in succession. The people were all in arms. The banks of the Ohio were crowded with men and boys, incessantly shooting at the pilgrims, which flew lower as they passed the river. Multitudes were thus destroyed. For a week or more, the population fed on no other flesh than that of Pigeons, and talked of nothing but Pigeons.

It is extremely interesting to see flock after flock performing exactly the same evolutions which had been traced as it were in the air by a preceding flock. Thus should a Hawk have charged on a group at a certain spot, the angles, curves, and undulations, that have been described by the birds, in their efforts to escape from the dreaded talons of the plunderer, are undeviatingly followed by the next group that comes up. Should the bystander happen to witness one of these affrays, and, struck with the rapidity and elegance of the motions exhibited, feel desirous of seeing them repeated, his wishes will be gratified if he only remain in the place until the next group comes up.

As soon as the Pigeons discover a sufficiency of food to entice them to alight, they fly around in circles, reviewing the country below. During their evolutions, on such occasions, the dense mass which they form exhibits a beautiful appearance, as it changes its direction, now displaying a glistening sheet of azure, when the backs of the birds come simultaneously into view, and anon, suddenly presenting a mass of rich deep purple. They then pass lower, over the woods, and for a moment are lost among the foliage, but again emerge, and are seen gliding aloft. They now alight, but the next moment, as if suddenly alarmed, they take to wing, producing by the flapping of their wings a noise like the roar of distant thunder, and sweep through the forest to see if danger is near. Hunger, however, soon brings them to the ground. When alighted, they are seen industriously throwing up the withered leaves in quest of the fallen mast. The rear ranks are continually rising, passing over the main-body, and alighting in front, in such rapid succession, that the whole flock seems still on wing. The quantity of ground thus swept is astonishing, and so completely has it been cleared, that the gleaner who might follow in their rear would find his labour completely lost. Whilst feeding, their avidity is at times so great that in attempting to swallow a large acorn or nut, they are seen gasping for a long while, as if in the agonies of suffocation.

On such occasions, when the woods are filled with these Pigeons, they are killed in immense numbers, although no apparent diminution ensues. About the middle of the day, after their repast is finished, they settle on the trees, to enjoy rest, and digest their food. On the ground they walk with ease, as well as on the branches, frequently jerking their beautiful tail, and moving the neck backwards and forwards in the most graceful manner. As the sun begins to sink beneath the horizon, they depart *en masse* for the roosting-place, which not unfrequently is hundreds of miles distant, as has been ascertained by persons who have kept an account of their arrivals and departures.

Let us now, kind reader, inspect their place of nightly rendezvous. One of these curious roosting-places, on the banks of the Green river in Kentucky, I repeatedly visited. It was, as is always the case, in a portion of the forest where the trees were of great magnitude, and where there was little under-wood. I rode through it upwards of forty miles, and, crossing it in different parts, found its average breadth to be rather more than three miles. My first view of it was about a fortnight subsequent to the period when they had made choice of it, and I arrived there nearly two hours before sunset. Few pigeons were then to be seen, but a great number of persons, with horses and wagons, guns and ammunition, had already established encampments on the borders. Two farmers from the vicinity of Russelsville, distant more than a hundred miles, had driven upwards of three hundred hogs to be fattened on the Pigeons which were to be slaughtered. Here and there, the people employed in plucking and salting what had already been procured, were seen sitting in the midst of large piles of these birds. The dung lay several inches deep, covering the whole extent of the roosting-place. Many trees two feet in diameter, I observed, were broken off at no great distance from the ground; and the branches of many of the largest and tallest had given way, as if the forest had been swept by a tornado. Everything proved to me that the number of birds resorting to this part of the forest must be immense beyond conception. As the period of their arrival approached, their foes anxiously prepared to receive them. Some were furnished with iron-pots containing sulphur, others with torches of pine-knots, many with poles, and the rest with guns. The sun was lost to our view, yet not a Pigeon had arrived. Everything was ready, and all eyes were gazing on the clear sky, which appeared in glimpses amidst the tall trees. Suddenly there burst forth a general cry of "Here they come!" The noise which they made, though yet distant, reminded me of a hard gale at sea, passing through the rigging of a close-reefed vessel. As the birds arrived and passed over me, I felt a current of air that surprised me. Thousands were soon knocked down by the pole-men. The birds continued to pour in. The fires were lighted, and a magnificent, as well as wonderful and almost terrifying, sight presented itself. The Pigeons, arriving by thousands, alighted everywhere, one above another, until solid masses were formed on the branches all round. Here and there the perches gave way under the weight with a crash, and, falling to the ground, destroyed hundreds of birds beneath, forcing down the dense groups with which every stick was loaded. It was a scene of uproar and confusion. I found it quite useless to speak, or even to shout to those persons who were nearest to me. Even the reports of the guns were seldom heard, and I was made aware of the firing only by seeing the shooters reloading.

No one dared venture within the line of devastation. The hogs had been penned up in due time, the picking up of the dead and wounded being left for the next morning's employment. The Pigeons were constantly coming and it was past midnight before I perceived a decrease in the number of those that arrived. The uproar continued the whole night; and as I was anxious to know to what distance the sound reached, I sent off a man, accustomed to perambulate the forest, who, returning two hours afterward, informed me he had heard it distinctly when three miles distant from the spot. Towards the approach of day, the noise in some measure subsided long before objects were distinguishable, the Pigeons began to move off in a direction quite different from that in which they had arrived the evening before, and at sunrise all that were able to fly had disappeared. The howlings of the wolves now reached our ears, and the foxes, lynxes, cougars, bears, racoons, opossums, and pole-cats were seen sneaking off whilst eagles and hawks of different species, accompanied by a crowd of vultures, came to supplant them, and enjoy their share of the spoil.

It was then that the authors of this devastation began their entry amongst the dead, the dying, and the mangled. The Pigeons were picked up and piled in heaps until each had as many as he could possibly dispose of, when the hogs were let loose to feed on the remainder.

Persons unacquainted with these birds might naturally conclude that such dreadful havoc would soon put an end to the species. But I have satisfied myself, by long observation, that nothing but the gradual diminution of our forests can accomplish their decrease, as they not unfrequently quadruple their numbers yearly, and always at least double it. In 1805 I saw schooners loaded in bulk with Pigeons caught up the Hudson River, coming in to the wharf at New York, when the birds sold for a cent apiece. I knew a man in Pennsylvania, who caught and killed upwards of 500 dozens in a clap-net in one day, sweeping sometimes twenty dozens or more at a single haul. In the month of March, 1830, they were so abundant in the markets of New York, that piles of them met the eye in every direction. I have seen the Negroes at the United States Salines or Saltworks of Shawanee Town, wearied with killing Pigeons, as they alighted to drink the water issuing from the leading pipes, for weeks at a time; and yet in 1826, in Louisiana, I saw congregated flocks of these birds as numerous as ever I had seen them before, during a residence of nearly thirty years in the United States.

The breeding of the Wild Pigeons, and the places chosen for that purpose, are points of great interest. The time is not much influenced by season, and the place selected is where food is most plentiful and most attainable, and always at a convenient distance from water. Forest-trees of great height are those in which the Pigeons form their nests. Thither the countless myriads resort, and prepare to fulfill one of the great laws of nature. At this period the note of the Pigeon is a soft *coo-coo-coo-coo*, much shorter than that of the domestic species. The common notes resemble the monosyllables *kee-kee-kee-kee*, the first being the loudest, the others gradually diminishing in power. The male assumes a pompous demeanour, and follows the female, whether on the ground or on the branches, with spread tail and drooping wings, which it rubs against the part over which it is moving. The body is elevated, the throat swells, the eyes sparkle. He continues his notes, and now and then rises on the wing, and flies a few yards to approach the fugitive and timorous female. Like the domestic Pigeon and other species, they caress each other by billing, in which action, the bill of the one is introduced transversely into that of the other, and both parties alternately disgorge the contents of their crop by repeated efforts. These preliminary affairs are soon settled, and the pigeons commence their nests in general peace and harmony. They are composed of a few dry twigs, crossing each other, and are supported by forks of the branches. On the same tree from fifty to a hundred nests may frequently be seen: —I might say a much greater number, were I not anxious, kind reader, that however wonderful my account of the Wild Pigeon is, you may not feel disposed to refer it to the marvellous. The eggs are two in number, of a broadly elliptical form, and pure white. During incubation, the male supplies the female with food. Indeed, the tenderness and affection displayed by these birds towards their mates, are in the highest degree striking. It is a remarkable fact, that each brood generally consists of a male and a female.

Here again, the tyrant of creation, man, interferes, disturbing the harmony of this peaceful scene. As the young birds grow up, their enemies, armed with axes, reach the spot, to seize and destroy all they can. The trees are felled, and made to fall in such a way that the cutting of one causes the overthrow of another, or shakes the neighbouring trees so much, that the young Pigeons, or *squabs*, as they are named, are violently hurled to the ground. In this manner also, immense quantities are destroyed.

The young are fed by the parents in the manner described above; in other words, the old bird introduces its bill into the mouth of the young one in a transverse manner, or with the back of each mandible opposite the separations of the mandibles of the young bird, and disgorges the contents of its crop. As soon as the young birds are able to shift for themselves, they leave their parents, and continue separate until they attain maturity. By the end of six months they are capable of reproducing their species.

The flesh of the Wild Pigeon is of a dark colour, but affords tolerable eating. That of young birds from the nest is much esteemed. The skin is covered with small white filmy scales. The feathers fall off at the least touch, as had been remarked to be the case in the Carolina Turtle-dove. I have only to add, that this species, like others of the same genus, immerses its head up to the eyes while drinking.

In March, 1830, I bought about 350 of these birds in the market of New York, at four cents apiece. Most of these I carried alive to England, and distributed them amongst several noblemen, presenting some at the same time to the Zoological Society.

This celebrated bird is mentioned by Dr. Richardson as "annually reaching the 62nd degree of latitude, in the warm central districts of the Fur Countries, and attaining the 58th parallel on the coast of Hudson's Bay in very fine summers only. Mr. Hutchins mentions a flock which visited York Factory and remained there two days, in 1775, as a very remarkable occurrence. A few hordes of Indians that frequent the low flooded tracts at the south end of Lake Winnipeg, subsist principally on the Pigeons, during a part of the summer, when the sturgeon-fishery is unproductive, and the *Zizania aquatica* has not yet ripened; but farther north, these birds are too few in number to furnish a material article of diet." Mr. Townsend states that this species is found on the Rocky Mountains, but not on the Columbia River, where the Band-tailed Pigeon, *Columba fasciata* of Say, is abundant. Whilst in Texas, I was assured that the Passenger Pigeon was plentiful there, although at irregular intervals. In the neighbourhood of Boston it arrives, as Dr. T. M. Brewer informs me, in small scattered flocks, much less numerous than in the interior of that State.

THE LAST

OF A

SPECIES

William Bridges

Audubon thought the passenger pigeon in no danger of disappearance. But disappear it did, and we know exactly when.

T HE whole world was beginning to take fire on the first day of September, 1914, so it is understandable why the death of a pigeon in the Cincinnati Zoological Garden passed, if not quite unnoticed, at any rate with a minimum of general interest. The Cincinnati *Enquirer* gave it a third of a column; no doubt the wire associations sent a paragraph to other American newspapers. I cannot find that the New York *Times*, usually receptive to significant news, bothered about the little obituary, for the Battle of the Marne was in the making that September day and the extinction taking place in western Europe transcended, in news value, the extinction of any bird.

Nevertheless, all of us interested in animal life must wish that some editor with a sharpened sense of history—natural history—had assigned a reporter to record every minute detail of the drama that was taking place in Cincinnati, because the dying pigeon was Martha, the last Passenger Pigeon in the world. The very last of a race, sole relic of flocks comprising uncounted billions of individuals.

It was an opportunity for someone to record an event that may never occur again—the final exit of a species before human eyes. Other forms of wild life will go out of existence; many large and spectacular creatures are almost surely doomed today. But in all probability they will drift from existence into nonexistence while no man watches or is aware, just as the Great Auk and the Carolina Parrakeet and the Heath Hen disappeared, and we will realize they are gone irretrievably only when the

From *Animal Kingdom*. Bulletin of the NYZS, October 18, 1946.

last known individual fails to appear in its accustomed haunts. The stars, whispering leaves, the bright eyes of some small startled animal may be the only witness of their passing.

Our chance to see a species expire came only with the Passenger Pigeon, for its circumstances were unique. In 1914 it had already vanished as a wild bird, a stealthy and obscure disappearance, but the race had lingered a long time in captivity and the approach of its doom could be seen and measured and recorded. For once, we could know to the hour and minute when a great phase of American life came to an end.

But much as we regret it now, no reporter kept a deathwatch beside Martha's cage and sought out all the ascertainable facts of her life, and as things stand, the published and scattered accounts are confused and conflicting. After the lapse of only thirty-one years and while the guardians of her last hours are still alive, it has been difficult to reconstruct accurately and in detail the story of her end and her apotheosis.

In running down as much of the story as is still recoverable, I have had the cordial assistance of Director Joseph A. Stephan of the Cincinnati Zoological Garden, of his father, General Manager Emeritus Sol A. Stephan, and of Dr. Herbert Friedman, Curator of Birds of the U. S. National Museum.

To set the stage for the exit of Martha, it is necessary to recall what the Passenger Pigeon was, and something about its natural history. A whole generation has grown up since the last captive bird died and the wild birds had disappeared more than a generation before 1914, so that there are many grown men and women today who never heard of the Passenger Pigeon. Mention it, and they think of the Carrier Pigeon or the Homing Pigeon.

The Passenger Pigeon, despite its name, did not carry messages nor did it have a highly developed homing instinct. It was something entirely different from the specialized breeds of the common domestic pigeon; it was a true wild pigeon, native only to North America. Slender-tailed, bluish, with a slaty-blue head and breast of purplish-brownish-red, it was big and handsome. It had a wingspread of almost two feet and it weighed about 12 ounces.

The "Passenger Pigeon," it was called, presumably because it was constantly wandering over areas of several hundred square miles in search of food, or making sun-darkening flocks to its roosting or nesting grounds. In the early years of the last century the wild pigeon flocks roamed almost the whole of the United States where the hardwood forests existed, and they consumed unbelievable quantities of acorns, beechnuts, chestnuts and other tree seeds, of blueberries, huckleberries, raspberries, wild cherries, pokeberries and even caterpillars and other insects.

In 1832 the conservative ornithologist Alexander Wilson estimated that a single flock he encountered near Frankfort, Kentucky, contained *at least* 2,230,270,000 birds. Audubon cited equally prodigious flocks. Wilson's birds, if they ate only one pint of beech mast each in the course of a day, would consume 34,847,968 bushels a day.

Their nesting sites in Kentucky, Indiana, Michigan and elsewhere in the Middle West have been described by competent naturalists in the early and middle years of the last century. Millions of pigeons nested in the same forest. Over an area of a hundred square miles every tree would be loaded with nests, often as many as a hundred in a single tree. Great branches would break from the weight of the nesting birds.

Concentrated as they were in flocks, roosts and nests, their extermination was easy. Netters could take 3000 birds at the spring of a single trap. The methods of slaughter, for market or for sport, were many and varied and often cruel and wanton. By the "seventies" the vast flocks were gone from many parts of the country and by the "Eighties" the end was in sight everywhere.

In 1879 dead Passenger Pigeons were selling for 35 to 40 cents a dozen on the Chicago market. Live birds that could be fattened and fed up for increased tenderness were worth $1 to $2 a dozen.

Already voices were crying in the wilderness, warning that the Passenger Pigeon was not an inexhaustible resource. In 1878 or 1879 (the record is confused), the Cincinnati Zoological Society bought four pairs of live Passenger Pigeons near Petoskey, Michigan, and paid the (comparatively) exhorbitant price of $2.50 a pair. These were put on exhibition in the Zoo and were, it appears, the progenitors of the last, ultimate survivor of their race.

As I said before, I wish some trained reporter had nominated himself Historian to the Last Passenger Pigeon, for the printed records are sadly in conflict. Edward Howe Forbush, the notable ornithologist of "The Birds of Massachusetts," thought the sole survivor in the Cincinnati Zoo had come (as I read his rather ambiguous remarks), from the Whittaker flock in Milwaukee.

Ruthven Deane attributed the last bird to the Whitman flock in Chicago (*The Auk*, 1911, page 262)—and, incidentally, stated that she was "about fourteen years old" then (1911). All the Cincinnati Zoo sources I have seen indicate that Martha was 29 years old at the time of her death.

(On second thought, maybe it would have been better to have *two* trained reporters keeping the history of Martha—each one checking on the other!)

The moot point of Martha's age (29 years is a remarkably advanced age for a pigeon), probably depends on whether one believes she came from some late generation of the Whittaker-Whitman flocks, or whether one accepts the Stephan family version of her origin—for both Director Joseph Stephan and his father have repeatedly and positively asserted that Martha was a direct descendant of the Cincinnati Zoo's own birds, that she was hatched in the collection, and passed her whole life within the confines of the Zoo.

The conflicting evidence extends even to the time of her death—some accounts saying 1 o'clock in the morning, some 1 o'clock in the afternoon. It has even been said that Martha died on September 2 instead of September 1.

Unable to reconcile all these contradictory statements, I wrote to Director Stephan and by return post came a sheaf of longhand and typewritten notes that his father had compiled around the time of Martha's demise. They, I thought, would settle matters once and for all. Instead, they offered some new contradictions!

Once more I queried the amiable Director of the Cincinnati Zoo, and his reply (airmail special delivery), was as specific as anyone could wish. He had even, I noticed, put a new and boldly black ribbon on his typewriter. There could be no question of illegibility.

"Martha died," he wrote, "at 5:00 P.M. September 1, 1914. My father, Sol A. Stephan, Director of Animals, now 96 years old, and myself were with her at death, as she was very feeble and had to be assisted to eat.

"Martha was hatched at the Cincinnati Zoo with many others, but outlived her sisters and brothers. She was named after Martha Washington. We still have the aviary covered with the same wire, that caged all the Passenger Pigeons and also have a sign erected to indicate that. Of course these birds were outdoors 12 months a year, with protection from the strong winds.

"I as a boy would take the eggs that dropped out of nests and put them under tame pigeons to hatch in my pigeon loft. Sometimes when they were about to hatch I put them in a Passenger Pigeon nest to let them finish the incubation, and when hatched, they mothered them O.K.

"On Sundays we would rope off the cage to keep the public from throwing sand at her to make her walk around; during her last five or six months she was not able to fly up to her perch."

So much for the time and date of Martha's death. I know of no one better qualified than Director Stephan and his father to say exactly when it occurred.

The United States Weather Bureau tells me that September 1, 1914, was a partly cloudy day in Cincinnati, with no rain but a fairly high humidity of 74 per cent, and a temperature range of 72 to 89 degrees. A warm, rather muggy day, it would appear, typical of so many midwestern summer days. The problem of what to do with Martha's body —long since promised to the Smithsonian Institution—must have required an immediate answer. I had seen a statement somewhere (which

Dr. Friedman of the Smithsonian had been unable to confirm), that she was frozen in a block of ice for shipment to Washington.

Director Stephan was positive about that:

"I took her to the Cincinnati Ice Co. plant personally and supervised the placing of her body in a tank of water, suspended by her two legs, and froze her body into a 300-lb block of ice," he wrote me.

Martha reached the United States National Museum on the morning of September 4, and the experts—taxidermists and anatomists—immediately went to work on it. A full account of the anatomical work was subsequently published (with a ghastly plate of the skinned carcass), in *The Auk* (1915, page 29), by Dr. Robert Wilson Shufeldt, sometime Honorary Curator of the Smithsonian Institution and in 1914 an associate in zoology.

"I found," he wrote, "the bird to be an adult female in the moult, with a few pin feathers in sight, and some of the middle tail feathers, including the long, central ones, missing . . . It had the appearance of a specimen in good health, with healthy eyes, eye-lids, nostrils, and mouth-parts. The feet were of a deep, flesh-colored pink, clean and healthy, while the claws presented no evidences indicative of unusual age, though not a few of wear."

Eventually the anatomists and the taxidermists did their work and Martha was ready to be presented to posterity that would never see her kind again in flesh.

"This specimen is still on exhibition in the U. S. National Museum," Dr. Friedman wrote. "The bird is mounted perched on a branch of a tree which, in turn, is inserted in an old-fashioned mahogany stand. The specimen is shown in our synoptic series of North American birds with no special trimmings. There is no background and the bird is not in a case by itself. The case is one of those which has glass on both sides and consequently there are two labels, one on either side of the bird. These labels read as follows:

"*Ectopistes migratorius* (Linnaeus)
Passenger Pigeon.

Exterminated. Formerly very abundant throughout a large part of North America. This is the last known individual. It died in captivity in September, 1914.

"*Ectopistes migratorius* (Linnaeus)
Passenger Pigeon.

Last of its race. Died at Cincinnati Zoological Garden, September 1st, 1914.

Age 29 years.

Presented by the Cincinnati Zoological Garden to the National Museum.
Adult female, 236650."

Such are the few stray bits of information that may now be gleaned about Martha's life and death. Thirty years ago a historian could have garnered other, and more pertinent, facts. I wish he had—but I wish even more that the grandparents of the present generation had not thought the Passenger Pigeon was indestructable.

SHOREBIRD

SHOOTING OF

YESTERYEAR

Peter Matthiessen

The publicity generated by the turn-of-the-century crusade against the slaughter at southern wading-bird rookeries had a lasting impact on the American consciousness. The more widely ranging destruction of our shorebirds, on the other hand, remains unknown even to many active conservationists. Peter Matthiessen concentrates on a particular gentleman shooter in telling that disheartening story.

THE pond at Sagaponack, where I live, has its source in the small woodland stream which drains Poxabogue Pond and Little Poxabogue, further inland. From the west windows of my house, a fringe of trees parting the fields winds into view; here Sagg Pond, like a wide meadow river, curls down through miles of warm potato country to the sea. The Long Island farmland fills the landscape to the north and west and spreads toward the southward; Sagg Pond appears again, turned back upon itself by the hard white of the dunes, by the hard blue of the sea horizon. The pond bends like the shank of a great hook; it is now a mile across. But seasonally, in storm or flood, the pond is open to the sea. Then this lower reach is salt, a place of tidal creek and shallow flat which is today, as it has always been, a haunt of shorebirds.

On the fourth of July of 1870, a Boston gentleman, George H. Mackay, killed twenty-seven woodcock at "Poxybang Pond"; a few days later, thirty-nine "dowitch" were gently slain at Sagaponack. The woodcock still comes to Poxabogue and the dowitcher to Sagaponack, though the dowitcher—its odd name may derive from "Deutscher snipe," due to its popularity, in Revolutionary times, among the Hessians—is now protected legally from guns, a circumstance which Mr. Mackay, one of the rare naturalist-sportsmen in an epoch of mighty game hogs, would doubtless find astonishing. Mackay and his contem-

From *The Shorebirds of North America*. New York: Viking, 1967.

poraries pursued the shorebirds with such vigor that when he died, in 1928, the hosts that flew down the long seacoasts of his youth had been reduced to fugitive small bands.

On September 28 of 1964, after a day and night of onshore winds, a flock of sixty-eight golden plover pitched into the potato field between my house and Sagaponack Pond; in that small flock at Sagaponack there flew more golden plover than the total I had seen in twenty years. Yet Audubon once reported a flight of "millions" of golden plover near New Orleans, of which some 48,000 were killed in a single day: the golden plover is thought to have been even more numerous than the Eskimo curlew, whose multitudes have been compared to the great flights of the passenger pigeon. From colonial times, plover and curlew had been hunted in spring and fall, but they suffered no fatal diminishment until the last part of the nineteenth century when, with the fading of the wild pigeon, the market guns were turned upon shorebirds and waterfowl. Even the least sandpiper met a violent end when the larger species were in short supply, though its minuscule roast would scarcely make a mouthful, bones and all: in one account, ninety-seven of these "ox-eyes" were cut down with a single shot.

But the plover and curlew were the favorite birds, not only because of their great numbers and fine taste but because they were unsuspicious to a fault. The Eskimo curlew would circle back over the guns, calling out to its fallen companions, a habit it shared with the dunlin, dowitcher, and many others. That the dunlin was called the "simpleton" on Long Island indicates the low esteem in which its brain was held (the piping plover was known as the "feeble" and the willet as the "humility," but the plover's name is derived from its call, and that of the willet from a family trait of feeding in the "humble mud"), and the buff-breasted and solitary sandpipers were celebrated far and wide for stubborn innocence. (Dr. Elliott Coues, taking advantage of a rare convention of solitary sandpipers, once collected seven of this species, shooting one at a time, before the eighth and last, suspecting that something was amiss, took leave—"I will add in justice to his wits," wrote Dr. Coues, "in a great hurry.")

Under the circumstances, one wonders that any shorebirds survived into the present century. Not only were they trapped and shot, but great numbers of knots and other species were taken by "fire-lighting," a nocturnal practice much in favor on Long Island's Great South Bay and elsewhere, in which the resting flocks, blinded but undismayed by a bright beam, stood by patiently while market men stepped forth from punts and wrung their necks. Night hunting took such a toll of a then common source of public nourishment that Massachusetts in 1835 passed a law forbidding the take of "Plover, Curlew, Dough-bird, and

Chicken-bird" after dark: the Dough-bird was the Eskimo curlew, and the Chicken-bird was the ruddy turnstone.

A decade later, Rhode Island passed a law forbidding spring shooting of woodcock and snipe, but this admirable and precocious measure on behalf of the two species which least needed it was repealed in the face of public outrage, and for the next seventy years almost nothing was done to slow the destruction of the shorebirds, whose narrow migration paths, close-flocking habits, and chronic foolishness contributed heavily to their own decline.

By the turn of the century, George Mackay was growing concerned about the shorebirds, which were rapidly disappearing from his hunting circuit. Mackay's notes on the fall migrations of the Eskimo curlew and golden plover for the four years 1896–1899 are among the first warnings we have of the curlew's rapid disappearance, even though a "fute" at Montauk in 1891 was the last of this species ever seen on Long Island (four were reported at Montauk in September of 1932, but the sighting is not generally accepted), and in New England, after 1897, no more than three were seen again in a single flock. In that same year, Mackay inquired publicly: "Are we not approaching the beginning of the end?" though his private journal reveals that he was still blazing away at shorebirds of all descriptions and was out before dawn in vain pursuit of the very bird whose passing he so lamented. "Although hopeless," he writes, "I was driving over the western plover ground at daylight, hoping to find a few tired birds." In this period, "fire-lighted" knots still sold in Boston for ten cents a dozen.

Whether uneasy or discouraged at the meager sport, Mackay did little hunting after 1897, and later he was to lead campaigns against spring shooting. But in 1916, at a time when the golden plover was fast following the Eskimo curlew toward oblivion, Mackay and his party "succeeded in shooting" one forlorn specimen at Nantucket where, a half-century before, both curlew and plover had appeared in such waves as to "almost darken the sun." And he was still at it in October of 1921, flanked now by younger generations of Mackays. "We saw in all eight Black-breast plovers, young birds, and I shot four. On picking them up, one proved to be a young Golden plover (pale-belly). If I could have a little practice I feel I could come back to my old shooting form fairly well." One can't help but feel affection for this doughty old gentleman —he was then very close to eighty—who led in the public fight for the protection of the shorebirds without once questioning his private right to kill them.

George Mackay's last shorebird, a ruddy turnstone, was shot illegally in 1922; the species had come under the protection of the Federal Migratory Bird Treaty Act four years earlier. Within the decade, all shorebirds except the snipe and woodcock had been removed from the list of game birds. But the Eskimo curlew had already passed the point of no return (though it has made a miraculous reappearance every time it has been mourned and buried; two Eskimo curlews were reported at Galveston Island, Texas, as recently as 1963, and a solitary specimen, in September of the same year, was shot by a hunter in Barbados), and the Hudsonian godwit and buff-breasted sandpiper, the long-billed curlew and golden plover are still dangerously reduced. Probably these species will remain uncommon, for their breeding and wintering grounds in both Americas are ever more threatened by man, but they are no longer fluttering at the edge of the abyss. Even the stilt sandpiper, never abundant, was recently reported in Saskatchewan in a flight estimated at 4000.

The Eskimo curlew excepted, the Hudsonian godwit is the one North American shorebird whose future is precarious at present. In 1926 hope for the species had been all but abandoned. ("The passing of this bird must be a cause for regret among sportsmen and nature lovers alike. . . .") A decade later, the godwit had almost vanished. In recent years it has recuperated and is even common here and there in spring in the Mississippi Valley, but the flock of twenty-four that I watched (with Robert Clem) one misty August afternoon of 1963 on the salt flats of Monomoy Island, south of Cape Cod, represented a large percentage of the Hudsonian godwits that still occur on the coasts of the Atlantic in the fall: except for a solitary bird that came one Indian summer to Sagaponack, they were the only Hudsonian godwits I have ever seen.

The last entry of Mackay's *Shooting Journal*, for August 16 of 1922, concludes as follows:

At noon we picked up and went up to the house on Third Point, where we had dinner, Bunt having dug a bucket of clams. As usual we had a strong S.W. breeze to return with. The day was fine but very hot.

And we close the book with the warm breath of summer tide flats in our nostrils and a vague longing for those blue-and-golden days of vanished Augusts when the great bird companies that no man will see again disappeared southward into the ocean mists.

HAT BIRDS

IN THE

HAUT MONDE

Frank M. Chapman

The rookery shooting mentioned above was undertaken for the nuptial plumes of egrets and herons to be used for millinery purposes. But wading birds were not the only victims of high fashion, as the eminent ornithologist Frank M. Chapman discovered when, just over a century ago, he sallied forth on New York City's 14th Street to see just what women were wearing on their hats.

THE slaughter of birds for millinery uses had now reached a stage when several species were threatened with extinction in this country. Egrets, Terns and Gulls were being killed on their nesting grounds. Even our native song birds were not spared and Thrushes, Warblers, Vireos, Flycatchers and others were commonly used in hat ornamentation.

Few people knew one bird from another. The goods the milliners provided, if they were becoming and in the mode, were worn without question, and only a handful of ornithologists realized where we were heading.

Under the leadership of George Bird Grinnell, William Dutcher, J. A. Allen and George B. Sennett, a committee of the American Ornithologists' Union was formed to tell the public of the danger of this traffic, awaken sentiment in favor of conservation, and secure the passage and enforcement of laws designed adequately to protect our birds. . . .

The streets of New York City do not offer a productive field for the ornithologist but . . . I determined to secure some definite information concerning the number and kinds of birds that were then actually being worn. At that time Fourteenth Street was the most frequented shopping thoroughfare. There, notebook in hand, I recorded, when I

From *Autobiography of a Bird-Lover.* New York: D. Appleton-Century, 1933.

could identify them, the names of birds which, usually entire, were seen on the hats of passing women. In the light of existing conditions the result seems incredible. It is probable that few if any of the women whose headgear formed part of my record, knew that they were wearing the plumage of the birds of our gardens, orchards and forests. This fact alone is a measure of the surprising growth in our popular knowledge of birds which has occurred since that period. Even under the urge of fashion, unrestrained by law, where could one find to-day a woman who would consent to wear the bodies of familiar native birds on her hat? . . . As a matter of history I present here the list of birds identified and the number seen of each during two late afternoon walks.

Robin, four
Brown Thrasher, one
Bluebird, three
Blackburnian Warbler, one
Blackpoll Warbler, three
Wilson's Warbler, three
Scarlet Tanager, three
Tree Swallow, one
Bohemian Waxwing, one
Cedar Waxwing, twenty-three
Northern Shrike, one
Pine Grosbeak, one
Snow Bunting, fifteen
Tree Sparrow, two
White-throated Sparrow, one
Bobolink, one
Meadowlark, two
Baltimore Oriole, nine
Purple Grackle, five
Blue Jay, five

Swallow-tailed Flycatcher, one
Kingbird, one
Kingfisher, one
Pileated Woodpecker, one
Red-headed Woodpecker, two
Flicker, twenty-one
Saw-whet Owl, one
Mourning Dove, one
Prairie Hen, one
Ruffed Grouse, two
Bob-white, sixteen
California Valley Quail, two
Sanderling, five
Greater Yellowlegs, one
Green Heron, one
Virginia Rail, one
Laughing Gull, one
Common Tern, twenty-one
Black Tern, one
Grebe, seven

THE

GUY BRADLEY

STORY

Charles M. Brookfield

---

*Even today the attempt to enforce wildlife laws often meets local resistance,
and for early Audubon Society wardens working alone among the remote
wading-bird rookeries, confronting renegade shooters sometimes ended—as
it did with Guy Bradley—in violence.*

ACROSS the calm waters of Florida Bay a series of distant shots
cracked faintly in the still summer air. It was the eighth of July;
the year 1905. Young Guy Bradley, Audubon Warden of Monroe County,
reached for his .32 caliber revolver, gave his wife, Fronie, a hasty
kiss, the two small sons a pat on the head, jumped into his boat, and took
off toward the sound of shooting. Near Oyster Keys he could see a
schooner anchored. Bradley recognized the boat—Walter Smith's. This
was to be a dangerous business—the arrest of a tricky violator who had
already threatened to kill him.

As Bradley drew closer, a man aboard the schooner fired a shot in
the air. The warning was heeded by the rookery raiders ashore—two
men came off in a skiff, one carrying dead birds. But they were too
late. Before the schooner could get underway, Bradley's boat was along-
side.

"I want that boy—the one with the birds," called Bradley. "He's
under arrest."

"You ain't got no warrant. I'll be damned if you'll get him," answered
the man with the rifle who stood on the schooner's deck above Bradley.

Two shots rang out. The little .32 ball lodged in the schooner's mast
but the heavy Winchester rifle bullet entered the left side of Bradley's
neck, ranging downward through his body. The little boat bearing a

crumpled body slowly drifted with the gentle southeast breeze. A thin red stream trickled through the floor-boards and mixed with the bilge-water below. The schooner sailed away.

The chain of events leading up to this tragedy began years before, shortly after the Chicago fire, when Edwin Ruthven Bradley brought his wife, Lydia, and two sons to Florida.

Arriving in the state about 1870, the Bradleys were Florida pioneers. The eldest boy, Louis, was four, and little Guy still a baby. The Bradleys settled in the pine woods near Orlando, cleared the land and started a citrus grove, but Edwin who had been a post office employee in Chicago, had a hankering to be near salt water. They moved to Melbourne, Florida, then to Lantana. Old grandfather E. C. F. Bradley, a civil engineer who had laid out many of Chicago's streets, came south to avoid cold winters and to visit the family in Lantana.

Although Edwin's two boys, Louis and Guy, spent most of their time hunting and fishing and had little formal education, their father became for a time Dade County Superintendent of Schools. This position, in that day, could not have been too arduous, for though the county stretched along the coast from the St. Lucie River to Florida Bay, the population in 1880 was but 257 persons. No doubt Guy Bradley picked up some knowledge of surveying from his grandfather. Their mother taught both boys to play and read music. Louis played the "big fiddle" and Guy the "little fiddle." With others, they formed a string band that played for dances and parties at the big hotel in Palm Beach. Each young man received five dollars to play all night. Guy Bradley became quite a musician.

Development of Florida's east coast was well under way in the early 1890s when Edwin Bradley became assistant superintendent of the Florida Coast Line Canal and Transportation Company, then engaged in dredging the East Coast Canal. He met J. E. Ingraham and became agent for the Florida East Coast Land Company, later the Model Land Company. The Bradleys, lured by free land, moved again from church and school to the remote Cape Sable country. Edwin and the boys each "took up" one quarter mile of waterfront, as all the settlers had agreed, extending as far back from the shore as they cared to go. Settlers grew potatoes, tomatoes, and eggplants without fertilizer in the rich hammock land, and raised numbers of chickens. Produce was carried by sailboat to Key West and sold. Those who were less industrious lived by fishing and hunting egrets for their plumes.

By 1900 the settlement at Flamingo could boast a post office and a schoolhouse with one teacher. Edwin Bradley was postmaster and his son Louis sailed the mailboat to Key West. W. R. Burton opened a general store, the only one in Flamingo, and married Edwin Bradley's daughter, Margaret. Their descendents live in Miami today. One day a strange west coast schooner put in at Flamingo with two brothers named Vickers and their sister, Fronie, aboard. Guy Bradley fell in love with Fronie. They married and within a few years two sons, Ellis and Morrel, arrived to add to their happiness.

Commercialization and "living off the country" always takes toll of wildlife. It was not surprising that by 1900 our beautiful plume birds —American and snowy egrets—were almost extinct in Florida. The rate of slaughter was tremendous. In the nesting season of 1892 just one of the many "feather merchants" in Jacksonville shipped 130,000 bird "scalps" (skins with the feathers on) to New York for the millinery trade! The big profits from the sale of egret scalps went to the milliners. Plume hunters got only $1.25 per scalp at Brickell's store on the Miami River. Even so, if a thousand parent birds were shot at a rookery, the heartless effort was well repaid. Several thousand young birds starving to death in the nests meant little where such pay was involved. Whites and Indians raided and killed with no thought of the future. Since the parent birds have plumes only in the nesting season, killing for plumes brought death to the season's young. Florida had no effective law to prevent the slaughter.

A small group of earnest conservationists began fighting this destruction. In May of 1901, William Dutcher, first president of the National Committee of Audubon Societies and Chairman of the Committee on Bird Protection of the American Ornithologists' Union, came to Tallahassee, secured the introduction of a model non-game bird bill and advocated its passage before the Florida State Legislature. The bill was enacted into law and is still the basis for bird protection in Florida.

In those days there was no Florida Game and Fresh Water Fish Commission. The Governor appointed one "game warden" for each county on recommendation of the county commissioners. But Monroe County included vast stretches of wilderness—mangrove and everglades—on the mainland. Key West, the only town and the county seat, was an island. One warden could not be very effective.

The National Association of Audubon Societies, as the National Audubon Society was then called, at its own expense, employed four men to guard the remaining egret rookeries in Florida. One of these first Audubon wardens was Guy M. Bradley, and he was faithful and courageous at his job. When the ornithologist, Frank M. Chapman, returned from a trip to a rookery with Guy Bradley in 1904, the New York *Sun* quoted Chapman as follows: "That man Bradley is going to be killed sometime. He has been shot at more than once, and some day they are going to get him."

Sanford L. Cluett, vice president of Cluett, Peabody and Company, had known Guy Bradley since 1888 in Palm Beach. In 1905 Mr. Cluett visited Flamingo and talked with his friend. Years later he wrote: "I spent several days there, and Guy told me of his connection with the

Audubon Society—and further told me that he was going to arrest a poacher who was a dangerous character. This matter worried him much, and he showed me his nickel-plated, I believe, .32 caliber pistol which he carried. I told him I thought it was altogether inadequate. We said good-bye on my leaving there—in fact, he came out in his rowboat with his little boy to say farewell."

Exactly what happened on that July day in 1905 will never be known. After the shooting, Walter Smith and his sons sailed to Key West. Guy's boat drifted into Sawfish Hole, near East Cape Sable. Here his body was found by the Roberts boys who were attracted to the spot by a flock of vultures wheeling in the air overhead.

Smith, in default of $5000 bond, was held in jail in Key West pending action of the grand jury. The National Association of Audubon Societies retained State Senator W. Hunt Harris of Key West and Col. J. T. Saunders of Miami to assist the prosecution. Two weeks later the newspapers carried headlines: *Indignant Neighbors Burn Smith's House—Flamingo People Incensed Over Killing of Guy Bradley*. With Key West dateline, the story went on: "The Negro and his wife, who were occupying Smith's house since he came to give himself up, were ordered to move out, and as soon as they were out the torch was applied and everything that would burn was destroyed. This act shows that the residents of Flamingo are indignant over the killing of Guy Bradley and that it would be unwise for Smith to return there, if he is released."

And Smith was released—five months later. The prosecution failed, despite the additional legal talent, and the testimony of S. L. (Uncle Steve) Roberts. "Uncle Steve" quoted Smith as admitting that in April Bradley had arrested Smith for shooting in the rookery, that Smith had a Winchester rifle, and had told him that if Bradley ever attempted to arrest him again, he would certainly kill the warden. The grand jury at Key West "deemed the evidence of the State insufficient to bring the accused to trial and failed to present a true bill." For Smith, this was the same as an acquittal.

But Guy Bradley did not give his life in vain. His death focused national attention on bird protection. Florida conservationists were outraged. President William Dutcher spoke for the National Association of Audubon Societies: "Every movement must have martyrs, and Guy Bradley is the first martyr to bird protection. A home is broken up, children left fatherless, their mother widowed, a faithful and devoted warden cut off in the movement. Heretofore the price had been the life of birds. Now human blood has been added." The National Association of Audubon Societies raised funds and bought a house in Key West for Guy's widow, Fronie, and the children.

The killing of Bradley, followed by the brutal murder of Audubon Warden McLeod by bird plume hunters near Charlotte Harbor, South

Carolina, in 1908, caused a shift in the conservation battlefront. The Audubon Society struck at the very heart of the traffic in bird "scalps" —the millinery trade in New York. The "Audubon Plumage Bill" was introduced in the Legislature at Albany. T. Gilbert Pearson, President of the Society, successfully spearheaded the fight for passage of this bill to outlaw the commercial use of wild bird feathers in New York State. Signed by Governor Charles Evans Hughes in 1910, the bill was enacted into law.

It is a great source of satisfaction that the Cape Sable country, scene of Guy Bradley's efforts and death and home of the wild birds he died to save, is preserved forever within the boundaries of the Everglades National Park. Ill-considered drainage canals ruined the land for farming by letting spring tides flood it with salt water. Hurricanes destroyed most of the original buildings, but the village lingered on for a time as a group of fishermen's shanties on stilts.

Out on the lonely sand beach of East Cape Sable stands a gravestone inscribed:

GUY M. BRADLEY

1870–1905

Faithful Unto Death

As Game Warden of Monroe County
He Gave His Life for the Cause
to Which He Was Pledged.

HAWK MOUNTAIN:

A

RAPTOR SHOOTER'S

PARADISE

Michael Harwood

Every autumn thousands of people—ranging from the merely curious to confirmed hawk watchers—trek to the lookouts of Pennsylvania's famous Hawk Mountain, hoping to catch a good flight of raptors moving down the Appalachian ridges. A more tranquil mountaintop cannot be imagined. In the 1920s and early '30s, however, the throngs on these same lookouts were engaged in an altogether different—and louder—sort of fun. The accomplished contemporary environmental writer Michael Harwood interviewed several local old-timers who had themselves participated in the early hawk-shooting sprees.

O F an evening, early in the 20's, the men would gather in the store beside the Little Schuylkill and the railroad. "That time," remembers Charles Mohl, "there was always 15, 16 fellas there. We didn't have no place to sit down most of the time, unless they had a barl or a nail keg. . . ." They sat around, talking about the deer hunting on the mountain, or the grouse shooting. . . .

When the gathering at the store took place on a Saturday night in the fall, and the weather was turning cold, promising a north wind for the next day, there might well be talk of going hawk shooting. Hunting was illegal in Pennsylvania on a Sunday—except when you were hunting "vermin"—and hawks were treated as vermin not only in practice but in law. So in the morning, or perhaps after the noon meal, they got in their cars or hiked up the dreadful dirt road across the mountain until they reached a steep and rocky trail that led up to the quarry. The quarry was now defunct, and had been since the 1890's—the sand, it is said, had to be milled too much and it had too much iron in it, and then

From *The View from Hawk Mountain*. New York: Charles Scribner's Sons, 1973.

the sandhouse burned down. From the quarry, they climbed out onto the North Lookout, which they called the Point, to see which way the hawks were flying. If the wind was in the northwest, the birds might be coming right overhead, and the men would stay put and start shooting. There was no need for them to hide behind the boulders. The hawks, Charles Mohl says, "came right up to you. Sometimes you thought they'd crawl in your barl." If the wind had backed around toward the east or south overnight, the hawks might be leaving the ridge before they reached the Point and flying across the Kettle toward the other outcroppings, and then the gunners worked their way down there, sometimes all the way to the road. On a good, strong north wind, especially in October, the sharpshins might be streaming along the north face of the mountain, hugging the treetops, and the Slide would be the place to stand. The quarrymen had cleared the Slide for some distance on either side of the tracks, to protect them from falling trees, and the scrub oak and rhododendron and laurel had not yet grown up very far. You'd go down there "a piece way," and pick off the hawks as they cleared the trees in front of you.

It was great fun. "It was nothing to go up there with two or three boxes of shells and get rid of them. The hawks usually came in flocks. Fellow lived over here used to say they leave them out in bagsful, and when a flock came he says, 'Here come another bagful.' "

The Drehersville shooters tried to keep the place pretty much to themselves. They didn't do much talking about it, certainly not out of town. But the secrecy didn't last. As Charles Mohl remembers it, one Sunday afternoon, a gang was collecting to go up the mountain, and a man from Schuylkillhaven, who knew the whole crowd, saw them standing around with their guns.

"He says, 'Where you going, boys?' We told him hawk shooting. 'Yes,' he says, 'hawk shooting.' Someone says, 'Does you want some?' 'Yes, I'll take all you get.' He didn't think we'd shoot but one, and he could have it mounted. 'All right.' And that was all that was said, and we went up, and it just happened to be a good day, and we brought these hawks along down. We got a box—a wooden box; that time, everything came in barls or wooden boxes—and this box was, I'd say, between three and four feet long, two feet high, and about two feet wide, as close as I can remember. And we threw these hawks in there, and it was all but full. We sent it to him, and that was where the blunder came in. He had a shoe factory out there, and we sent it collect, by express. And the man from the express company brought it in, and who was there but a shoe manufacturer from Pottsville. He seen this, and he was a hunter, and the next thing you knew, we had more company up there than you can place a stick at. *Everybody* was there. The game warden wanted to go up. He wasn't no shooter; he couldn't shoot. He gave his shells to everybody and his gun to anybody that didn't have none. He says, 'Shoot, and here are the shells.' And we shot a bunch of hawks, and so he got them together and hung them on a string in a ring, and he stood in the middle of them. And they took a picture of him. There was a bunch— I'd say was 25, 30, maybe 50 hawks, and they had those pictures in the Philadelphia *Record* and they had them in I don't know what-all papers. That brought more in, and more. It was nice up there, and people just came from all over and everywhere—and spoiled the whole works."

The operation became big-time, with shooting on the weekdays as well as on the weekends. Some of the hunters—including the shoeman from Pottsville and his various brothers and cousins—would carry up whole cases of shells and store them out of the weather under rocks, so that they didn't have to tote up ammunition every trip. A local sport-ing-goods store took a truck up there on weekends, parked on the road, and opened for business. The shoemen brought along extra guns, loaded them, and as the day's shooting began, they would tell their companions, "Ah, if they come fast, boys, don't be afraid to pick up one of these and keep firing." The shooting could be so good that the guns overheated, and if you didn't accept the shoemen's invitation, or bring along an extra gun or two of your own, you might use a specially made handle for the barrel of your gun, to protect your forward hand from the heat of the barrel—that is, said lean, old Charles Mohl drily, rap-ping his cane on the arms of his metal lawn chair, if you didn't respect your gun. "Some people don't care for their guns. They just keep on firing. If you have any respect for your gun, you leave some hawks go through, sometimes."

"It wasn't even safe no more to go up," he said. "When this thing was advertised, it wasn't nothing to be 50 hunters up there." Some days there were 300 or 400 shooters blazing away at one time. At least one man I know—Charles Thomas, who now runs an antique store in nearby Hamburg—and surely more men than he, could personally ac-count for more than 100 hawks some days. . . . When he looked down into the scrub below the shooting stand on a good day, Charley Thomas says, the down feathers from the bellies of the shot hawks "would hang in the branches, and I swear to Christ, it looked like a cotton tree. And *stink!*—"

HAWK MOUNTAIN

BECOMES A

SANCTUARY

Maurice Broun

Word of the annual hawk slaughter reached conservationists, and, in 1934,
under the guiding spirit of Rosalie Edge, nearly 1,400 acres of mountaintop
and forest were purchased for $2.50 an acre. But would the new Hawk
Mountain Sanctuary become a sanctuary in fact? Mrs. Edge hired a young
ornithologist named Maurice Broun, who, with his wife Irma, was des-
tined to spend over three decades on the mountain. Here Broun recalls that
first dicey autumn, when about the only weapons he had to use against the
shooters were bluff and bad weather.

DREHERSVILLE [we found] was a cluster of tidy houses surrounding
a tiny church. Hardly a soul was in sight. Hushed tranquility,
deep repose, the feeling that all was well with the world pervaded the
little village. This was not at all what we had anticipated; this was alien
to what we had read about: blood and thunder, and swarms of gun-
toting men.

I decided that we had better run into Schuylkill Haven, some twelve
miles toward Pottsville, to call on the real estate agent. We had hoped to
learn from him about the mountain. We also needed quantities of "no
trespassing" posters.

My first act in Schuylkill Haven was to phone four local newspapers,
requesting each to carry a notice, for three successive days, announcing
the new status of the mountain property, that it was henceforth an
inviolate wildlife sanctuary, and that the trespassing laws would be
enforced. Then we called on Gordon Reed, the agent for the property.
Oh, yes, he knew all about the mountain and all about the hawk-shoots;
and he succeeded in filling us with gloom. I told him that I was about to
put up "no trespassing" posters along the road, especially at the beginning of the trail that led through the woods to the shooting stands.

From *Hawks Aloft*. New York: Dodd, Mead & Company, 1948.

When we parted, Mr. Reed suggested, "After you get your posters up, take my advice and *scram!*"

Early morning found me putting up posters along the rocky road. Where did the bounds of the property run through the woods? Not even the neighboring owners could tell exactly. Five years later a costly survey revealed to us the extent of the 1398 acres. For the time being, it was necessary to post both sides of a stretch of road one and a half miles; for the road, a public thoroughfare, bisected the Sanctuary. It was dreadfully hot. I was surprised that no hunters had come. I did not know that it was too early in the season, nor did I realize that the hawk-hunters knew just when to flock the mountain.

By mid-afternoon the lonely road flaunted posters every few yards. A local game warden, apparently startled by my newspaper notices which had just been printed, came to find out what it was all about. The warden tried to impress me with the utter futility of my job. "Wait till the coalminers from Tamaqua come along; then you'll see," he warned me. While we argued, two carloads of hunters drove up—the vanguard. There was much guttural, explosive language from the visitors. But they left the mountain, bewildered, to say the least. In the days to follow I was to meet many such men, many of whom I tried to reason with as to why hawks should not be killed indiscriminately. Generally, these men were irritated, unwilling to listen. The game warden, a man named Jones, concluded his visit with the statement that I had the hardest job on my hands that I'd ever have in my life. "You can't stop those guys from shooting hawks up here," he said, despite the fact that I had already done so, before his eyes!

It suddenly came to me that, after all, in spite of our right, our duty to stop the hawk-shooting, we were, from the standpoint of the hunters, meddlesome outsiders, and as such we were bound to arouse indignation. Of course, it did not matter to the hunters that most of the hawks also came down from New England and New York. Did they ever give a thought to the rights of others?

Before the close of the day I prepared a thousand word statement— "A New Deal for Hawks"—defending the action of the Emergency Conservation Committee in leasing the mountaintop to prevent the killing of hawks. It hammered out the theme of unjust persecution and the economic importance of the hawks. Every trip up and down the mountain was agony to tires, but I sent the article off the same evening to three local newspapers, whose combined circulation exceeded 200,000. The article promptly appeared in print, and was copied in other newspapers, as far away as Scranton.

Daybreak of our third day on the mountain found me patrolling the road. I was anxious to see some hawks, but was utterly ignorant of the hawk-flights and their *modus operandi.* And, naïvely, I expected to see hunters at that ridiculous hour. During the night someone had ripped off most of the "no trespassing" posters.

As I patrolled the road that day, replacing posters, I was impressed with the countless numbers of old cartridge shells scattered along a quarter-mile stretch of road above the present entrance to the sanctuary. In the early afternoon I was thrilled to see my first flight of hawks, some fifty birds, including three bald eagles, three peregrine falcons, a few broad-wings and sharp-shins, all passing fairly low over the road.

During the day three more cars came up, with seven inquiring faces, and shotguns ready for business. But they departed promptly. One of the men made a slurring remark about the "New York chiselers going to hog all the shooting."

The following morning I found that every single one of my sixty-odd posters along the road had been removed. It began to rain, for which I rejoiced, since no one was likely to venture up the mountain to make trouble. I drove into Hamburg, the nearest large town, to obtain more posters, and to make contact with game wardens and the State Police. I thought, naïvely, that I could obtain official protection on weekends. I went over to the police barracks and learned that the police had their hands full with strikes in the local industries.

The weekend was upon us. I drove up the mountain after breakfast and in a drizzling rain I managed to nail up an entirely new set of posters. The weather cleared in the early afternoon. A few hawks passed low over the road. Only two cars appeared, each emptying gunners—five in one car. These men asked if they could walk to the pinnacle, and I allowed them to do so, without their guns. Returning, an old man in the group had this to offer: "A fellow doesn't want a gun up there; he should bring a pair of field glasses and a camera." These were the first heartening words I had heard on the mountain since our arrival.

Sunday brought raw, nasty weather, which suited me immensely. At 5 A.M. I was at my post of duty on the mountain road, expecting hunters and the promised trouble. Nothing happened, except the weather, and obligingly it poured all through the day.

Looking back on those early, disquieting experiences, I marvel at our great good luck with the weather. Providentially, torrents of rain fell on three successive weekends, and the anticipated hordes of hawk-killers did not materialize. The game wardens had warned me, however, that early October would bring plenty of hawks and plenty of trouble in the form of toughs from the coal region.

Mrs. Edge and her son Peter came out to the mountain in the middle of the second week to see how everything had been going. The situation was well in hand, and we had had no trouble—not yet—but it behooved us to engage a deputy sheriff, I advised Mrs. Edge. Obviously we must secure the services of someone who was authorized to make arrests, if necessary. I had already begun to cast around for the right man and, through the help of a sympathetic notary in a nearby town, I hoped to engage Bob Kramer, if Mrs. Edge approved. She did. The cost of maintaining Kramer for ten weeks was another worry for Mrs. Edge, but she did not hesitate. Bob Kramer, of nearby Auburn, a sturdy man of forty-two, good-humored and dependable, possessed an important weapon which I lacked: the Pennsylvania Dutch tongue. He had been engaged in police work for years. Kramer would have agreed to work for us on weekends only, but we took him on daily, beginning the end of September. I also engaged a surveyor, who successfully determined our important west boundary, the one nearest the hunters of Drehersville.

Meanwhile I continued my vigil, day after day, at the entrance to the sanctuary, where few hawks are seen unless the wind is in a southerly quarter. All sorts of men with high-powered rifles and shotguns came to indulge in the old "sport," only to learn that on *this* mountain it was a thing of the past. A few hunters came from New Jersey, and two from Delaware. My tongue wagged incessantly those first few weeks. It was no fun trying to convince those men of the folly of shooting hawks. Many were surly, and some went off with pent-up truculence. My only weapons that entire season was a ready tongue and a bold front—under which I sometimes quailed! But Kramer had a gun which was respected.

The evening of the seventeenth two young men said they had been gunning a few miles up the ridge, during the afternoon. They asked me whether or not I had seen the big hawk flight. No, I had not. Then I learned that they had counted almost two thousand hawks passing high over the ridge that afternoon; a broad-wing flight, I gathered. I was chagrined that I had missed the spectacle. Not until October 7th did I make daily visits to the mountain summit to observe the wonderful hawk-flights, while Kramer patrolled the road.

The possibility of an "invasion" of hunters now became very real. Kramer's daily presence had deterred the local hotheads from forcing their way, but I was advised that it might be necessary for me to stand guard at the old shooting-stands on the crest of the mountain. From there it was possible to observe the various approaches to the summit, through the woods from the north or from the west.

One day I learned almost with disbelief that a certain obstreperous character in Drehersville, who worked cheek by jowl with the officials of the numerous hunting clubs, had been obtaining sworn affidavits from many of the local farmers that the hawks often came down and carried off young pigs! This same man killed a red-tailed hawk and, to taunt us, he hung the bird, with wings spread, from the girder of the little bridge over which we passed twice daily. There the bird hung for about ten days. I took a picture of it which helped us in our money-raising campaign.

Now a great hullabaloo was raised in gunning circles throughout two counties against the out-of-state "chiselers." The farmers in the vicinity made the loudest squawk. They not only resented us and our assumed arrogance in taking over "their" mountain, they resented the name "Hawk Mountain" and claimed that there never had been such a place. Local newspapers belabored us and carried the usual stale message that the hawks were killing off game. A great to-do was made by the Pottsville merchant "sportsman" who used to come up the mountain on weekends, his truck loaded with cartridges to sell. We learned that the local sportsmen's clubs, representing 15,000 hunters, had engaged a lawyer to search all land titles and find loopholes which might break Mrs. Edge's lease, and to buy the mountain, if possible. The hunters were holding frequent meetings to decide what to do.

A few days later, the agitated hawk-shooters, though still contemplating the purchase of "Hawk Mountain," leased a considerable tract of land near Port Clinton. I saw their advertisement in a newspaper, urging gunners to kill hawks in this new place, about four miles down the ridge, and offering gunners "a new line of shells, at $.60 a case." Kramer investigated the Port Clinton hawk-shoots. These could be serious on days when the wind was easterly, but at no time was the slaughter comparable to that which had occurred formerly on our mountain. The place was also much more difficult of access.

Most of the hunters that I encountered had been killing hawks on this mountain for many years. Most of them were obdurate in their opinion of hawks in general and, they insisted, all hawks should be exterminated. It was useless to argue that the hawks do not feed while migrating, and that the good habits of the birds of prey involved mainly rodents. One farmer, in spite of his carping, allowed his large flock of white leghorns to roam the fields at the foot of the mountain. Why, I asked the gunners, were there so many grouse drumming in these upland woods? Here, at the greatest concentration point for hawks in the entire country, the ruffed grouse abounded; one day I had counted thirty-three of the birds in different parts of the Sanctuary. Rabbits, quail and pheasants were plentiful in the excellent cover of the old fields in the vicinity of Drehersville. But perhaps I was "seeing things," for the hawks kill off the game!

In early October much of the opposition had quieted, but it looked like the calm before the storm, and throughout the month Kramer and I anticipated trouble daily. With the fourth week approaching, a group of local hunters was planning to mob Kramer and me and force their way to the summit.

Late Friday afternoon two husky young men, built like fullbacks, appeared without guns at the Sanctuary. I was pleasantly surprised to learn that they had been recruited by Richard Pough to help us protect the place for a week or so. Pough, one of the "discoverers" of the hawk-shoots, had been in constant touch with Mrs. Edge. Knowing only too well what we might be up against with the lawless elements among the hawk-shooters, Pough generously arranged to have Charlie French and Dudley Wagar, both of Philadelphia, help us.

The following day it poured again—the fourth soggy Saturday! The four of us, Kramer, the newcomers and I spent a few hours on the mountain road, nevertheless, hunched in our cars. We even turned away a few hunters who had come from Reading.

Sunday, October 7th brought beautiful weather and ideal hawking conditions. Kramer and Wagar took the road, while French and I posted ourselves at the summit rocks. It was a day of many surprises, and some drama—but not the drama we had expected. We had plenty of company, some of it very talented. Ten members of the Delaware Valley Ornithological Club, of Philadelphia, including Richard Pough, Samuel Scoville, Jr., the writer, Julian K. Potter, the ornithologist, and Jacob B. Abbott, the artist, were among the observers at the Lookout that day. The hawk flight was disappointing—only a hundred birds of thirteen species. But to me it was tremendously exciting to see so many kinds of hawks. A special feature was an adult golden eagle. The great bird came obligingly close, an eye-opener to the ornithological gathering—and the first of many golden eagles that were to lure bird watchers from all over the country.

Early in the afternoon we heard some shooting on the ridgetop, about a half mile directly behind us. Charlie French and I and one of the D.V.O.C. men took off through the woods and presently reached the west boundary of the Sanctuary. There, on the edge of our line, marked by "no trespassing" posters, were ten men, two of them perched high in a tree, blazing away at occasional hawks passing just out of shotgun range. The men were just off the Sanctuary property. There was nothing I could do, except perhaps to wait until they killed a protected species (ten ospreys and a bald eagle were the only "protected" birds that passed), and then I would prosecute the killer. So we leaned against a tree and waited, silently. The shooting stopped, the men were maddened that we just stood there and stared at them. Each passing minute increased the tension till one of the men snapped, "Well, whatcha goin' to do about it?" I replied, "Just stay here and see what you fellows might do." The fellow lowered his gun, came up to me menacingly and said, "I'll knock your—block off." For a moment it looked like a fight—and it might have been bad business, three unarmed men against ten with guns and hot tempers—but the fellow suddenly stopped and spluttered, "You damn hawk-lovers; you're just a bunch of barbarians."

Returning to the Lookout, I found more visitors. A "mob" had indeed come! That day seventy-four men, women and children climbed to the Lookout to enjoy the beautiful scenery and the birds. It was an inspiring sight, and it augured well for the successful outcome of our "new deal for the hawks." At the entrance, Kramer had turned away thirty-two gunners, including a few women. Ten times that number of gunners might have been on hand that day had we not spent the previous weeks impressing the hunting elements that we meant business on the mountain. Pleasant weekends thereafter brought increasing numbers of bird-students and protectionists to enjoy the hawking.

Hawk-hunters, some of them hard-bitten fellows who looked as though they would as soon shoot a mother-in-law as a hawk, continued to come late into November—a month *after* the opening of the small game season—so deep-rooted was the urge to follow this perverse and cruel "sport." But in spite of all the threats and warnings and the hubbub of the shotgun squads, we had a singularly peaceful time of it along the old mountain road. At the summit, in the few weeks that it was possible to observe the hawk-flights, we had the satisfaction of seeing more than ten thousand hawks pass safely; not a single bird was killed.

THE

RESURRECTION

OF THE

WILD TURKEY

Ted Williams

All of us appreciate finding an honest-to-god success *story in the on-going —and generally depressing—saga of wildlife conservation. Ted Williams here reports on the remarkable man-assisted recovery of the wild turkey, the king of North American game birds.*

E VERY now and then we do something right, you know," announced my friend Carl Prescott, who supervises fish and wild-life management for the Commonwealth of Massachusetts and who sometimes gets a trifle annoyed with environmental writers. I scratched my head, chewed my pen, scowled as if in deep thought, then asked him if it was the new linoleum. But I knew what it was. It was wild turkey restoration.

In Massachusetts and dozens of other states this is some of the good news that game managers say gets skipped over. There are, of course, other successes—Atlantic salmon restoration and bald eagle hacking programs—but these are more dramatic, and a lot gets written about them. People need to pay attention to wild turkey restoration because it casts so much other game and fish department activity into proper per-spective—the put-and-take stocking of cock pheasants, for instance. It shows what can be done. It's a prime example of wildlife management gone right.

There are only two species of turkey: *Meleagris gallopavo* of North America, domesticated by Indians about two thousand years ago, and the smaller, more colorful *Meleagris ocellata* of southern Mexico and Central America. Other species, now extinct, lived on both New World

From *Audubon*, January, 1984.

continents, but apparently turkeys have never occurred naturally anywhere else.

By 1930 things looked mighty bleak for wild turkeys. All five subspecies of *gallopavo*—the Florida and eastern and, in the West, the whiter,
shorter-legged Merriam's, Rio Grande, and Mexican—were at an all-
time low. The total population, confined to twenty-one states, was
probably somewhere in the neighborhood of 20,000. Habitat destruction—the razing of old forests—is commonly believed to be the cause of
the wild turkey's demise. But this catchall theory for wildlife decline
seems a bit too pat in this situation, and it has recently come under fire
by some pretty knowledgeable authorities. Among them is veteran turkey biologist Lovett Williams, who makes the following observation in
his new publication, THE BOOK OF THE WILD TURKEY:

"The blame for the turkey's decline during the 1800s has usually been
placed on forest fires, deforestation, and agriculture. It is true that a
large part of the turkey's habitat in the northeastern United States became unsuitable, but that happened after local turkey populations had
already been eliminated. In early America, the gun came before the ax,
and excessive exploitation depleted turkey populations well in advance
of the more material signs of civilization, just as it did in the cases of the
bison and the panther. The early activities of human settlement, including lumbering, family farming, pasture clearing, naval stores, and
woods burning, practiced in the proportions to be expected in the 1800s,
could only have improved much of the eastern hardwood forest as turkey habitat. It is now a moot point because overhunting was soon followed by the pressures of urban human occupation and the forest of
change that went with it. I will always believe, however, that the wild
turkey could have survived that in good shape if it had not been
overhunted."

The habitat-destruction theory is also suspect in that the scrub resulting from forest removal turns out to be not-bad turkey habitat. Turkeys
weren't supposed to be able to tolerate such conditions, but since restoration has been under way they have defied the experts. "The birds
have been more adaptable than we thought," declares John Lewis, wildlife research supervisor of the Missouri Department of Conservation.
Missouri is one of the states that has led the way in turkey restoration
and (along with Florida) actually finished the job. "We moved birds up
to the [sparsely forested] northern part of Missouri in the early 1960s,
and they've done very well there. We felt that turkeys needed large
blocks of fairly extensive timber, but this is not the case. They're doing
much better in areas with less timber than we ever thought possible."

In addition to overhunting, alien diseases imported with European
poultry may have had a lot to do with the wild turkey's decline. This

has recently been suggested by blackhead-infected birds found dead in areas where farmers had been spreading poultry manure on the fields.

But if some of the reasons for the wild turkey's decline are a bit obscure, all the reasons for its return are immediately obvious. Granted, there has been some good luck, as when land-use patterns resulted in pole timber and abandoned farmland growing up into prime turkey woods. Mostly, though, there has been good management.

America's wild turkey population has increased 10,000 percent in the last half-century—from 20,000 to 2 million. And today the birds are found in every state except Alaska—including Hawaii, California, Nevada, Idaho, Oregon, Washington, the Dakotas, and Minnesota, states where there is no record of their occurring previously. There are now an estimated 1.5 million turkey hunters in the United States, and turkey hunting is second in popularity only to deer hunting.

The good management didn't come easily. It had to be learned through years of trial and error, and it had to bubble up through a smothering scum of politics.

Rare is the article written about the wild turkey or bald eagle that fails to mention up front that Ben Franklin recommended the wild turkey for the national symbol. This is false. He recommended the *barnyard* turkey, and he did so not because it was a native American or because, as he wrote, the bald eagle was "a Bird of bad moral Character," "very lousy," and "a rank coward." He did so because barnyard turkeys were then, as now, ugly, dirty and stupid, and because he was a wag. But in addition to being ugly, dirty, and stupid, barnyard turkeys also do not respond to confinement by bashing themselves to death against wire, and it was this attribute that endeared them to the politicians.

It was obvious even to the politicians that a barnyard turkey could not tough it out in the real world long enough to be shot by a hunter. But the managers reasoned that if they could breed a little of its manageability into the wild turkey, they could mass-produce the birds in game farms and stock them as cannon fodder—much like they already did with ring-necked pheasants—or for restoration.

They tried it, and it didn't work. The trouble was that the birds needed all their wildness for survival in the wild, and even a trace of domestic blood usually doomed them. They survived just long enough to distribute their various diseases and infirm genes among the wild population, dragging it down, too.

In Pennsylvania, the most politicized of all turkey states, band returns on game-farm stock indicated an overall survival rate of 1.1 percent during the first six months following release. For winter releases, long-term band recoveries were nine times greater for wild stock than for game-farm stock. For summer releases, long-term returns for wild stock were fifteen times greater.

Similar results were obtained in West Virginia. From 1957 through 1959 a private hunting club in the southeastern part of the state released more than two hundred game-farm birds. Beginning in 1957 the area's annual hunting kill, which had averaged about twelve, started to fall. By 1960 it was averaging about two.

A survey by the National Wild Turkey Federation revealed that of 354 restoration attempts by twenty-three states using 350,000 game-farm turkeys there have been 331 total failures, i.e., wipeouts. This finding was published in 1978, but as early as 1944 wildlife biologist A. Starker Leopold had figured out that nature and game farms selected turkeys for precisely opposite reasons, and that survival in one precluded survival in the other. By 1959 this was so obvious that New York abandoned turkey farming in favor of trapping and transferring wild birds. In February that year, the turkey federation hosted its first National Wild Turkey Symposium in Memphis. One of the speakers, Leonard Foote of the Wildlife Management Institute, vented his spleen as follows: "Sickels . . . Hardy, Gilpin, and others presented crystal-clear evidence of the futility of playing with game-farm stock when restoration is the objective. Why some states continue, even for the sake of experimentation, is almost beyond my comprehension."

But continue they did. Though the biologists had long known it was worse than a waste of money, the politicians and the management bosses—who, together, called the shots—didn't want to risk offending the hunting-license buyers. Pennsylvania used to defend its put-and-take turkey stocking on the grounds that it was done only where *wild* turkeys weren't, and that the game-farm stock was 95 percent wild. But the game-farm turkeys wandered vast distances (preferring to travel by road and cleared right-of-way), and the five percent of barnyard blood— like the five percent of drowned rat marinating in a keg of 95 percent-pure wine—rendered everything worthless.

The stocked turkeys were obscene pantomimes of the original items. One researcher determined that after two months in the wild some birds still allowed humans to approach to within six feet before showing alarm. At last, pressure from the great outside world of modern wildlife management became so intense that most state-sponsored stocking of game-farm turkeys ceased. In 1980 the revolution even spread to Pennsylvania, where the Game Commission, in a move that indicated it had absorbed at least some of the lesson, voted to convert its turkey factory to a pheasant factory.

Maryland, for the express purpose of humoring one well-connected individual, attempted in 1981 to establish a population of game-farm stock in the central part of the state, and achieved spectacular failure.

Doubtless, some politician somewhere again will coerce or seduce a state into releasing game-farm turkeys, but for all intents and purposes it is finally over.

What is not over, however, is *private* release of game-farm turkeys. This is a problem in a lot of states, especially those that haven't officially outlawed it. Any turkey hunter or turkey fancier who wants to have "wild turkeys" in his back forty can flip through any poultry magazine and order eggs, chicks, or poults. But *real* wild turkeys are state property and can't be bought or sold, a fact which keeps the mail-order business booming. Instead of containing five percent barnyard blood—hopeless tainting, as aptly demonstrated by the states—the mail-order birds may contain 50 percent. Some are actually white. The written word cannot convey the absurdity of their behavior. They strut along the yellow stripes on highways, eat tomatoes from backyard gardens, defecate copiously on cartops and housetops, attack children and motorcycles. From my contact at the Minnesota Division of Fish and Wildlife word arrived that a flock of more than a hundred privately stocked game-farm turkeys had just burned down a barn by shorting out the electric wires upon which it roosted each night. The public observes such behavior and, as one New Jersey biologist put it, asks questions such as, "How can you have a hunting season on such a stupid bird?" and "Why bother restoring such silly creatures to the wild?"

"If we really knew how many turkeys were being stocked around the country by so-called do-gooders, it'd probably scare both of us to death," the Wild Turkey Federation's research director, James Kennamer, told me. "These game breeders will raise these birds; and they're clean and in good shape when they hatch from the egg. And I have no doubt that they're doing a good job. But then John Doe out here buys the chicks and raises them in wire pens, and he's got them in with all his chickens and guinea fowl and peafowl and the rest, and they pick all this stuff up. And then he turns them loose.

"I was doing some research over in the Mississippi Delta where they had a good turkey population, and this game warden living in the area had a domestic gobbler and a few [semi-wild] hens. The wild birds would come in and take the hens and whip the old gobbler. And I remember one year he only had one tail feather left. But the bottom line was I kept telling the guy he was asking for problems. Not only was he polluting the gene pool by letting the hens go wild, but he had this domestic turkey that was immune to blackhead and other diseases transmitting them to the wild birds. The following year they had a dieoff and found turkeys dead in the woods, which is very hard to do."

The states had learned a lot about what constitutes good turkey management well before they were able to practice it to any great extent.

Part of the recipe called for seeding depleted turkey range with genuinely wild turkeys, but first they had to *catch* the wild turkeys. Killing one of these birds requires some luck, lots of time, and prodigious hunting skill. Trapping a whole flock *alive* seemed impossible.

At first the states tried live traps, with scant success. Then they tried rigging drop nets over winter feeding stations, but the nets didn't work very well, and the turkeys would come to the bait only during severe winters. Finally, in the late 1950s, biologists in several states took to trapping turkeys with waterfowl "cannon nets" propelled by rockets or mortars.

I saw it done once. Jim Cardoza, a wildlife biologist with the Massachusetts Department of Fisheries, Wildlife, and Recreational Vehicles and one of the nation's top authorities on wild turkeys, had camouflaged the net with grass, scattered the corn, packed the plastic bag of explosive pellets into each of the two heavy metal rockets, rigged the ignition wires, screwed on the perforated, salt-shaker-lid backs, jammed the supporting steel rods in the dirt at the proper angle, then tucked me into the big, wild woods that shroud Boston's Quabbin Reservoir. Hours passed. I fell asleep to the hypnotic buzz of cicadas starting in one treetop and finishing in another.

And I awoke just in time to see Cardoza's hand easing toward the plunger and about a dozen wild turkeys, a beautiful bronze in the late afternoon sunlight, bending over the bait. There was a hideous explosion, and Cardoza and I were up and running toward the thrashing lumps under the net. I was appalled at the damage to the birds. Clumps of feathers with skin still attached were woven into the mesh. Later, when we released the birds at the transfer site, two limped badly. But we had done well. The damage had been inevitable and relatively minor. The big danger, Cardoza told me, is the turkeys' detecting you and coming up from the bait just as you fire. When this happens they literally lose their heads.

Another modern capture device is drugged bait, but occasionally the birds lurch drunkenly into the woods, where they become easy marks for dogs and wild predators. And sometimes they overeat and O.D. When this happens you've got to grab them fast, slice open their crops, squeeze out the bait, then stitch up their necks. Can cannon nets and chemicals really be efficient means of trapping wild turkeys? To this day they remain the *most* efficient. That's the difference between game-farm turkeys—which don't mind humans, provided they stay six feet away—and wild turkeys.

With the advent of the cannon nets states committed themselves to intensive trap and transfer programs. The same 1978 survey that recorded 331 failures out of 354 restoration attempts by twenty-three states using 350,000 game-farm birds also revealed 685 successes out of 841 restoration attempts by thirty-two states using just 26,500 *wild* birds. The game-farm birds had established themselves marginally on 630 square miles. The wild birds had established themselves strongly on 300,000 square miles.

The managers' learning process was not quite over, though. Many states tried to help their newly transferred wild turkeys by feeding them through the winter, thereby short-circuiting the natural selection process, facilitating the spread of disease, and providing splendid opportunities for predators and poachers. Even in mild weather, feeders had to be kept full or the turkeys would forget where they were when conditions became severe. Gradually the incredible toughness of wild turkeys became apparent. In one experiment—which would have sent the Humaniacs into orbit had they known about it—a wild turkey survived twenty-four winter days without food or water. Two other equally cruel experiments established that wild turkeys can recover near-normal fecundity after two weeks of starvation and 40 percent weight loss.

Once the harmful effects of winter feeding became known, the states quickly abandoned it. Massachusetts' Jim Cardoza was among the biologists who helped spread the word. "Weakened, poor-quality birds were surviving and subsequently breeding, thus lowering the vigor of the stock," he wrote in one of his many reports. "The wild turkeys were becoming dependent on artificially provided grains rather than adapting to the natural foods, and potential disease-transmission conditions were created by concentrating birds in a small area."

Weaned from its debilitating welfare diet, the wild turkey proliferated at an even faster clip, surging into vacant habitat, astonishing biologists with its vigor and survivability.

Vermont released seventeen wild New York birds during the winter of 1968–69. The following winter it released fourteen more. By 1973 the flock had expanded to 600, and in-state trap and transfer began. That same year, 579 Vermont turkey-hunting permits were issued. Now there are so many turkeys in Vermont that anyone who asks for a permit gets one. Vermont also has found the resolve to scrap its small but scandalously wasteful put-and-take pheasant program in order to channel the money to programs of real and lasting value. Like turkey restoration. Recently retired Vermont Fish and Game Commissioner Ed Kehoe told me that there was "a lot of pressure" on his department to keep the pheasants coming. "But," he said, "the program was just too expensive." It cost the state about twenty-five dollars for each bird shot by a hunter. At first there was much screaming and tearing of hair, but once wild turkeys started repopulating the state the sportsmen forgot all about pheasants.

In most states there has been great support for turkey restoration, from the non-hunting public as well as from sportsmen, and it is this support that has made and is making the programs so successful, particularly on private land. Missouri, for instance, elected not to advertise that it wished to release wild turkeys on privately owned turkey range. Instead, the Wildlife Division quietly seeded the information around the state. In this fashion the genuinely interested, genuinely committed landowners were selected out. Once they approached the division, asking if they might be *allowed* to have wild turkeys on their land, John Lewis would survey the proposed transfer site. If he liked the looks of it, he would have the locals sign a petition to protect "their" turkeys from outsiders. "There was a little basic psychology involved here," he told me. "The people really got involved in the program. The birds became theirs, not the [state] government's." Last year, Missouri completed its twenty-fourth spring gobbler season, in which slightly over 19,000 birds were taken.

In Massachusetts the wild turkey population has increased from thirty-seven New York birds released in 1972 and 1973 to an estimated three or four thousand in 1983. There have been four spring gobbler seasons, and the annual hunting kill is approaching two hundred.

In the southern national forests the wild turkey population has increased 500 percent in the past twenty years, and the annual hunting kill during this period has climbed from about 1,300 to 10,000. Real wild turkeys are booming just about everywhere.

Of course, there are still threats to wild turkeys—factory farming, urbanization, and predatory logging being chief among them. But, for once, it looks as if things are going to get better before they get worse. The age of the wild turkey in America is at hand, again. The managers have done something right. Celebrate.

CAN THE LOON

COME BACK?

Judith McIntyre

Unalterable facts of breeding biology have much to say about the relative difficulty of restoring the numbers of threatened species. The wild turkey, for example, may average a dozen young a year, young which quickly attain breeding age, while the common loon typically produces but two chicks, chicks which mature more slowly. (An extreme example of bad reproductive numbers is the hapless California condor, which produces one egg every second year, and which requires years longer than most birds to attain reproductive maturity.)

The jury is still out on the common loon conservation movement. Biologist Judith McIntyre, who has made this bird her special study for two decades, reports on the efforts being made to bolster breeding success in the southern part of the loon's nesting range.

THERE she sat, looking like a spectator at Wimbledon, her head turning from side to side as she followed the action in front of her. But this loon, sitting on her eggs on an island in an Adirondack lake, was not watching tennis balls whizzing across a grassy court. Instead, the lady of the lake was viewing an endless stream of boats and canoes moving up and down the reservoir. Despite the commotion, she never left her nest. Neither did her mate when it was his turn to sit on the eggs.

This odd sight was more than a mere curiosity, for it was evidence of a remarkable comeback. Nearly 20 years ago, when I began trying to unravel the mysteries of the common loon, I found elusive, shy birds that slipped underwater at the least provocation, even if it meant leaving their eggs to predators. And as a result, the invasion of vacation cottages and outboard motors into the birds' lakeside nesting grounds was causing loon populations to shrink all across the country.

Was the loon's wonderful and eerie cry sounding its own death knell by luring people to the wilderness? The statistics, showing declines of up to 75 percent since 1900 in some states, were grim. But in the early

From *National Wildlife*, August–September, 1986.

1980s, along with other researchers, I began to notice a surprising change in the behavior of the creatures. Like the tennis spectator bird, loons were learning to live near people. Now, while the loon still faces threats from acid rain and other pollutants, the bird is once again, as Henry Thoreau once wrote, "making the woods ring with his wild laughter."

Loons are aquatic birds, highly specialized for life in the water. Powerful legs, set far to the rear of their streamlined bodies, enable them to dive swiftly after fishy prey. But the adaptations that make loons marvelous swimmers do little for their walking ability. Vulnerable on land, they build their nests right at the water's edge.

Measuring less than 5 feet from tip to tip, loon wings are small for a bird that weighs between 8 and 14 pounds. To compensate, the birds must fly very fast, over 75 miles per hour, with wings beating 260 times every minute. They do a lot of flying, both during migration, when they travel from summer breeding grounds in northern United States and Canada to coastal areas as far south as Florida, and en route to and from ritualized "social gatherings" at regular intervals in the summer. No one knows exactly why 4 to 20 birds have daily get-togethers, but we believe it may be preparation for group migration.

During most of the summer, loons can only be seen alone, in pairs, or with one or two chicks in tow. Pair members share all parental responsibilities. They both build the nest, incubate the eggs, feed and carry the young on their backs and defend them against predators and other loons. Since the young are flightless until they are 11 to 12 weeks old, they must hatch by late June or early July at the latest. Otherwise, they might not be ready to leave breeding grounds before the lakes begin to freeze in October.

In the 1800s, the common loon, one of the five loon species that nest in the northern hemisphere, bred all across the United States from New England to northern California. But people soon began to take a heavy toll of the birds. During the late 1800s, loon shooting was considered great "sport." The birds dive so quickly that it was thought to be a challenge to hit one before it disappeared underwater. For a long time loons won, but as guns improved, the birds became the losers. Gunners lined the sides of Buzzard's Bay in Massachusetts every spring. On mornings when conditions were just right, the shooting was frightful. Dead loons were not eaten, nor were they used for anything else.

By 1968, when I began my studies, who still heard the laughter of the loon in Massachusetts? Or in Iowa or California? Loons did pass through as they migrated to Maine, New Hampshire and other more northern sites, but they no longer summered in states like Indiana, Connecticut or Iowa.

Even where they still bred, their population was shrinking. Thirty percent fewer lakes in New York hosted nesting pairs in 1978 than in 1960. And in New Hampshire, one estimate suggested that 75 percent of the loon population had been lost since the turn of the century.

The reasons for the decline, however, were not clear. Shooting had largely ended by the early 1900s, and now loons are protected. In addition, pesticides such as DDT, which had caused the downfall of so many other birds, did not reach high enough concentrations in the body tissues of most loons to cause significant problems.

Loons, however, did raise fewer and fewer young each summer on lakes where human activity was high and summer cottages numerous, so it seemed to me that people pressure might be the major cause of the decline. I began my research hoping to find out to what extent human recreational pursuits did conflict with the loon's ability to nest and raise young. Specifically, I wanted to learn if loons could adapt. Was their behavior so stereotyped and inflexible that they were doomed by a changing world? Or could they modify their habits given time and removal of direct threats?

My initial results were discouraging. In 1970, I was watching a nesting loon in Minnesota when two canoes drew near. The threat of humans so close caused the bird to flatten, lean over the nest edge and slide quietly into the water. All seemed peaceful to the unsuspecting people paddling along the shoreline. They did not spot the loon nest. But as I peered through my spotting scope, a little nose, followed by a little masked face, poked out from a stand of cattails. This time the nest *was* sighted. Little masked eyes blinked, little nose twitched and little fingers picked up the loon eggs. Biting into each egg, the raccoon enjoyed a hearty lunch. In the lake, the loon rolled and preened, unaware it would have no eggs to sit on when it returned to its nest.

Finding more evidence was not easy, as muddy roads hindered my progress and a series of broken canoes, broken outboard motors and broken paddles caused additional problems. Eventually, a broken heart was added to the list: I repeatedly saw loons lose their eggs to a parade of predators. Everywhere I looked the answer seemed the same—people, too many people.

Then I began to look deeper. Who was losing eggs and why? I found that in the absence of people, loons spend more than 99 percent of their time on nests during the four weeks of incubation. During the short periods of time when the adults are away, the eggs have no protection. They are not covered with down and nest material like duck eggs, nor hidden or concealed behind rocks. They are out in the open, easy to spot. And because the birds cannot walk on land, they have to build their nests at the water's edge, near the path of passing boaters.

Loons were obviously not going to start covering their eggs to protect them from predators. But might they be able to recognize and use better nesting sites? Since islands are the safest sites, I decided to test this idea by building artificial islands with the help of John Mathisen, the biologist at the Chippewa National Forest in Minnesota, and his staff. The platforms were small structures of sedge mat that were anchored in four- to six-foot-deep water.

The loons loved them. If there were no natural islands present, they used our little hand-built ones, deserting shoreline sites they had used for years.

More importantly, the loons seemed to be learning to stay on their nests when people approached. Suddenly, the future looked much brighter.

Since then, with the help of artificial islands and strong preservation efforts, the bird has proven that it is indeed adaptable enough to survive. The loon population in New Hampshire, for instance, has increased from 200 adults in 1975 to almost 300 in 1985, and the number of young being raised has nearly doubled. Hundreds of enthusiastic volunteers organized by the state's Loon Preservation Committee help by monitoring nesting sites and maintaining artificial islands.

In Minnesota's Boundary Waters Canoe Area, where loon numbers dropped dramatically in the 1960s, loons have made a similar comeback. Jim Titus, now with the Oregon Extension, discovered that the birds moved away from popular camping islands and initiated new sites where they had not previously nested. In addition, loons that used lakes with heavy canoe traffic became so good at staying on their nests that Titus labeled them "stickers."

In my own study of loons on a busy reservoir in New York's Adirondack Park and on a northern Saskatchewan lake, I have even found that birds that nest along traffic lanes are often more successful at raising young than those in more remote areas. It is something that I would not have predicted many years ago, and may explain why numbers of loons are increasing across the country.

But the continuing story of the loon is not an altogether happy one. In 1983, Laurence Alexander, then with The Nature Conservancy, called attention to a massive die-off of loons off the Gulf coast of Florida. More than 3,000 birds died. Scientists are not completely sure what happened, but they suspect that high levels of mercury may have made the birds susceptible to disease.

Another threat comes from acid rain. Graduate student Gary Dulin of Central Michigan University discovered last year that loons nesting on acidified Michigan lakes could not find enough fish to feed their young as they grew older. By the second month after hatching, many of the chicks were starving.

Another researcher, Karl Parker, found that loons on acidified Adirondack lakes were forced to care for their offspring long after the normal period of parental feeding. And Robert Alvo of Trent University discovered that loons had completely deserted the most acidified lakes in Ontario, and were only partially successful raising young on lakes just starting to become acidic.

If we cannot blunt the threat from acid rain, we lose more than just a bird. The loon is an indicator species, telling us what is happening to its aquatic habitat. But even more important, loons are symbols of the wilderness. If their mournful, wild laughter continues to ring out through misty dawns, then it is easy to believe that all is right with the world. If that eerie call disappears, it is an ominous warning for all of us.

BOSQUE DEL APACHE

Roger Morris

---

*In an increasingly man-dominated world, wildlife conservation depends
more and more on protected chunks of habitat, especially national parks
and wildlife refuges. Roger Morris details the conservation role of New
Mexico's Bosque del Apache, and some of its problems as well.*

A HUNDRED miles south of Albuquerque in central New Mexico, the
Rio Grande wanders through a desolate landscape where even
the faint presence of man is remote and ominous. Bordering each bank
is monotonous desert, sparsely studded with mesquite, salt brush and
stunted piñon pine. To the west, beyond a stony-gray mountain peak,
lie the antennae of the world's greatest array of giant radio-telescopes,
listening in computer silence for messages from distant stars. To the
northeast is the misty silhouette of the Manzanos, one of the nation's
largest storage sites for nuclear bombs. It is a gritty surreal wasteland, a
stark fastness that seems almost like an alien world.

Travel just a few more miles down the Rio Grande, however, and a
magical transformation occurs. The riverbanks suddenly become green
and alive, cushioned by thick groves of cottonwoods and saltcedar that
defy the desert. Vast expanses of fields and marsh grass glisten green
and gold in the sun. The silence is broken by the sound of beating
wings and the raucous calling of birds, while deer and rabbits quietly
slip between the cottonwoods. It is as if a chunk of the Chesapeake
Bay's rich shoreline had been transported to the New Mexican desert.

This is the Bosque del Apache, long a haven in a weary land for both
humans and animals. Pre-Columbian nomads once sought a respite
from the Chihuahuan Desert in its verdant glens; now the Bosque is a
winter home for such endangered species as whooping crane and bald
eagle—and one of the most successful refuges in the often-besieged National Wildlife Refuge System.

But Bosque has not always been so untroubled. In its 50-year history
as a federal refuge, the "Woods of the Apache" has suffered from natural disaster and severely degraded habitat. Its tranquil forests and
marshes have been the scene of bitter controversy. And therein lies a

From *National Wildlife*, February–March, 1986.

tale of how authorities at one refuge managed to balance the conflicting demands of wildlife and people.

The story begins in 1936 when the U.S. government purchased 57,191 acres along nine miles of the Rio Grande. The land had been heavily grazed and farmed, but its cottonwood savannah still provided a rich wildlife habitat. Then, in 1941, there was an ecological catastrophe. A rare flood of the Rio Grande caused the river to jump two miles west, ripping out virtually all of the cottonwood trees and depositing up to 30 feet of silt over the fertile marshes. Animals disappeared and many of the birds stopped coming to the Bosque. In 1941, for example, only 17 sandhill cranes wintered in the valley, in part because of loss of habitat in their northern nesting grounds.

Wildlife officials began to restore the habitat, building dikes and impoundments to create and maintain new forests and marshes. Slowly the plants and animals came back. But their return brought a new problem: conflicts between people and wildlife. To the farmers whose lands bordered on the refuge, the rapidly increasing populations of birds that descended on their fields to feed were like plagues of locusts. In addition, the water being used to re-create the marshes was water taken away from the farmers' irrigated fields.

As a result, tensions in the valley ran high throughout the 1940s and early 1950s. "They were rough times," remembers one farmer. "We asked ourselves whether the government cared more for the birds and animals than it did for our families." Finally, refuge managers hit upon solutions. They cut back on the size of impoundments in order to leave more water for farmers. In addition, they began to farm parts of the refuge itself in order to entice the birds away from neighboring fields. At first, the refuge staff did the farming; later the government hired local sharecroppers to till the fields. Today, 1,300 acres are under cultivation in a rotation of corn, sorghum, winter wheat and alfalfa. One third of the crop is left for wildlife; the other two thirds provide a substantial income for farmers and their families in the neighboring small town of San Antonio. Even more revenue for the townspeople comes from the large number of tourists that have begun to visit Bosque. Now, the local people have a strong financial incentive to protect "their" refuge.

At the same time, the refuge managers have improved the habitat with a new network of canals and ponds. For wildlife, the results have been dramatic. The population of Bosque's sandhill crane, for example, has risen to more than 20,000—a recovery aided by protection of the birds' nesting grounds and migratory routes as well.

The wonder is there to be seen and heard every autumn. In late October, the soft "krooo, krooo" cries of the sandhill cranes begin to break the desert stillness as the birds arrive in magnificent flocks, some a mile long. Throughout the winter, they forage in the fields and grass, roosting quietly at night in the protection of the refuge marshes.

The New Mexico sanctuary has also played a vital role in an extraordinary "foster parent" program to ward off extinction of the majestic whooping crane. By the early 1940s, only 15 of the five-foot-tall birds were left and the species seemed doomed. Then, in a bold scheme of wildlife adoption, made possible by the success of the sandhills at Bosque, biologists began to place whooper eggs in sandhill nests at Gray's Lake National Wildlife Refuge in northwest Idaho. The young whoopers migrated south with their sandhill "parents" and hopefully will soon begin to breed. This winter, the flock is expected to number about 30, second only to the 80 to 90 whoopers that winter in the Aransas National Wildlife Refuge and the surrounding area on the Gulf Coast.

While the whooping and the sandhill cranes represent the desert refuge's most notable triumphs, they are scarcely alone. More than 290 species of birds and dozens of other types of animals find temporary or permanent homes in the Bosque. Bald eagles and peregrine falcons soar on the winds of fall, winter and spring. Thirty thousand snow geese and 20,000 ducks forage in field and marsh, while fish-eating mergansers patrol the ponds. White-winged doves and Gambel's quail "play" hide and seek with bobcats, raccoons and coyotes in the shrubs and tall grass. And up above, porcupines, Cooper's hawks and short-eared owls perch on saltcedar branches like preachers in their pulpits.

Drawn by this incredible bounty of life, visitors are traveling to Bosque in increasing numbers. The majority are bird watchers who hike out into the refuge in chill of dawn or sunset during the months of November to February. "The Bosque is a refuge where you can readily see the birds at close range," explains Lynn Greenwalt, a former director of the Fish and Wildlife Service.

Everything possible is done to protect the birds. Visitors, for example, are required to stay on a 15-mile looping trail that provides close-up views of the animals. The hunting season is carefully scheduled to protect the whooping cranes as they fly into or leave the refuge—and each hunting blind is equipped with a two-way radio so that rangers can warn hunters when whoopers enter their area.

But Bosque has also been fortunate compared to many other National Wildlife Refuges. It has escaped the PCB dump that has contaminated Crab Orchard in Illinois and the condominiums that have blocked crucial migration routes at Jackson Hole in Wyoming. No off-road vehicle enthusiasts are demanding the right to scar the landscape, as at Chincoteague in Virginia. And pressure to overgraze, a problem plaguing a number of refuges, has been minor. Investigative reporters from the *Sacramento Bee*, who recently analyzed Bosque's mud and water, did find elevated levels of selenium, one particularly toxic component of the agricultural runoff that turned Kesterson in California into an avian graveyard. But Bosque's managers claim not to be worried by the newspaper's findings. "We've had some agricultural runoff and some levels of chemicals above normal," says FWS assistant regional director Gerald Stegman, "but nothing that could be called a problem."

Ironically, the biggest threat to Bosque may come not from people, but from nature. The 1941 flood of the Rio Grande carried seeds of saltcedar, a Mediterranean ornamental which had been recently introduced into the American Southwest, into the refuge's marshes and cottonwood groves. Now, thick stands of the wildly prolific, incorrigible tree are spreading all over Bosque del Apache, despite the best efforts of chainsaw-wielding refuge workers. "We're just trying to break even," says refuge manager Bill Hutchinson. "Fire doesn't kill the cedar and if we don't cut back all we can, it would soon take over the impoundments."

For now, the Bosque thrives as never before, an oasis of food, water and space for the irreplaceable winged refugees from northern winters. But the startling and soothing beauty of the preserve is a reminder of the desert's harshness just beyond the boundary—and of the precariousness of the miracle.

FIFTY YEARS OF PROGRESS—

THE NATIONAL AUDUBON SOCIETY

John H. Baker

In this interesting historical piece, former National Audubon Society president John H. Baker reminds us of the context out of which the modern conservation movement arose.

WHEN the National Association of Audubon Societies for the Protection of Wild Birds and Animals, Inc. was launched in January 1905, market gunning and sport shooting, practically without restriction, were widespread in the United States. Quite a few states, as a consequence of local Audubon movements, had adopted the Audubon model law protecting songbirds, so that the practice, commonly prevailing before the 1890s, of using robins, meadowlarks, and other songbirds for food, had been largely stopped. But there was almost no protection of non-game species of wildlife, other than songbirds, and very little protection of game.

Commercial dealers in game were doing a thriving business. I remember very well watching gunners shooting small sandpipers for the pot on the beaches in the early 1900s. The eggs of coastal nesting birds such as gulls, terns, and skimmers were being widely used locally for food. The commercial traffic in wild bird plumage, mainly for millinery purposes, was bringing millions of dollars annually into the coffers of the importers and wholesalers.

There was at that time no soil conservation concept or recognition of the need for governmental action. There certainly was no water conservation concept; everyone seemed to think there always would be plenty of water for all purposes. The forest conservation concept was just developing. There was little concept of wildlife conservation outside of the small groups constituting the then-organized Audubon Societies. There was little, if any, awareness of the interdependence of wildlife, plants, soil, and water, or their relation to human progress. The beneficial role of predatory animals was not at all appreciated and even today, may I say, it is little appreciated. Our children's children may look back on the present destructive attitude toward predatory animals with the same feeling we have today about those who shot small sandpipers for the pot, used robins and meadowlarks for food, or wore the plumage of wild birds as hat trimmings.

The wildlife protective organizations in existence toward the end of the last century, and early in this one, tended to be highly specialized in objectives. As a consequence, there were apt to be conflicts that tended to weaken the whole movement. I have, in the past, likened this situation to one in which the theoretical Society for the Preservation of the Chickadee was constantly warring with the theoretical Society for the Preservation of Sunflower Seeds.

Appreciative uses of the out-of-doors—other than to view the scenery, hike, hunt or fish were, generally, not indulged in. Certainly there was no training of teachers in effective presentation of nature and conservation subjects from the outdoor approach. True, there was teaching of nature study, but almost wholly from the indoor laboratory approach and not outdoors in nature's laboratory.

While the original stated purposes of the National Association included the protection of other animals than birds, the great bulk of the Society's activities, and of the interest of its members and affiliated societies, concerned bird protection. There was need to develop public opinion to support the passage of basic laws restricting or ending the slaughter of wild birds and other animals. Insofar as the commercial traffic in wild bird plumage was concerned, it was a long battle. The key actions were: (1) the passage in New York State in 1910—New York City being the place of business of more than 90 per cent of the importers and dealers in such plumage—of a law banning possession for sale, offering for sale, and sale of the plumage of wild birds; (2) the Federal Tariff Act of 1913 banning the importation into the United States of wild bird plumage with, however, certain provisions that provided loop-holes; (3) the Federal Migratory Bird Treaty Act of 1918, giving power to the federal government to prescribe allowable take, if any, of those families and species of birds defined in that Act as migratory; (4) the 1941 New York State law eliminating legal loop-holes of which advantage had been taken; and (5) the 1952 amendment of the Federal Tariff Act for the same purpose. In obtaining the passage of these basic bird protective laws the National Association of Audubon Societies played a leading part.

It might well be said that during nearly the first half of the Society's existence we were in the era of protection, and that in the second half we have been in the era of conservation.

With the growth of public awareness of the recreational pleasures to be derived from appreciative use of the out-of-doors, new industries have developed, providing ever better cameras and projectors, binoculars, nature books, bird nesting boxes, feeding stations, and field guides for identification, not only of birds and flowers, but of trees, mammals, insects, reptiles, and all other forms of plant and animal life. There is no question that the National Audubon Society has played a substantial part in the development of such public interest. At the turn of the century anyone who was interested in observing birds was apt to be regarded as odd; now almost everyone is apologetic if he does not know one bird from another.

During the second half of your Society's existence the scope of objectives and program has been greatly widened in recognition of the fact, learned from experience, that with increasing population pressure, neither birds nor plants can, in the long run, be saved from extinction through protection alone; recognition that it is essential to preserve the carrying capacity of their habitats in terms of food, cover and water; recognition of the complex interrelationships of soil, water, plants, and wildlife, and their direct impact upon human progress.

As recently as 25 years ago, there were no summer camps for the training of teachers and other youth leaders to present nature and conservation subjects from the outdoor approach, and none that stressed the interrelationships of the resources. There were no wildlife tours by station wagon and boat under guidance of trained naturalists and conservationists, taking people into the field to observe first-hand the existing soil, water, plant, and wildlife conditions in an area, in order to learn of the history and results of man's alteration of that environment; to see what a national park, monument, federal, state, or private refuge or sanctuary is like; and to learn something of the management problems in connection with them.

There were no nature educational centers in the vicinity of great metropolitan populations where groups of school children and scouts might be taken by busloads with their teachers and leaders. Here they go out on the trails under the guidance of well-qualified nature and conservation teachers, receive instruction while visiting trailside museums, and so better their chances of living healthy and happy lives, and of helping, as voting citizens, to preserve those resources and environments on which their health and happiness depend. It is not merely to increase recreational pleasures that your Society strives to develop public conservation opinion. It is, in the last analysis, to prevent human impoverishment through promoting human progress.

Although bird lectures, and some on other animals, were given in
the early part of this century, the volume was small. Usually they were
not presented by organizations, but by individual lecturers seeking personal profit or acclaim. The big jump in public attendance at wildlife and
conservation lectures came with the development of Audubon Screen
Tours in the past ten years, now reaching an estimated 700,000 persons
annually in North America.

The organization of children in schools and other groups into clubs
receiving informative leaflets about birds began as far back as 1910, and
surely has been an outstanding factor in our generation in the development of public opinion favoring conservation. It was only during the
past 20 years, however, and to some extent very recently, that the scope
of the informative material furnished both the children and their teachers
and leaders was broadened to include the protection of habitats and the
interrelationships of all renewable resources.

It might be said that a primary objective of all of the new programs
of the second half of your Society's existence has been to provide opportunity to members and other friends to participate in doing, as distinct
from being urged, told, or aroused.

While the value of intangibles has surely been recognized to some
degree ever since man was released from cave-man status, it is only in
this century that an appreciation of those intangible values has received
volume expression; for example, the value of a sunset, a snow-capped
range of mountain peaks, human health and happiness. Every year more
and more people realize that it is not only impossible but unreasonable
to attempt to evaluate intangibles in dollars or other monetary terms.

We are still far from our goal. No doubt there will be new develop-
ments in regard to policy and objectives with succeeding generations,
but it would seem that, insofar as the scope of your Society's objectives
is concerned, it now "covers the waterfront." Governments may come
and go and policies change, but the need for conservation, like the law
of supply and demand, goes on forever. Conservation affects profoundly
the physical, spiritual, and economic welfare of every man, woman,
and child, bar none, everywhere and always.

To me it seems that the greatest progress in conservation in our generation has been the growing recognition of its basic relation to human
progress. With this has come the broadening of horizons and the scope
of the operations and goals of the organizations working in the conservation vineyard.

It is easy to be pessimistic, in the face of human population pressures
and the obstacles of human fear and greed, but it is truly remarkable how
much progress has been made in so little time. It takes stamina, persist-

ence, determination, and faith to keep forging ahead toward our objectives. It is gratifying to realize that every day the Society enjoys the encouragement of more and more people. We have hitched our wagon to a star, and we intend to keep on "going places" in the attainment of our goals.

MAN-MADE

THREATS

TO BIRDLIFE

Christopher Leahy

It is easy for us to feel superior to our recent forbears, who had no experience with hands-on environmental education and who had never heard the word "ecology." Unhappily, our increased understanding of biotic systems has not led to a safer world for those systems. Christopher Leahy points out some of the more important ways in which we persistently—often increasingly—threaten the biota with which we share this planet.

I T has been a long time since we could claim that humankind was locked in an equal life-or-death struggle with nature. In fact, long after nature surrendered to our tools, machines, master plans, and fecundity, we continued to "conquer" her—if not out of necessity precisely, then for profit and pleasure. The rightness of this urge to exploit the biosphere was bolstered by the notion, popular in Western religions, that the earth was created for our benefit.

By the late nineteenth century the expiration of several bird species and the impending man-induced doom of a number of others made it clear to a few people that men with rapacious appetites for killing represented a mortal threat to wildlife. In the first half of this century these "conservationists" managed to convince the public at large that this was true, that it was a bad thing, and that legislation should be passed to rigidly restrict the killing of animals. Today in North America the major threat to wildlife is no longer the clear, direct one of men killing animals, but the rather more insidious and ill-defined one of a sophisticated technology working beyond our control killing organisms gradually, indirectly, in ways we didn't predict and in many cases still don't understand. "Conservationists" have become "environmental-

From *The Birdwatcher's Companion: An Encyclopedic Handbook of North American Birdlife*. New York: Hill & Wang, 1982.

ists," having realized that the new dangers threaten ourselves as well as other animals.

With this brief historical perspective, consider the following man-made threats to birdlife.

HUNTING. Shooting for the game markets as well as for sport and individual use in the late nineteenth and early twentieth century is generally credited with the extinction of the Passenger Pigeon and the Heath Hen and the mortal decline of the Eskimo Curlew. It also drastically reduced the numbers of many other native shorebirds and upland game birds before effective conservation laws were passed. The Great Auk was hunted to extinction for its eggs, meat, and feathers, and populations of Great, Snowy, and Reddish Egrets and Roseate Spoonbills were drastically reduced by plume hunters between about 1875 and 1900. Game and conservation laws now restrict hunting to certain species of birds (chiefly the ducks, geese, grouse, pheasants, quail, rails, and doves); to certain clearly defined seasons; to a limited number of birds; and to licensed hunters using approved methods. In North America responsible hunters now consider themselves conservationists and support research on and propagation of game species and protection of their habitat.

The most popular upland game bird on the continent is the introduced Ring-necked (Common) Pheasant, which is reared in large numbers in captivity and released for the benefit of sportsmen.

HABITAT DESTRUCTION. This may be the single greatest threat to wildlife on the planet. It occurs in direct proportion to population growth and development, though it takes many forms: draining of wetlands for highway construction, destroying prairie lands for agriculture, clearing second-growth woodland for house lots, cutting down primeval redwood forest for lumber. It was a major factor in the decline of the Whooping Crane, Everglade Kite, and (probably) Bachman's Warbler and the probable extinction of the American Ivory-billed Woodpecker and Dusky Seaside Sparrow. It is particularly threatening to species with highly restrictive habitat preferences: prairie chickens need short-grass prairie, Red-cockaded Woodpeckers need diseased pine trees, Golden-cheeked Warblers need virgin stands of cedar, Seaside Sparrows need salt marshes. Without these specific requirements, the birds which depend on them will likely perish.

There has been considerable public sympathy recently for the preservation of unique habitats in North America, as people have recognized their intrinsic beauty as well as their value in maintaining biological diversity. This is commendable, but it should not be allowed to mask the fact that habitat destruction elsewhere in the world (e.g., the chopping of tropical rain forest at the rate of about 30 acres per minute) is of more than just local concern. Wood Thrushes and Hooded Warblers, which breed in North America, winter almost exclusively in Middle American rain forests. Furthermore, it has been argued that the survival of tropical forests is crucial to such fundamental matters as the planet's oxygen supply, its climate, and its genetic diversity—about 50 percent of the world's species of plant and animal life occur exclusively in tropical rain forest, a habitat covering only about 6 percent of the earth's surface.

PESTICIDES AND OTHER CHEMICAL POISONS. The careless use of highly toxic chemicals to control arboreal and agricultural insect pests stands as one of the chief follies of the modern era. Those who continue to urge heavy reliance on non-specific, highly toxic, persistent pesticides argue that they are the most effective and efficient means of controlling pest insects such as mosquitoes, caterpillars, and leaf beetles. Opponents reply that such pesticides are: (1) insufficiently specific, killing "good" insects as well as "bad" along with other insect-controlling organisms such as birds, amphibians, etc., and potentially destabilizing entire ecosystems, making them highly vulnerable to unpredictable new problems; (2) difficult to control in application, especially when sprayed from airplanes and carried by winds away from target areas; (3) highly persistent and mobile both in soil, whence it is washed into bodies of water, and in animal tissue, where it accumulates and increases in concentration as it is passed up a food chain (pesticide residues have been detected in the tissue of humans living in the remotest reaches of the earth); (4) often applied carelessly and without sufficient warrant, as when thousands of acres are sprayed in a knee-jerk reaction to an outbreak of eastern equine encephalitis, in a futile attempt to kill the mosquitoes that may bear the disease, instead of requiring and enforcing the inoculation of horses, which would stop the disease in mid-cycle; (5) effective against noxious insects *only in the short term,* since insect populations readily produce resistant generations which in turn require the use of even deadlier pesticides or heavier applications of the original one.

DDT (dichlorodiphenyltrichloroethane), once considered a miracle chemical essential to man's struggle against competitive insects, has been shown to have been the principal cause of the precipitous decline of certain bird species in North America during the 1960's and early 1970's as well as being implicated in human health problems. DDT washed by rain from uplands into lakes and rivers became highly concentrated in the tissues of large fish. Bird species, especially the Brown Pelican, Bald Eagle, and Osprey, feeding heavily on these, accumulated still higher concentrations—enough in some cases to kill the birds outright. A more insidious effect of the pesticide was to create a hormone imbalance in the birds' systems which inhibited the ability to produce calcium for eggshells. Affected females laid soft-shelled eggs, which could not survive incubation, or even eggs with no shells at all. Peregrine Falcons feeding on fish-eating ducks and insectivorous birds also fell prey to the DDT miracle. The decline in populations of the four species mentioned above during years of maximum DDT use was dramatic, as has been the recovery of some populations since the ban on DDT in 1972.

Because of the persistence of DDT, we may continue to discover more subtle but no less pernicious side effects of its indiscriminate use for a long time to come. And DDT is only one of many toxic chemicals which were ladled freely into the environment, the effects of which, in many cases, we are just beginning to discover. Among those proven dangerous are aldrin, dieldrin, endrin, toxaphene, BHC (benzene hexachloride) HCB (hexachlorobenzene), heptachlor epoxide, PCB's (polychlorinated biphenyls), and that most obscene of chemical weapons applied in Vietnam by Dr. Strangelove—Agent Orange.

Another ugly twist to this sad story is that some American chemical corporations, forbidden to sell their poisons in North America, have not scrupled at passing them off on third world countries to the detriment of the latter's people and wildlife. One need not expect corporations profiting from the export of DDT to appreciate the fact that North American migrant birds are still being exposed to pesticide poisoning on their Latin American wintering grounds.

A more direct form of poisoning kills Golden Eagles and other raptors drawn to poisoned carcasses of "controlled" prairie dogs set out to attract coyotes.

LEAD POISONING. One of the oldest and most severe man-made threats to many game-bird species is lead pellets from shotgun cartridges, the inevitable remains of the thousands of rounds of ammunition spent during the hunting season. Fatal lead poisoning has been recorded in a wide range of gallinaceous birds and waterfowl, which ingest the shot along with other GRIT. But particularly susceptible are those species of dabbling ducks that feed largely on the hard, round seeds of aquatic plants to which shot pellets bear a strong resemblance. Terres notes the case of 110,000 Mallards succumbing to lead poisoning *on a single occasion* in Illinois, and Bellrose estimates that waterfowl deaths from this source may account for 2–3 percent of North American populations.

Lead toxins enter the bloodstream of their victims via the stomach and intestinal walls after being pulverized from the shot pellets in the gizzard. Effects include liver and kidney damage and paralysis of the muscles of the digestive tract. Within a few days affected birds develop diarrhea and begin to lose their appetite; they soon become pathetically weak and unable to function normally but may take three weeks or more to die of starvation. A single lead pellet is sufficient to cause death in some instances, but dead ducks found in heavily hunted areas normally contain 10–40 times this number. Each season thousands of tons of lead shot are added to what has been accumulating in wetlands in significant amounts for more than a century.

The solution to the problem is, of course, the replacement of lead shot with an acceptable, non-toxic substitute. A soft iron shot has been tested on birds in the laboratory with good results, but legislation banning the use of poisonous ammo has not been passed to date. The issue puts the commitment of the hunting community to sound conservation practices to a clear test—one they have yet to pass.

OIL SPILLS. It does not require much imagination to understand that petroleum, sea water, and swimming birds do not mix well. Loons, grebes, tubenoses, sea ducks, alcids, and other oceangoing species which are caught in the thick phlegm of an oil spill quickly become hopelessly mired, totally unable to function, and thus are doomed to a slow death by starvation, exposure, and poison. Even birds with apparently negligible oil stains may be dangerously liable to total loss of body heat because the oil creates a gap in the insulation system that maintains a bird's body temperature on the cold ocean. Ingestion of oil can also kill —postmortem examinations of some alcids found dead on beaches with no oil at all on their plumage have revealed lung and intestinal tissue clotted and destroyed by oil.

In recent years, conservationists have had all too many opportunities to experiment with techniques of cleaning oiled birds. After a major oil spill, hundreds of thousands of dead and dying seabirds wash up on our beaches—probably a small fraction of those that perish offshore. And in spite of improved cleaning methods, the survival rate among oiled birds is very low.

The millions of tons of oil which we have put into the oceans was not all spilled by accident. Much of it results from the deliberate flushing of tanks and oily bilges at sea. In the winter of 1956, a year in which no major oil spills were reported, 7,500 fatally oiled seabirds washed up on the beaches of Nantucket Island (Massachusetts) alone. This form of pollution has been "limited" by international convention, but no one suggests that the practice has been effectively curtailed. Think of this the next time you get "tar" on your feet at the beach.

In the current panic to exploit native oil resources here, some are willing to risk the living resources of offshore fishing banks for a problematical and very limited return of petroleum. On Georges Bank off the coast of New England, the fishery and the large concentrations of whales and seabirds which are attracted by it are being wagered against the possibility of finding enough oil to meet the energy needs of the U.S. for 3–4 weeks.

It is still common for people to sigh in relief when a euphoric newscaster reports that the latest oil spill is being blown or carried "out to sea" away from bathing beaches. We still know very little about the long-range effects of oil on the marine environment, but we do know that when the oil sinks to the bottom of the ocean, it has a devastating and long-term effect on benthic (bottom-dwelling) organisms. . . .

COMPANION ANIMALS. The dogs, cats, rats, pigs, goats, and other animals which have followed the spread of Western civilization around the world have at times posed serious threats to wildlife. Their arrival has been particularly devastating among endemic island species such as the Laysan Island Rail, which, due to the absence of predators on its native island, had lost the ability to fly. However, any burrow-nesting or ground-nesting bird is potentially threatened by these animals. Pigs, for example, were a factor in the decline of the Bermuda Petrel or Cahow (*Pterodroma cahow*) and rats often menace petrel, tern, and alcid colonies. Suburban neighborhoods, which may support several dogs and/or cats per household, are treacherous breeding areas for songbirds.

MAN-MADE STRUCTURES. Skyscrapers and television towers represent hazards to low-flying nocturnal migrants. Especially on foggy nights, the bright lights of city buildings may attract thousands of birds which become disoriented, unable to find their way out of the maze of reflecting glass, and often kill themselves by flying into windows in their panic. Mortalities at television towers, ceilometers, and the like are the result of birds migrating at night under low ceilings being attracted and baffled by the lights and striking the towers and guy wires. Johnston and Haines record two particularly disastrous nights in early October 1954 during which over 100,000 migrant birds were killed in only 25 localities sampled from New York to Georgia. Picture windows also exact their toll—although the number of birds killed at any given window is small, the aggregate is undoubtedly enormous. A reasonable estimate of birds killed annually in North America by encounters with buildings, picture windows, and TV towers undoubtedly runs in the millions. Golden Eagles, Mute Swans, Red-tailed Hawks, and other large birds are often killed or fatally injured by flying into or being electrocuted by high-tension power lines.

AUTOMOBILES. In the 1960's it was estimated that about 2.5 million birds were killed annually in collisions with automobiles in *Britain*. The number of birds killed on North America's much more extensive network of highways must be staggering.

BEACH RECREATION. Relatively few species (mainly sand plovers and some terns) breed in what might be called "Frisbee" or "sunbathing" zones of public beaches, and in many instances these areas are recognized and protected from the ravages of feet and tires. Perhaps of greater concern is the need for long-distance shorebird migrants to rest and feed relatively undisturbed at a number of points during their long journeys. Increased development of beach real estate and public demand for recreational access are making such quiet havens scarce along the coast of North America. Clearly there is a compromise to be reached between the legitimate claims of beach users and the equally valid interests of shorebirds. Conceivably banning motorized traffic from most beach areas would find wide support among most beachgoers as well as environmentalists.

INTRODUCED BIRDS. Alien bird species brought to North America for reasons ranging from the wildly frivolous to the well-intentioned and pseudo-scientific have at times threatened populations of native birds. . . .

THREATENING THE WHOLE. As noted earlier, the most alarming of today's man-made threats to birdlife are more subtle but also more far-reaching than the simple destructiveness of men shooting birds. One reason so many people have recently become interested in the welfare of the world's wildlife is that our own fate is inextricably involved with that of our fellow organisms. We may survive "frail" species such as the Bachman's Warbler or the blue whale, but there are other creatures such as the cockroach which have already demonstrated greater staying powers than our own.

Listed above are a few of the many threats to the environment which *we* have posed quite recently. They are ones which relate particularly to birdlife and in ways which have been clearly documented. Many others, such as air pollution, acid rain, disposal of chemical and nuclear wastes—both alone and in combination—gnaw inexorably away at the abundance and diversity of earthly life. This self-inflicted corrosion afflicts not only our physical well-being but also what we alone have the ability to appreciate—the overall quality of life.

It has long been traditional among coal miners to take a caged canary down into the shaft with them. When the canary falls off its perch— killed by lethal fumes—it's time to get out. If we wake up one morning to find birds falling off their perches, it will be too late to correct earlier miscalculations. And, of course, there is nowhere else to go.

permission of Henry Holt and Company, Inc. HOUGHTON MIFFLIN COMPANY. Excerpts from *Watching Birds* by Roger R. Pasquier. Copyright © 1977 by Roger F. Pasquier. Reprinted by permission of Houghton Mifflin Company. ALFRED A. KNOPF, INC. Excerpt from *Bird Behavior* by Robert Burton. Copyright © 1985 by Robert Burton. Excerpt from *Encyclopedia of North American Birds* by John K. Terres. Copyright © 1980 by John K. Terres. Reprinted by permission of Alfred A. Knopf, Inc., a division of Random House. NICK LYONS BOOKS. Excerpt from *Natural Acts* by David Quammen. Copyright © 1985 by David Quammen. Reprinted by permission of Nick Lyons Books. NATIONAL WILDLIFE FEDERATION. Excerpt from "A Louder Voice in the Wilderness" by Judith McIntyre in *National Wildlife Magazine*, August/September 1986. Excerpt from "Winter Oasis" by Roger Morris, in *National Wildlife Magazine*, February/March 1986. Copyright 1986 by the National Wildlife Federation. Reprinted by permission. NORTH POINT PRESS. Excerpt from "The Long-Legged House," in *Recollected Essays*, copyright © 1981 by Wendell Berry. Published by North Point Press and reprinted by permission. CHARLES SCRIBNER'S SONS. Excerpt from *The View From Hawk Mountain* by Michael Harwood. Copyright © 1973 by Michael Harwood. Excerpt from *Arctic Dreams* by Barry Lopez. Copyright © 1986 by Barry Holstun Lopez. Reprinted by permission of Charles Scribner's Sons, a division of Macmillan, Inc. SIERRA CLUB BOOKS. Excerpts from *Idle Weeds* by David Rains Wallace. Copyright © 1980 by David Rains Wallace. Reprinted with permission of Sierra Club Books. UNIVERSITY OF MINNESOTA PRESS. Excerpts from *Travels and Traditions* by H. Albert Hochbaum. Copyright © 1955 by H. Albert Hochbaum. Reprinted by permission of University of Minnesota Press. Viking Penguin, Inc. Excerpt from *The Nesting Season* by Helen Cruickshank. Text © Copyright © 1979 by Helen Cruickshank. Excerpt from *The Wind Birds* by Peter Matthiessen. Copyright (text) © 1967, 1973 by Peter Matthiessen. Reprinted by permission of Viking Penguin, Inc. WILLIAMS, TED. Excerpt from "Resurrection of the Wild Turkey," in *Audubon Magazine*, January 1984. Copyright © 1984 by Ted Williams. Reprinted by permission of the author. AMERICAN ASSOCIATION OF RETIRED PERSONS. "Eagle Man" by Ted Shane, condensed from *Lifetime Living*, January 1953. Copyright by Lifetime Living, Inc. Reprinted by permission of the American Association of Retired Persons. AUDUBON NATURALIST SOCIETY. "The American Career of Alexander Wilson, Father of American Ornithology," by Elsa G. Allen, from *Atlantic Naturalist*, Vol. 8, No. 2, November–December, 1952. Copyright © 1952 by Audubon Naturalist Society of the Central Atlantic States, Inc. Reprinted by permission. AUDUBON MAGAZINE. "Wings Across the Moon" by Robert J. Newman, from *Audubon Magazine*, July–August 1952. "Presidential Bird" by Richard L. Scheffel, from *Audubon Magazine*, May–June 1961. "Snobber-Sparrow de Luxe: A Picture Story" by Edwin Way Teale, from *Audubon Magazine*, November–December 1944. "Care and Feeding of Wild Birds" by John K. Terres, from *Audubon Magazine*, Vol. 51, 1949. Reprinted by permission. BRIDGES, WILLIAM. "The Last of a Species" by William Bridges, from *Animal Kingdom*, the magazine of the New York Zoological Society. Reprinted by permission of William Bridges. BROOKFIELD, CHARLES M. "The Guy Bradley Story" by Charles M. Brookfield, from *Audubon Magazine*, July–August 1955. Reprinted by permission of Charles M. Brookfield. DODD, MEAD & COMPANY. "The Story of Hawk Mountain" by Maurice Broun, from *Hawks Aloft*. Copyright 1949 by Maurice Broun. "Birds Over America" from *The Big Day* by Roger Tory Peterson. Copyright 1948 by Roger Tory Peterson. "Bird Invasion" from *Days without Time* by Edwin Way Teale. Copyright 1948 by Edwin Way Teale. Reprinted by permission. DOUBLEDAY & COMPANY, INC. "The Hardy Horned Owl," "Old Sicklewings," from *Footnotes on Nature* by John Kieran. Copyright 1947 by John Kieran. Reprinted by permission. FRONTIERS. "White House Bird Watcher" by Bates M. Stovall, from *Frontiers*, the Magazine of the Academy of Natural Sciences, Philadelphia, Pennsylvania. Reprinted by permission. HARPER & BROTHERS. Excerpts from *Spring in Washington* by Louis J. Halle. Copyright 1947, 1957 by Louis J. Halle, Jr. Reprinted by permission. HATCH, ROBERT MCCONNELL. "The Master of Our Woods" by Robert McConnell Hatch, from *New*

Hampshire Bird News, Vol. 7, No. 1, January 1954. Reprinted by permission of Robert McConnell Hatch and the Audubon Society of New Hampshire. HOLT, RINEHARD & WINSTON, INC. "The Hawk and the Tern" from *The Outermost House* by Henry Beston. Copyright 1928, 1949, copyright renewed © 1956 by Henry Beston. "And I Ought to Know" from *How to Become Extinct* by Will Cuppy. Copyright 1941 by Will Cuppy. HOUGHTON MIFFLIN COMPANY. Excerpt from "Birds of Massachusetts" from *Natural History of the Birds* E. H. Forbush. Copyright 1927 by the Commonwealth of Massachusetts. JAEGER, EDMUND C. "Does the Poor-Will Hibernate?" by Edmund C. Jaeger from *The Condor*, Vol. 50, No. 1, January–February 1948. Reprinted by permission of Edmund C. Jaeger. ALFRED A. KNOPF, INC. "The Trumpeter Swan" by Sally Carrighar, from *One Day at Teton Marsh*. Copyright 1947 by Sally Carrighar and the Curtis Publishing Company. Specially adapted and abridged for this usage, with the permission of Alfred A. Knopf, Inc. "Wilderness Music" from *The Singing Wilderness* by Sigurd F. Olson. Copyright © 1956 by Sigurd F. Olson. Reprinted by permission. LAWRENCE, LOUISE DE KIRILINE. "The Voluble Singer of the Treetops" by Louise de Kiriline, from *Audubon Magazine*, May–June 1954. Reprinted by permission of the author. MACMILLIAN COMPANY. Excerpt from *Wings at My Window* by Ada Clapham Govan. Copyright, 1940, by The Macmillan Company. "On Watching an Ovenbird's Nest" by Margaret Morse Nice, from *The Watcher at the Nest*. Copyright, 1939, by The Macmillan Company. "An Adventure with a Turkey Vulture," "The Harris's Sparrow's Eggs," "Titania and Oberon" by George M. Sutton, from *Birds in the Wilderness*. Copyright, 1936, by The Macmillan Company. Reprinted by permission. MILLER, ROBERT CUNNINGHAM. "Bird Voices of Autumn" by Robert Cunningham Miller, from *Pacific Discovery*, September–October 1951. "Wings of the Storm" by Robert Cunningham Miller, from *Pacific Discovery*, September–October 1951. Reprinted by permission of California Academy of Sciences. "How to Get Along with Birds" by Robert Cunningham Miller, from *National League for Women's Service Magazine*, March 1950. Reprinted by permission of the Women's City Club, San Francisco. MURCHIE, JR., GUY. "The Perfect Flying Machine" from *Song of the Sky* by Guy Murchie, Jr. Reprinted by permission of Guy Murchie, Jr. NATURE HISTORY. "The Bird Doctor" by Paul H. Fluck, from *Nature*, June 1956. OXFORD UNIVERSITY PRESS, INC. "Arctic Rendezvous" from *Under the Sea-Wind Arctic* by Rachel L. Carson. Copyright 1941 by Rachel L. Carson. "March: The Geese Return" from *A Sand County Almanac: and Sketches Here and There* by Aldo Leopold. Copyright 1949 by Oxford University Press, Inc. Reprinted by permission. THE READER'S DIGEST. "Birds Live in Nature's Invisible Cage" by John and Jean George, condensed in *Reader's Digest* from *Christian Science Monitor*. Copyright 1959 by Christian Science Monitor. Reprinted by permission. WILLIAM SLOANE ASSOCIATES. "Most Dangerous Predator" from *The Forgotten Peninsula* by Joseph Wood Krutch. Reprinted by permission. VIKING PRESS. Excerpt from *Birds against Men* by Louis J. Halle Jr. Copyright 1938 by Louis J. Halle.